Diversity and First Nations Issues in Canada

John Roberts

Darion Boyington

Shahé S. Kazarian

2008
Emond Montgomery Publications Limited
Toronto, Canada

Copyright © 2008 Emond Montgomery Publications Limited. All rights reserved. No part of this publication may be reproduced, stored in a retrieval system, or transmitted, in any form or by any means, photocopying, electronic, mechanical, recording, or otherwise, without the prior written permission of the copyright holder.

Emond Montgomery Publications Limited
60 Shaftesbury Avenue
Toronto ON M4T 1A3
http://www.emp.ca

Printed in Canada.

We acknowledge the financial support of the Government of Canada through the Book Publishing Industry Development Program (BPIDP) for our publishing activities.

Acquisitions and developmental editor: Peggy Buchan
Marketing director: Dave Stokaluk
Copy editors: Karen Rolfe and Jamie Bush
Production editor: Jim Lyons, WordsWorth Communications
Assistant production editor: Debbie Gervais, WordsWorth Communications
Proofreader: David Handelsman, WordsWorth Communications
Typesetter: Nancy Ennis, WordsWorth Communications
Indexer: Paula Pike, WordsWorth Communications
Cover designer: Susan Darrach, Darrach Design

Library and Archives Canada Cataloguing in Publication

Roberts, John A., 1944-

　　Diversity and First Nations issues in Canada / John Roberts, Darion Boyington, Shahé S. Kazarian.

Includes index.

ISBN 978-1-55239-194-5

　　1. Police-community relations—Canada. 2. Multiculturalism—Canada.
3. Native peoples—Canada. 4. Law enforcement—Canada. 5. Police—Canada.
I. Boyington, Darion II. Kazarian, Shahe S., 1945- III. Title.

HV8157.R63 2008　　　　　　363.2'30971　　　　　　C2007-904057-8

Contents

PART I DIVERSITY ISSUES IN CANADA

CHAPTER 1 A Portrait of Canadian Diversity 3
The Concept of Multiculturalism 3
The Concept of Diversity 3
Four State Ideologies 4
    Multiculturalism Ideology 4
    Civic Ideology 4
    Assimilation Ideology 4
    Ethnist Ideology 4
Canada and the Concept of Multiculturalism 5
Canadian Society in Brief 6
Concept of the State 7
Concept of the Host Community 7
Acculturation Orientations of Host Communities 8
Acculturation Orientations of Settler Groups 8
History of Immigration and Diversity in Canada 9
Refugee Policies 10
Canada's Aboriginal Peoples 12
Immigration Trends 13
    Ethnic Origins 13
    Visible Minorities 17
    Other Immigration Trends 18
    Implications for Diversity 20
Developing a Canadian Identity 22
Chapter Summary 23
Key Terms 23
References 24

CHAPTER 2 Law Enforcement Culture in a Diversity Context 27
Introduction 27
Diversity and Police 27
Diversity Ideologies and Policies in Law Enforcement 29
Police Culture 30

Demographic Police Profile	30
Law Enforcement Knowledge of Cultural Groups	31
Improving Law Enforcement in Diverse Communities	32
Recruiting Members of Diverse Communities	32
Context of Law Enforcement	32
Core Values in Policing	35
Police–Community Interface	37
Police Culture in a Diversity Context: Police Abilities, Knowledge, and Skills	40
Chapter Summary	42
Key Terms	42
References	43

CHAPTER 3 Human Rights and Freedoms ... 45

Introduction	45
International Human Rights and Freedoms	45
Human Rights in Canada: Federal	47
Canadian Human Rights Act	47
Canadian Charter of Rights and Freedoms	47
Human Rights in Ontario	56
Human Rights Code	56
Human Rights Commission Policies and Initiatives	59
Human Rights and Law Enforcement	62
Human Rights and Freedoms: Post-9/11	64
Human Rights and Freedoms: Police Abilities, Knowledge, and Skills	64
Chapter Summary	66
Key Terms	67
References	67

CHAPTER 4 Cultural Diversity Values, Beliefs, and Practices ... 69

Introduction	69
Concepts of Culture, Ethnicity, Race, and Minority	70
Culture	70
Ethnicity	71
Race	71
Minority	71
Cultural Beliefs and Practices: Specific Cultural Groups	72
Aboriginal Peoples	72
Non-Visible Ethnic Minority Peoples	75
Visible-Minority Ethnic Peoples	76
Stereotypes and Prejudices	79
Alcohol, Aboriginal People, and the Law	79
Alcohol and Stereotyping	80
Women in the Workplace	80

The Black Experience 81
South Asians 82
Cultural Diversity Values, Beliefs, and Practices:
    Police Abilities, Knowledge, and Skills 83
Chapter Summary 84
Key Terms 84
References 85

CHAPTER 5 Religious Diversity 87

Introduction 87
What Is Religion? 88
Religious Beliefs and Practices 88
    Bahá'í Faith: Embracing All Nations, Creeds, and Colours 90
    Buddhism: Seeking Enlightenment 91
    Christian Science: Healing Through Divine Laws 92
    Christianity: Love Your Neighbour 93
    Hinduism: Museum of Religions 93
    Islam: There Is No God but God 94
    Jehovah's Witnesses: Spreading the Word 96
    Judaism: First Monotheistic Religion 96
    Shintoism: The Way of the Gods 98
    Sikhism: Religion of Disciples 99
    Taoism: Universal Energy in Balance 100
    Aboriginal Spirituality: Respect Mother Earth 100
Religious Diversity: Police Abilities, Knowledge, and Skills 103
Chapter Summary 105
Key Terms 105
References 105

CHAPTER 6 Policing with Diversity Competency 107

Introduction 107
Police–Community Perceptions 108
    Self-Perception of Police 108
    Community Perception of Police 108
Diversity Initiatives in Canadian Society 110
Positive Diversity Management in Policing 110
    Diversity as a Strategic Advantage in Policing 111
    Police Training in Race Relations and Cultural Sensitivity 111
    Police Training in Anti-Racism 114
Policing with Diversity Competency: Police Abilities, Knowledge, and Skills 114
Chapter Summary 119
Key Terms 120
References 120

CHAPTER 7   Family Violence and Mental Health Issues 123

Introduction 123
Definition of Family Violence 123
Family Violence and the Law 124
How Big a Problem is Family Violence? 124
    Abuse Among Adults 124
    Abuse: Children and Youth 124
    Abuse: Older Adults 125
Diversity and Family Violence 125
    Sex and Family Violence 125
    Immigrants and Refugees and Family Violence 126
Explanations for Family Violence 127
Barriers to Leaving Violent Relationships 128
Social Responses to Family Violence 128
    Supports and Services 128
Police Response to Family Violence 129
Family Violence and Mental Health Issues:
    Police Abilities, Knowledge, and Skills 130
Mental Illness and Homelessness 130
    Concept of Mental Illness 131
Mental Health Legislation 131
    Mental Health Act: Ontario 131
Mental Disturbances and Police Response 132
    Substance-Related Disorders 132
    Mood Disorders and Suicidal Behaviour 133
    Schizophrenia 136
    Mental Retardation 137
Policing Mental Illness: Police Abilities, Knowledge, and Skills 137
Chapter Summary 140
Key Terms 140
Family Violence References 141
Mental Health Issues References 142

PART II   FIRST NATIONS ISSUES IN CANADA

CHAPTER 8   Pre-Contact 147

Introduction 147
World View 147
Foundations of the Mainstream World View 148
    Religious Creation Story 148
    Scientific Creation Story 149
    Migration Theories 149

Philosophy and Governance 151
      Locke's Theory of Land Ownership 152
First Nations 153
Oral Tradition 153
      Written Records of First Nations History 155
Creation Stories 155
      Concepts of Land and Spirituality 155
      Community Organization 156
      International Organization 157
Conclusion 158
References 158

CHAPTER 9   First Contact 171

Introduction 171
Las Casas and the Indians 171
Canada 173
The Royal Proclamation 176
The Fur Trade 177
Changes to Native Communities 179
Conclusion 180
Key Terms 180
References 181

CHAPTER 10   Western Expansion and Treaties 183

Introduction 183
Treaties Background 183
Numbered Treaties 185
Western Expansion 187
Vanishing Race 189
Thirst for Land 190
Assimilation Legislation 192
The Indian Act 192
      Imposed System of Government 193
      Gender Discrimination Within the Act 194
      Tax Exemption 195
      Changes Through Time 195
1951: Changes to the Act 197
Conclusion 199
Key Terms 199
References 200

CHAPTER 11 Children and the Residential Schools ... 203

Introduction ... 203
Education as a Tool for Assimilation ... 204
Problems Within the System ... 205
Health Conditions ... 208
Abuse Within Residential Schools ... 209
Aftermath of Schools ... 213
Attempts at Resolution ... 214
Recognition of Wrong ... 216
The Sixties Scoop ... 217
Cultural Genocide ... 219
Conclusion ... 220
Key Terms ... 220
References ... 221

Chapter 12 Lingering Socio-economic Issues ... 225

Introduction ... 225
Case Study ... 225
Native Demographics ... 230
    Aboriginal Growth Rates ... 230
    Decrease in Birth Rate ... 231
    Increase in Life Expectancy ... 231
    Aboriginal Youth and Median Age ... 232
    North American Indian Seniors ... 232
    Reinstatement of Native Status Through Bill C-31 ... 233
    Provincial Distributions of North American Native Populations ... 233
    Native Migration to Cities ... 233
    Elementary and Secondary Education ... 234
    Post-Secondary Education for Natives ... 236
Physical Health ... 237
    Infant and Child Mortality ... 237
    Adult Mortality and Morbidity ... 238
    Common Health Problems ... 239
Mental Health Problems ... 240
    Suicides ... 240
    Alcoholism ... 241
    Other Substance Abuse ... 242
    Living Conditions ... 243
    Living Arrangements: Children Under 15 ... 244
    Administration of Health Services ... 245
Socio-economic Status ... 246
    Employment ... 246
    Income ... 248
    Social Assistance ... 250

Delivery of Services and Programs 250
Off-Reserve Aboriginal Populations 251
Conclusion 252

CHAPTER 13 Current Issues Over Land 261
Introduction 261
Background 262
Historical Case Law 262
Constitution 265
Aboriginal Title to Land 268
Recent Case Study 271
Working Together 273
Land Claims 274
Ontario 276
Conclusion 277
Key Terms 277
References 278

CHAPTER 14 Aboriginal People and the Criminal Justice System 287
Introduction 287
Native Overrepresentation in the Criminal Justice System 287
Alcohol and Criminality in Native Communities 289
Systemic Problems 292
Culture Conflict and Alternative Justice 294
Proposed Solutions 295
    Indigenization 296
    Sentencing Reforms 298
    Corrections and Conditional Release Act 300
    Culturally Appropriate Programs in Custody 300
Conclusion 301
Key Terms 302
References 303

Glossary 311

Index 317

Acknowledgments 321

Introduction

Diversity and First Nations Issues in Canada is a unique book. In two separate sections, it deals first with diversity issues and law enforcement and, second, with First Nations issues. It is intended as a text for those who teach issues in diversity and First Nations peoples as a one-semester course. The book is student-friendly, with exercises throughout the text and a comprehensive terminology list at the end of each chapter.

The first section, "Diversity Issues in Canada," is taken in large part from Shahé Kazarian's best-selling *Diversity Issues in Law Enforcement*, 3rd ed., with expanded sections on human rights legislation, Canadian diversity, and stereotypes and prejudices. The section begins with an introduction to the basic concepts of diversity, multiculturalism, and human rights; it moves to an explanation of minority perceptions, identity, and stratification in Canada; and then continues with a discussion of law enforcement and human rights. The section ends with a discussion of mental illness and homelessness and the implications of these issues for law enforcement. Throughout the section, the focus is on the relationship between law enforcement and diverse communities in Canada.

The second section, "First Nations Issues in Canada," contains a significant amount of new material. This section discusses First Nations peoples in pre-contact North America with the purpose of understanding the culture before its collision with European culture. The significant differences in worldviews between First Nations and European cultures provide insight into both cultures and the effects of colonization on First Nations peoples and Europeans alike.

There is a significant discussion about the exclusion of Native children from Canadian schools, ongoing as late as 1945, which describes how the poorly run, poorly funded, government residential schools schools for Natives were operated by an assortment of religious denominations. Repercussions from this era still linger today, with ensuing criminal and civil lawsuits against the federal government making headlines on a regular basis.

The section ends with a discussion of contemporary issues in Native culture, focusing on the years of First Nations' exclusion from the Canadian political system and on the issues of land claims, which are commonly misunderstood by Canadian society.

Common to both sections is the argument that both First Nations peoples and non-white or marginalized populations in Canada share in common not only the hardships of discrimination, but a common historical experience of being members of populations subjects to a European, mostly British-based society, caught up in the effects of Canadian nationalist movements.

John Roberts
Hamilton, Ontario
June 2007

PART I
Diversity Issues in Canada

CHAPTER 1

A Portrait of Canadian Diversity

CHAPTER OBJECTIVES

After completing this chapter, you should be able to:

- Understand the concepts of multiculturalism and diversity.
- Discuss the four state ideologies of host countries.
- Define Canada's concept of multiculturalism.
- Understand Canadian society, immigration trends, and Canadian diversity.

THE CONCEPT OF MULTICULTURALISM

The term **multiculturalism** has different meanings and evokes a variety of attitudes and emotions. Multiculturalism may be interpreted as *a celebration of cultural diversity* or *a description of the actual cultural diversity of a population*. Multiculturalism as a celebration of diversity and as a fact is characteristic of many countries, including Australia, the United Kingdom, and the United States. Multiculturalism may also be interpreted as a national ideology and a state policy, a stance unique to Canada (Kazarian, 2001, p. 27). Canada is the first nation to enshrine a multiculturalism policy in its constitution (Kazarian, 2001, p. 26).

multiculturalism
a policy relating to or designed for a combination of several distinct cultures

THE CONCEPT OF DIVERSITY

Diversity refers to the variety of human qualities among different people and groups (University of Maryland, 2000). Diversity has two dimensions: primary and secondary. *Primary* dimensions include age, **ethnicity**, gender, physical abilities and qualities, race, and sexual orientation. *Secondary* dimensions include educational background, geographic location, income, marital status, parental status, religious beliefs, and work experience. Secondary dimensions are assumed to be alterable (Kazarian, 2001, p. 4).

diversity
the variety of human qualities among different people and groups

ethnicity
refers to country of origin and may involve distinct elements that are shared, such as language, religion, and customs

FOUR STATE IDEOLOGIES

Host cultures apply one of four prevailing ideologies to their own members and to people they accept as immigrants and refugees. These ideologies are the multiculturalism ideology, civic ideology, assimilation ideology, and ethnist ideology.

Multiculturalism Ideology

multiculturalism ideology
ideology that recognizes and supports people of diversity in maintaining or promoting their diversity, providing that their practices do not clash with the laws of the nation

values
standards or principles; ideas about the worth or importance of certain qualities, especially those accepted by a particular group

The **multiculturalism ideology** recognizes and supports people of diversity in maintaining or promoting their diversity, provided that their practices do not clash with the criminal and civil laws of the nation. Four main principles are associated with this ideology. First, people of diversity are expected to adopt the public **values** of the nation: the democratic ideals, constitutional and human rights provisions, and civil and criminal codes of the state. Second, the multiculturalism ideology protects the private values of individual citizens. Private values are personal attitudes and activities of individuals in terms of domestic, interpersonal, and associative relations, such as those in the workplace or in clubs and service organizations. Third, the state recognizes multicultural values and protects these values from interference from both others and the state. Thus, the state values the efforts of immigrants to maintain their cultural and linguistic distinctiveness, provided that their conduct is within the boundaries of the laws of the state. Fourth, the multiculturalism ideology endorses state funding for ethnocultural activities of both citizens and newcomers on the grounds that both groups contribute to the state through taxation.

Civic Ideology

civic ideology
ideology that subscribes to multiculturalism ideology principles but does not support state funding to maintain and promote ethnocultural diversity

The **civic ideology** subscribes to the multiculturalism ideology principles except for state funding to promote and maintain ethnocultural diversity. Great Britain is an example of a state that supports civic ideology.

Assimilation Ideology

assimilation ideology
ideology that expects people of diversity to relinquish their culture and linguistic identity and adopt the culture of the host state

The **assimilation ideology** is a homogenization or "melting pot" ideology. This ideology expects people of diversity to relinquish their cultural and linguistic identities and to adopt the culture of the host state. In return, the state promises to protect the private values of individual citizens but reserves the right to limit expression of some domains of private values, particularly those that pertain to immigrant minorities. The United States is a state that espouses assimilation.

Ethnist Ideology

ethnist ideology
ideology that expects people of diversity to assimilate, but the state defines which groups should assimilate and thus which ones are not rightful members of the state

The **ethnist ideology** is similar to the assimilation ideology except that the state defines which groups should or should not assimilate. Germany is one state that espoused ethnist ideology (Kazarian, 2001, pp. 26–27).

EXERCISE 1

1. Which of the four state ideologies is practised by Canada? Give reasons for your answer.

2. After each of the following statements, indicate whether the statement represents a multiculturalism, civic, assimilation, or ethnist ideology, or a combination of ideologies:

   a. Individuals from diverse countries should be encouraged to maintain their cultural heritages.

   b. Canada is a better place because people of various ethnic backgrounds come to live here.

   c. Canadians would be better off if all immigrants abandoned their cultural and linguistic identities.

   d. The government should not support ethnic radio, television, or newspapers in ethnic languages.

   e. Canada should be selective in which immigrants it accepts.

   f. Multiculturalism is Canada's main source of political, economic, and social wealth.

   g. Immigrants should be forced to learn English or French.

   h. Newcomers should combine the best of their heritage culture with the best of the host culture.

   i. Multiculturalism is "mosaic madness."

   j. The host state should recognize foreign professional (for example, medical) credentials as equivalent to Canadian credentials.

CANADA AND THE CONCEPT OF MULTICULTURALISM

Canada has been defined by its dominant cultures. This occurred in three distinct stages:

1. Canada as a Colony of the British Empire

   a. Sovereignty was exercised by an external authority in England.

   b. Canadians had only limited democratic rights, and were governed by a political elite.

   c. The dominant cultures were English and French, although the British sought to assimilate the French.

2. Canada as an Independent "White Dominion" in the British Empire/Commonwealth

   a. Sovereignty was increasingly exercised within the Dominion.

   b. Canadians had full democratic rights, and were governed by Parliament.

   c. The dominant culture was British, although immigrants began arriving to colonize the West.

   d. The policy of assimilation and commitment to the British Empire still imposed a cultural uniformity on the nation (with the exception of Quebec). Canadians were British subjects until 1947.

3. Canada as a Fully Sovereign and Independent Nation-State

   a. Canada became completely independent of British sovereignty (1931–1949).

   b. The divide between French and English was temporarily settled through constitutional reform.

   c. European immigration slowed, and people from all parts of the world began to immigrate to Canada.

   d. The subsequent immigration boom caused a substantial demographic shift in the latter half of the 20th century.

   e. The assimilation of French Canadians and Aboriginal peoples was replaced by concepts of multiculturalism.

CANADIAN SOCIETY IN BRIEF

Canada is caught on the horns of a dilemma in terms of diversity issues. On the one hand, Canadians live in a rights-based culture that suggests all citizens should be treated equally under civil law, and that no one will receive any unearned benefits from the state or society because of identity. This is the rule of law upon which Canada was founded.

On the other hand, Canada the nation, and the dominant ideas of what the nation is and who belongs in it, is determined by historical and cultural factors that are inconsistent with the fundamental equality of rights culture.

The tension between these two positions can be understood in the context of formal and informal multiculturalism. Formal multiculturalism was inaugurated as a policy of the federal government by Prime Minister Trudeau in 1971. The policy was formalized into a legal and bureaucratic structure under the *Canadian Multiculturalism Act* of 1988, and further protections for minorities are enshrined in s. 15 of the *Canadian Charter of Rights and Freedoms*. These formal policies and laws are put in place to address the needs of new Canadians and disadvantaged groups. However, as a liberal democratic and rights-based political community, the Canadian government had to interpret multiculturalism as a policy from the per-

CHAPTER 1   A Portrait of Canadian Diversity   7

> **EXERCISE 2**
>
> After examining the three stages of multiculturalism in Canada, can you give reasons why the third stage of Canada's multicultural policy was the result of the first two stages?

spective of universal rights. This meant that these policies treated all cultures and individuals on the assumption that everyone was fundamentally equal; thus, the formal policy of multiculturalism could not, and did not, address the problem of fundamental inequalities and **discrimination** in Canadian society.

Informal multiculturalism, on the other hand, refers to the popular ideas and the cultural factors that determine people's attitudes toward diversity. Informal multiculturalism takes social diversity in Canada as a given—as a well-known social fact—and suggests that explanations for the relative lack of success of people from disadvantaged groups can be explained by the persistence of discriminatory and stereotypical attitudes rather than by the failings of particular formalized policies. It follows, then, that the persistence of popular discriminatory and stereotypical attitudes has to be examined, as do the ways in which the imbalances of power between minority and majority populations work themselves out in daily life (Baxter, 2003).

discrimination
process by which a person is deprived of equal access to privileges and opportunities available to others

CONCEPT OF THE STATE

A census is a powerful tool, because, in part, it helps define the nation by labelling the citizens within it. Canada is a nation built upon immigration, and there is an intimate connection between immigration and multiculturalism in this country (Fleras, 1994).

These issues will be discussed in later chapters. It is important to look at diversity in Canada from a social and historical perspective to examine not only the stereotypes and prejudices that must be overcome, but also particular relations between diverse groups and law enforcement agencies, and First Nations peoples and the law.

CONCEPT OF THE HOST COMMUNITY

A **host community** is sometimes called the host culture or nation, dominant culture or society, or majority culture. A host community consists of people with different **settlement patterns**. The people may have either lived on the land—that is, as settlers or members of a First Nation—or may have come from other parts of the world to live together and form the culturally diverse character of the host nation.

Host communities comprise groups of people who have the power and influence to change societal attitudes toward the remaining groups in society. The host community sets the tone for how the rest of society views and deals with the less powerful *other*. For example, a host culture such as Canada may cease to view marriage exclusively as a sacred heterosexual institution and will change its views to recognize the rights of gay and lesbian communities, and will introduce legislation allowing for gay and lesbian marriages. Host communities also determine immigration

host community
comprises groups of people who have the power and influence to shape attitudes toward the remaining groups in society

settlement patterns
the variety of ways people physically establish themselves in a country, whether born there or as immigrants

policies—that is, who is a desirable addition to the host culture and who is undesirable. Finally, by assimilating newcomers and expecting them to accept the patterns of the host community, host communities alter the settlement and adaptation patterns of those they accept as newcomers.

ACCULTURATION ORIENTATIONS OF HOST COMMUNITIES

Host communities adopt one or more of the following acculturation orientations toward immigrants:

- An **integrationist** host community encourages immigrants to adopt important features of the host culture and values as well as maintain aspects of their heritage culture.

- An **exclusionary** host community is intolerant of the wishes of immigrants or other cultures to maintain their heritage cultures, and does not allow them to adopt features of the host culture. Host community members welcome newcomers with ambivalence.

- An **assimilationist** host community demands that immigrants relinquish their cultural identity and adapt totally to the host culture. Assimilation refers to the social process whereby members of different ethnic communities participate in ethnocultural institutions other than those of the ethnic community to which they belong (Kallen, 2003). Over time, members of the host culture consider those who have been culturally absorbed to be full-fledged citizens.

- A **segregationist** host community distances itself from immigrants or other cultures but allows them to maintain their heritage culture. Members of the host community believe that immigrants "can never be incorporated culturally or socially as rightful members of the host society" (Bourhis, Moise, Perreault, & Senecal, 1997).

integrationist
supportive of immigrants' adopting features of the host culture while maintaining aspects of their heritage culture

exclusionary
intolerant of immigrants' heritage culture and of immigration in general

assimilationist
intolerant of immigrants' heritage culture, demanding that they relinquish the culture and adopt the host culture

segregationist
opposed to immigrants and other cultures, preferring that immigrants return to their countries of origin

ACCULTURATION ORIENTATIONS OF SETTLER GROUPS

Acculturation refers to those "phenomena which result when groups of individuals having different cultures come into continuous first-hand contact, with subsequent changes in the original cultural patterns of either group or both groups" (Berry, 1990, 1998). In this process, each population acquires from the other new cultural attributes that may eventually be absorbed into its own system. Immigrants exhibit one of four modes of acculturation, which together form the acronym MASI:

- **Marginalization** involves the simultaneous rejection of one's country of origin and the host culture. Those who are marginalized are disenchanted with their own cultural identity and the alternative identity accorded by the host culture.

acculturation
process of change in the cultural patterns of an ethnic group as a result of contact with other ethnic groups

marginalization
simultaneous rejection of the culture of origin and the host culture

- **Assimilation** represents rejection of one's culture in favour of absorption into the host culture.

- **Separation** involves individual rejection of the host culture and maintenance of one's culture of origin.

- **Integration** involves embracing the host culture and continued maintenance of one's culture of origin.

Integration is the most preferred and desired mode of adaptation. Integrationists show good psychological adjustment and personal satisfaction, which is an important consideration not only from an economic perspective, but also from the perspective of law and order, because members of ethnic groups who are integrated are perceived as less likely to engage in disorderly or criminal activity. Most significantly, integrationists do not practise separation or isolation from the host culture, nor does their cultural identity lessen their commitment to the welfare of the host nation (Berry & Sam, 1997).

assimilation
to absorb groups of different cultures into the main culture

separation
individual rejection of the host culture and maintenance of the culture of origin

integration
embrace of the host culture of settlement and continued maintenance of culture of origin

HISTORY OF IMMIGRATION AND DIVERSITY IN CANADA

The 2001 Census reports that Canada receives approximately 200,000 immigrants a year. Immigration began with the arrival of English and French explorers and settlers. At first contact between Aboriginal peoples and European peoples, there were 56 Aboriginal nations speaking more than 30 languages. The French and English colonized the eastern part of what is now Canada, and signed treaties with First Nations peoples acknowledging Aboriginal nationhood.

In 1867, the English and French languages were given constitutional status at Confederation. Bilingualism became the core of Canada's approach to diversity. From the late 1800s to the mid-1900s, Canada's immigration policy was based on supplying a labour pool for settlement and agriculture; after this, immigration policy was based on establishing a Canadian industrial base. Canada recognized the right of minorities to maintain their culture and traditions, with some exceptions, such as the Japanese during World War II.

In 1950, as a result of the Massey-Levesque Commission, which linked cultural diversity and Canadian identity, ethnocultural diversity gradually came to be understood as an essential ingredient in a distinct Canadian society. At that time, 92 percent of Canada's population growth was the result of birth rate. By 2001, immigration had outpaced the natural birth rate, and accounted for 53 percent of overall population growth.

The 1960 *Canadian Bill of Rights* outlawed discrimination by federal agencies based on the grounds of race, national origin, colour, religion, and gender. The *Immigration Act* of 1960 reflected this policy by stating that immigrants were not to be refused entry into Canada on the grounds of race, national origin, colour, or country of origin. This Act resulted in more immigration from southern Europe, Africa, and the West Indies.

The *Official Languages Act* of 1969 required the government to give equal status, rights, and privileges to both official languages in federal institutions. It further required that these institutions must serve Canadians in the official language of their choice.

The 1970s and 1980s saw substantial numbers of refugees admitted to this country, in some cases as a result of Canada's official multiculturalism policy, established in 1971, which provided for programs and services to help individuals from diverse cultures overcome barriers to their full participation in Canadian society.

The 1982 *Canadian Charter of Rights and Freedoms* granted parents who are members of an English or French linguistic minority in the communities where they live to have their children educated in the official language of their choice. Section 27 of the Charter stated that the courts were to interpret the constitution in a manner that would preserve and enhance the multicultural nature of Canada:

> 27. This Charter shall be interpreted in a manner consistent with the preservation and enhancement of the multicultural heritage of Canadians.

Jean Chrétien, as minister of justice, commented on the importance of the Charter in protecting the rights of a multicultural and ethnically diverse population:

> In a free and democratic society, it is important that citizens know exactly what their rights and freedoms are, and where to turn for help and advice in the event that those freedoms are denied or those rights infringed. In a country like Canada—vast and diverse, with 11 governments, 2 official languages, and a variety of ethnic origins—the only way to provide equal protection for everyone is to enshrine those basic rights and freedoms in the Constitution. (1982, p. v)

The concept of diversity expanded from language, ethnicity, race, and religion to include gender, sexual orientation, ability, and age. The rights of diverse groups are enshrined in other Canadian legal responses to diversity, including the following federal legislation:

- the *Canadian Human Rights Act*,
- the *Employment Equity Act*, and
- the *Canadian Multiculturalism Act*.

Provinces have responded to diversity issues by passing similar legislation, including pay equity acts, and developing programs to promote diversity. On the international stage, Canada is signatory to, among others, the

- *Universal Declaration of Human Rights* and
- *International Covenant on Economic, Social and Cultural Rights*.

REFUGEE POLICIES

Canada has been home to refugees since before Confederation. The United Empire Loyalists, for example, flocked to Canada (along with many non-British subjects) during the American Revolution in 1776. Similarly, Puritans found refuge in Canada in the 1600s after suffering religious persecution in England. Scots settled in Canada after the Highland Clearances of the 1600s, the Irish during the potato famine of the 1800s, Russians as a result of the Bolshevik Revolution, and Armenians after 1923.

Like many other countries, Canada has continued its humanitarian tradition with respect to refugees. The past four decades, however, have witnessed a shift from a predominately east-west refugee pattern to a north-south pattern (Nef & da Silva, 1991). Thus, refugees after World War II were primarily from Eastern Europe, while many currently originate from countries such as Somalia, Cambodia, Vietnam, and Guatemala.

Welcoming refugees should be seen not as an immigration issue, but as a human rights issue. Article 1 of the 1951 *United Nations Protocol Relating to the Status of Refugees* (United Nations, 1983) defines a refugee as any person who

> owing to well-founded fear of being persecuted for reasons of race, religion, nationality, membership of a particular social group or political opinion, is outside the country of nationality and is unable, or owing to such fear, is unwilling to avail himself of the protection of that country; or who, not having a nationality and being outside the country of his former habitual residence as a result of such events, is unable or, owing to such fear, is unwilling to return to it.

The 1976 Canadian *Immigration Act* formalized the prevailing ad hoc approach to refugee determination and selection to form a **refugee policy**. The Act identified three options to granting qualified refugees permission to resettle in Canada: overseas selection, special programs, and inland refugee-status determination. Canada is currently moving away from government-assisted refugees and supporting private sponsorship.

refugee policy
humanitarian policy, based on the United Nations definition of a refugee, that assesses eligibility for entry to a country based on refugee status

Immigration and refugee policies need periodic changes, such as viable solutions for dealing with security concerns and executing valid orders of deportation of criminals. Amendments passed in 1995 to the *Immigration Act* have made it easier to deport a permanent resident with a serious criminal background.

In 1996, a review of Canada's refugee and immigration policy was initiated to make fundamental policy reforms and introduce new legislation, resulting in the reintroduction of the *Immigration and Refugee Protection Act* in 2001. This Act and its accompanying regulations were to represent a simpler, more modern and coherent law and legislation; to better respond to Canada's global challenges of the 21st century; to ensure that Canada can preserve immigration as a source of diversity, richness, and openness to the world; to enhance Canada's advantage in the global competition for skilled workers; to maintain and enhance its strong humanitarian tradition; to deter migrant trafficking and to punish those who engage in this form of slavery; and to maintain confidence in the integrity of the immigration and refugee protection program.

EXERCISE 3

Examine the following quotation. Do you feel that acceptance and respect for diverse cultures have to be legislated? With increasing immigration, would this respect and acceptance not follow naturally as diversity became more common? Give reasons for your answer.

> "Canada's approach to diversity is based on the belief that the common good is best served when everyone is accepted and respected for who they are, and that ultimately makes for a resilient, more harmonious and more creative society" (Canadian Heritage, 2001).

CANADA'S ABORIGINAL PEOPLES

As mentioned at the beginning of this chapter, there was a significant Aboriginal presence in what is now Canada when the first Europeans arrived. Aboriginal cultures were greatly affected by contact with Europeans. From the beginning of contact, Aboriginal nations were at a disadvantage. They faced social changes, new technologies, and imported diseases, as well as the Europeans' quest for new lands. Unfortunately, cultural and traditional changes and the erosion of Aboriginal sovereignty were inevitable.

The French and the British were the main European influences in North America from the 1500s to the early 1900s. They competed for dominance by establishing settlements. Both sides courted First Nations peoples in their quest for trade and in their battles with each other over control of the North American continent. European settlement gradually pushed First Nations peoples off the land, and Aboriginals became dependent upon Europeans for their livelihoods. Hunting skills disappeared, languages were lost, traditions were abolished, and Aboriginals were looked upon as wards of the government, since the government considered that Aboriginals were no longer able to take care of themselves. Missionaries moved in to "save" the lost Aboriginal souls, one result of which was the infamous residential school system in which many Aboriginal children were physically and sexually abused.

In the second half of the 20th century, oppressed peoples around the world challenged the remnants of colonialism and demanded equality. Some proclaimed their independence and forged new nations. Others, like the First Nations, Inuit, and Métis of Canada, demanded the right to sovereignty and self-determination within the framework of Canada (Roberts, 2006).

Attempts to address the needs of Canada's Aboriginal peoples began in 1973 and first recognized Aboriginal land rights based on a group's traditional use and occupancy of the land. In 1982, the *Charter of Rights and Freedoms* recognized and affirmed the treaty rights of Aboriginal peoples to protect their cultures, traditions, and languages. In 1996, the Royal Commission on Aboriginal Peoples presented a comprehensive five-volume report to Parliament identifying the legal, political, social, economic, and cultural issues that need to be addressed to ensure the future survival of Canada's First Nations, Inuit, and Métis. Two years later, the government responded with an action plan to work in partnership with Canada's Aboriginal peoples to improve health, housing, and public safety; strengthen economic development; and assist with the implementation of self-government. As of 2007, much remains to be done (Heritage Canada, 2006).

Aboriginal culture will be lost if modern governments do not help protect it. In both North America and Australia, hundreds of Aboriginal languages and cultural practices are either extinct or endangered. Aboriginal culture and language are intimately connected to the land; by removing the rights of Aboriginals to freely hunt, fish, or travel, the culture is being lost (University of Maryland, 2000).

CHAPTER 1 A Portrait of Canadian Diversity

> ### EXERCISE 4
>
> Conduct a research study into some of the problems facing Aboriginal peoples today. Use headings such as
>
> a. loss of language,
>
> b. health issues,
>
> c. interaction with the justice system,
>
> d. education levels,
>
> e. unemployment,
>
> f. urban migration, and
>
> g. land claims issues.
>
> How is the government involved in dealing with these issues, and how are Aboriginal peoples dealing with these issues apart from government?

IMMIGRATION TRENDS

This section examines immigration into Canada after the turn of the 21st century. Unless otherwise indicated, statistics are from Statistics Canada, "2001 Census: Analysis Series."

Ethnic Origins

More than 200 different ethnic origins were reported in the 2001 Census. Ethnic origin, as defined in the census, refers to the ethnic or cultural group to which an individual's ancestors belonged.

The list of origins reported includes cultural groups associated with Canada's Aboriginal peoples, and groups associated with the founding of Canada, such as the French, English, Scottish, and Irish. The list also reflects the history of immigration to Canada in the past 100 years, with groups such as German, Italian, Chinese, Ukrainian, Dutch, Polish, and others. Changes in the sources of immigrants to Canada have resulted in emerging new ethnic origins from eastern Europe, central Asia, the Middle East, Africa, and Central and South America.

These tables reveal that

- The People's Republic of China has replaced the United Kingdom as the leading country of birth for immigrants between 1991 and 2001, as compared with 1961 and before.

- Of the 10 leading countries of birth previous to 1961, only Poland (down to 2.4 percent of immigrants from 5 percent) and the United States (down to 2.8 from 3.9 percent) remain on the 1991–2001 list.

TABLE 1.1 Population by Selected Ethnic Origins, by Province and Territory (2001 Census) (Canada)

	Total responses	Single responses	Multiple responses
		number	
Total population	29,639,035	18,307,545	11,331,490
Ethnic origin			
Canadian	11,682,680	6,748,135	4,934,545
English	5,978,875	1,479,525	4,499,355
French	4,668,410	1,060,760	3,607,655
Scottish	4,157,210	607,235	3,549,975
Irish	3,822,660	496,865	3,325,795
German	2,742,765	705,600	2,037,170
Italian	1,270,370	726,275	544,090
Chinese	1,094,700	936,210	158,490
Ukrainian	1,071,060	326,195	744,860
North American Indian	1,000,890	455,805	545,085
Dutch (Netherlands)	923,310	316,220	607,090
Polish	817,085	260,415	556,665
East Indian	713,330	581,665	131,665
Norwegian	363,760	47,230	316,530
Portuguese	357,690	252,835	104,855
Welsh	350,365	28,445	321,920
Jewish	348,605	186,475	162,130
Russian	337,960	70,895	267,070
Filipino	327,550	266,140	61,405
Métis	307,845	72,210	235,635
Swedish	282,760	30,440	252,325
Hungarian (Magyar)	267,255	91,800	175,455
American (USA)	250,005	25,205	224,805
Greek	215,105	143,785	71,325
Spanish	213,105	66,545	146,555
Jamaican	211,720	138,180	73,545
Danish	170,780	33,795	136,985
Vietnamese	151,410	119,120	32,290

Source: http://www40.statcan.ca.

TABLE 1.2 Place of Birth by Period of Immigration, Canada, 2001

	Before 1961		1961–1970		Period of immigration 1971–1980		1981–1990		1991–2001[1]	
	Number	%	Number	%	Number	%	Number	%	Number	%
Total immigrants	**894,465**	**100.0**	**745,565**	**100.0**	**936,275**	**100.0**	**1,041,495**	**100.0**	**1,830,680**	**100.0**
United States	34,805	3.9	46,880	6.3	62,835	6.7	41,965	4.0	51,440	2.8
Europe	809,330	90.5	515,675	69.2	338,520	36.2	266,185	25.6	357,845	19.5
Asia	28,850	3.2	90,420	12.1	311,960	33.3	491,720	47.2	1,066,230	58.2
Africa	4,635	0.5	23,830	3.2	54,655	5.8	59,715	5.7	139,770	7.6
Caribbean, Central and South America	12,895	1.4	59,895	8.0	154,395	16.5	171,495	16.5	200,010	10.9
Oceania and other countries	3,950	0.4	8,865	1.2	13,910	1.5	10,415	1.0	15,385	0.8

[1] Includes data up to May 15, 2001.

Source: http://www12.statcan.ca/english/census01/products/analytic/companion/etoimm/tables/canada/period.cfm.

TABLE 1.3 Top 10 Countries of Birth, Canada, 2001

	Immigrated before 1961 Number	%		Immigrated 1991–2001[1] Number	%
Total immigrants	894,465	100.0	**Total immigrants**	1,830,680	100.0
United Kingdom	217,175	24.3	China, People's Republic of	197,360	10.8
Italy	147,320	16.5	India	156,120	8.5
Germany	96,770	10.8	Philippines	122,010	6.7
Netherlands	79,170	8.9	Hong Kong, Special Administrative Region	118,385	6.5
Poland	44,340	5.0	Sri Lanka	62,590	3.4
United States	34,810	3.9	Pakistan	57,990	3.2
Hungary	27,425	3.1	Taiwan	53,755	2.9
Ukraine	21,240	2.4	United States	51,440	2.8
Greece	20,755	2.3	Iran	47,080	2.6
China, People's Republic of	15,850	1.8	Poland	43,370	2.4

[1] Includes data up to May 15, 2001.

Source: http://www12.statcan.ca/english/census01/Products/Analytic/companion/etoimm/tables/canada/pobtop.cfm.

TABLE 1.4 1990s' Immigrants by Source Country and Proportion Speaking a Non-Official Language, Canada, 2001

	Number	Percentage speaking non-official language most often at home	Percentage with no knowledge of the official languages
Total 1990s' immigrants	1,830,680	61.1	9.4
Top 10 countries of birth			
China, People's Republic of	197,355	88.4	29.1
India	156,120	70.6	14.7
Philippines	122,015	46.8	1.1
Hong Kong, Special Administrative Region	118,385	87.9	7.7
Sri Lanka	62,590	73.4	7.3
Pakistan	57,990	67.7	6.2
Taiwan	53,750	86.8	12.7
United States	51,440	9.7	1.2
Iran	47,075	76.0	6.8
Poland	43,370	73.1	7.3
Other countries	920,590	50.9	6.4

Source: http://www12.statcan.ca/english/census01/products/analytic/companion/etoimm/tables/canada/offlang.cfm.

TABLE 1.5 Distribution of 1990s' Immigrants Compared with Distribution of Total Population, Canada, Provinces and Territories, 2001

	1990s' immigrants	Total population in Canada	Ratio of 1990s' immigrants to total population[1]
Canada	100.0%	100.0%	
Newfoundland and Labrador	0.1%	1.7%	0.1
Prince Edward Island	0.0%	0.5%	0.1
Nova Scotia	0.6%	3.0%	0.2
New Brunswick	0.2%	2.4%	0.1
Quebec	13.4%	24.0%	0.6
Ontario	55.8%	38.1%	1.5
Manitoba	1.8%	3.7%	0.5
Saskatchewan	0.6%	3.2%	0.2
Alberta	7.1%	9.9%	0.7
British Columbia	20.2%	13.1%	1.5
Yukon Territory	0.0%	0.1%	0.4
Northwest Territories	0.0%	0.1%	0.3
Nunavut	0.0%	0.1%	0.1

[1] This ratio shows whether the proportion of 1990s' immigrants living in a given province or territory is higher than the proportion of the total population living in that province or territory. For example, if 5% of 1990s' immigrants live in a given province and the same proportion (5%) of the total population lives there, then the ratio will be 1.0.

Source: http://www12.statcan.ca/english/census01/products/analytic/companion/etoimm/tables/provs/immsh.cfm.

- Of the nearly two million immigrants to Canada in the 1990s, nearly 10 percent had no knowledge of English or French. This number was led by the People's Republic of China, with 29.1 percent of immigrants having no knowledge of the two official languages, followed by India with 14.7 percent.

- Ontario retained its status as the largest receiving province for immigrants. In 1991, 23.7 percent of all immigrants went to Ontario, a figure that increased to 26.8 percent in 2001. The number of immigrants going to British Columbia increased from 22.3 percent in 1991 to 26.1 percent in 2001. In summary, nearly 53 percent of all immigrants went to either Ontario or British Columbia in 2001.

Visible Minorities

Combined, the three largest **visible-minority** groups in 2001—Chinese, South Asians, and Blacks—accounted for two-thirds of the visible-minority population. Chinese was the largest visible-minority group, surpassing one million for the first time. A total of 1,029,400 individuals identified themselves as Chinese, up from 860,100 in 1996. They accounted for 3.5 percent of the total Canadian population and 26 percent of the visible-minority population.

visible minority
persons, other than Aboriginal peoples, who are non-Caucasian in race or non-white in colour

Chinese comprised the largest proportion of the visible-minority population in British Columbia (44 percent), Alberta (30 percent), and Saskatchewan (29 percent). Ontario had the highest number of Chinese (481,500), but they comprised the second-highest proportion (22 percent) of the visible minorities in that province, behind South Asians (26 percent).

The first major wave of Chinese immigration to Canada occurred in the late 1800s when Chinese labourers arrived in western Canada to build the Canadian Pacific Railway, although Chinese had immigrated as early as 1858 for the Gold Rush in British Columbia. For decades following the railway's completion, Chinese immigration was discouraged: the federal government imposed a $50 tax on Chinese immigrants that later rose to $500. About 81,000 Chinese immigrants paid $23 million to enter Canada between 1885 and 1923. The *Chinese Exclusion Act* followed, barring Chinese immigration altogether until the Act was repealed in 1947. In 2006, the Canadian government apologized and offered reparations to Chinese immigrants, although few of the original immigrants were still alive. Until the 1960s, restrictions on Chinese immigration kept their numbers relatively small. Since then, immigration from Hong Kong and the People's Republic of China has made the Chinese one of the fastest-growing visible-minority populations.

Between 1996 and 2001, the number of Chinese immigrants increased 20 percent. The number of South Asians, the second-largest visible-minority group, rose 37 percent. The 2001 Census enumerated 917,100 South Asians, up from 670,600 in 1996; South Asians represented 3.1 percent of Canada's total population and 23 percent of the visible-minority population. South Asians accounted for at least one-quarter of the visible-minority populations in Ontario, Newfoundland and Labrador, and British Columbia.

The census enumerated 662,200 Blacks in 2001, up 15 percent from 573,900 in 1996. This third-largest visible-minority group represented 2.2 percent of the country's total population and 17 percent of the visible-minority population. Many Blacks have a history in Canada dating back several centuries. In 2001, Blacks were a proportionally large component of the visible-minority population in the Atlantic provinces and in Quebec.

Canada's visible-minority population also comprised Filipinos (8 percent), Arabs and West Asians (8 percent), Latin Americans (5 percent), Southeast Asians (5 percent), Koreans (3 percent), and Japanese (2 percent). Combined, their total population of about 1.2 million represented one-third of the total visible-minority population in 2001 (Statistics Canada, 2001).

Other Immigration Trends

- As of May 2001, 18.4 percent (5.4 million) Canadians were born outside Canada. This is the highest percentage of the population that is foreign born since 1931, when 22.2 percent of the population fit that category. Only Australia has a larger percentage of its population that is foreign born (Statistics Canada, 2001).

- Immigrants to Canada are increasingly from Asia: 58 percent of all immigrants between 1991 and 2001 came from Asia and/or the Middle East; 20 percent came from Europe; 11 percent from the Caribbean or

CHAPTER 1   A Portrait of Canadian Diversity

> **EXERCISE 5**
>
> Research one of the dominant visible-minority groups in Canada (Chinese, South Asians, or Blacks) and list reasons the group may have immigrated to Canada. Use the headings
>
> - social conditions in country of origin
> - economic conditions in country of origin
> - religious freedom concerns
> - employment opportunity concerns
> - educational opportunity concerns
> - health concerns
>
> Discuss ways in which immigration to Canada may have either alleviated or failed to alleviate some of these conditions or concerns.

Central or South America; 8 percent from Africa; and 3 percent from the United States (Statistics Canada, 2001).

- China is the leading country of birth of new Canadians, followed by India, the Philippines, Hong Kong, Sri Lanka, Pakistan, and Taiwan. Together, these Asian countries accounted for more than 40 percent of immigration in the 1990s.

- European immigration has declined steadily since the period before 1961, when it constituted 90 percent of all immigration. In 2001, European immigration accounted for less than 12 percent of the total immigrant population of Canada.

- Immigration is an urban phenomenon: 94 percent of all immigrants who came to Canada in the 1990s live in one of Canada's metropolitan areas, and 73 percent of those immigrants live in Toronto, Montreal, and Vancouver. In contrast, only about 30 percent of the total Canadian population live in these metropolitan areas.

- Toronto is the main stopping point for new Canadians. Over 40 percent of all new Canadians in the past two decades have moved to Toronto. From 1991 to 2001, immigrants constituted 17 percent of Toronto's population. Markham became the first municipality in greater Toronto where more than half of the population comprises immigrants, with 56 percent visible minorities. More than 40 percent of the population of Toronto suburbs Mississauga, Brampton, Vaughan, and Richmond Hill were new immigrants (Carey, 2003).

- Of all immigrants in the 1990s, 63 percent were of working age. This reflects official immigration policy, which seeks to use immigration to fill gaps in the workforce.

- Sixty-one percent of the immigrants of the 1990s reported that neither of Canada's official languages was their first language, nor were they languages that were used at home. However, only 10 percent reported being unable to use either English or French.

- In 2001, over four million Canadians (13.4 percent) identified themselves as visible minorities.

- There has been a threefold increase in the number of people who identify themselves as visible minorities since 1981. Although the general Canadian population growth has been about 4 percent, the visible-minority population has grown by 25 percent for the period 1981 to 2001.

- Seventy-three percent of all immigrants to Canada are visible minorities. Almost 60 percent of visible-minority immigrants in the last 10 years were from Asia, with 20 percent from the Caribbean, Central and South America, and Africa. Toronto and Vancouver both have 37 percent visible-minority populations, the largest group being Asians. Ontario cities Hamilton and Windsor have nearly 25 and 22 percent visible-minority populations, respectively (Canadian Council on Social Development, 2003).

- The Aboriginal population of Canada is 4.4 percent of the Canadian population, up from 3.8 percent in 1966. Canada has the second-largest Aboriginal population next to New Zealand.

- By 2016, visible minorities will account for 20 percent of the Canadian population (Baxter, 2003, pp. 5–8).

Implications for Diversity

There has been a fundamental transformation in Canadian immigration since 1961. The "Old Canada," a country that resists multiculturalism, is predominantly rural, conservative, and white, and opposes social change, is still present, but is under pressure from a diverse number of ethnicities. This will have a profound effect on the ways people communicate, and on the ways public services will be delivered. Changes in communication will include recognizing cultural barriers to communication, adopting communications methods of diverse cultures, requiring bi- or trilingualism in public service and business workers, and acknowledging the implications of communicating on a global scale.

Before 1961, the Canadian government consciously attempted to retain the British nature of Canadian society. Canadian culture was bound by relatively strict morals and manners, and profound differences of opinion or culture would not be tolerated. The cultural emphasis was on work, the accumulation of wealth, the written word, codified laws and regulations, and punctuality.

After 1961, immigration resulted in the development of a society where social morals and manners were more diverse, dynamic, and fluid. Communication is expressed differently; words have to be understood in the context in which they are spoken.

These fundamental changes to Canadian lifestyles present a challenge to Canadian civil authorities. How can we expect someone from a small African community to become integrated into Canadian culture? How can we expect that person to understand something as complicated as Canada's *Criminal Code*? Most people who have been in Canada for more than three generations tend to take their understanding of what is socially acceptable, legal or illegal, or simply right and wrong, for granted, because they have been raised within this cultural context. Most Canadians who have been here for some time also assume that the predominant "rules of the game" in Canada are "natural" or "the best possible alternatives." These concepts are now being challenged, and the question of "What is a Canadian?" remains to be settled.

Immigrants face a number of challenges. Poverty, for instance, remains high among immigrant groups. The children of immigrants and visible minorities are twice as likely to live in poverty as other Canadian children. Almost one in two recent immigrant children live in poverty (Brown, 2005).

> Here in one of the wealthiest countries in the world, with the lowest unemployment rate in 30 years, it seems an irony that so many [immigrant] children still live in poverty. All of these groups are growing ... [O]ur national policy is to increase the number of immigrants ... but at the most basic levels of food and housing and income, these groups are being marginalized. (Laurel Rothman, Campaign 2000)

One of the many reasons for this poverty is the fact that male immigrants face barriers to good jobs. Earnings of recent immigrant men working full-time fell 7 percent in the period 1980–2000, while earnings of Canadian-born men rose 7 percent. Discrimination is still playing a big part in hiring, despite the law. The shortage of doctors in Ontario, and the shortage of skilled workers across the country, could be eased by the recognition of professional qualifications of immigrants. Low wages earned by immigrants put a strain on social services, and the employment situation is causing some immigrants to return to their homelands because they can't make a living here. For many immigrants, Canada is no longer a land of milk and honey (Fragomeni, 2003).

EXERCISE 6

Two problems facing immigrants—poverty and lack of acceptable credentials—are mentioned in the previous paragraph. List some of the other problems faced by immigrants, and give examples of each.

DEVELOPING A CANADIAN IDENTITY

Demographic trends indicate that more and more people are self-identifying as "Canadian." In the 2001 census, the most frequently reported ethnicities were

- Canadian (11.7 million),
- English (6 million),
- French (4.7 million),
- Scottish (4.2 million),
- Irish (3.8 million),
- German (2.7 million),
- Italian (1.3 million),
- Chinese (1.1 million),
- Ukrainian (1.1 million), and
- North American Indian (1 million) (Statistics Canada, 2001, pp. 11–12).

Self-identification is important, because it reflects values. From 1996 to 2001, over 30 percent of the population identified themselves as "Canadian."

This fact might suggest optimism toward identifying a Canadian identity. However, a study done by Rodolf Kalin and John W. Berry suggests that the majority of those who identify themselves as "Canadian" are members of the Charter groups (English and French). Slightly over one-half of people from other ethnic heritages chose to identify themselves as "Canadian."

It is likely that as successive generations of immigrant families live in Canada, they will lean more toward the "Canadian" identity label. According to the 2002 *Ethnic Diversity Survey*, immigrants were more likely than people born in Canada to report a stronger sense of belonging to their ethnic or cultural group, and immigrants who had recently arrived indicated that their ethnic or cultural ancestry was important to them (Statistics Canada, 2002, p. 1). As an example, there are more than 250 ethnic newspapers and magazines produced in the Toronto area alone. Their mission is to inform, to build community, and, as time goes on, to be passed on to the next generation (Ross, 2003, p. B1).

However, while the first generation of immigrants had the strongest sense of belonging to an **ethnic group**, that sense of ethnicity declined considerably by the third generation (Statistics Canada, 2002, p. 3). Identification with Canada increases with time in Canada, and participation in non-ethnic organizations also increases with time in Canada. Multiculturalism and cultural diversity seem to be working for Canada, and, rather than assimilating immigrants, it is likely that a true Canadian identity will emerge, taking into account the values of the various ethnic groups that contribute to Canadian society, as the Canadian identity becomes stronger. As Hassan Zerehi, publisher of an Iranian newspaper in Toronto, puts it:

> When an ethnic group first settles here, its members would likely cheer for their Homeland's team in a soccer match against a side representing Canada. Eventually, this changes. "Now we would want Canada to win." (Ross, 2003, p. B7)

ethnic group
group of individuals with a shared sense of peoplehood based on presumed shared socio-cultural experiences and/or similar characteristics

The search for a Canadian identity is likely premature. But when it does emerge, it will be characterized by openness, tolerance, multiculturalism, and diversity. It won't be a negaive "we're not like the United States" type of identity, but a positive identity of different heights, textures, and contours, where people of all sizes, shapes, and colours will be free to live their cultures and faiths to form part of the Canadian identity. There is still a way to go, but it's happening.

EXERCISE 7

How would you define the Canadian identity? What is a Canadian? How does a Canadian differ from citizens of any other country in the world? How do Canadians differ from Americans? Be specific in your answers, and give concrete examples.

CHAPTER SUMMARY

Canada is a diverse, multicultural country that encourages diverse groups to retain their cultures and cultural practices. The process of embracing diversity has been lengthy, beginning in colonial times, and reaching the stage where Canada now accepts in excess of 200,000 immigrants yearly. The People's Republic of China is now the leading country of birth for immigrants, and Chinese, South Asians, and Blacks form the largest visible-minority population. This trend has many implications for the development of a Canadian identity.

KEY TERMS

multiculturalism

diversity

ethnicity

multiculturalism ideology

values

civic ideology

assimilation ideology

ethnist ideology

discrimination

host community

settlement patterns

integrationist

exclusionary

assimilationist

segregationist

acculturation

marginalization

assimilation

separation

integration

refugee policy

visible minority

ethnic group

REFERENCES

Baxter, P. (2003). A portrait of Canadian diversity. Unpublished manuscript. Barrie, ON: Georgian College.

Berry, J.W. (1990). Psychology of acculturation: Understanding individuals moving between cultures. In R.W. Brislin (Ed.), *Applied cross-cultural psychology* (pp. 232–252). Newbury Park, CA: Sage.

Berry, J.W. (1998). Acculturation and health: Theory and research. In S.S. Kazarian & D.R. Evans (Eds.), *Cultural clinical psychology: Theory, research and practice* (pp. 39–60). New York: Oxford University Press.

Berry, J.W., & D. Sam. (1997). Acculturation and adaptation. In J.W. Berry, M.H. Segal, & C. Kagitcibasi (Eds.), *Handbook of cross-cultural psychology: Social behavior and applications.* Vol. 3 (pp. 291–326). Needham Heights, MA: Allyn and Bacon.

Bourhis, R.Y., L.C. Moise, S. Perreault, & S. Senecal. (1997). Towards an interactive acculturation model: A social psychological perspective. *International Journal of Psychology* 32: 369–386.

Brown, L. (2005, November 24). Native, minority kids twice as likely to be poor. *The Hamilton Spectator*, p. A11.

Canadian Council on Social Development. (2003). Census shows increasing diversity of Canadian society. http://www.ccsd.ca/pr/2003/diversity.htm.

Canadian Heritage. (2001). Canadian diversity: Respecting our differences. http://www.pch.gc.ca/progs/multi/respect_e.cfm.

Carey, E. (2003, February 11). Census shows 905 home to more immigrants. *The Toronto Star*. http://www.thestar.com.

Carmichael, A. (2006, April 19). Chinese Canadians being consulted on apology. The Canadian Press. *The Hamilton Spectator*, p. A11.

Chrétien, J. (1982). *Canadian Charter of Rights and Freedoms: A Guide for Canadians.* Ottawa: Supply and Services.

Cultures Canada. (2003, July 23). A day to celebrate Canadian diversity. http://www.culturescanada.ca.

Fernandez, J.P. (1991). *Making a diverse workforce: Regaining the competitive edge.* Lexington, MA: Lexington Books.

Fleras, A. (1994). Multiculturalism as society-building: Doing what is necessary, workable and fair. In M. Charlton & P. Barker (Eds.), *Contemporary political issues* (pp. 25-40). Scarborough, ON: Nelson.

Fleras, A. "Engaging in diversity." In Baxter (2003). p. 32.

Fragomeni, C. (2003, October 9). Male immigrants face barriers to high-paying jobs. *The Hamilton Spectator*, p. A12.

Heritage Canada. (2006). *Annual report on the operation of the Canadian Multiculturalism Act: 2004–2005.* http://www.multiculturalism.pch.gc.ca.

Holborn, L.W. (1975). *Refugees: A problem of our time: The work of the United Nations High Commission for Refugees 1951–1972.* Metuchen, NJ: The Scarecrow Press.

Immigration and Refugee Protection Act. http://laws.justice.gc.ca/en/I-2.5.

International Debate Education Association. Treatment of Aboriginals. (2003, January 23). http://www.idebate.org/debatabase_topic_index.php.

Kalin, R., & J.W. Barry. (2000). Ethnic and self-identity in Canada: Analyses of 1974 and 1991 national surveys. In M.A. Kalbach & W.E. Kalbach (Eds.), *Perspectives on ethnicity in Canada* (pp. 88–110). Toronto: Harcourt Brace.

Kalinowski, T. (2003, October 12). Celebrating cultures in classes. *Toronto Star*, p. A4.

Kallen, E. (2003). *Ethnicity and human rights in Canada: A human rights perspective on race, ethnicity, racism and systemic inequality.* New York: Oxford University Press.

Kaprelian, E. (1982). Armenians in Ontario. *Polyphony* 4: 5–11.

Kazarian, S. (2001). *Diversity issues in law enforcement* (2nd ed.). Toronto: Emond Montgomery.

Kazarian, S.S. (1997). The Armenian psyche: Genocide and acculturation. *Mentalities* 12: 74–87.

Kymlicka, W. (1995). *Multicultural citizenship: A liberal theory of minority rights.* New York: Oxford.

Multiculturalism at work. (2002, April 19). *Montreal Gazette,* http://www.antiracistaction.ca/montreal4192002d.html.

Nef, J., & R. da Silva. (1991). The politics of refugee generation in Latin America. In H. Adelman (Ed.), *Refugee policy: Canada and the United States* (pp. 52–80). North York, ON: York Lanes Press.

Roberts, J. (2006). *First Nations, Inuit, and Métis peoples: Exploring their past, present, and future.* Toronto: Emond Montgomery.

Ross, O. (2003, November 2). All the world's a page. *Toronto Star*, pp. B1, 7.

Statistics Canada. (2001). 2001 Census: Analysis Series. Canada's ethnocultural portrait: The changing mosaic. http://www.statcan.ca/bsolc/english/bsolc?catno=96F0030X2001008.

Statistics Canada. (2002). Ethnic Diversity Survey 2002. *The Daily.* http://www.statcan.ca/English/dai.quo.

Statistics Canada. (2005). Canada at a glance 2005. Catalogue no. 12-581-XPE. http://www.statcan.ca.

United Nations. (1983). *Convention and protocol relating to the status of refugees: Final act of the United Nations Conference of Plenipotentiaries on the Status of Refugees and Stateless Persons and the text of the 1951 Convention Relating to Refugees. Resolution 2198 adopted by the General Assembly and the text of the 1967 Protocol Relating to the Status of Refugees.* New York: United Nations.

University of Maryland. (2000). *Diversity database.* http://www.umd.edu/diversity.

CHAPTER 2

Law Enforcement Culture in a Diversity Context

CHAPTER OBJECTIVES

After completing this chapter, you should be able to:

- Recognize the importance of diversity in law enforcement settings.
- Explain police culture in terms of a demographic police profile, the context of policing, and core values.
- Discuss law enforcement within the contexts of social and cultural diversity.

INTRODUCTION

Law enforcement officials serve and protect many diverse groups in Canada's **pluralistic** society, a society comprising many cultural groups in one country. More than 200 different ethnic origins were reported in the 2001 Census question on ethnic ancestry, including First Nations peoples, Inuit, and Métis, as well as French and English (Statistics Canada, 2001). Needless to say, law enforcement is imbedded in **diversity**. This chapter discusses the concept of diversity in relation to law enforcement services, and discusses models of policing and the police culture. Diversity is viewed as an asset to law enforcement rather than a liability.

pluralism
state of having many cultural groups in one country

diversity
variety of human qualities among different people and groups

DIVERSITY AND POLICE

Recognizing cultural diversity is an important component of the philosophies of many police services, to the extent that some police services have a diversity component as part of their officers' yearly evaluations. The section of the Hamilton Police Service evaluation form relating to diversity is shown on the following page.

FIGURE 2.1 Diversity Component of Hamilton Police Service Officers' Evaluation

10 Valuing Diversity:

Valuing Diversity is the ability to understand and respect the practices, customs, values and norms of individuals, groups and cultures other than one's own. It is not restricted to employment equity, but includes the ability to respect and value diverse points-of-view, and to be open to others of differing backgrounds or perspectives. It includes seeing diversity as beneficial to the Hamilton Police Service. It also implies the ability to work effectively with a wide cross-section of the community representing diverse backgrounds, cultures, and/or socio-economic circumstances.

Expectations:	☐ Requires Improvement ☐ Meets Exceeds: ☐ (d) ☐ (e)
(a) Accepts Diversity	Is willing to accept and respect the practices, customs, values and norms of other individuals or groups. Is open to others of different backgrounds or perspective. Responds openly when approached by others.
(b) Values Differences or Diversity	Values diversity and actively seeks out opportunities to gain new knowledge and understanding of individuals/groups through learning and active community participation and involvement. Recognizes prejudices and systemic barriers which may exist within the current environment.
(c) Monitors and Modifies Own Behaviours	Monitors and evaluates own beliefs and behaviours with regard to prejudices and personal bias. Practices new behaviours that reflect an understanding and appreciation of diversity.
(d) Challenges Others	Openly and directly addresses issues or situations that may not support diversity and tolerance of others. Holds people accountable for their actions to ensure that their behaviour reflects an appreciation and acceptance of diversity. Educates others of the value of diversity, and teaches tolerance and openness to diverse ideas and backgrounds.
(e) Actively Promotes Diversity	Actively promotes the value of diversity through planned and visible activities aimed at building sensitivity to, and support for, others. Actively promotes and supports programs that are designed to increase diversity within the Hamilton Police Service.

Supporting Evidence:

Comments:

TABLE 2.1 Principles of the Ontario Police Services Act

Declaration of principles

Police services shall be provided throughout Ontario in accordance with the following principles:

1. The need to ensure the safety and security of all persons and property in Ontario.
2. The importance of safeguarding the fundamental rights guaranteed by the *Canadian Charter of Rights and Freedoms* and the *Human Rights Code*.
3. The need for co-operation between the providers of police services and the communities they serve.
4. The importance of respect for victims of crime and understanding of their needs.
5. The need for sensitivity to the pluralistic, multiracial and multicultural character of Ontario society.
6. The need to ensure that police services are representative of the communities they serve.

Source: *Police Services Act*, RSO 1990, c. P.15, s. 1.

Diversity is incorporated in two of the six principles of the Ontario *Police Services Act*: the principle of sensitivity to the pluralistic, multiracial, and multicultural character of Ontario society, and the principle of ensuring that police services are representative of the communities they serve.

EXERCISE 1

After reading the sections on multiculturalism in table 2.1 and after reading the diversity evaluation practised by the Hamilton Police Service, do you feel that every police service in Canada should have an evaluation of this nature? Should a similar evaluation be given to customs and corrections officers? Should an evaluation be carried out at all, given the fact that understanding diversity is part of the job for law enforcement officers? Are there items other than those listed in the Hamilton Police Service evaluation that should be included? Give reasons for your answers.

DIVERSITY IDEOLOGIES AND POLICIES IN LAW ENFORCEMENT

Nations around the world are increasingly experiencing diversity but holding different attitudes toward people of diversity (see "Four State Ideologies" in chapter 1). Canada is unique in having a constitutionally enshrined multiculturalism policy that is inspired by a diversity framework.

Law enforcement agencies in pluralistic societies are part of, rather than apart from, the diversity mosaic. For example, law enforcement agencies in Ontario are cultural communities within a community of millions of people of diversity. Multiculturalism and human rights legislation provide the legal foundation for a diversity law enforcement framework and a core infrastructure for protecting individual and collective rights for diversity sustenance and enhancement. Every individual in

Canada has the right to democratic citizenry, to full and equal participation in society, and to the preservation of his or her diversity. These rights are optimized when both the letter and spirit of diversity policies are honoured (Kazarian, 2001, p. 35).

POLICE CULTURE

People in law enforcement live for the safety and protection of all citizens within their jurisdiction. Police officers, for instance, spend countless hours controlling crime; maintaining the law, peace, and order; responding to neighbourhood problems; assisting people in crises; helping to solve a wide range of social issues; and contributing to the enhancement of people's quality of life. Rather than merely doing their jobs, police officers *live* their jobs—that is, they think of their jobs as part of their personalities.

The list of functions performed by police leads to an exploration of the meaning of the **police culture**. Police culture is defined, in part, as the expression of common values, beliefs, and attitudes of police within a police context (Waddington, 1999). In 2000, 56,000 police officers were members of the police culture in Canada (Statistics Canada, 2000). In the sections below, we explore police culture by examining the demographic police profile, context of policing, and core values in policing.

police culture
attitudes, values, and beliefs in police organizations that influence police reactions and behaviours within the police services and on the street

EXERCISE 2

Notwithstanding the definition of "police culture" given above, how do you think the general public would define the term "police culture"? Would this definition differ from one given by a person in a visible-minority group?

DEMOGRAPHIC POLICE PROFILE

Police services now strive to represent the diversity of the communities that they serve and protect. Nevertheless, it is a historical reality that police services in pluralistic Western countries, including Canada, Australia, the United Kingdom, and the United States, were not representative of the diversities within those countries. For example, males tended to be overrepresented in police services (called police "forces" until relatively recently), resulting in the perception of the police as a **white machismo culture**. This is a culture in which white skin colour, masculinity, and hierarchy are emphasized, while non-whites, women, and non-traditional sexual orientation are devalued. Police officers who subscribe to the "culture of masculinity" (Waddington, 1999) have a "gladiator mentality" and have "the sense of a crime-fighting mission that provides ideological justification for authority that is exercised against fellow citizens."

white machismo culture
culture in which whiteness, masculinity, and hierarchy are emphasized and diversity, women, gays and lesbians, and horizontality are devalued

There is evidence to suggest that law enforcement continues to be a male-dominated culture. While the situation is slowly being corrected in Canada, a chronic gender imbalance does remain in 2007. This is a paradoxical situation considering the positive impact of women in policing, including the reduction in police brutality, the increased desire to deal with the problem of violence against women, and the increased emphasis on conflict resolution rather than the use of force. Police services in Canada continue to target women as potential recruits in order to overcome this gender imbalance.

Inequalities in other primary dimensions of diversity—for example, ethnicity, race, and sexual orientation—also exist in law enforcement. To put the entire blame for unequal representation on law enforcement agencies is unfair. The absence of visible minorities in law enforcement is at least partly due to non-white immigrant families and Aboriginals not encouraging their children to consider law enforcement as a worthwhile and satisfying career. Visible-minority immigrants may believe that policing is not a good career due to a lack of knowledge of professional opportunities and career advancement offered by law enforcement, or these minorities may prefer that their children pursue more traditional professions that are given high social status by the minority communities.

The reluctance of minority immigrant families to consider law enforcement as a career option for their children may also be due to these families' negative experiences with law enforcement in their countries of origin. Finally, the reluctance of immigrant, non-white families to consider law enforcement as a career may be due to their misperception that *all* law enforcement agencies are pervaded by the white machismo culture. These and other reasons provide the impetus for law enforcement agencies to develop more inclusive recruiting strategies to heighten the interest of diverse groups in law enforcement as a career. People of diversity need to learn more about law enforcement, while law enforcement agencies need to reach out to people of diversity and educate them on the benefits of a career in law enforcement.

EXERCISE 3

Some soul searching is required in this exercise. Do you consider law enforcement to be a male-dominated profession; in other words, is it still a white machismo culture? Are women and visible minorities being targeted as potential recruits in order to truly overcome gender and diversity inequality, or is this merely window dressing to deflect criticism of law enforcement hiring practices? If you believe that the white machismo culture still prevails, do you think that this culture will disappear as older law enforcement officers retire, or is the culture ingrained in law enforcement?

Law Enforcement Knowledge of Cultural Groups

Law enforcement representatives have the ultimate authority to arrest or admonish someone suspected of a crime. Discretion based on cultural knowledge at the police level is much more significant than what happens in the courts. Individual officers have the opportunity to create positive public relations if they demonstrate cultural sensitivity and respect toward members of an ethnic community. Awareness of and sensitivity to cultural issues can have a significant impact on the criminal justice system, in which police have the power to either inflame or calm the people involved in a particular incident. In certain types of situations, officers can rethink traditional police methods in order to be as effective as possible. This involves knowledge of ethnic communities and a desire to establish a positive and trustworthy image in those communities (Katz, 2003, p. 23).

Improving Law Enforcement in Diverse Communities

Police services and police officers can improve law enforcement in their communities by remembering the following tips:

- Make positive contact with community group members from diverse backgrounds.

- Allow the public to see the police as much as possible in a non–law enforcement role.

- Make a conscious effort to treat all segments of society justly and fairly.

- Remember that criminal activity is not linked to any particular ethnic group.

- Make a particular effort to show the positive side of law enforcement to minority groups.

- Avoid discussing a suspect's racial or cultural background with the public.

- Take responsibility for discussing the role of the police officer and police procedures to members of ethnic communities.

- Take the initiative to improve relationships with ethnic groups within your community (Shusta, 2005, p. 31).

Recruiting Members of Diverse Communities

The Toronto Police Service is making an effort to recruit more visible-minority women. In January 2006, the service held an information session at Charles O. Bick College in Toronto for 40 women of South and West Asian backgrounds, primarily to familiarize them with the physical testing required of all applicants. These included clearing an obstacle course and dragging a 150-pound dummy 24 feet in 2 minutes, 42 seconds. The women also practised handcuffing using an arm restraint simulator.

Constables in charge of recruiting both South Asian men and women for the service, as well as people from the gay, lesbian, bisexual, and transgender communities, feel that the physical testing keeps many of these people from applying. Only about 200 officers of the 5,000-member Toronto Police Service are visible minorities as of early 2006. It is hoped that another 300 can be recruited (Battacharya, 2006, p. A6).

CONTEXT OF LAW ENFORCEMENT

Police do their best to fight crime and put criminals behind bars. However, no modern society is free of crime. Crime is not easily eradicated, and public fear of crime in many parts of the world continues to be high (US Department of Justice, 1999).

In Canada, 2,384,247 *Criminal Code* offences were reported in 2002, an increase of 0.4 percent over 2001. The offences break down as shown in table 2.2. Figure 2.2 illustrates the trend in the crime rate in Canada over the period 1967–2002.

Policing is a lifestyle, not just a career; police take their profession to heart, and make many sacrifices. Analysis of police work shows five important characteristics: shift work, long work hours, crisis-driven and unpredictable public contacts, public scrutiny, and work-related injuries (Kirschman, 1997).

Police officers and many law enforcement officials work shifts. Shift work is difficult; in addition to contributing to sleep disturbance, shift work raises potential issues of isolation, reduced quality time with family, and more difficult family

TABLE 2.2 Reported Crime Statistics

	1984	1994	2004
Total *Criminal Code* offences[1]	**2,147,656**	**2,646,209**	**2,571,860**
Property crimes	1,408,663	1,524,519	1,274,931
Crimes of violence	179,396	303,745	302,257
Other crimes	559,597	817,945	994,672
Selected offences			
Homicide	667	596	622
Assault	149,931	268,270	270,181
Sexual assault	14,793	31,706	23,534
Prostitution	1,024	5,575	6,493
Break and enter	356,912	387,867	274,717
Motor vehicle theft	76,613	159,469	169,544
Fraud	122,775	103,243	97,091
Drugs	54,950	60,153	97,135

[1] Excluding all *Criminal Code* traffic offences, such as impaired driving.

Source: Statistics Canada (2006, p. 7).

FIGURE 2.2 Crime Rate for Canada

Rate per 100,000 population

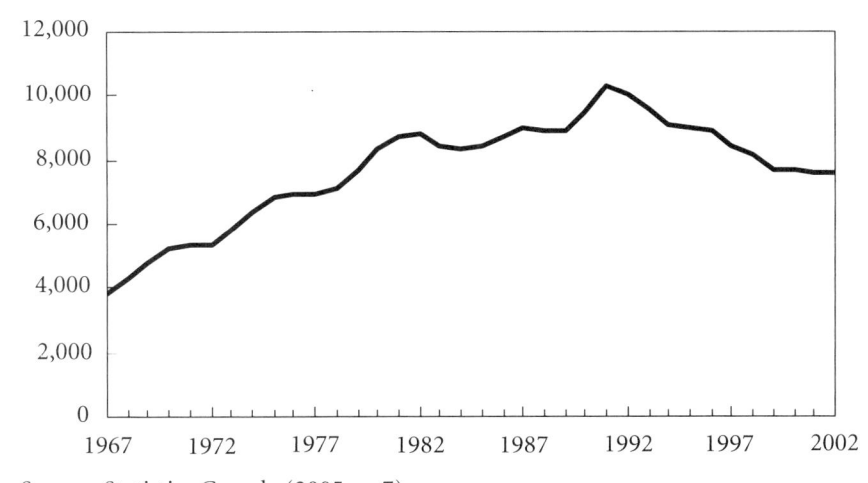

Source: Statistics Canada (2005, p. 7).

scheduling. Many marriages of law enforcement officials end in divorce; it is difficult to balance the demands of the profession with family, friends, and leisure time.

Police work involves long hours and is unpredictable, by virtue of crises and emergency responses. While the variety and spontaneity of police work is alluring, it is not without its drawbacks (Kirschman, 1997). First, the unpredictability of the work may interfere with planned family activities. Second, the unpredictability causes stress in the family through the host of emotions the police officer may express when he or she returns home. These emotions may range from irritability to simply being glad to be alive.

Law enforcement officials, especially police, are likely to experience public scrutiny of their work. For example, the often intrusive coverage of police and the criticisms police receive from the media and the community can be sources of stress for police, their partners, and their children. One recent example of public scrutiny and media criticism of the police occurred during the Caledonia, Ontario, Aboriginal land dispute in 2006. The public and the media were particularly critical of the Ontario Provincial Police for not enforcing the law equally between the Aboriginal people and non-Aboriginals involved in the dispute. In one case, television cameramen were allegedly attacked by Aboriginal protestors while a number of OPP officers stood by and did nothing. Two rallies by non-Aboriginals over this alleged preferential treatment for Aboriginal protestors led to additional police involvement in the dispute.

In addition, law enforcement work involves the use or threat of violence. People in law enforcement encounter violent individuals, who put the officers' safety at risk. Law enforcement officials may also have to use force, as is commonly seen in corrections or police settings. People may die in the process. Police view the *necessary* shooting of a person not as killing a person, but as terminating violence. The vast majority of law enforcement officials strive to beat crime and not criminals, although an extreme few may still exhibit **ego forcing**, the use of unnecessary force to boost a macho self-image.

ego forcing
use of unnecessary force to boost macho self-image

Finally, law enforcement work is often associated with on-the-job injuries, making physical fitness a crucial component in all law enforcement work. Regular physical exercise is an important protective factor against work-related injuries.

EXERCISE 4

Although statistics indicate that crime is generally on the decline across the country, do you think the general public believes that crime is being reduced? Are statistics being used to manipulate the public into feeling safer on the streets and in their homes, while some types of crime are actually on the rise? Can statistics be used to encourage the hiring of more police officers? Does crime appear to be declining in your neighbourhood, or do you feel that the statistics apply to somewhere else?

CORE VALUES IN POLICING

A very positive aspect of police culture is that it is a collectivist culture. Police value one another for safety, mutual support, and quality of life. A number of **core values** are associated with the collectivist police culture: self-control, cynicism, respect for authority, hypervigilance, and a code of silence (Crank, 1997; Kirschman, 1997; Stansfield, 1996; Williams & Henderson, 1997). These core values may be adaptive (healthy) for police officers but they may also be maladaptive (unhealthy—that is, they may interfere with quality of life). They are mentioned here not as a criticism but to raise awareness of their potential influence on police behaviour and quality of life.

Police officers may value **self-control**, which entails suppressing verbal and non-verbal expressions of emotion. Police self-control of emotions is developed by virtue of training and prolonged exposure to the distresses and despairs of life. Self-control serves three important functions: enhancing self-image, controlling others, and saving face. Self-control enhances police self-image by allowing officers to appear knowledgeable, fearless, and in control. Self-control enables police to maintain an emotional distance in carrying out their work and to control others who require such control—for example, calming victims of a serious traffic accident. In the absence of self-control, officers' ability to cope with situations in which they are hit, spat on, or humiliated is likely to be compromised. Finally, self-control enables police to sustain the respect and support of their fellow officers by refraining from displaying negative emotions in their presence.

While self-control is a protective strategy for police, overcontrolling emotions—that is, showing no emotion, regardless of feelings or the situation—may interfere with spontaneity and intimacy in interpersonal and family relations. In addition to social remoteness, emotional overcontrol and numbness may prevent self-growth by shutting off normal and appropriate expression. Police need to learn not to keep everything inside all the time, because what is inside may pollute their body and mind.

Cynicism is a second core value in police culture. **Cynicism** is the belief that everyone in the world is primarily motivated by selfishness (Kirschman, 1997; Neiderhoffer, 1967; Skolnick, 1966). Police become cynical because of their prolonged exposure to the worst in human behaviour. The four stages of cynicism are overidealism, frustration, disenchantment, and full-blown "hardened" world view. The hardened world view can contribute to denying goodness in people, assuming a behavioural pattern of overprotecting self and family, and having an isolationist ("blue wall") social style that accepts only fellow cops (Skolnick, 1966).

Respect for authority is a third core value in police culture. Police are trained to develop **respect for authority**. This core value provides simplicity, clarity, and comfort for police in fulfilling their role and executing their duties. The positive function of respect for authority, however, may prove dysfunctional; non-compliance from other people in the line of duty or at home can represent a violation of respect for authority. Such non-compliance is a source of frustration for police, may be perceived by them as a sign of personal incompetence, and may cause them to overreact.

Hypervigilance is a fourth core value in police culture. **Hypervigilance** entails the belief that survival of police and of others depends on police ability to view everything in the environment as potentially life threatening and dangerous. Officers are "urged, warned, required, and rewarded for developing a habit of scanning

core values
values of self-control, cynicism, respect for authority, hypervigilance, and code of silence associated with the collectivist police culture

self-control
suppression of verbal and non-verbal expressions of emotion

cynicism
belief that the primary motivation behind human behaviour is selfishness

respect for authority
core value stemming from the prevailing paramilitary organizational structure of police services, which provides simplicity, clarity, and comfort for police in fulfilling their role and executing their duties

hypervigilance
belief that survival of police and of others depends on police ability to view everything in the environment as potentially life-threatening and dangerous

the environment for cues to danger" (Kirschman, 1997, p. 27). The scanning behaviour associated with hypervigilance

> becomes so finely tuned that even mild danger alerts the officer's autonomic nervous system. The cop experiences this as "buzz": a general sense of aliveness, high energy, vitality, and alertness. This state of physiological elevation becomes its own reward, like a runner's high. This is what cops mean when they talk about police work getting "into their blood" or about becoming addicted to their own adrenalin. (Kirschman, 1997, pp. 27–28)

While hypervigilance helps police execute their duties and survive real or potentially dangerous situations, their alarmist world view may interfere with their ability to discriminate lethal situations from innocuous ones. Kirschman (1997, p. 28) points out that

> [t]he problem arises when cops become so hypervigilant that they actually search for an opportunity to get involved in an emergency because they need that hit of adrenalin to avoid feeling depressed or listless. Or they develop a sense of superiority to anyone—including their family members—who doesn't share their alarmist point of view.

code of silence
core value of withholding information from anyone who is not a member of the police culture

The **code of silence** is a fifth core value in police culture. It is consistent with the brotherhood police image—that an attack on one is an attack on all (Skolnick, 1966)—and entails the value of withholding information from anyone who is not a member of the police culture. Those who are excluded include the public, the courts, and police services management (Stansfield, 1996, p. 170). While the code of silence is both informal and unofficial, its basis, according to Stansfield, is the official police "oath of secrecy" as stated in many police services acts, including that of Ontario:

> The oath or affirmation of secrecy to be taken by a police officer, auxiliary member of a police force, special constable or First Nations Constable shall be in the following form:
>
> > I solemnly swear (affirm) that I will not disclose any information obtained by me in the course of my duties as (*insert name of office*), except as I may be authorized or required by law. (O. reg. 144/91, s. 4)

The vast majority of police officers are professional and ethical in their conduct. The code of silence, however, may exert a powerful influence on police behaviour, including potentially leading them to commit perjury. Police who break the code of silence are called various names, including "rat," "stool pigeon," "squealer," and "the one who tells." In extreme cases, those who breach the code of silence are penalized and ostracized by other police to affirm commitment to the value of police solidarity represented by the code (Stansfield, 1996).

> **EXERCISE 5**
>
> Examine each of the core values described above. Rank each of them in order of what you consider to be important as far as essential police values are concerned. For example, how important is the "code of silence"? Is it an effective value in reducing crime, or is it merely a value established to separate law enforcement personnel from the general public and "not let the public in" to the world of the police culture? Does hypervigilance lead to crime reduction, or is it paranoia?

POLICE–COMMUNITY INTERFACE

The responsibility for providing police services is shared by municipal, provincial, and federal governments. In Canada, the majority of police (63 percent) belong to municipal police services. In 2000, there were about 183 officers per 100,000 population (Statistics Canada, 2000). Many police services in North America have adopted the motto "To serve and protect." These serving and protecting functions—or the **police–community interface**—are presumed to be extended to all community residents, regardless of their culture, race, ethnic origin, religion, sex, age, sexual orientation, or physical or mental ability. A recent international survey involving 11 Western industrial nations showed that satisfaction with police performance was highest in Canada. In fact, the study found that "Canadians love their cops far more than the English love their famed British Bobby" (Durkan, 1998, p. A9). Nevertheless, issues in policing in multicultural contexts continue to evolve. Common concerns being addressed in police departments around the world include internal organizational structure and culture, and the police–community interface.

police–community interface
represented by the motto "To serve and protect," the principle that police functions are presumed to be afforded to all community residents regardless of their culture, race, ethnic origin, religion, sex, age, sexual orientation, or physical or mental ability

> **EXERCISE 6**
>
> What does the motto "To serve and protect" mean to you? Discuss this motto in a diversity context.

Two primary approaches have dominated policing in the global village: the police force approach and the police services approach (Fleras, 1992; Williams & Henderson, 1997). A summary of both approaches is provided in table 2.3. The **police force approach** has assumed a management structure and culture in which a reactive, crime control mandate is emphasized so that police are seen as warrior cops, and police effectiveness is measured by such indicators as number of random patrols to deter criminal activity, response rate to police calls, number of arrests and convictions, and citizen satisfaction surveys (Fleras, 1992). An underlying assumption of the crime control approach is that streets and neighbourhoods can be reclaimed only by a strong centralized police department that promotes a police culture that is hard on crime. Potential negative consequences of the crime control approach to policing are isolation from the community and the people served and police harbouring an us-versus-them mentality.

police force approach
emphasizes a reactive, crime control mandate that measures police effectiveness by such indicators as number of random patrols to deter criminal activity, response rate to police calls, number of arrests and convictions, and citizen satisfaction surveys

TABLE 2.3 Police Force Approach Versus Police Services Approach

Police force	Police services
Crime fighting	Crime preventing
Incident-drive	Problem-driven
Reactive	Proactive
Us versus them	Partner with community
Centralized	Decentralized
Hierarchical	Flattened
Diversity-blind	Diversity-responsive
Inwardly focused	Outwardly focused

police services approach emphasizes problem solving, crime prevention, and partnerships between police and communities

On the other hand, the **police services approach** has assumed a structure and a culture in which new core knowledge, skills, and abilities are identified to enhance police officers' effectiveness in performing their duties. The Ministry of Solicitor General Strategic Planning Committee on Police Training and Education (1992) lists 20 police abilities, knowledge sets, and skills (PAKS) that are of strategic importance to future police organizations.

1. ability to accept and work with community diversity,
2. ability to service victims,
3. ability to use force appropriately,
4. ability to reform community policing,
5. ability to act ethically and professionally,
6. ability to solve problems,
7. knowledge of crime prevention strategies,
8. knowledge of human behaviour,
9. knowledge of political systems and processes,
10. knowledge of other agencies,
11. communication skills,
12. interpersonal skills,
13. sensitivity skills,
14. conflict avoidance skills,
15. resolution skills,
16. mediation skills,
17. officer safety skills,
18. personal skills,
19. organizational development skills, and
20. team-building skills.

CHAPTER 2 Law Enforcement Culture in a Diversity Context

A key area of strategic learning and an important aspect of the police services approach is **community policing principles** or problem-solving policing principles. An underlying assumption of the crime prevention model is that streets and neighbourhoods can be reclaimed by promoting a police culture that is inclusive of the rank and file as well as of civic empowerment (Williams & Henderson, 1997). Empowerment entails openness on the part of the administration (from the chief on down) to input from the rank and file as well as embracing partnerships with communities. The proactive and problem-solving orientation of the police services approach provides for identifying and solving problems, resolving the underlying causes of disputes, preventing future recurrences, and eliminating the need for arrests and convictions except when necessary (Clyderman, O'Toole, & Fleras, 1992). Principles associated with problem-solving policing and community policing are listed in table 2.4. Examples of problem-solving and community policing programs are Crime Stoppers and Neighbourhood Watch.

community policing principles
principles associated with the police services approach that provide for identifying and solving problems, resolving the underlying causes of disputes, preventing future recurrences, and eliminating the need for arrests and convictions except when necessary

EXERCISE 7

While the police services approach seems to be taking hold in many police services across the country (which is one of the reasons they are called "services" rather than "forces"), can you see some aspects of the police force approach that should be retained? Are police services seen to be softer on crime because of their "kinder, gentler" approach? Will the police services approach be more effective than the police force approach in dealing with crack houses, organized crime, sexual assaults, homicides, and the like? Can you come up with an effective combination of the police services approach and the police force approach that might cover all situations?

Community policing is not universally accepted and is resisted within some law enforcement circles (Lewis, Rosenberg, & Sigler, 1999). This resistance is partly due to the perception that community policing is "feminized" policing in that it abandons the traditional "masculine" crime-fighting approach (Miller, 1999). Needless to say, this perception is false. Community policing does not betray policing history—it enhances traditional law enforcement and makes policing more responsive to the culturally diverse public.

Technological changes have had profound effects on the police–community interface. Cars and computers contributed to the shift from a proactive approach to policing to a reactive approach. As described by Williams & Henderson (1997), the bond between officers who "walked the beat" and members of the community provided a natural climate for public safety and crime prevention. In contrast, the use of cars and computerized communications systems minimizes routine police contact with customers, reduces police problem-solving opportunities, allows for reactive and prioritized police responses to calls, and violates the fundamental principle articulated by Sir Robert Peel, a British politician credited with founding modern policing, in 1829—namely, that "the public are the police and the police the public."

TABLE 2.4 Principles of Community Policing

- Empowering police officers and supervisors to solve community issues without having to seek a stamp of approval from the police hierarchy.

- Actively listening, at all police levels, to community issues, concerns, and solutions.

- Providing needs-based police services determined by public input.

- Adopting a style of internal police management that is responsive to the recruitment of police with attributes and skills conducive to effective community-oriented policing.

- Applying a people-oriented philosophy to the organization of police services, to law interpretation, and to law enforcement.

- Communicating with citizens in languages they understand, including mandatory police acquisition of second languages for the purposes of communication and minimization of conflict, doubt, and distrust.

- Selecting and training police officers to ensure that the best people are entrusted with the job of policing.

- Using police officers the best way possible, including who is assigned to a variety of jobs and a variety of neighbourhoods.

- Ensuring that the men and women of a police service reflect the cultural diversity of the community served.

- Assigning officers to work with residents, schools, and community groups for the purpose of resolving community issues.

- Treating employees of police services fairly by fostering an environment within the ranks that is free of sexual harassment, discrimination, and bias.

Source: Williams & Henderson (1997, pp. 219–220).

POLICE CULTURE IN A DIVERSITY CONTEXT: POLICE ABILITIES, KNOWLEDGE, AND SKILLS

Police serve and protect a diverse public. In their day-to-day lives, police may encounter individuals from a variety of cultural groups, languages, genders, ages, socio-economic classes, religions, sexual orientations, and physical and mental abilities, and with different levels of psychological well-being. This diversity dictates a diversity-oriented policing structure and function.

The vast majority of police see diversity as a valuable part of their challenging and rewarding police lifestyle. People of diversity are vital and contributing members of the communities served and protected by police. Principle 5 of the Ontario *Police Services Act* envisions a police service that is sensitive "to the pluralistic, multiracial and multicultural character of Ontario society" (s. 1). Putting this principle into practice requires that the diversity of the communities be reflected within the police services from the highest to the lowest rank. This is for the benefit of not only those communities but also the police. There is evidence that diversity within police forces and provision of diversity-appropriate services *enhance* police safety and respect from the visible-minority communities.

The Community Policing Consortium (1996) identifies the following specific benefits to adopting a **diversity policing framework**:

- reduction in the frequency of injuries to law enforcement officers and citizens,
- decrease in the number of citizen complaints and lawsuits against police,
- improvement in police–community relations,
- recognition and appreciation of the value of diversity to police services and its use as an asset rather than a liability, and
- effective response to major demographic changes in communities served.

The amount of admiration and respect that people of diversity have for police work should not be underestimated. The prevailing strategy for dealing with diversity issues in pluralistic societies in general and policing in particular has been the negative approach, in which victims assume the role of victimizer. Using police training courses and police–community conflicts as platforms for bitter criticism and attacks is counterproductive to policing and police–community relations at best and destructive at worst. It is more important to create the necessary dialogue for solving problems and resolving conflicts.

Police must be aware that it is time to partner with people of diversity to salvage an already strained relationship. There are indications that societies and police are paying more heed to diversity. Table 2.5 lists a number of initiatives in support of efforts to diversify policing and to address diversity issues in policing.

Four core values are identified with diversity policing: affirming and valuing diversity; assuming a police–community climate that validates diverse perspectives; empowering diverse voices within and outside the police service in goal setting, problem solving, and decision making; and promoting a police culture that respects the rights of people of diversity, police safety, and the person.

diversity policing framework
affirms and values people of diversity; assumes a police–community climate that validates diversity; empowers voices of diversity within and outside the police force in goal setting, problem solving, and decision making; and promotes a police–community culture that is respectful of the rights of people of diversity, police safety, and the person

EXERCISE 8

List the advantages of community policing to people of diversity. Is community policing an effective way to encourage people of diversity to become more interested in law enforcement as a career?

The remaining chapters of this book address a variety of diversity issues in policing to rethink policing in a diversity context and engender six policing competencies: analytical thinking, effective communication, flexibility, self-confidence, self-control, and relationship building. The process of rethinking policing in this way can evoke highly charged emotions when one is exposed to controversial issues and positions. While this process can lead to better personal understanding and growth, interpersonal relations, and policing effectiveness, it can also be confusing and painful at times. However, personal and interpersonal growth are worth it, and the process can be made easier by generating a climate of self-respect, respect for others, dialogue, patience, hard work, and willingness to grow.

TABLE 2.5 Diversity Initiatives in Policing

- Relaxing weight and height requirements for recruits.
- Increasing recruitment of people of diversity (for example, women and those from diverse cultures and sexual orientations) and those with higher education.
- Introduction of race relations training programs.
- Introduction of cultural awareness training programs.
- Introduction of diversity awareness training programs.
- Implementation of anti-racism and anti–sexual harassment programs.
- Improvement in communication between police and people of diversity.
- Increased citizen participation in crime prevention initiatives.
- Increased community involvement in review of police activity (for example, civilian review boards).
- Introduction of police, ethnic, and cultural exchange (PEACE) programs.
- Creation of Aboriginal policing programs to improve Aboriginal–police relations and quality of policing services to Aboriginal peoples.
- Inclusion of courses on diversity issues in policing as part of police foundations programs.

CHAPTER SUMMARY

Because society is culturally pluralistic and composed of diverse groups, a diversity policing framework is required. Police culture and organization affect the approach to policing and thus police–community relations. The diversification of policing promotes a police–community interface that respects diversity and enhances police safety.

KEY TERMS

pluralistic

diversity

police culture

white machismo culture

ego forcing

core values

self-control

cynicism

respect for authority

hypervigilance

code of silence

police–community interface

police force approach

police services approach

community policing principles

diversity policing framework

REFERENCES

Battacharya, S. (2006, February 19). Police college puts Asian women through its hurdles. *The Toronto Star*, p. A6.

Canadian Charter of Rights and Freedoms. Part I of the *Constitution Act, 1982*, RSC 1985, app. II, no. 44.

Canadian Council on Social Development. (2003). Census shows increasing diversity of Canadian society. http://www.ccsd.ca/pr/2003/diversity.htm.

Clyderman, B.K., C.N. O'Toole, & A. Fleras. (1992). *Police, race and ethnicity*. Toronto: Butterworths.

Community Policing Consortium. (1996, June). Cultural diversity 1. http://www.communitypolicing.org/cultural/index.html.

Crank, J.P. (1997). *Understanding police culture*. Cincinnati, OH: Anderson.

Criminal Code. RSC 1985, c. C-46, as amended.

Durkan, S. (1998, March 24). Canadian cops top the list in most-popular survey. *The London Free Press*.

Feminist Majority Foundation. National Center for Women and Policing. (1999). *Equality denied: The status of women in policing, 1999*. Arlington, VA: Author.

Fleras, A. (1992). From enforcement to service: Community policing in a multicultural society. In B.K. Clyderman, C.N. O'Toole, & A. Fleras (Eds.), *Police, race and ethnicity* (pp. 69–126). Toronto: Butterworths.

Katz, L. Personal communication. December 15, 2003. In Robert M. Shusta et al. (2005). *Multicultural law enforcement* (3rd ed.). Upper Saddle River, NJ: Pearson/Prentice-Hall.

Kazarian, S. (2001). *Diversity issues in law enforcement* (2nd ed.). Toronto: Emond Montgomery.

Kirschman, E. (1997). *I love a cop: What police families need to know*. New York: The Guilford Press.

Lewis, S., H. Rosenberg, & R.T. Sigler. (1999). Acceptance of community policing among police officers and police administrators. *Policing: An International Journal of Police Strategies and Management* 22: 5670–5688.

Miller, S.L. (1999). *Gender and community policing: Walking the talk*. Boston: Northeastern University Press.

Ministry of Solicitor General Strategic Planning Committee on Police Training and Education. (1992). *PAKS*. Toronto: Author.

Mullan, B. Chief, Hamilton Police Service. (2005). Officer evaluation form.

Neiderhoffer, A. (1967). *Behind the shield*. NY: Anchor Books.

Peel, R. (1829). Nine principles of policing. http://www.civitas.org.uk.

Police Services Act. RSO 1990, c. P.15, as amended.

Roberts, J. (2006). *Communications for law enforcement professionals.* Toronto: Emond Montgomery.

Shusta, R.M. (2005). *Multicultural law enforcement* (3rd ed.). Upper Saddle River, NJ: Pearson/Prentice-Hall.

Skolnick, J. (1966). *Justice without trial.* New York: Wiley.

Stansfield, R.T. (1996). *Issues in policing: A Canadian perspective.* Toronto: Thompson Educational.

Statistics Canada. (1996a). Population by aboriginal group. *1996 Census.* http://www.statcan.ca/english/Pgdb/People/Population/demo39a.htm.

Statistics Canada. (1996b). Population by mother tongue. *1996 Census.* http://www.statcan.ca/english/Pgdb/People/Population/demo18a.htm.

Statistics Canada. (1999). Crimes by type of offence. http://www.statcan.ca/english/Pgdb/State/Justice/legal02.htm.

Statistics Canada. (2000). Number of police officers and population per police officer. http://www.statcan.ca/english/Pgdb/State/Justice/legal05.htm.

Statistics Canada. (2001). Ethnic origin (232), sex (3) and single and multiple responses (3) for population, for Canada, provinces, territories, census metropolitan areas and census agglomerations, 2001 Census—20% sample data. *2001 Census.* Catalogue no. 97F0010XCB2001001.

Statistics Canada. (2006). *Canada at a glance, 2006.* Catalogue no. 12-581-XPE. http://www.statcan.ca.

University of Maryland. (2000). Equity and diversity of the University of Maryland. http://www.umd.edu/diversity.

US Department of Justice. (1999). *Criminal victimization and perceptions of community safety in 12 cities 1998.* http://www.ojp.usdoj.gov/bjs/abstract/cvpcs98.htm.

Waddington, P.A.J. (1999). Police (canteen) sub-culture. *British Journal of Criminology* 39: 287–309.

Williams, W.L., & B.B. Henderson. (1997). *Taking back our streets: Fighting crime in America.* NY: Lisa Drew/Scribner.

CHAPTER 3

Human Rights and Freedoms

CHAPTER OBJECTIVES

After completing this chapter, you should be able to:

- Explain how human rights legislation influences people's individual and collective rights and freedoms.
- Discuss the impact of relevant policies and legislation on the recognition of rights of people of diversity.
- Discuss policing in the context of human rights and freedoms and 9/11.

INTRODUCTION

The evolution of civil rights has influenced political and civil structures and processes around the world, and has inspired the character of nations and the quality of life of their people. Human rights and freedoms are discussed in this chapter for four main reasons. First, they form important parts of the collective conscience of nations. Second, they provide the international community with basic standards by which nations can identify and measure equality and fairness. Third, understanding human rights and freedoms is paramount to the ability of police to fulfill their mandate. Fourth, human rights and freedoms illustrate the tension between democratic community law enforcement and dictatorship policing invoked by the terrorist threats and acts of some groups against Western countries.

INTERNATIONAL HUMAN RIGHTS AND FREEDOMS

The idea of human rights has been traced back to the ancient Greeks and Romans. However, the concept as understood today seems to have been nurtured at the beginning of the 13th century. In 1215, England's *Magna Carta*, or Great Charter, symbolized a cry against oppression. This document, a response to the misuse of power by the monarchy and royal officials, addressed such issues as unfair and arbitrary taxes imposed on the people, their inability to have a fair hearing of their complaints, and other problems. The *Magna Carta* inspired future instruments on human rights and freedoms. Liberty and equality were at the core of these documents, which declared the right of people, for example, not to be imprisoned arbitrarily, to pursue happiness, to own property, and to enjoy free speech.

In 1948 the General Assembly of the United Nations set down the *Universal Declaration of Human Rights* (Office of the United Nations High Commissioner for Human Rights, 1948), whose 30 articles recognize the equality and dignity of all people, and accord to them inalienable human rights, including rights to freedom, security, personal expression, an adequate standard of living, and education. Recently, a UN Human Rights Council replaced the UN Human Rights Commission. Even though the 47-member council includes a fraction of the countries that Western nations have criticized for violating human rights, in the words of Kofi Annan, the former Secretary General of the UN, "This council represents a great chance for the UN, and for humanity, to renew the struggle for human rights" (Editorial, 2006).

EXERCISE 1

Before beginning this section, read the 10 statements below. Indicate whether you agree or disagree with each statement, and give reasons. Do you think that each of the situations would be covered under some aspects of Canadian human rights legislation? As you go through this chapter, come back to these statements and indicate which act, code, right, or policy addresses each situation.

1. As a society, we should restrict the definition of spouse to opposite-sex couples.

2. If women want to breast-feed their infants, they should do so in the privacy of their homes rather than in public.

3. A Christian country should demand that all of its public school students say the Lord's Prayer in the morning before starting classes.

4. The policy of adoption agencies to permit adoption of a child only by parents with similar religious beliefs or cultural background seems discriminatory.

5. Gay or lesbian couples should not have the same rights as heterosexual married couples.

6. Human rights provisions in many countries are nothing but efforts to "window dress" diversity.

7. Criminals are getting away with murder by relying on human rights and freedoms provisions.

8. Like the right to decide on abortion, each woman has the right to circumcise her son or daughter.

9. Employers should have the right to drug test all potential employees.

10. The law should protect police officers more so that they can do their jobs without constant fear of reprisal.

HUMAN RIGHTS IN CANADA: FEDERAL

Canadian Human Rights Act

The *Royal Proclamation* of 1763 gave provincial legislatures in Canada the right to pass laws in relation to property and civil rights, and local private matters. The Proclamation was followed by the *British North America Act, 1867* (BNA Act), which provided for confederation. It was renamed the *Constitution Act 1867*. The *Canadian Bill of Rights* was introduced in 1960 to protect individual rights and freedoms. In 1977, the federal government passed the **Canadian Human Rights Act**, in which discrimination based on "race, national or ethnic origin, colour, age, sex, marital status, disability or conviction for an offence for which a pardon has been granted" was prohibited. The Act was amended in 1996 to include sexual orientation as a prohibited ground of discrimination. The Act has recently undergone a comprehensive review by the Canadian Human Rights Act Review Panel (2000).

In s. 40(1), the Act stipulates that "any individual or group of individuals having reasonable grounds for believing that a person is engaging or has engaged in a discriminatory practice may file with the [Canadian Human Rights] Commission a complaint in a form acceptable to the Commission." The **Canadian Human Rights Commission** is a government agency with the mandate to investigate human rights complaints and to develop policies and address issues pertaining to discrimination based on disability, race, religion, sex, and sexual orientation; employment and pay equity; and Aboriginal peoples. For example, the commission has developed policies on drug testing in the workplace (1999), HIV/AIDS (2000), harassment in the workplace (1998), and the *Employment Equity Act* (1995).

> **Canadian Human Rights Act**
> prohibits discrimination based on race, national or ethnic origin, colour, age, sex, marital status, disability, sexual orientation, or conviction for an offence for which a pardon has been granted
>
> **Canadian Human Rights Commission**
> federal body responsible for investigating and adjudicating complaints of violations of the *Canadian Human Rights Act*

Canadian Charter of Rights and Freedoms

The **Canadian Charter of Rights and Freedoms** was introduced in the *Constitution Act, 1982*. The Charter entrenches *minimum* rights for Canadian citizens. The 10 basic rights and freedoms enshrined in the Charter and applied to all governments—federal, provincial, and territorial—are summarized in table 3.1.

GUARANTEE OF RIGHTS AND FREEDOMS AND FUNDAMENTAL FREEDOMS

Section 1 of the Charter guarantees rights and freedoms to all Canadians subject to reasonable and legal limits, and s. 2 lists the **fundamental freedoms** (see table 3.1). The Charter guarantees freedom of speech, and freedom of the press and other media. Past laws that (1) required newspapers to reveal their sources of news; (2) banned the propagation of certain political ideologies by closing down any premises used for that purpose; (3) prohibited the distribution of any book, pamphlet, or tract without permission of a chief of police; and (4) restricted a religious group from its right to free expression and religious practice are contrary to the spirit of the Charter. Finally, the Charter ensures the right of Canadians to gather in peaceful groups and protects their freedom of association. It is important to underscore the fact that these freedoms are not absolute. For example, freedom of speech is subject to laws governing libel and slander in recognition of the fact that

> **Canadian Charter of Rights and Freedoms**
> part of the Canadian constitution that establishes the protection of basic rights and freedoms deemed essential to the maintenance of a free and democratic society and a united country
>
> **fundamental freedoms**
> freedom of conscience and religion; freedom of thought, belief, opinion, and expression, including freedom of the press and other media of communication; freedom of peaceful assembly; and freedom of association

TABLE 3.1 Basic Rights and Freedoms Enshrined in the Canadian Charter of Rights and Freedoms

1. Guarantee of rights and freedoms
2. Fundamental freedoms
3. Democratic rights
4. Mobility rights
5. Legal rights
6. Equality rights
7. Official languages of Canada
8. Minority language educational rights
9. Enforcement
10. General

Source: *Canadian Charter of Rights and Freedoms*, part I of the *Constitution Act, 1982*, RSC 1985, app. II, no. 44.

an absolute right to freedom of speech fails to protect the rights of others. We can see the wisdom of such a qualification when faced with hate literature against particular groups in Canadian society.

DEMOCRATIC RIGHTS

In addition to enshrining certain fundamental freedoms for everyone in Canada, the Charter gives all Canadian citizens **democratic rights** to vote or run in an election (s. 3) and the assurance that no government has the right to continue to hold power indefinitely without seeking a new mandate from the electorate (s. 4). It should be noted that s. 46 of the Ontario *Police Services Act* states, "No municipal police officer shall engage in political activity, except as the regulations permit." The regulations state that a serving police officer may run for office only if granted a leave of absence: "A municipal police officer may be a candidate, or may seek to become a candidate, in a federal or provincial election or in an election for municipal council only while on a leave of absence granted under subsection (2) O. Reg. 89/98, s. 1."

democratic rights
rights to vote or run in an election and the assurance that no government has the right to continue to hold power indefinitely without seeking a new mandate from the electorate

MOBILITY RIGHTS

The **mobility rights** granted to Canadian citizens and permanent residents in s. 6 of the Charter assure them the freedom to enter, remain in, or leave the country. This section also allows them to live and seek employment anywhere in Canada. Nevertheless, provinces have the right to set residence requirements for certain provincial social and welfare benefits, and to apply employment requirements to both newcomers and long-time residents.

mobility rights
freedom to enter, remain in, or leave the country, and to live and seek employment anywhere in Canada

LEGAL RIGHTS

The **legal rights** section (ss. 7–14), known as the lawyers' section, provides basic legal protection to safeguard Canadian citizens in their dealings with the state and its justice system (see the box on page 50). More specifically, Canadian citizens'

legal rights
basic legal protections to safeguard Canadian citizens in their dealings with the state and its machinery of justice

> ## GUARANTEE OF RIGHTS AND FREEDOMS
>
> 1. The *Canadian Charter of Rights and Freedoms* guarantees the rights and freedoms set out in it subject only to such reasonable limits prescribed by law as can be demonstrably justified in a free and democratic society.
>
> ## FUNDAMENTAL FREEDOMS
>
> 2. Everyone has the following fundamental freedoms:
>
>   a. freedom of conscience and religion;
>
>   b. freedom of thought, belief, opinion and expression, including freedom of the press and other media of communication;
>
>   c. freedom of peaceful assembly; and
>
>   d. freedom of association.
>
> Source: *Canadian Charter of Rights and Freedoms*, part I of the *Constitution Act, 1982*, RSC 1985, app. II, no. 44.

right to life, liberty, and security prohibit the use of not only unreasonable search or seizure but also unreasonable manner of executing these functions—for example, police use of unnecessary force. These legal rights also guarantee that no one will be detained or held arbitrarily. Thus, a police officer has to show reasonable cause for detaining an individual.

The legal rights on arrest and detention protect Canadian citizens from arbitrary or unlawful actions by law enforcement agencies. When being held or arrested by any authority, people have the right to be informed of the reasons for their being taken into custody, the right to be instructed of their right to contact and consult a lawyer without delay, and the right to have a court determine quickly whether the detention is lawful. Finally, the legal rights ensure that no individual is subjected to cruel and unusual treatment or punishment.

EQUALITY RIGHTS

Section 15, **equality rights**, states categorically that all Canadians, regardless of their race, national or ethnic origin, colour, religion, sex, age, or mental or physical disability, are equal before the law and are to enjoy equal protection and benefit of the law (see the box on page 51). However, this equality right may be undermined by a citizen's inability to pay for a defence. For example, a successful defence against an impaired driving charge can easily cost $10,000, and many people cannot afford that. Even if a citizen elects to act as his own counsel to avoid a costly defence, the right is still imperilled because defending oneself considerably diminishes the likelihood of a successful outcome. Sexual orientation is not specifically mentioned in this section, but a Supreme Court ruling in 1995 made sexual orientation a protected ground of discrimination.

equality rights
rights of all Canadians, regardless of race, national or ethnic origin, colour, sex, age, or mental or physical disability, to be equal before the law and to enjoy equal protection and benefit of the law

LEGAL RIGHTS

7. Everyone has the right to life, liberty and security of the person and the right not to be deprived thereof except in accordance with the principles of fundamental justice.

8. Everyone has the right to be secure against unreasonable search or seizure.

9. Everyone has the right not to be arbitrarily detained or imprisoned.

10. Everyone has the right on arrest or detention

    (a) to be informed promptly of the reasons therefor;

    (b) to retain and instruct counsel without delay and to be informed of that right; and

    (c) to have the validity of the detention determined by way of habeas corpus and to be released if the detention is not lawful.

11. Any person charged with an offence has the right

    (a) to be informed without unreasonable delay of the specific offence;

    (b) to be tried within a reasonable time; ...

    (d) to be presumed innocent until proven guilty ... ;

12. Everyone has the right not to be subjected to any cruel and unusual treatment or punishment.

13. A witness who testifies in any proceedings has the right not to have any incriminating evidence so given used to incriminate that witness in any other proceedings, except in a prosecution for perjury or for the giving of contradictory evidence.

14. A party or witness in any proceedings who does not understand or speak the language in which the proceedings are conducted or who is deaf has the right to the assistance of an interpreter.

Source: *Canadian Charter of Rights and Freedoms*, part I of the *Constitution Act, 1982*, RSC 1985, app. II, no. 44.

EQUALITY RIGHTS

15(1) Every individual is equal before and under the law and has the right to the equal protection and equal benefit of the law without discrimination and, in particular, without discrimination based on race, national or ethnic origin, colour, religion, sex, age or mental or physical disability.

(2) Subsection (1) does not preclude any law, program or activity that has as its object the amelioration of conditions of disadvantaged individuals or groups including those that are disadvantaged because of race, national or ethnic origin, colour, religion, sex, age or mental or physical disability.

Source: *Canadian Charter of Rights and Freedoms*, part I of the *Constitution Act, 1982*, RSC 1985, app. II, no. 44.

EXERCISE 2

What are the implications of human rights and freedoms to the following duties of law enforcement officials?

1. preserving the peace
2. preventing crimes and other offences, and providing assistance and encouragement to other persons in the prevention of crimes and other offences
3. assisting victims of crime
4. apprehending criminals, other offenders, and others who may lawfully be taken into custody
5. laying charges, prosecuting, and participating in prosecution
6. executing warrants and performing related duties
7. performing the lawful duties assigned by their superiors
8. completing prescribed training

OFFICIAL LANGUAGES OF CANADA

Sections 16 to 22 confirm that English and French are Canada's two **official languages** but do not require any member of the public to become bilingual (see the box on pages 52–53). Rather, these sections give people the right to communicate in either language with the federal government, to receive federal government services in the official language of their choice, and to use either language in Parliament or in all courts of law that are under federal jurisdiction.

official languages
English and French, as confirmed by the Charter, which guarantees that the federal government can serve members of the public in the official language of their choice

OFFICIAL LANGUAGES OF CANADA

16(1) English and French are the official languages of Canada and have equality of status and equal rights and privileges as to their use in all institutions of the Parliament and government of Canada.

(2) English and French are the official languages of New Brunswick and have equality of status and equal rights and privileges as to their use in all institutions of the legislature and government of New Brunswick....

17(1) Everyone has the right to use English or French in any debates and other proceedings of Parliament.

(2) Everyone has the right to use English or French in any debates and other proceedings of the legislature of New Brunswick.

18(1) The statutes, records and journals of Parliament shall be printed and published in English and French and both language versions are equally authoritative.

(2) The statutes, records and journals of the legislature of New Brunswick shall be printed and published in English and French and both language versions are equally authoritative.

19(1) Either English or French may be used by any person in, or in any pleading in or process issuing from, any court established by Parliament.

(2) Either English or French may be used by any person in, or in any pleading in or process issuing from, any court of New Brunswick.

20(1) Any member of the public in Canada has the right to communicate with, and to receive available services from, any head or central office of an institution of the Parliament or government of Canada in English or French, and has the same right with respect to any other office of any such institution where

(a) there is a significant demand for communication with and services from that office in such language; or

(b) due to the nature of the office, it is reasonable that communications with and services from that office be available in both English and French.

(2) Any member of the public in New Brunswick has the right to communicate with, and to receive available services from, any office of an institution of the legislature or government of New Brunswick in English or French.

> 21. Nothing in sections 16 to 20 abrogates or derogates from any right, privilege or obligation with respect to the English and French languages, or either of them, that exists or is continued by virtue of any other provision of the Constitution of Canada.
>
> 22. Nothing in sections 16 to 20 abrogates or derogates from any legal or customary right or privilege acquired or enjoyed either before or after the coming into force of this Charter with respect to any language that is not English or French.
>
> Source: *Canadian Charter of Rights and Freedoms*, part I of the *Constitution Act, 1982*, RSC 1985, app. II, no. 44.

MINORITY LANGUAGE EDUCATIONAL RIGHTS

Section 23 of the Charter uses three main criteria to identify the rights of Canadian citizens of the English- and French-speaking minorities in each province to allow education of their children in their own language (see the box on page 54). The first criterion is *mother tongue*. The Charter stipulates that individuals whose first learned and still understood language is French and who live in a mainly English-speaking province have the constitutional right to have their children educated in French; those whose mother tongue is English and who live in a mainly French-speaking province have the right to have their children educated in English. The second criterion is the *language in which the parents were educated in Canada*. The Charter stipulates that individuals who were educated in English or French and live in a province where that language is in the linguistic minority have the right to send their children to a school that uses that minority language. The third criterion relates to the *language in which other children in the family are receiving or have received their education*. The Charter protects the right of children whose siblings have received primary or secondary school instruction in either official language to be educated in the same language. In a separate section (s. 29), the Charter guarantees the establishment and operation of religious schools and provides them immunity from other provisions. Thus, the Charter ensures that neither the freedom of conscience and religion provision nor the equality rights provision can override existing constitutional rights with respect to the establishment and state financing of religious schools.

ENFORCEMENT

Section 24 allows a person or group whose rights have been denied or infringed upon by law or by action taken by the state to apply to a court for a remedy (see the box on page 54). An example of a potential infringement is police breaking into and searching a person's premises and discovering incriminating evidence. In such a circumstance, the courts could exclude the evidence in a subsequent trial in which it is alleged that a right under the Charter was infringed, or the courts could rule that admission of the evidence brings the administration of justice into disrepute.

> ## MINORITY LANGUAGE EDUCATIONAL RIGHTS
>
> 23(1) Citizens of Canada
>
> > (a) whose first language learned and still understood is that of the English or French linguistic minority population of the province in which they reside, or
> >
> > (b) who have received their primary school instruction in Canada in English or French and reside in a province where the language in which they received that instruction is the language of the English or French linguistic minority population of the province,
>
> have the right to have their children receive primary and secondary school instruction in that language in that province.
>
> > (2) Citizens of Canada of whom any child has received or is receiving primary or secondary school instruction in English or French in Canada, have the right to have all their children receive primary and secondary school instruction in the same language.
>
> Source: *Canadian Charter of Rights and Freedoms*, part I of the *Constitution Act, 1982*, RSC 1985, app. II, no. 44.

> ## ENFORCEMENT
>
> 24(1) Anyone whose rights or freedoms, as guaranteed by this Charter, have been infringed or denied may apply to a court of competent jurisdiction to obtain such remedy as the court considers appropriate and just in the circumstances.
>
> (2) Where, in proceedings under subsection (1), a court concludes that evidence was obtained in a manner that infringed or denied any rights or freedoms guaranteed by this Charter, the evidence shall be excluded if it is established that, having regard to all the circumstances, the admission of it in the proceedings would bring the administration of justice into disrepute.
>
> Source: *Canadian Charter of Rights and Freedoms*, part I of the *Constitution Act, 1982*, RSC 1985, app. II, no. 44.

GENERAL RIGHTS OF ABORIGINAL PEOPLES, MULTICULTURALISM, AND RIGHTS OF WOMEN

The rights of Canada's Aboriginal peoples (Indian, Inuit, and Métis), enshrinement of Canada's multicultural character, and the rights of women are contained in ss. 25, 27, and 28 of the Charter, respectively (see the box on page 55).

Section 25 recognizes and affirms **Aboriginal peoples' rights** to preserve their culture, identity, customs, traditions, and languages, and any special rights that they have currently or rights that they may acquire in the future. (Section 35 of the

---

Aboriginal peoples' rights
rights of Canada's Aboriginal peoples to preserve their culture, identity, customs, traditions, and languages, and any special rights that they have currently or may acquire in the future

> **GENERAL**
>
> 25. The guarantee in this Charter of certain rights and freedoms shall not be construed so as to abrogate or derogate from any aboriginal, treaty or other rights or freedoms that pertain to the aboriginal peoples of Canada including
>
>   (a) any rights or freedoms that have been recognized by the Royal Proclamation of October 7, 1763; and
>
>   (b) any rights or freedoms that now exist by way of land claims agreements or may be so acquired. ...
>
> 27. This Charter shall be interpreted in a manner consistent with the preservation and enhancement of the multicultural heritage of Canadians.
>
> 28. Notwithstanding anything in this Charter, the rights and freedoms referred to in it are guaranteed equally to male and female persons.
>
> Source: *Canadian Charter of Rights and Freedoms*, part I of the *Constitution Act, 1982*, RSC 1985, app. II, no. 44.

constitution recognizes and affirms existing Aboriginal and treaty rights. This section also ensures that any new benefits that Aboriginal peoples may gain from a settlement of land claims would not run afoul of the general equality rights as set out in the Charter.)

Section 27 provides a constitutionally unique provision by enshrining the multicultural character of Canadian society—that is, the maintenance and enhancement of Canada's **multicultural heritage**.

Finally, s. 28 ensures that all rights in the Charter are guaranteed equally to both sexes. Including this provision in the Charter ensures that it cannot be overridden by a provincial legislature or by Parliament.

Federal human rights legislation is not without its detractors. In the autumn of 2006, the debate in Britain over wearing of the *niqab*, or face veil, by Muslim women, appeared in the Canadian press. It came on the heels of claims that leaders of the large Indo-Canadian population in British Columbia were turning a blind eye toward domestic violence. The preceding year (2005) saw an acrimonious dispute in Ontario over whether Muslims could use Islamic *sharia* courts to settle family disputes.

Fighting over cultural practices and symbols is nothing new in Canada. Sikhs went to the Supreme Court to win the right for male police officers to wear turbans and male students to wear ceremonial daggers known as *kirpans*. However, new to the arguments is an underlying tension between some cultural practices of recent immigrants and the mainstream values of Canadian liberal democracy, such as equality between the sexes. It is generally agreed that immigrants should be able to maintain their cultural and religious practices, but that these practices should not be tolerated when they infringe on women's rights.

multicultural heritage
the unique and constitutionally enshrined character of Canadian society

> ### EXERCISE 3
>
> 1. You apprehend a citizen with limited English and French. You do not speak her language yourself, but as an officer it is your duty to inform her of her right to know the reasons for taking her into custody, her right to contact and consult a lawyer forthwith to obtain legal advice, and her right to have a court determine quickly whether her detention is lawful.
>
>   a. What human rights and freedoms provisions would guide your decision in handling this case?
>
>   b. What action would you take in this situation?
>
> 2. You take a Sikh man into custody. From your course on diversity issues in policing, you remember that a Sikh religious practice entails carrying a *kirpan* (ceremonial dagger).
>
>   a. What human rights and freedoms provisions would guide your decisions in dealing with this man and his *kirpan*?
>
>   b. What action would you take in this situation?

HUMAN RIGHTS IN ONTARIO

Human Rights Code

At the time that the *Canadian Bill of Rights* was enacted, the provinces developed their own human rights codes. Due to space limitations, the focus in this section is on the Ontario *Human Rights Code*, which was enacted in 1962.

In its preamble, the **Ontario *Human Rights Code*** recognizes that "the inherent dignity and the equal and inalienable rights of all members of the human family is the foundation of freedom, justice and peace in the world and is in accord with the *Universal Declaration of Human Rights* as proclaimed by the United Nations." Part I of the Code, which deals with **freedom from discrimination**, is provided on pages 57-58. Individuals who believe their rights have been infringed under the Code can file a complaint with the **Ontario Human Rights Commission** (OHRC). Part IV of the Code outlines the complaint process. The commission investigates complaints of discrimination to settle the complaints between the parties or permit litigation of the cases at the Human Rights Tribunal of Ontario and higher courts. In 2005–6, the Ontario Human Rights Commission mediated, investigated, or otherwise completed a total of 2,117 individual complaints of discrimination, and referred a total of 170 cases to the Human Rights Tribunal of Ontario for a hearing (OHRC, 2006). The commission also saw the legislature of Ontario pass a bill to end mandatory retirement and allow, as of December 2006, employees the choice to continue working past age 65.

Ontario *Human Rights Code* Ontario statute that protects the dignity and worth of every person and provides for equal rights and opportunities without discrimination that is contrary to law

freedom from discrimination part I of the Ontario *Human Rights Code*, which grants freedom from discrimination with respect to services, goods, facilities, accommodation, contracts, employment, and occupational associations, and freedom from sexual solicitation in the workplace and by those in a position of power

Ontario Human Rights Commission provincial body responsible for investigating and adjudicating complaints of violations of the Ontario *Human Rights Code*

ONTARIO HUMAN RIGHTS CODE

PART I: FREEDOM FROM DISCRIMINATION

Services

1. Every person has a right to equal treatment with respect to services, goods and facilities, without discrimination because of race, ancestry, place of origin, colour, ethnic origin, citizenship, creed, sex, sexual orientation, age, marital status, family status or disability.

Accommodation

2(1) Every person has a right to equal treatment with respect to occupancy of accommodation, without discrimination because of race, ancestry, place of origin, colour, ethnic origin, citizenship, creed, sex, sexual orientation, age, marital status, family status, disability or the receipt of public assistance.

Harassment in accommodation

(2) Every person who occupies accommodation has a right to freedom from harassment by the landlord or agent of the landlord or by an occupant of the same building because of race, ancestry, place of origin, colour, ethnic origin, citizenship, creed, age, marital status, family status, disability or the receipt of public assistance.

Contracts

3. Every person having legal capacity has a right to contract on equal terms without discrimination because of race, ancestry, place of origin, colour, ethnic origin, citizenship, creed, sex, sexual orientation, age, marital status, family status or disability.

Accommodation of person under eighteen

4(1) Every sixteen or seventeen year old person who has withdrawn from parental control has a right to equal treatment with respect to occupancy of and contracting for accommodation without discrimination because the person is less than eighteen years old.

Idem

(2) A contract for accommodation entered into by a sixteen or seventeen year old person who has withdrawn from parental control is enforceable against that person as if the person were eighteen years old.

Employment

5(1) Every person has a right to equal treatment with respect to employment without discrimination because of race, ancestry, place of origin, colour, ethnic origin, citizenship, creed, sex, sexual orientation, age, record of offences, marital status, family status or disability.

Harassment in employment

(2) Every person who is an employee has a right to freedom from harassment in the workplace by the employer or agent of the employer or by another employee because of race, ancestry, place of origin, colour, ethnic origin, citizenship, creed, age, record of offence, marital status, family status or disability.

Vocational associations

6. Every person has a right to equal treatment with respect to membership in any trade union, trade or occupational association or self-governing profession without discrimination because of race, ancestry, place of origin, colour, ethnic origin, citizenship, creed, sex, sexual orientation, age, marital status, family status or disability.

Sexual harassment

Harassment because of sex in accommodation

7(1) Every person who occupies accommodation has a right to freedom from harassment because of sex by the landlord or agent of the landlord or by an occupant of the same building.

Harassment because of sex in workplaces

(2) Every person who is an employee has a right to freedom from harassment in the workplace because of sex by his or her employer or agent of the employer or by another employee.

Sexual solicitation by a person in position to confer benefit, etc.

(3) Every person has a right to be free from,

   (a) a sexual solicitation or advance made by a person in a position to confer, grant or deny a benefit or advancement to the person where the person making the solicitation or advance knows or ought reasonably to know that it is unwelcome; or

   (b) a reprisal or a threat of reprisal for the rejection of a sexual solicitation or advance where the reprisal is made or threatened by a person in a position to confer, grant or deny a benefit or advancement to the person.

Reprisals

8. Every person has a right to claim and enforce his or her rights under this Act, to institute and participate in proceedings under this Act and to refuse to infringe a right of another person under this Act, without reprisal or threat of reprisal for so doing.

Infringement prohibited

9. No person shall infringe or do, directly or indirectly, anything that infringes a right under this Part.

Source: Ontario *Human Rights Code*, RSO 1990, c. H.19, as amended.

Human Rights Commission Policies and Initiatives

The Ontario Human Rights Commission has issued a number of policies to clarify or complement the Code, some of which are described below. In advancing its various policies, the commission makes reference to harassment, a poisoned environment, and constructive discrimination. As defined in the Code (part II, s. 10(1)(e)), **harassment** is a "course of vexatious comment or conduct that is known or ought reasonably to be known to be unwelcome." A poisoned environment is one in which a person or a group of people are treated differently for reasons related to prohibitory grounds, such as gender, race, and sexual orientation. According to the Code (part II, s. 11(1)), **constructive discrimination** refers to "a requirement, qualification or factor … that is not discrimination on a prohibited ground but that results in the exclusion, restriction or preference of a group of persons who are identified by a prohibited ground of discrimination." A requirement, qualification, or factor is not discriminatory if it can be established that it is reasonable and bona fide (in good faith) in the circumstances. Two conditions are required to establish bona fide: first, it must be demonstrated that there is an objective relationship between the selection criteria and the job in question, and, second, it must be shown that the standards required for the job are imposed in good faith.

The following sections describe some Ontario Human Rights Commission policies.

harassment
comments or conduct toward another person that is unwelcome

constructive discrimination
discrimination that results from some criterion that seems reasonable but effectively excludes, restricts, or favours some people contrary to human rights laws

POLICY ON DISCRIMINATION AND HARASSMENT BECAUSE OF SEXUAL ORIENTATION

Discrimination on the grounds of sexual orientation and same-sex partnership status is prohibited. *Sexual orientation* is "more than simply a 'status' that an individual possesses; it is an immutable personal characteristic that forms part of an individual's core identity. Sexual orientation encompasses the range of human sexuality from gay and lesbian to bisexual and heterosexual orientations" (OHRC, 2000a). This policy was updated (OHRC, 2006) to include the March 2005 amendments to the Code in which marital status was redefined to be inclusive of same-sex conjugal relationships; to reflect the rights of same-sex marriage partners; to improve understanding of discrimination experienced by lesbian, gay, and bisexual individuals; and to assist organizational development of harassment-free environments.

On May 20, 1999, the Supreme Court of Canada found the "opposite sex" definition of "spouse" in part III of Ontario's *Family Law Act* to be unconstitutional. In response to the Supreme Court's decision, Ontario introduced Bill 5, which received royal assent on October 28, 1999. This bill amended the *Family Law Act* to allow its provisions governing support obligations to apply to same-sex partners. Bill 5 also amended the Ontario *Human Rights Code* by defining the term "marital status" to include "same-sex partnership status" and the term "spouse" to include "same-sex partner." "Same-sex partner" is further defined to mean the individual with whom a person of the same sex is living in a conjugal relationship outside marriage. Similarly, "same-sex partnership status" is defined to mean the status of living with an individual of the same sex in a conjugal relationship outside marriage.

POLICY ON DISCRIMINATION AND HARASSMENT BECAUSE OF GENDER IDENTITY

In this policy (OHRC, 2000b), sex under the Ontario *Human Rights Code* is interpreted to include *gender identity*. Gender identity is not the same as sexual orientation, but diverges from a person's birth-assigned identity (almost exclusively transgenderists and transsexuals). The personal attributes associated with gender identity include self-image, physical and biological appearance, behaviour, and gender-related conduct. The term "transgendered" refers to "people who are not comfortable with or who reject, in whole or in part, their birth-assigned gender identities" (OHRC, 2000b). Transgendered people include transsexuals, cross-dressers, and intersexed individuals.

POLICY ON SEXUAL HARASSMENT AND INAPPROPRIATE GENDER-RELATED COMMENTS AND CONDUCT

This policy (OHRC, 1996c) provides the fundamental human right to freedom from sexual harassment and other forms of unequal treatment expressed through demeaning comments and actions based on gender. The policy clearly distinguishes between accepted social interaction or consensual relations and behaviour that is known or ought reasonably to be known to be unwelcome. Also, the policy provides a framework for educational initiatives (for example, the development of training materials and anti-harassment policies) by employers and others.

There are two views of *sexual harassment*. In a narrow context, sexual harassment is defined as an objectionable comment or conduct of a sexual nature. In a broader context, sexual harassment is defined as conduct that is not overtly sexual in nature but is related to the person's gender, and demeans or causes personal humiliation or embarrassment to the recipient. In most cases men are the harassers of women. However, there are women harassers of men, and sexual harassment between members of the same sex is known to occur.

A person can be guilty of sexual harassment or discrimination without making explicit reference to gender or sex. Sexual discrimination may involve gender-based harassing comments or conduct. The comments or actions do not have to be made with the intention to discriminate for them to be considered violations of human rights. For example, an employer may indirectly harass a female employee, with the intent to discourage her from continuing her employment in a particular position, because of her gender.

Specific examples of sexual harassment and inappropriate gender-related comments and conduct include the following (OHRC, 1996c, s. 6):

    i) gender-related comments about an individual's physical characteristics or mannerisms;

    ii) unwelcome physical contact;

    iii) suggestive or offensive remarks or innuendoes about members of a specific gender;

    iv) propositions of physical intimacy;

    v) gender-related verbal abuse, threats, or taunting;

    vi) leering or inappropriate staring;

    vii) bragging about sexual prowess;

    viii) demands for dates or sexual favours;

ix) offensive jokes or comments of a sexual nature about an employee, client, or tenant;

x) display of sexually offensive pictures, graffiti, or other materials;

xi) questions or discussions about sexual activities;

xii) paternalism based on gender which a person feels undermines his or her self-respect or position of responsibility;

xiii) rough and vulgar humour or language related to gender.

This policy is consistent with laws in several countries on workplace discrimination and harassment. A harassment-free work environment is one that does not tolerate a hostile or abusive atmosphere where an employee is subjected to offensive remarks, behaviour, or surroundings that create intimidating, hostile, or humiliating working conditions.

POLICY ON RACIAL SLURS AND HARASSMENT AND RACIAL JOKES

This policy (OHRC, 1996b) endorses the right of every individual to live and work in an environment that is free of race-related demeaning comments and actions. The policy defines as discriminatory acts or expressions that are manifested through slurs, jokes, or behaviour intended to demean a person because of his or her race. *Racial harassment* involves offensive, humiliating, derogatory, or hostile acts or expressions that are racially based. A comment or conduct need not be explicitly racial in order to constitute racial harassment. The term "race" in the policy refers to all of the race-related grounds (that is, race, ancestry, colour, and ethnic origin) and to citizenship, place of origin, and creed.

EXERCISE 4

1. What are the implications of sexual harassment for the harasser?

2. What are the implications of sexual harassment for the victim?

3. How can sexual harassment be prevented?

4. How can harassment on the Internet be prevented? Is online harassment of people based on age, gender, sexual orientation, and so on, protected through human rights legislation? What about the right to freedom of speech?

POLICY AND GUIDELINES ON RACISM AND RACIAL DISCRIMINATION

This policy (OHRC, 2006) updates and significantly expands on the policy on racial slurs and racial jokes. The policy describes a number of considerations for the determination of racial discrimination. The policy also stresses the importance of development of an organizational culture that respects human rights and prevents racial discrimination.

In April 2006 Ontario introduced a bill to reform its overloaded human rights complaint system, although some groups representing the disabled, the poor, and visible minorities feared that the proposal to streamline the complaint process would shut out the vulnerable people it is supposed to help. Ontario's 40-year-old human rights system, once the envy of the world, now sees some complaints taking years to be resolved. Nevertheless, these groups suggest that changes to the bill to reform the system would make it more difficult for the vulnerable to make complaints; cynics see changes to the legislation as nothing more than a government cost-cutting measure ("Human Rights," 2006).

HUMAN RIGHTS AND LAW ENFORCEMENT

The United Nations Centre for Human Rights developed international human rights standards specific to law enforcement. The standards address policing ethics and legal conduct, policing in democracies, non-discrimination in law enforcement, police investigations, arrest, detention, the use of force and firearms, civil disorder, states of emergency, armed conflict, protection of juveniles, community policing, and police violations of human rights, as well as the human rights of women, refugees, non-nationals, victims, police command, and management.

Police legislation in Canada is consistent with international standards and federal and provincial laws regarding human rights and freedoms. In its declaration of principles, the **Ontario *Police Services Act*** (Hamilton & Shilton, 1992) stipulates that police services shall be provided at the provincial level in accordance with the safeguards that guarantee the fundamental rights enshrined in the *Canadian Charter of Rights and Freedoms* and the Ontario *Human Rights Code* (principle 2).

> **Ontario *Police Services Act*** stipulates that police services shall be provided throughout Ontario in accordance with the safeguards that guarantee the fundamental rights enshrined in the *Canadian Charter of Rights and Freedoms* and the Ontario *Human Rights Code*

EXERCISE 5

The vast majority of police officers protect the rights and freedoms of citizens. In rare cases, police abuse their authority. Three types of police abuse of authority have been identified:

- Physical abuse/excessive force. This involves the use of more force than is necessary to effect an arrest or search, or the "wanton use of any degree of physical force against another by the police officer under the colour of the officer's authority."

- Verbal/psychological abuse. "Relying on authority inherently vested in them based on their office, police verbally assail, ridicule, harass, and/or place persons who are under the actual or constructive dominion of the officer in a situation where the individual's esteem and/or self-image is threatened and/or diminished; threat of physical harm under the supposition that a threat is psychologically coercive and instills fear in the average person."

- Violation of civil rights. This includes "any violation of a person's constitutional rights, federally protected rights, and provincially protected rights even though the person may not suffer any apparent physical or psychological damage in the purest sense."

Read each police action below, and indicate the nature of the abuse: PA if it is physical abuse/excessive force, VPA if it is verbal/psychological abuse, or VCR if it is a violation of civil rights.

a. stopping a car without justifiable reason

b. punching a citizen

c. kicking a suspect

d. spraying mace

e. hitting a citizen with a flashlight

f. using deadly force

g. hitting a citizen with a baton

h. overtightening handcuffs

i. "bumping" a citizen's head as the citizen is entering a police car

j. holding someone incommunicado during interrogation

k. conducting a search without a justifiable reason

l. calling a citizen derogatory names

m. not allowing a person held for interrogation to consult an attorney

n. imposing a police-dominated atmosphere during interrogation

o. sexually harassing a female suspect in custody

p. not taking someone into custody because of his or her race

q. booking a lesbian or gay person because of the person's sexual orientation

r. taking someone into custody without legal grounds

s. harassing a citizen because of the colour of his or her skin

HUMAN RIGHTS AND FREEDOMS: POST-9/11

In the aftermath of the terrorist attacks on the United States on September 11, 2001, the Canadian government's preoccupation with national and international security issues, and partnership with the United States and law enforcement agencies to address internal and external security threats became most salient. The heightened sensitivity to security threats and the legislative changes related to law enforcement created tension between civil liberties and police powers. While the root causes of terrorism remained unclear, several candidates were considered: the violent nature of some aspects of the Muslim religion, poverty, the marginalization of Muslim and Arab immigrants and their communities by democratic Western countries, cynicism invoked by violation of democratic principles and values preached by democratic countries and their support of dictatorial regimes, and differential application of human rights standards to nations construed as friendly allies and those that were deemed unfriendly.

HUMAN RIGHTS AND FREEDOMS: POLICE ABILITIES, KNOWLEDGE, AND SKILLS

The importance of human rights and freedoms to people's quality of life is increasingly recognized. Many countries are actively involved in serving and protecting the human rights and freedoms of their citizens, and law enforcement plays a significant role in these initiatives. Police services operate in contexts of international, national, and provincial human rights provisions that enshrine basic individual and collective rights and freedoms at social and institutional levels. The intent of these provisions is a collective conscience for the protection of democratic citizenship and societal justice. The human rights and freedoms acts, codes, and policies are more than just principles and goals—they are designed to change a culture that is plagued by human rights violations, complaints and inquiries, court actions, disciplinary hearings, and penalties into one that treasures and preserves equal treatment and protection under the law.

A police culture in which all police officers uphold the letter and the spirit of human rights laws and foster a climate that is committed to the fundamental values of justice, respect, acceptance, and harmonious coexistence befits the dignity of the profession.

Nevertheless, the focus of law enforcement on counterterrorism and national security is challenging from the perspectives of both human rights and community policing. More specifically, terrorist threats and acts in Western countries such as Canada, the United Kingdom, Spain, and the United States have challenged the role of law enforcement and resulted in tension between human rights and freedoms and the imperative of law and order. On the one hand, law enforcement agents are expected to honour human rights standards, respect the civil rights of citizens, and establish a trusting relationship with the communities they serve and protect. On the other hand, they are also expected to fulfill the imperative of law and order and do whatever is necessary to prevent threats to national security.

The imperative of law and order is also challenging to law enforcement from the democratic community policing perspective. The dilemma for law enforcement

EXERCISE 6

The Maher Arar Case

Identify and explain what you see as human rights violations in the following case study.

Maher Arar is a Canadian software engineer. On September 26, 2002, during a stopover in New York en route from Tunis to Montreal, Arar was detained by American authorities who may have been acting upon false and misleading information supplied by the Royal Canadian Mounted Police (RCMP). Despite carrying a Canadian passport, he was deported to Syria, held in solitary confinement in a Syrian prison where he was regularly tortured for over a year, and eventually released and returned to Canada in October 2003.

Arar's case reached new heights of controversy when an Ottawa journalist wrote an article on November 8, 2003, containing information leaked to her from an unknown security source, possibly within the RCMP. This information suggested that Arar was a trained member of an al-Qaida terrorist cell. The RCMP raided the journalist's house while investigating the leak. The raid was widely denounced and led to a public inquiry.

The episode strained Canada–US relations and led to a public inquiry in Canada, which cleared Arar and was sharply critical of the RCMP, other Canadian government departments, and the United States over its treatment of Arar. The United States did not participate in the inquiry, but maintained that Arar's removal to Syria was legal. Human rights groups dispute this.

Arar's ordeal has raised questions concerning the role of various government officials. RCMP Commissioner Giuliano Zaccardelli resigned in December 2006 over contradictions in his testimony to the House of Commons Committee on Public Safety and National Security with respect to what he knew at the time and what he told government ministers.

(Source: http://www.cbc.ca/news/background/arar.)

---

services, which are empowered with issues of national security, protection of civil order, and the war against terrorism, is that they are expected to partner with the very people and communities that they serve and protect but whom they may deem a threat to national security. Having national security as a priority challenges policing that balances civil liberty and civil order.

Thus, law enforcement in the 21st century is challenged by two fundamentally antagonistic approaches to policing: democratic community policing and democratic dictatorship policing. Democratic community policing honours the imperatives of law and order and due process while democratic dictatorship policing honours the imperative of law and order disproportionate to the imperative of civil liberties. It could be argued that civilized and democratic nations and their law enforcement services cannot make "any allowance for those who seek to profit by terror ... a lesson when ignored or forgotten, leads to the ruin of civilized living" (Mansur, 2006, p. F6).

EXERCISE 7

A police service allows a Sikh officer to wear his turban on duty, and allows Aboriginal officers to continue their practice of wearing braids down to the top of the armpit to connect with Mother Earth.

a. Is the police service justified in its decision? Explain.

b. Do you consider these practices to be examples of the erosion of national symbols in Canadian culture? Why or why not?

c. Do you consider the actions of the police service as kowtowing to the whims of human rights activists?

d. Do you think these decisions will lead nudists to challenge the dress code policy?

e. Can you think of other practices or events that some people might consider evidence of the erosion of national symbols? Justify your choices.

f. What relevance, if any, do human rights and freedoms provisions have in influencing the decisions of a police service? What relevance, if any, do human rights and freedoms codes have on other potential challenges to Canadian culture—for example, a woman's right to go topless in public?

CHAPTER SUMMARY

Human rights laws and policies enshrine basic rights and freedoms and protect both citizens and social justice, treating with equity and respect all citizens, regardless of their culture, race, religion, gender, age, sexual orientation, gender identity, socio-economic status, or physical or mental ability. The response of governments to the 9/11 terrorist attacks has increased the tension between the imperatives of national security and law and order on the one hand and civil liberties on the other.

THE GREAT DEBATE

Post-9/11 events involving law enforcement brought the issue of civil liberty versus national security to a head. Have one group take the position that individual rights should take precedence over national security. Have the second group take the position that national security should take precedence over civil liberty. Include in the debate situations in which police confront the dilemma of having to balance the rights of individuals against law and order.

KEY TERMS

Canadian Human Rights Act

Canadian Human Rights Commission

Canadian Charter of Rights and Freedoms

fundamental freedoms

democratic rights

mobility rights

legal rights

equality rights

official languages

Aboriginal peoples' rights

multicultural heritage

Ontario *Human Rights Code*

freedom from discrimination

Ontario Human Rights Commission

harassment

constructive discrimination

Ontario *Police Services Act*

REFERENCES

Canadian Bill of Rights, SC 1960, c. 44.

Canadian Charter of Rights and Freedoms, part I of the *Constitution Act, 1982*, RSC 1985, app. II, no. 44.

Canadian Human Rights Act, RSC 1985, c. H-6, as amended.

Canadian Human Rights Act Review Panel. (2000). Promoting equality: A new vision. http://www/chrareview.org/frp/frp-toce.html.

Canadian Human Rights Commission (CHRC). (1999). Policy on drug testing. http://www.chrc-ccdp.ca/legis&poli/drgpol-poldrg.asp.

Canadian Human Rights Commission (CHRC). (2000). Policy on HIV/AIDS. Publications & Policies, Employment Equity Branch. http://www.chrc-ccdp.ca/ee.

Canadian Human Rights Commission (CHRC) in cooperation with Human Resources Development Canada and Status of Women Canada. (1998). *Anti-harassment policies for the workplace: An employer's guide.* http://www.chrc-ccdp.ca/publications/default-en.asp.

Centre for Human Rights (n.d.). *International human rights standards for law enforcement.* Geneva: United Nations High Commissioner for Human Rights.

Commission on Systemic Racism in the Ontario Criminal Justice System. (1994). *Report on youth and street harassment: The police and investigative detention.* Toronto: Queen's Printer for Ontario.

Constitution Act, 1982, RSC 1985, app. II, no. 44.

Criminal Code, RSC 1985, c. C-46, as amended.

The Economist. (2006). Canada: One nation or many? In *The Hamilton Spectator* (2006, 18 November), p. A24.

Editorial. *International Herald Tribune.* (2006, June 24–25), p. 6.

Family Law Act, RSO 1990, c. F.3, as amended.

Hamilton, J.F., & B.R. Shilton. (1992). *Police Services Act, 1993.* Toronto: Carswell.

Human Rights Code, RSO 1990, c. H.19, as amended.

Human rights system needs more tinkering. Comment. (2006, November 19). *The Toronto Star*, p. A16.

Law Commission of Canada. (2006). Crossing borders: Law in a globalized world. Discussion Paper. Ottawa: Queen's Printer.

Leeder, J. (2006, July 27). His nightmare began on 9/12. *Toronto Star*, p. A1, A13.

Maher Arar. http://www.cbc.ca/news/background/arar.

Mansur, S. (August, 19, 2006). Trudeau right to crush terror. *The London Free Press*, p. F6.

Office of the United Nations High Commissioner for Human Rights. (1948). *Universal declaration of human rights.* http://www.unhchr.ch/udhr/lang/eng.htm.

Ontario Human Rights Commission (OHRC). (1996a, April 9). Policy on female genital mutilation (FGM). See Policies under Publications Online. http://www.ohrc.on.ca/en/resources/publications.

Ontario Human Rights Commission (OHRC). (1996b, June 19). Policy on racial slurs and harassment and racial jokes. http://www.ohrc.on.ca/en/resources/publications.

Ontario Human Rights Commission (OHRC). (1996c, September 10). Policy on sexual harassment and inappropriate gender-related comments and conduct. http://www.ohrc.on.ca/en/resources/publications.

Ontario Human Rights Commission (OHRC). (2000a, January 11). Policy on discrimination and harassment because of sexual orientation. http://www.ohrc.on.ca/en/resources/publications.

Ontario Human Rights Commission (OHRC). (2000b, March 30). Policy on discrimination and harassment because of gender identity. http://www.ohrc.on.ca/en/resources/publications.

Ontario Human Rights Commission (OHRC). (2006). Ontario Human Rights Commission annual report 2005–2006. Toronto: Author.

Police Services Act, RSO 1990, c. P.15, as amended.

Rosenthal, E. (2006, June 2). Study tracks genital cutting's deadly legacy. *International Herald Tribune*, p. 4.

CHAPTER 4

Cultural Diversity Values, Beliefs, and Practices

CHAPTER OBJECTIVES

After completing this chapter, you should be able to:

- Explain the concepts of culture, race, and ethnicity.
- Understand core cultural values, beliefs, and practices.
- Refine your understanding of specific cultures in the context of the post-9/11 environment.
- Understand the concepts of prejudice and stereotyping.

INTRODUCTION

Canada's over 30 million inhabitants reflect a cultural, ethnic, and linguistic mosaic not found anywhere else on earth. Each year, close to 200,000 immigrants from all over the globe choose Canada as their host country and become law-abiding citizens. These immigrants are drawn by Canada's quality of life and "its reputation as an open, peaceful and caring society that welcomes newcomers and values diversity" (Canadian Heritage, 2004).

Canada is a federation of 10 provinces and 3 northern territories. Eighty percent of the country's population live in urban areas (Sustainability Reporting Program, 2004). Canada's geographic, political, and domestic boundaries are challenging to Canadian police work. Each geographic region offers the challenges of distance, urban populations, and climate considerations; on the political side, some communities are served by federal services, some by regional services, and others by city services, with individual laws and bylaws applying; domestically, urban boundaries and, in some areas, the challenges of dense populations offer their own unique problems. In combatting crime, protecting civil order, and contributing to international strategies against terrorism, police encounter many different types of people from all walks of life.

Attempts to describe Canada's diversity invariably mask the complexity of each group's historical development and the important cultural similarities and cultural differences among them. Equally important, such descriptions ignore the richness of the lives of individuals. Nevertheless, an understanding of and respect for specific diversities can improve social relations and strengthen national identity, and enhance security and lawful conduct in a free and democratic civil society. This chapter focuses on issues of diversity, namely, ethnicity, race, and culture. More specifically, it discusses the core values, beliefs, and practices associated with a selection of ethnocultural groups and the challenges for policing in the aftermath of the terrorist attacks on the United States on September 11, 2001.

> **EXERCISE 1**
>
> 1. What implications does focusing on cultural differences rather than similarities have for law enforcement?
>
> 2. How would you go about involving police and the community to develop and implement policing approaches that are responsive to ethnic and racial groups?

CONCEPTS OF CULTURE, ETHNICITY, RACE, AND MINORITY

There is a great deal of confusion over the terms "culture," "ethnicity," "race," and "minority." A major problem is that these terms are used interchangeably (Kazarian, 1998). A good example is the way the English and the French are called Canada's "two founding races." As pointed out by Lagasse (1967), both cultural groups belong to the same Caucasian race.

Culture

Culture can be defined narrowly as folk tradition or, in its anthropological sense, as synonymous with ethnoculture (Kallen, 2003). Both definitions refer to the distinctive ways of viewing and doing things shared by members of a particular ethnic community and transmitted by them from one generation to the next through the process of enculturation (distinctive ethnic socialization). In a broader sense, **culture** refers to the pattern of behaviour and results of behaviour that are shared and transmitted among the members of a particular society (Linton, 1945). Triandis (1990) refers to culture as "the man-made part of the environment" (p. 36) and describes two aspects: the objective (for example, roads and bridges) and the subjective (beliefs, attitudes, norms, roles, and values). Individuals have unique world views that are shaped by their culture. These world views affect how they think, feel, act, communicate, and interpret their personal and social environments. Culture is a learned phenomenon; it is acquired, for the most part, through the ordinary process of growing up and participating in the daily life of a particular ethnic community (Kallen, 2003).

culture
pattern of behaviour and results of behaviour that are shared and transmitted among members of a particular society

Ethnicity

The term **ethnicity** (also called ethnic identity) is used to define individuals or a group's identification with a cultural origin (for example, British or Armenian) within a culturally pluralistic context (for example, Canada); thus, a group may define itself as British-Canadian or Armenian-Canadian. Ethnicity can be symbolic—that is, by expressing an attachment to and pride in one's ethnic origin—or behavioural—that is, by participating in ethnic activities and passing one's culture from generation to generation. Census Canada defines ethnic origin as "the ethnic or cultural group(s) to which an individual's ancestors belonged" (Statistics Canada, 2001). While ethnicity refers to identifying with a cultural community at the group or individual level, "cultural group" refers to individuals who share a cultural heritage but do not necessarily identify with it. For example, someone may be a member of the Estonian cultural group but consider herself or himself Canadian. Canadian in this context is a legal definition given to one when the government of Canada, through its immigration policy, bestows upon an individual legal rights and privileges associated with the label and identity Canadian. While cultural group is inherited, ethnicity develops through the process of learning and socialization. Globalization and intermarriages among ethnic groups are contributing to the emergence of multiple ethnic ancestries and identities.

ethnicity
individual or group identification with a culture of origin

Race

The word "race" first occurs in the English language about CE 1500. A study of its etymology shows that it was adopted from the French word *race*, which is connected to the Italian words *razza* and the Spanish word *raza*. Beyond this its origin is obscure (Kallen, 2003). It was not until the 18th century, however, that the term was used to indicate major divisions of humankind by stressing certain common physical characteristics such as skin colour (Kallen, 2003). In essence, race is an approach to categorizing people according to common ancestry or origin, based on physical characteristics. At the same time, race is a social concept that can be rejected as a means of dividing people.

Originally, **race** was used to refer to both biological characteristics (as in "white race," "black race," "yellow race," or "red race") and cultural traits and values (as in "peasant race") (Berry & Laponce, 1994). The term is increasingly used to refer to such groupings as language, national origin, ethnicity, culture, and religion. It has become so all-encompassing that it has lost its value as a defining term. Social scientists and others stick to the definition of race as physical or biological.

race
classification based on biological or cultural traits

Minority

A minority (or subordinate) social category has subordinate social status relative to the majority, and its members wield a lesser degree of political and economic and/or social power (Kallen, 2003, p. 284). For example, Blacks in South Africa constitute the majority of the population numerically, but hold the minority power politically, economically, and socially. The term "minority" is not and should not be reduced to a racial classification of those who are not white. Any racial group can hold the majority power in any given society, and have bestowed upon it the term or concept "majority group."

The term "minority" is used to refer to groups that are seen as having less social, political, and economic power than the host group. The minority group status may be based on race, religion, political affiliation, nationality, or some other characteristics that are different from the majority group in question. In Canada, a **visible minority** is defined as individuals, other than Aboriginal peoples, who are non-Caucasian in race or non-white in colour (Employment and Immigration Canada, 1987, p. B-3). This definition is used solely for the purposes of employment, to hire those groups that are underemployed, under-represented, or not represented in the government and private sector areas of employment.

visible minority
individuals, other than Aboriginal people, who are non-Caucasian in race or non-white in colour

The Canadian Council on Social Development reported in 2003 that almost 60 percent of visible-minority immigrants to Canada in the past 10 years were from Asia, with 20 percent from the Caribbean, Central and South America, and Africa. By 2001, Canada's visible-minority population had reached four million people. Toronto and Vancouver both have 37 percent visible-minority populations, the largest group being Asian. Hamilton, Ontario has nearly 25 percent visible-minority population, while Windsor, Ontario, has 22 percent. Close to 94 percent of visible-minority immigrants settled in urban areas, with 44 percent of Toronto's population born outside Canada (Canadian Council on Social Development, 2003).

> **EXERCISE 2**
>
> Newcomers to Canada are often vulnerable to victimization and may fear police because of experiences with police corruption and brutality in their countries of origin. What would you do to maximize newcomer adherence to the law and cooperation with police when serious crimes occur in their neighbourhoods?

CULTURAL BELIEFS AND PRACTICES: SPECIFIC CULTURAL GROUPS

Canada is a multicultural and multi-ethnic society comprising more than 200 ethnic groups. The nation's cultural groups can be classified into three major categories: Aboriginal peoples, non-visible ethnic minority peoples, and visible-minority ethnic peoples. A list of the top 10 groups representing the three major categories is provided in table 4.1. In the present section, the three major cultural groups and major subgroups within them are described briefly for the purpose of discussion. (Note that many smaller groups are not discussed because of space limitations. A single chapter simply cannot begin to cover the international world within Canada.)

Aboriginal Peoples

Aboriginal peoples comprise 3.4 percent of the population in Canada. The Aboriginal community is growing almost twice as fast as the rest of the population in Canada and 50 percent of Aboriginal peoples live in cities across the country. The

TABLE 4.1 Top Ten Ethnic Groups in Canada, 2001

	percent
Canadian	39.4
English	20.2
French	15.8
Scottish	14.0
Irish	12.9
German	9.3
Italian	4.3
Chinese	3.7
Ukrainian	3.6
North American Indian	3.4

Source: Statistics Canada (2001).

majority of Aboriginal peoples report being North American Indian (referred to as First Nations in this book) (62 percent), followed by Métis (30 percent), and Inuit (5 percent). Ontario is home to 188,315 Aboriginal people.

At the time of European contact, more than 56 Aboriginal nations existed, speaking more than 36 languages (Canadian Heritage, 2004). Aboriginal peoples in Canada continue to confront unique socio-cultural and economic challenges including loss of their Aboriginal language, high rates of poverty, and discrimination.

Infringements on the human rights of Aboriginal peoples date back to the first European contact, and violations such as the physical and sexual abuse many Aboriginal children suffered in the residential school system occurred as recently as a few decades ago. The effects on many individuals and communities are plainly evident; Aboriginal people suffer more poverty, poorer health, higher death and suicide rates, and far greater unemployment than do other Canadians.

In the modern era, attempts to address the needs of Canada's Aboriginal peoples began in 1973 when the Supreme Court of Canada first recognized land rights based on an Aboriginal group's traditional use and occupancy of land. In 1982, the *Canadian Charter of Rights and Freedoms* recognized and affirmed the treaty rights of Aboriginal peoples to protect their cultures, customs, traditions, and languages. In 1996, the Royal Commission on Aboriginal Peoples presented a comprehensive five-volume report to the Parliament of Canada identifying the legal, political, social, economic, and cultural issues that need to be addressed to ensure the future survival of Canada's First Nations, Inuit, and Métis peoples. Two years later, the federal government responded with *Gathering Strength: Canada's Aboriginal Action Plan*, a proposal to work in partnership with Canada's Aboriginal peoples to improve health, housing, and public safety; strengthen economic development; and assist with the implementation of self-government (Canadian Heritage, 2004). Some changes and successes were realized, but many opportunities for partnerships between the government and Canada's Aboriginal peoples still remain.

Aboriginal ethics, values, and rules of behaviour have contributed to the development of cooperation and harmonious interpersonal relationships among Aboriginal peoples and in the past ensured their individual and collective survival in harsh natural environments. Differences between individualistic and collectivistic cultures are shown in table 4.2. To sustain a cooperative and friendly social climate for survival, Aboriginal peoples assumed a social pattern of behaviour that dictated the suppression of conflict (Brant, 1990). According to Brant (1990), conflict suppression among the members of an extended family, clan, band, or tribe was established through ethics, or the application of harmony-promoting principles of behaviour. Aboriginal ethics or principles of behaviour, which still apply today, are listed in table 4.3.

TABLE 4.2 Differences Between Individualist and Collectivist Cultures

Individualism	Collectivism
Pursuit of one's own goals	Loyalty to one's group
Nuclear family structure	Extended family structure
Self-reliant	Group-reliant
Time and energy invested for personal gain	Time and energy invested for group gain
Receptive to career changes	Relatively unreceptive to career changes
Relatively little sharing of material/non-material resources	Sharing of material/non-material resources
Emphasis on competition	Emphasis on cooperation
Relatively non-conformist	Conformist
Mistrust of authority	Respectful of status and authority

TABLE 4.3 Aboriginal Ethics of Behaviour

Non-interference	Physical, verbal, and psychological coercion are avoided, as is exertion of pressure by means of advising, instructing, coercing, or persuading.
Non-competitiveness	Rivalry is averted and social embarrassment of individuals is prevented.
Emotional restraint	Both positive (joy and enthusiasm) and negative (anger and hostility) emotions are suppressed.
Sharing	Generosity is encouraged while hoarding material goods is discouraged.
Concept of time	There is a belief in "doing things when the time is right."
Attitude toward gratitude and approval	Gratitude and approval are rarely shown, verbalized, or expected.
Principle of teaching by modelling	To learn, one is *shown* how rather than *told* how. Actions convey useful and practical information.

Source: Brant (1990), p. 536.

Aboriginal peoples believe that *non-interference* helps promote positive relations between people. It takes the form of permissiveness in the context of adult–child relationships. Brant (1990, p. 535) describes the following:

> A Native child may be allowed at the age of six, for example, to make the decision on whether or not he goes to school even though he is required to do so by law. The child may be allowed to decide whether or not he will do his homework, have his assignment done on time, and even visit the dentist. Native parents will be reluctant to force the child into doing anything he does not choose to do.

Non-competitiveness is a way of avoiding conflict between groups and between individuals. Aboriginal cultures are collectivist cultures that emphasize group harmony over individual success.

Emotional restraint is considered desirable because it promotes self-control and discourages the expression of strong and violent feelings. However, suppressing emotions may contribute to alcohol abuse as an outlet for some individuals. Domestic violence and violence within the community that result from intoxication are serious issues for Aboriginal peoples living on reserves.

Sharing is consistent with Aboriginal collectivist cultures. In addition to its historical survival value, sharing helps to suppress conflict by minimizing the likelihood of greed, envy, arrogance, and pride within the community. It also contributes to equality and democracy. Personal striving for prosperity and success and acquiring education and other assets require individuals to give up the ethic of sharing. Aboriginal society is therefore likely to discourage or disapprove of individual ambition. In addition, individual ambition has resulted in the "skimming of Native society" (Brant, 1990), where young, talented Native people or those with a postsecondary education leave the reserve to live in non-Aboriginal society and marry non-Aboriginals.

The *concept of time* in contemporary Aboriginal life is another manifestation of the need for harmonious relationships (Brant, 1990). Aboriginal people are unlikely to be inconvenienced or annoyed by delays in starting scheduled meetings or social functions.

Gratitude and approval are rarely expressed. Both are considered superfluous because doing something for someone else carries its own intrinsic reward.

Teaching in Aboriginal culture is done by modelling.

In Aboriginal cultures *excellence is expected at all times*. A negative consequence of this core value is performance anxiety. Aboriginal people may avoid taking risks for fear of making mistakes or subjecting themselves to public scrutiny. In Aboriginal cultures, praise and rewards for being good are not expected because being good is what one expects from oneself. Praise is likely to be seen as deceitful, or as embarrassing in group contexts when the praise is not given to the whole group. Praise that is not shared with peers is seen as disharmonious to peer relationships.

Non-Visible Ethnic Minority Peoples

Non-visible ethnic minority groups represent those that are not listed in Employment and Immigration Canada (1987). They include the two founding peoples of Canada, the English and the French, and a host of other cultural groups from Europe including Germans, Italians, the Dutch, Australians, and New Zealanders.

As indicated in table 4.1, English, French, Scottish, and Irish are the most frequently reported non-visible ethnic minority groups in Canada. In this section we focus mainly on the French and the English.

People of French heritage are likely to value their language and its preservation, their French culture and its distinctiveness, their families, and, in some cases, their religion.

While there are differences among the English, Scottish, Irish, and Welsh cultures, they share several common values. These are listed in table 4.4 under the heading "British." People of British and Irish cultures are individualistic, as manifested in their emphasis on the work ethic, self-reliance, emotional reserve, the nuclear family structure, privacy, democracy, and mistrust of authority.

Visible-Minority Ethnic Peoples

Visible minorities constitute 13.4 percent of the Canadian population (Statistics Canada, 2001). The increase in people of visible minorities between 1996 and 2001 was six times faster than the increase in the general population of the country. In 1981, 1 in 20 Canadians was a visible minority; in 2001, it was 1 in 7. Thus, almost four million individuals who identify themselves as visible minorities have made Canada their home; 3 out of 10 visible-minority people were born in Canada; and Chinese, South Asians, and Blacks constitute the three largest visible-minority groups, accounting for two-thirds of the visible-minority population. In terms of urban settlement, 36.9 percent of the population of Vancouver, 36.8 percent of the population of the Toronto Census Metropolitan Area (GTA), and 13.6 percent of

TABLE 4.4 Comparison of Cultural Values and Practices

British	Black	Latino	Asian
Individualism	Collectivism	Collectivism	Collectivism
Nuclear family structure	Extended family system	Familism (*la familia*)	Extended family system
Individual initiative and risk taking	Family strength	Family honour	Group decision making
Achievement orientation	Education	Importance of process over outcome	Obligation to group
Competition	Cooperation	Cooperation	Cooperation
Work ethic, task-and-outcome orientation	Black language, soul, and oral tradition	*Dignidad*—Spanish pride, personal reputation, opinions of others, and saving face	Harmonious interpersonal relationships
Materialism	Religion	Religion	Spiritualism
Rationalism	Emotional expressiveness	Emotional expressiveness	Indirect expression of emotions
Direct communication	Direct communication	Indirect communication	Indirect communication
Assertiveness	Openness, directness	Courtesy, tact, and diplomacy	Fatalism, patience, and formality

the population of Montreal are visible-minority people. In the GTA, 25 percent of Chinese and 25 percent of South Asians are foreign born, as are 20 percent of Blacks, 8 percent of Filipinos, 6 percent of Arabs and West Asians, 5 percent of Latin Americans, 3 percent of South East Asians, 3 percent of Koreans, and 1 percent of Japanese.

> **EXERCISE 3**
>
> Law enforcement officials want to be respected for their abilities and professionalism, not for their cultures. What moral dilemmas could law enforcement officials from, say, an English, Asian, or Black culture encounter in dealing with co-workers or suspects from the same culture, and those from other cultures?

BLACK PEOPLES

According to the 2001 Census, a total of 662,215 people identified themselves as Black (Statistics Canada, 2001). Blacks have a long and tragic history of colonization and slavery. The beginnings of their slavery in the United States are traced to 1619. A trickle of Africans brought from England to work as farm labourers swelled to a slave population in the millions. Similarly, a fairly loose labour system evolved into a "system of chattel slavery that tried to control nearly every aspect of the slaves' lives" (Wheeler & Becker, 1994, p. 170).

The French brought African slaves to Canada in the early 1600s. In 1689, the settlers of New France were given explicit permission to import more slaves from Africa. Thousands of Blacks settled in the Maritimes beginning in 1776. Many of those individuals came with their white masters fleeing the American Revolution, but many also came as free people. Slavery was legalized in Canada in 1709 and outlawed in 1834, at a time when Canada was under British rule. While Blacks were invited to settle on Vancouver Island in 1859, segregated schools continued to exist in many parts of Canada until 1964. (More historical detail on people of African heritage in North America is provided in Kazarian, 2001.)

Blacks are a heterogeneous group of people who nonetheless share several cultural values (see table 4.4), including collectivism, directness and spontaneity, expressiveness, and high regard for family and religion (Blank & Slipp, 1994; Gaines, 1997). The negative image of the Black family as dysfunctional decontextualizes Black social life, and ignores strengths within the extended family system. Any child who repeatedly hears the larger society's pronouncement that his or her colour is ugly; that he or she is subjected to a low-income, inner-city environment; and that he or she is exposed to criminal activity and victimization is a vulnerable child. While the resilience of Blacks in the face of slavery, segregation, and racist theories and practices is a source of pride and inspiration, their battle against discrimination is ongoing.

LATIN AMERICAN PEOPLES

People of Latin American heritage come from a variety of Latin countries and constitute many races and cultures. As an umbrella term, "Latino" identifies people who claim Spanish-speaking ancestry. Other terms that are used include "Chicano" and "Hispanic." A list of core values and practices of Latin American culture is provided in table 4.4.

The majority of people of Latin American heritage are Roman Catholic. According to Gaines (1997), *la familia*, not machismo, is central to Latino culture. Familism has such a strong influence on interpersonal behaviours in Latino culture that "when the two sets of value [machismo and familism] come into conflict, familism tends to prevail" (p. 51). A more appropriate portrayal of the Latino male is that of *dignidad*—Spanish pride.

ASIAN PEOPLES

People of Asian heritage come from various countries—for example, China, Southeast Asia, Japan, Korea, the Pacific Islands, and the Philippines. Even though Asian peoples constitute a heterogeneous group, they share some core cultural values and practices, summarized in table 4.4. Confucianism, Buddhism, Hinduism, Taoism, and Islam have influenced these values and practices. Family and group loyalties are fundamental to Asians. The Asian self is seen as an extension of the family and the in-group. Family loyalty is practised through filial piety—children honouring their parents.

ARAB PEOPLES

The fastest-growing visible-minority groups in Canada are Arabs and Western Asians. The majority of people of Arab heritage living in Canada are Lebanese, Syrian, Egyptian, Chaldean/Iraqi, and Palestinian/Jordanian. Even though there are Christian Arabs, the majority are Muslim. The various Arab groups share the Arabic language, although there are some differences in vocabulary and accent.

Arab culture is a culture of honour and shame, and a self-construct that is interdependent. This influences and guides the behaviour of nuclear and extended family members. Female premarital sex and loss of virginity before marriage bring shame and dishonour to the family. Medical conditions may also be a source of shame for the family. As in many other cultures, mental illness may be concealed because of the shame it may bring to the family and the potential limits it may place on the marriage opportunities of other family members.

EXERCISE 4

Explain the behaviour of the police officer in the following scenario. Role-play the situation and share your thoughts and feelings with the group.

> A police officer arrested two Muslim women who were wearing *niqabs* (veils) as they walked from a local mosque to a convenience store. The officer frisked the women, handcuffed them, and took them to the police station on the grounds that wearing a mask in public is against the law. The women were released without charge.

Source: Khouri (1996).

STEREOTYPES AND PREJUDICES

A **stereotype** is a usually oversimplified conception or belief about a person, group, event, or issue considered to typify or conform to an unvarying pattern or manner. Stereotypes indicate that the object of the stereotype is lacking any individuality. A **prejudice** is an adverse judgment or opinion formed beforehand or without knowledge or examination of the facts. It's a preconceived preference, idea, or bias. Being prejudiced is the act or state of holding unreasonable preconceived judgments or convictions. Usually these include irrational suspicion or hatred of a particular group, race, or religion.

Prejudices cause people to judge prematurely and irrationally, and influence their own thinking and that of others into becoming biased against someone or something. Prejudices affect people detrimentally, often forming the foundations of, among other things, racist and sexist attitudes.

stereotype
conventional, formulaic, and usually oversimplified conception, opinion, or belief about a person, group, event, or issue considered to typify or conform to an unvarying pattern or manner

prejudice
an adverse judgment or opinion formed beforehand or without knowledge or examination of the facts

ALCOHOL, ABORIGINAL PEOPLE, AND THE LAW

Aboriginal people are grossly overrepresented in Canada's criminal justice system. For example, the incarceration rate for Aboriginal peoples in Ontario is about four times that of the population at large; Aboriginal peoples comprise about 2 percent of Ontario's population, but about 8 percent of the prison population. This situation is even worse in other areas of the country. For example, in Saskatchewan, Aboriginal women are 88 times more likely to be arrested than non-Aboriginal women.

Most Aboriginal people are arrested for minor offences. Many of these offences are alcohol related and, in Ontario, many of the offences are for public intoxication or failure to pay fines related to the *Liquor Licence Act*. This problem is most acute in Kenora, Ontario where, before 2000, 50 percent of male Aboriginal admissions and 71 percent of female Aboriginal admissions to the Kenora prison system were for liquor-related offences (excluding impaired-driving charges). In Kenora, "street people" comprise a major portion of the jail population. These individuals may be incarcerated for several weeks or even months for the crime of public intoxication. Sometimes a street person may be "blackstriped" (given a ticket for drinking in public) twice in one day. It is possible for tickets to accumulate to the extent that a person may have to pay several hundred dollars in fines. With no hope of employment, street people cannot pay these fines, so they spend weeks in jail.

However, the relationship between alcohol use and criminal activity is seldom so direct. Many crimes are alcohol related, acts committed while a person was intoxicated. According to figures gathered by the Ontario Native Council on Justice, 71 percent of Native male inmates and 81 percent of Native female inmates felt that alcohol abuse was the major reason for their legal problems (Loucks, 1982; Moynes, 1999, p. 87).

ALCOHOL AND STEREOTYPING

There is no accurate estimate of how many Aboriginal people abuse alcohol. It appears that the number of non-drinkers is the same in non-Aboriginal and Aboriginal society—about 30 percent. Increased awareness of the importance of physical fitness and health among whites, and the increased awareness of the need to create healthy communities among Aboriginal people, will inevitably lead to an increase in the number of non-drinkers.

It is extremely difficult to determine the alcoholism rate for different Aboriginal communities; the very definition of "alcoholism" is subject to debate. It is known, however, that the incidence of alcohol abuse increases in northern or remote communities where feelings of isolation and a lack of recreational opportunities increase the likelihood that people will turn to alcohol as a way of decreasing boredom and increasing social interaction.

Alcohol abuse varies greatly between Aboriginal communities. Just as there are dry reserves, so too are there reserves where alcohol abuse is a major problem. In the final analysis, however, there is little hard evidence to suggest that Aboriginal alcoholism rates are any greater than those among the general population.

Despite these facts, the "drunken Indian" continues to be a powerful stereotype in mainstream society. Many whites and Aboriginal people believe that the latter "can't handle their liquor" or that "once they start drinking, they can't stop," or that, for biological reasons, Aboriginal people are, as a race, more susceptible to alcoholism and alcohol abuse. However, none of these stereotypes have any scientific basis. Alcohol abuse should be viewed as a result of Aboriginal social, psychological, and economic disadvantages, not as a cause of these factors (Moynes, 1999, p. 88).

WOMEN IN THE WORKPLACE

Of the 500 highest-paid executives in Canada's 100 largest public companies, only 23 are females. A study of the 2005 executive compensation filings of those companies, with revenues ranging from $2.2 billion to $30 billion a year, found that fewer than two dozen of the 497 CEOs, chief financial officers, and other top executives are women. That's 4.6 percent.

"We've heard a lot of talk over the past decade or so about women breaking through the glass ceiling," said Jay Rosenzweig, managing partner of Toronto executive search firm Rosenzweig & Company, the company that conducted the study. "But clearly these numbers speak volumes as to how much action—or inaction—has occurred in filling the highest executive positions with women. There remains great hesitancy to give women the keys to the top five executive officer jobs. ... The irony is that companies only hurt themselves by ignoring such a huge talent pool of women when promoting to the top."

This is the first time Canada's top five executives at the top 100 public companies have been scrutinized. But a study in 2004 by Catalyst Canada found that just more than 14 percent of all executives are women, and it will take 20 years to reach even one quarter. Women have been in the workforce in droves for several decades and now comprise 46.6 percent of workers. Yet the pace of change at the uppermost levels has been evolutionary rather than revolutionary.

The thin ranks of women at the leadership level is attracting the attention of some governments. As of January 1, 2006, Norway is requiring publicly traded companies to increase the number of women on their boards of directors within two years to at least 40 percent. Corporations that don't meet the target can be disbanded. To compare, only 9 percent of Canadian board seats are filled by women (MacLeod, 2006, pp. A1, A5).

In the federal election of January 23, 2006, women were no closer to achieving parity with men in the House of Commons. The Conservatives recruited fewer females to run in the election than other parties. Over the past 12 years of Liberal rule, the proportion of women in the Commons has barely increased, going from 18 percent when Jean Chrétien first became prime minister to 21 percent under Paul Martin. In 1993, the number of female candidates was actually higher than in the 2004 and 2006 elections. Back then, two of the five leaders, including the prime minister, were women, and that gave every party a stronger incentive to recruit female candidates.

There are fewer women on the election ballots today, and there are few future female contenders in sight for federal leadership positions. No political party establishment used the 2006 election to groom a female candidate for a future leadership post (Hebert, 2006, p. A10).

THE BLACK EXPERIENCE

One of the great myths of Canadian society is that it was a slavery-free society. Slavery had been practised in Canada since the first years of the 17th century, and was abolished in the British Empire in 1834. The passage of the *Fugitive Slave Act* in the United States in 1850 greatly increased the number of Blacks coming to Canada. However, these Blacks were unwelcome and were subjected to racial prejudice and ridicule both personally and in the Canadian public press. Even into the 19th century, Blacks were accused of being responsible for a disproportionate amount of crime.

The Canadian government had consistently resisted the immigration of Blacks. In the early 1900s, when the government was attempting to lure experienced farmers from the United States, the Immigration Branch informed its American agents that Blacks were not encouraged to emigrate. The government often rejected Blacks on medical or other non-racial grounds, in order not to be accused of overt racism (Baxter, 2003, p. 65).

The magnitude of the racism expressed by Canadians toward people of African descent cannot be minimized. In 1903, J.S. Woodsworth, the founder of the CCF political party, demonstrated a surprising antipathy toward Blacks. He asserted that the "very qualities of intelligence and manliness which are the essentials for citizens in a democracy were systematically expunged from the Negro race" (Henry & Tator, 2005, p. 66). There are other examples:

- 1785: Sheriffs in St. John, NB, were instructed to deny Blacks the right to vote.
- 1795: Blacks in St. John were denied fishing rights.

- 1830s: Some churches in Canada consigned Black worshippers to back galleries.

- 1850s: Blacks were denied admission to hotels in cities such as Chatham, Hamilton, and Windsor.

- 1850: The *Separate School Act* enabled whites to relegate Blacks to all-Black schools with only Blacks for teachers. The practice continued up to the 1960s.

- 1920s: The Ku Klux Klan grew to such an extent that there were 119 chapters throughout Canada.

- 1924: The City Commissioner of Edmonton banned all Blacks from public parks and swimming pools.

- 1918–1939: McGill University had racial segregation regulations that were maintained until well after World War II.

- 1954: A teacher was dismissed from a teaching position in Victoria, BC, for no other reason than he was married to a Jamaican woman.

In 1986, there were officially only 175,000 Blacks in Canada, or 0.7 percent of the population.

All of the provinces with significant Black populations had segregation laws on the books for most of the last century. In Ontario, school segregation continued to be legal until 1964, and residential segregation was imposed through restrictions imposed on deeds and leases—for example, when a black person applied for an apartment and was falsely told that it was already taken. Contemporary debates over discrimination in housing have their origins in these practices (Henry & Tator, 2005, p. 66). African-Canadians face particularly harsh obstacles to success. Aside from Aboriginal peoples, they are the most stigmatized of all visible minorities in Canada, and they have paid the price in terms of economic success and in relationships with the justice system (Baxter, 2003, p. 15).

SOUTH ASIANS

South Asians include anyone whose ancestry can be traced to the Indian subcontinent. The first South Asians who came to Canada were Sikhs. Although their numbers were very small (5,000 in 1908), white society reacted with the same animosity to them as it did to Blacks, Chinese, and Japanese. The presence of Sikhs in British Columbia at the turn of the century prompted talk of a "Hindu invasion" in the popular press. As World War I approached, white Canadians became even more obsessed with racial purity:

> To prepare ourselves for the irrepressible conflict, Canada must remain a White Man's country. On this western frontier of the Empire will be the forefront of the coming struggle … . Therefore we ought to maintain this Country for the Anglo-Saxon and those races which are able to assimilate themselves to them. If this is done, we believe that history will repeat itself and the supremacy of our race will continue. (Henry & Tator, 2005, p. 71)

This supremacist attitude led to the passage of a number of laws in British Columbia to bar South Asians from participating in elections, even though they were British citizens. Most people of Asian descent of any kind (whether British citizens or not) were denied the franchise in Canada. The loss of the right to vote had a negative economic impact on these people. Since Asian-Canadians were not included on voters' lists, they could not bid on government contracts, nor could they enter professions such as law, education, or medicine. South Asians did not get the franchise until the late 1940s (Baxter, 2003, p. 16).

EXERCISE 5

1. Consider a few of the stereotypes that you have encountered. What effects do you think stereotypes have on the quality of life of individuals and groups and on society generally?
2. What effects do you think stereotypes have on law enforcement?

CULTURAL DIVERSITY VALUES, BELIEFS, AND PRACTICES: POLICE ABILITIES, KNOWLEDGE, AND SKILLS

Culture, race, and ethnicity affect individual values, practices, and codes of conduct. Diverse values and customs enrich the quality of life of a country, but also have the potential to be a source of conflict, misunderstanding, and violence.

Ethnocultural groups and their community leaders have the responsibility to respect others' rights and freedoms, live peacefully with diversity, recognize that there is one secular law for all, obey the law of the land, and protect the civil order of the nation. Conflict and misunderstanding are more likely in contexts where certain groups are convinced that they are superior and that others are inferior or where different laws for different groups prevail. Ethnocultural groups and police need to recognize and sustain a core value that respects diversity—namely, **diversity equity**, which means that, while different groups exist, none are superior or inferior.

Police need to be vigilant in opposing distorted portrayals of ethnocultural groups and individuals. The demonization of Arabs generally and Arab communities in Western countries by some Canadians in the aftermath of 9/11 is illustrative. To such people, "Arab" and "Muslim Arab" have become synonymous with "terrorist," and the Arab–terrorist connection has been perpetuated on the grounds that some Arab communities and their leaders failed to express unequivocal condemnation of terrorism or were slow in making their declaration, or that some Muslims even reacted with jubilance to the 9/11 tragedy. Police need to remember that very few Arabs are fundamentalists, extremists, radicals, fascists, or terrorists and that terrorists are likely to defy demographic, racial, or ethnic profiles. They may spring out of all demographics—male and female, young and old, immigrants and citizens; and all colours and nationalities—African, Asian, European, Hispanic, and Middle Eastern. Colourblind and democratic law enforcement is required to protect civil order and curb terrorist threats. All those who pose a legitimate terrorist threat or threat to national

diversity equity
equity based on a belief that there are no superior or inferior cultural groups

security, regardless of their race, ethnicity, and religion, must be fair game for democratic policing measures, including screening, scrutiny, surveillance, and criminal prosecution. Symptomatic approaches to terrorist threats, however, may be limited in that they fail to eradicate the underlying causes of the problem. Sound police–community relations and mutually respectful and trusting attitudes and open communication are good ingredients for counterterrorism.

Police should be neither complacent nor overzealous. Protection of civil order is critical. Ethnocultural groups and their leaders must understand the security measures and practices of police; the reassurance of a democratic approach to policing is also essential. Resisting the tendency to identify a particular ethnic group with terrorism and incorporating and maintaining diversity equity in the police psyche promotes a world view that recognizes the humanity of people, nourishes the humanity of policing, and nurtures a climate of mutual trust that promotes a safe and a secure Canada.

EXERCISE 6

Consider how the following factors may influence your reactions to individuals from various ethnic groups:

1. your upbringing
2. media portrayal of specific religions
3. police culture
4. past personal experiences
5. a person's appearance
6. a person's skin colour

CHAPTER SUMMARY

It is important to keep in mind that cultural groups actually represent a variety of cultures and ethnic origins, as well as individuals with personal beliefs and attitudes. Stereotyping people is a simplistic and lazy substitute for getting to know and understand them. Focusing on people's similarities instead of their differences can help reduce conflict and misunderstanding. Establishing a mutually respectful and trusting relationship between law enforcement and cultural groups contributes to protection of civil order.

KEY TERMS

culture	stereotype
ethnicity	prejudice
race	diversity equity
visible minority	

REFERENCES

Baxter, P. (2003). A portrait of Canadian diversity: The 2001 census and its implications for multiculturalism. In *Issues in diversity and first nations policing*. Unpublished manuscript. Georgian College, Barrie, ON.

Berry, J.W., & J.A. Laponce. (1994). Evaluating research on Canada's multiethnic and multicultural society. In J.W. Berry & J.A. Laponce (Eds.), *Ethnicity and culture in Canada* (pp. 3–16). Toronto: University of Toronto Press.

Blank, R., & S. Slipp. (1994). *Voices of diversity: Real people talk about problems and solutions in a workplace where everyone is not alike.* New York: American Management Association.

Brant, C.C. (1990). Native ethics and rules of behaviour. *Canadian Journal of Psychiatry* 35: 534–539.

Canadian Council on Social Development. (2003). Census shows increasing diversity of Canadian society. http://www.ccsd.ca/home.htm.

Canadian Heritage. (2004). Canadian diversity: Respecting our differences. http://www.pch.gc.ca/index_e.cfm.

Canadian Press. (2000, November 10). Escaper, 73, "armed and dangerous." *The London Free Press*, p. A8.

Carey, E. (2003, February 11). Census shows 905 home to more immigrants. *The Toronto Star*. http://www.thestar.com.

Employment and Immigration Canada. (1987). *Profiles of Canadian immigration.* Ottawa: Supply and Services Canada.

Gaines, S.O.J. (1997). *Culture, ethnicity, and personal relationship processes.* NY: Routledge.

Hebert, C. (2006, January 23). More women ran 13 years ago. *The Hamilton Spectator*, p. A10.

Henry, F., & C. Tator. (2005). *The colour of democracy: Racism in Canadian society* (3rd ed.) Toronto: Nelson Thomson.

Kallen, E. (2003). *Ethnicity and human rights in Canada: A human rights perspective on race, ethnicity, racism and systemic inequality.* New York: Oxford University Press.

Kazarian, S.S. (2001). Health issues in North American people of African heritage. In S.S. Kazarian & D.R. Evans (Eds.), *Handbook of cultural health psychology*. San Diego: Academic Press.

Kazarian, S.S., & D.R. Evans. (1998). Cultural clinical psychology. In S.S. Kazarian & D.R. Evans (Eds.), *Cultural clinical psychology: Theory, research and practice.* New York: Oxford University Press.

Khouri, G. (1996, September 18). American-Arab Anti-Discrimination Committee press release. http://www.adc.org/adc/pressrelease/1996/18-sep-96.txt.

Lagasse, J.H. (1967). The two founding peoples. In Canada, Dominion Bureau of Statistics, *Canada one hundred, 1867–1967* (pp. 74–81). Ottawa: Queen's Printer.

Lett, A.H. (1968). A look at others: Minority groups and police–community relations. In A.F. Brandstaller & L.A. Radelee (Eds.), *Police and community relations: A source book* (pp. 121–128). Beverly Hills, CA: Glencoe Press.

Linton, R. (1945). *The cultural background of psychology*. New York: Appleton-Century.

Loucks, B. (1982). Preliminary response to the Ontario consultation paper on implementing Bill C-61, the *Young Offenders Act*. Toronto: Ontario Native Council on Justice.

Macleod, Meredith. (2006, January 19). Women still not reaching top rungs. *The Hamilton Spectator*, p. A1.

Markus, H.R., & S. Kitayama. (1991). Culture and self: Implications for cognition, emotion and motivation. *Psychological Review* 98: 224–253.

Moynes, J. (1999). Social competence and deviant behaviour. Native Community Care, Counselling and Development. Hamilton, ON: Mohawk College.

Moynihan, D.P. (1993). *Pandaemonium*. Oxford: Oxford University Press.

Race Relations Act 1976 (UK), c. 74.

Ripley, B. (2006, August 19). Terrorism defies comprehension, cure. *The London Free Press*, p. F5.

Statistics Canada. (2001). Canada's ethnocultural portrait: The changing mosaic. http://www.statcan.ca/menu-en.htm.

Sustainability Reporting Program. (2004). The urbanization of Canada. http://www.sustreport.org/signals/canpop_urb.html.

Triandis, H.C. (1990). Theoretical concepts that are applicable to the analysis of ethnocentrism. In R.W. Brislin (Ed.), *Applied cross-cultural psychology* (pp. 24–55). Newbury Park, CA: Sage.

Triandis, H.C. (1995). A theoretical framework for the study of diversity. In M.M. Chemers, S. Oskamp, & M.A. Costanza (Eds.), *Diversity in organizations: New perspectives for a changing workplace* (pp. 11–36). Thousand Oaks, CA: Sage.

Wheeler, W.B., & S.D. Becker. (1994). *Discovering the American past: A look at the evidence*. Volume I to 1877. Boston: Houghton Mifflin.

Winterdyk, J.A., & D.E. King (Eds.). (1999). *Diversity and criminal justice in Canada*. Toronto: Canadian Scholars' Press.

CHAPTER 5
Religious Diversity

CHAPTER OBJECTIVES

After completing this chapter, you should be able to:

- Explain the concept of religion.
- Recognize the multiple religious beliefs and practices in pluralistic societies.
- Discuss specific religious groups and their beliefs and practices.
- Analyze personal perspectives on religion.
- Use concepts of religious diversity to analyze and facilitate police–community interactions.

INTRODUCTION

This chapter discusses the concept of religion, describes the beliefs and practices of a number of religious groups with a view to increasing understanding of the expressions of these religions, and explains the experiences of Muslims, post 9/11, and their implications for enabling police to work better and smarter in protecting themselves and their fellow citizens.

Canada is a multicultural, multi-ethnic, multilingual, and multi-faith country. New immigrants to Canada have brought not only new cultures, ethnicities, and languages but also new faiths. In 2001, 43 percent of the population in Canada identified itself as Roman Catholic, 29 percent as Protestant, 2 percent as Muslim, and 1 percent each as Buddhist, Hindu, and Sikh. The changing sources of immigrants have also contributed to shifts in the country's religious makeup such that there have been decreases in the last decade in the number of Canadians reporting Protestant and Catholic religious affiliations and substantial increases in the number of Canadians reporting the religions of Islam, Sikhism, and Buddhism (Statistics Canada, 2001).

WHAT IS RELIGION?

religion
a spiritual belief system

All humans have basic needs that require satisfaction. **Religion** and spirituality identify ways of satisfying those needs. The spiritual needs identified by various religions and how they are satisfied vary, since each religious tradition evolves in a unique historical context. For example, Christianity identifies sin as a fundamental human issue and advocates salvation from sin. Buddhism, on the other hand, regards ignorance as the fundamental issue and prescribes enlightenment as the purpose. Religions use sacred speech and narrative (myth, prayer, song), sacred acts and rituals, and sacred places for religious expression (Forman, 1993).

> **EXERCISE 1**
>
> What implications does religious diversity have for both individual police and for police services?

RELIGIOUS BELIEFS AND PRACTICES

Religion plays a significant role in the lives of many people. Each religion has its own world view and concept of a higher power. Religions give individuals within a family of faith a common link to the past and the future (White, 1997). However, **religious beliefs** and **religious practices** in pluralistic societies have the potential to create divisiveness, animosity, and intolerance through ignorance, misunderstanding of religious doctrines, or differences in world views. For example, many Americans interviewed by CNN after the terrorist attacks on the United States on September 11, 2001 believed that America needed to go into Iraq and turn all Muslims living in Iraq into good Christians in order for them to be "saved" and be "humanized." The same can be said about the treatment of Canada's Aboriginal peoples by the colonizers, for Blacks during slavery, and most conquered or colonized people around the world. History is replete with examples of hegemonic Christianizing of colonized and dominated peoples. Thus, the history of a group's religious struggles against forms of domination will assist in a better understanding of the group's resistance, trust, and level of integration into mainstream society. To that end, exploring some major religions and the beliefs and practices associated with them is an important step in appreciating religions and developing an attitude of acceptance and respect.

religious beliefs
tenets of particular faiths

religious practices
concrete expressions of religious beliefs

Needless to say, not everyone has a religion or believes in religion. For example, atheists profess no particular religion and do not believe in a higher power. Similarly, agnostics believe in the impossibility of knowing God or determining how the universe began. Atheists and agnostics have their own values and codes of ethical conduct. They deserve as much recognition, respect, and protection as those with firm religious beliefs and practices.

The religions discussed in this chapter are listed in table 5.1. Needless to say, all religions cannot be discussed in a single chapter. Those that have been included have not been chosen because they are seen to be more significant or superior to a religion not discussed in the chapter, just as those that are excluded should not be seen as insignificant or inferior.

TABLE 5.1 Some Religions of the World

Religion	Number of believers in the world
Bahá'í Faith	5 to 6 million
Buddhism	376 million
Christian Scientists	500,000
Christianity	2.1 billion
Hinduism	1 billion
Islam	> 1.3 billion
Jehovah's Witnesses	> 12 million
Judaism	14 million
Shintoism	> 100 million
Sikhism	23 million
Taoism	not available
Wicca	> 100,000

EXERCISE 2

1. In the following section you will learn about a variety of religious beliefs and practices. Do you have any images of the following individuals before reading about them in the text? Share your reactions.

    a. a Muslim woman wearing a *niqab*

    b. a Chinese Buddhist

    c. a Christian Scientist

    d. a Jehovah's Witness

    e. a traditional Aboriginal man

    f. a Sikh wearing a turban

    g. a Hindu woman wearing a sari

    h. a Muslim man with a beard

    i. a white Protestant woman

    j. a Roman Catholic priest

2. Identify factors that may have contributed to your reactions to people from the various religious groups. Identify which factors are irrational, and which are rational.

Bahá'í Faith: Embracing All Nations, Creeds, and Colours

Bahá'u'lláh is the founder of the Bahá'í Faith, which is associated with the trinity of oneness of God, oneness of religion, and oneness of humanity. A Bahá'í is a follower of Bahá'u'lláh. This religion teaches that there is only one God; that there is only one religion, which is revealed progressively by God; and that all people are equal in the sight of God. The Bahá'í Faith endorses several other basic principles and practices, as follows (New York City Bahá'í Community, 1999):

- unity (oneness) of humankind;
- unity in the foundation of all religions, the great religions expressing a single divine plan;
- religion as the source of unity;
- religion as a progressive and evolutionary process;
- compatibility of science and religion;
- independent investigation of truth;
- equality of men and women;
- elimination of all forms of prejudice;
- universal peace;
- universal education;
- a universal auxiliary language—an international language everyone learns in addition to his or her mother tongue;
- spiritual solutions to economic problems; and
- an international tribunal.

The Bahá'í do not have a clergy. They consider the family the foundation of human society, marriage a means for the spiritual development of both partners, and morality as a direct influence on spiritual development and happiness. In addition to the Ten Commandments (see table 5.3, below), the moral code of the Bahá'í Faith dictates the following practices:

- avoiding backbiting and gossip, promiscuity, gambling, and alcohol and drug use;
- daily prayer and reading of holy writings;
- fasting;
- observing Bahá'í holidays;
- maintaining chastity before marriage;
- teaching the cause of God;
- contributing to the Bahá'í Fund, which supports the work of the faith;

- considering work a form of worship; and

- respecting and obeying the government of the land.

Buddhism: Seeking Enlightenment

In 2001, 300,300 Canadians identified themselves as Buddhists. Buddhism was founded in northern India by the ascetic Siddhartha Gautama (566–480 BC), who became Buddha, "the enlightened one." Gautama was from an aristocratic family but discovered suffering and left home to search for redemption from it. He saw the truth of salvation as he sat under a tree in deep meditation.

Buddhism is not a religion in the Western sense. Buddhists do not worship a creator God. Instead, they follow a path of practice and spiritual development for the full development and freedom of body, speech, and mind and that leads to the personal qualities of awareness, kindness, and wisdom; for insight into the true nature of life; and ultimately for Enlightenment or Buddhahood. The three basic tenets of Buddhist teaching are *impermanence* (nothing is fixed or permanent), *actions have consequences*, and *change is possible*. There are different types or levels of Buddhism, but all invoke non-violence, lack of dogma, tolerance of differences, and the practice of meditation.

Four Noble Truths are associated with Buddhism (Boeree, 2000):

1. Suffering is inherent in life.

2. Attachment to things and craving sensual pleasures are cause for suffering.

3. Release from suffering (Nirvana) is achieved by eliminating selfish, sensual, and material desires.

4. There is an Eightfold Path to achieve Nirvana:

    a. right view—understanding the Four Noble Truths;

    b. right aspiration—sincerely wanting to overcome attachment;

    c. right speech—avoiding slander and gossip;

    d. right action—conducting oneself morally;

    e. right livelihood—doing work that harms no one;

    f. right effort—focusing on good thoughts and nurturing good qualities;

    g. right mindfulness—integrating thoughts, body, and feelings to overcome desire; and

    h. right concentration—disciplining the mind through meditation.

The Four Noble Truths and the Eightfold Path translate into five rules of Buddhist living:

1. Avoid harm and be kind.

2. Avoid taking what is not given and be generous.

3. Avoid sexual misconduct and excess, and be content.
4. Avoid false speech and be truthful.
5. Abstain from intoxicants and be aware.

The Buddhist moral code forbids killing, stealing, lying, and sexual promiscuity. In marital relationships, husbands are expected to be respectful, faithful, and supportive of their wives. Wives are expected to show diligence, hospitality to relatives, and faithfulness to their husbands, as well as being respectful and supportive.

Christian Science: Healing Through Divine Laws

Christian Science aims to save the universe from evil and to heal disease by spiritual means alone. It is based on the words and works of Jesus Christ, draws its authority from the Bible, and follows the teachings of its founder, Mary Baker Eddy. Eddy's personal experience with spiritual healing through divine laws led to her discovery of the Science of Christianity that Jesus lived and taught. In 1875, she wrote and published *Science and Health with Key to the Scriptures*, which is used as a textbook and to prepare Christian Science practitioners for ministering Christian healing.

Christian Scientists subscribe to the belief that moral, spiritual, and physical healing can occur through *divine laws*—that is, through scientific prayer, or spiritual communion with God. Scientific prayer recognizes an ill person's direct access to God's love. Scientific prayer knows God, or divine Mind, as the only healer. It brings the transforming action of Christ, the idea of divine Love, to the ill person's consciousness. The ill person's transformed or spiritualized thought changes his or her condition.

Christian Science healing is a specific treatment distinct from faith healing, psychotherapy, Scientology, and positive thinking. Hypnotism, spiritualism, and suggestion are not part of Christian Science healing, nor are blind faith or control of one human mind over another. No formulas, chants, rituals, esoteric practices, or secret writings are associated with Christian Science healing (The First Church of Christ, Scientist, 2001).

While some authoritative sources assert that Christian Scientists reject medical treatment from physicians and hospitals (for example, White, 1997), the Christian Science community refers to the freedom of choice of its members in caring for themselves and their families, "just as anyone who normally resorts to medical care could choose to use spiritual means" (The First Church of Christ, Scientist, 2001). More specifically, Christian Science takes the position that those who "depart from the use of Christian Science by choosing some other kind of treatment" are "neither condemned by the Church nor dropped from membership."

Christian Science teaches strict adherence to the moral code of the Ten Commandments (see table 5.3, below) and Christ's Sermon on the Mount. The sermon speaks to seeking spirituality; being mild-tempered, peaceable, merciful, and a lover of righteousness; loving even those who are disliked; giving to the needy; being non-judgmental; and treating others as one would like to be treated. The sermon also condemns murder, being wrathful with others, adultery, lustful thoughts, and irresponsible divorce actions that break up homes and victimize children.

Christianity: Love Your Neighbour

Christianity is the most popular religion in the world. About 33 percent of the world's population is Christian. Christianity became a moral force in the first century CE.

Jesus of Nazareth is the central figure in Christianity. The basic Christian beliefs are stated in the Nicene Creed. Christians believe in one God; in one Lord, Jesus Christ, the son of God and saviour whose birth, death, and resurrection provide hope for eternal life with God; and in the Holy Spirit. The principle of love ("love your neighbour as yourself") represents the fundamental ethical instruction for Christians. Christians hold children in high regard and are obligated to support their church and to give to the poor.

A number of branches of Christianity date back to Christ's disciples (for example, Catholic and Orthodox). The Roman Catholic Church is the largest and most universal. In 2001, 43 percent of Canadians identified themselves with the Roman Catholic Church. The head of the Catholic Church is the Pope (Latin for "father") whose pronouncements are considered infallible. The Catholic Church opposes premarital sex, birth control, abortion, and the ordination of women.

In 2001, Protestant denominations comprised 29 percent of the Canadian population. Martin Luther (1483–1546), a German monk and reformer, sparked a major schism in the Catholic Church called the Protestant Reformation. He advanced the ideas that the Bible is the only rule of faith and practice, and that ordinary Christians are competent to profess their faith without adhering to the proclamations of popes. Luther's reformist movement resulted in the establishment of non-Catholic sects. Today, there are over 1,000 Christian denominations, which are often categorized into conservative, mainline, and liberal groups.

Hinduism: Museum of Religions

In 2001, 297,200 Canadians identified themselves as Hindu. *Hindu* is the Persian word for "India." India and the Ganges River make up the sacred geography of Hinduism. Hindus believe that God lives on the Ganges. Hinduism is called a "museum of religions" because of the immense diversity of its beliefs and practices. There is no specific founder or holy book that is Hinduism's basic scriptural guide.

Hinduism has four primary denominations: Saivism, Vaishnavism, Shaktism, and Smartism. Even though all of the denominations rely on the Vedas—the most sacred books of Hinduism—as scriptural authority, they hold divergent beliefs and are considered independent religions. Nevertheless, all four denominations share beliefs in dharma, all-pervasive divinity, one supreme being that is manifested in many deities (gods and goddesses), reincarnation, sacraments, the guru tradition, and yoga.

Dharma is a central concept in Hinduism. It refers to a way of life, the ritualization of daily life, or self-actualization.

No one particular deity is central to Hinduism. Hindus may worship a particular god (for example, Krishna) or goddess; a spirit, trees, and animals; or a Supreme Spirit. Of all the deities, Brahma, Vishnu, and Shiva are the most significant. *Brahma* is the creator of the universe and life; *Vishnu* the preserver of life, the guide of the cycle of birth and rebirth, and saviour of the world from evil; and *Shiva* the destroyer of all evil.

Reincarnation is a process of many births to attain knowledge and gain freedom from the cycle of reincarnation. In this process, *kharma* is resolved through successive lives. *Kharma* is the law of cause and effect, and Hindus believe that each person creates a personal destiny through his or her thoughts, words, and actions.

Gurus are teachers with superior spiritual knowledge, and they are considered essential guides for attaining that knowledge.

The word *yoga* means union, and it is a philosophy and discipline whose purpose is to unite the person's consciousness with divine consciousness. There are several levels, or types, of *yoga* (Himalayan Academy, 2000).

The following are other basic principles of Hinduism (Himalayan Academy, 2000):

- Spiritual transformation comes from personal discipline, good conduct, and meditation.
- All life is sacred, so individuals must practise non-injury.
- No particular religion is above all others.

Islam: There Is No God but God

Islam is one of the fastest-growing faiths in Canada, North America, and the Caribbean. The Muslim population more than doubled in the decade between 1991 and 2001 such that 579,200 people identified themselves as Muslims in 2001 (Statistics Canada, 2001).

Like Judaism and Christianity, Islam is also a one-God religion and the second most popular religion in the world. It may become the dominant religion of the world during the 21st century. Islam is a global faith that spans diverse races, nationalities, and cultures (Abu-Harb, 2001). One out of five people in the world is a Muslim.

In Arabic, *Islam* means achieving peace personally and spiritually through submission (surrender, obedience) to Allah (God) and commitment to His guidance. A *Muslim* is a person who has surrendered to the will of God. A person becomes a Muslim by believing and proclaiming that "There is none worthy of worship except God," and that "Muhammad is the Messenger of God." Muslims do not worship the Prophet Muhammad, but follow his teachings.

The Koran ("recitation") is the holy text of Islam. Muslims believe that the Koran contains the words of God communicated to Muhammad through the archangel Gabriel. They also believe that the Koran completes the Jewish and Christian scriptures rather than contradicts either.

Belief in fate is seen in the Islamic doctrine of predestination ("Nothing will befall us but what God has written down for us"). However, the Islamic doctrine of the hereafter, with its stress on reward and punishment, also requires that people assume responsibility for their deeds.

The two main Islamic sects are Sunni and Shiite, but there are other sects as well, including Sufi, Ismaili, and Druze. The five basic religious practices of Islam are listed in table 5.2.

Islam is not just a religion; it is a way of life. There is no artificial division between the secular and the sacred for Muslims; law is not separate from religion. Religious law, *fiqh*, relies on five sources: the Koran, Muhammad's way of life, oral

TABLE 5.2   The Five Pillars: Basic Religious Practices in Islam

Iman (faith)	Iman signifies the belief that the sole purpose of life is to serve and obey God through the teachings and practices of Muhammad. Mulsims are required to declare their faith by bearing witness that there is no God but Allah and that Muhammad is his final messenger.
Salat (prayer)	Muslims are required to pray five times a day: at dawn, noon, afternoon, evening, and night.
Zakat (alms giving)	A certain percentage of earnings is expected to go to the poor or needy. This obligation is based on the belief that everything belongs to Allah.
Siyam (fasting)	Fasting is beneficial for health, self-purification, and self-restraint; it reminds Muslims of their purpose in life and promotes empathy for poor and hungry people. All adult Muslims are expected to fast (abstain from food, drink, and sexual relations) from sunrise to sunset during the holy month of Ramadan.
Hajj (pilgrimage)	Adult Muslims with the physical and financial means are required to make at least one pilgrimage to Mecca (in Saudi Arabia), the birthplace of Islam, during the 12th month of the Islamic calendar.

traditions, reasoning, and community consensus. Proper food is known as *halal*. Muslims are prohibited from eating pork and consuming blood, alcohol, and animals that have not been slaughtered properly or those that have died naturally. Parents are highly respected, and caring for them in old age is seen as an honour and a blessing. Consequently, institutional homes for the elderly are virtually unknown in the Muslim world.

The Muslim community identifies the following myths associated with Islam:

- Muslims are a threat to the "new world order." The Western media's use of such terms as *jihad* (Holy War), Islamic fundamentalism, Islamic terrorism, fascist, and Islamic militia reflect stereotypes.

- The "sword of Islam" is forcing people to accept Islam.

- Muhammad is God's final messenger (Jesus is held in high esteem by Muslims).

- The God worshipped by Muslims is separate from the God of the Jews and Christians.

- All Muslims are Arabs.

- Islam oppresses women.

Even though, according to the Koran, men and women are equal before God and their roles are complementary, the West associates Islam with the subordination of women. According to Muslim theologians, governments, not Islam, oppress women.

Jehovah's Witnesses: Spreading the Word

Jehovah's Witnesses are recognized by their religious activity of going from house to house or standing on the streets with Bibles, Bible literature, and *Watchtower* and *Awake!* magazines. This religion originated in the United States, as did its founder, Charles Taze Russell (1852–1916). Jehovah's Witnesses have published and use their own version of the Bible known as the *New World Translation of the Holy Scriptures*. They have elders but no clergy. The following are basic beliefs and practices of Jehovah's Witnesses (Watch Tower Bible and Tract Society of Pennsylvania, 2001):

- There is only one God, Jehovah. Jesus is Jehovah's son and inferior to Him.

- The Bible is Jehovah's word and is the truth.

- The end of the world is imminent. God's Kingdom will be ushered in when the wicked are destroyed in the battle of Armageddon, God's war to end wickedness. Armageddon will restore paradise, purify the world, establish God's Kingdom on earth for 1,000 years, and destroy Satan, his demon forces, and all rebels against God.

- Accepting blood orally or intravenously violates God's divine law to "abstain from blood." So, Jehovah's Witnesses refuse to accept blood transfusions.

- The Memorial of Christ's Death is recognized at Passover as the only holiday that requires celebration. Other holidays are worldly or pagan.

- Christians must keep separate from the world. Jehovah's Witnesses dissociate themselves from politics because they regard the world as being under Satan's control, refuse formal allegiance to political systems, and interpret all pledges of allegiance to national emblems as idolatry. Jehovah's Witnesses do not run for public office, join the military, salute the flag, or vote in elections.

- Humanity was created, it did not evolve.

- Spiritual cleanliness, moral cleanliness, mental cleanliness, physical cleanliness, and clean speech must be maintained. The Bible teaches people to respect marriage, raise children with the right principles, and emphasize the importance of the family.

- Christians must publicly testify to spiritual truth. Jehovah's Witnesses assert that the more individuals and families they influence to live by Christian principles, the less crime, delinquency, and immorality will exist in society.

Judaism: First Monotheistic Religion

Judaism is about God, the *Torah*, and Israel. As a way of life, Judaism describes the relationship between God and the Jewish nation and their mutual obligations. The Hebrew Bible is called the *Tanach*. It consists of the *Torah* ("teaching"), the *Neviim* (prophets), and the *Ketuvim* (writings, or wisdom literature). As the central symbol

TABLE 5.3 The Ten Commandments

1. I the Lord am your God. ... You shall have no other gods beside Me.
2. You shall not make for yourself a sculptured image. ... You shall not bow down to them or serve them.
3. You shall not take in vain the name of the Lord your God.
4. Remember the Sabbath day and keep it holy.
5. Honour your father and your mother.
6. You shall not murder.
7. You shall not commit adultery.
8. You shall not steal.
9. You shall not bear false witness against your neighbour.
10. You shall not covet.

of Judaism, the *Torah* contains within it the 613 *mitzvot* (plural of *mitzvah*, commandments or divine rules of conduct) that God gave to the Jewish people. Ten of those *mitzvot*, the Ten Commandments, are listed in table 5.3.

Even though Judaism is more action than belief, several principles of faith are associated with this religion:

- God exists.
- God is one and unique, incorporeal, eternal, knower of the thoughts and deeds of persons, and rewarder of the good and punisher of the wicked.
- Prayer is directed to God alone and to no other. Even in prayer, Jews do not address God by name because naming God is an act of idolatry, which the *Torah* prohibits.
- Moses's prophecies and the words of the prophets are true.
- The written *Torah* and the oral *Torah* (teachings contained in the *Talmud* and other writings) were given to Moses (the greatest of the prophets), and there will be no other *Torah*. The *Talmud* ("study") contains commentaries on and interpretations of Jewish law, in addition to proverbs and parables.
- The Messiah will come, and the dead will be resurrected.

Judaism is described as a set of rules and practices known as *halakhah*, which means law, or "the path that one walks." Observing *halakhah* is believed to support spirituality in life. *Halakhah* consists of the 613 *mitzvot*, laws instituted by the rabbis (teachers), and long-standing customs. Needless to say, *halakhah* touches on every aspect of life, including relations to God, the Torah, other people, and animals; clothing; prayers and blessings; dietary law (*kashrut*); marriage, divorce, family, and sexual relations; and criminal law. Nevertheless, observing Jewish law is subordinate to preserving life. Jews live by the commandments, they don't die by them (Krauthammer, 2000). Food must be *kosher*. Pork is prohibited, as are all animals that do not chew their cud, wild birds, insects, and shellfish. Women are highly regarded, but certain restrictions on women apply in strict Jewish communities. The equal status of women to men in Judaism is supported by the view that God has no body and gender, and has both masculine and feminine qualities.

Four major movements or groups in Judaism follow:

- *Orthodox Judaism* views the *halakhah* as binding on Jews. Because God gave the *Torah* to Moses, its 613 *mitzvot* are divine and binding on all Jews. Of the four major movements, Orthodox Judaism is the most traditional. Men and women sit separately to worship, and women are not ordained as rabbis.

- *Conservative Judaism* views *halakhah* as binding on Jews, but believes in the evolutionary nature of the *Torah*. Consequently, conservative Jews change religious rules and practices over time. Conservative Judaism allows its members to ride in a car to attend service on the Shabbath (the day of rest, Saturday), permits the ordination of women as rabbis, and allows men and women to sit together during worship in Conservative synagogues. On the other hand, Conservative rabbis are unlikely to perform or attend a marriage between a born Jew and an unconverted non-Jew.

- *Reform Judaism* is a liberal religious movement that views Jewish law as non-binding. It allows individual autonomy and choice on the personal meaningfulness of religious laws.

- *Reconstructionist Judaism* views Judaism as a civilization. It does not view Jews as the chosen people and does not consider Jewish law to be binding.

Shintoism: The Way of the Gods

Shintoism is an ancient religion of Japan. Historically, it was the state religion of Japan; today it has 13 denominations.

Shinto means "way of the *kami*." *Kami* are "the sacred spirits that exist both in the celestial realm and in nature and human beings" (White, 1997, p. 98). *Kami* is also translated as "God" or "divinity." Shintoism is an animistic religion that sees the sacred in all things, including animals and plants, trees, and mountains. Human ancestors are also held in high regard. All forms of life are celebrated in Shinto, as is the connection among gods, people, and the world.

Shintoism has no written scriptures, formal teachings or dogma, or group worship. Instead, small shrines believed to be the homes of the *kami* are places for individual worship. Shinto festivals and rituals replace the sermons and study of scripture that characterize other religions. There are three elements of Shinto worship:

- purification, usually with water;

- offerings to the *kami*, usually money or food; and

- prayer or petition (a request for something).

Shintoism supports attitudes of respect for life, appreciation of beauty, and love of purity and simplicity.

Sikhism: Religion of Disciples

In 2001, 278,400 Canadians identified themselves as Sikhs. Sikhism is the religion of the state of Punjab in northern India. In Punjabi, *Sikh* means disciple or learner. Sikhs believe in human unity and equality of the sexes. They are anti-class and strive to eliminate all prejudices based on race, colour, and religion.

Sikhism was founded by Guru Nanak in 1469, who was succeeded by nine more gurus (teachers or authorities). The last one, Guru Gobind Singh, appointed as his successor the Sikh holy book the *Guru Granth Sahib*, which contains the writings of all 10 gurus. These scriptures are unique in being the head of the Sikh religion. There are no clergy in Sikhism. Table 5.4 lists the five principles of faith, five stages of spiritual development, five virtues, and five vices associated with Sikhism.

Khalsas are Sikhs who have gone through a special ceremony to dedicate themselves to the principles of Sikhism. The word "Khalsa" means pure. Sikhs are expected to be Khalsas or working toward becoming Khalsas. Khalsas must wear five articles of faith (Brar, 1998b):

- *Kesh*: Uncut hair, symbol of spirituality and dedication. Sikh men must wear a turban, a symbol of royalty and dignity; it is optional for Sikh women. The turban cannot be covered by anything else and cannot be replaced with a hat.

- *Kangha*: Comb, symbol of cleanliness and discipline.

- *Kara*: Steel bracelet, to remind its wearer to show restraint.

- *Kachha*: Undergarments, symbol of self-control and chastity.

- *Kirpan*: Ceremonial dagger or sword, symbol of dignity and the Sikh struggle against injustice. The *kirpan* is a religious symbol only and is never used as a weapon.

TABLE 5.4 Doctrines of Sikhism

Principles of faith	Stages of spiritual development
Human equality	Duty
Worship of God	Knowledge
Charity for the poor	Effort
Dignity of work	Grace
Service to others	Truth
Virtues	**Vices**
Faith	Lust
Truth	Greed
Compassion	Materialism
Patience	Conceit
Self-control	Anger

Taoism: Universal Energy in Balance

Taoism is China's oldest religion, dating back to 206 BCE. It is believed that Lao Tzu, who wrote the *Tao Te Ching*, founded this religion. The word "Tao" comes from a Chinese word for "the way." Taoism is a philosophy of life with great emphasis on non-aggression, non-competition, balance, the pursuit of health, and physical immortality. Its influence can be seen in such practices as acupuncture, Chinese herbal medicine, meditation, and the martial arts.

Until the 20th century, Taoism was the state religion of China. However, from 1911 on, because of political upheaval and the growth of Confucianism and Buddhism in China, Taoism began to wane. During the Chinese communist years that began in 1949, when religion was banned, many Taoist monks were imprisoned or killed, and Taoist temples were destroyed. Taoism almost died out entirely, but it has been enjoying a resurgence since the 1980s (The Taoist Restoration Society, 1999).

Taoists believe that Tao is an energy force that flows through all life. The goal of life is harmony between the individual and this universal energy.

The ancient yin and yang symbol represents Tao. Yin is the dark side and yang is the light side. The two sides symbolize pairs of opposites: good and evil, feminine and masculine, and so on. Taoists believe that yin and yang must be in balance in people. This balance is achieved through mental, physical, and spiritual health. Illness is believed to be caused by a lack of balance in the body's energy (ch'i). Practices such as meditation and Tai Chi help to restore the balance (Ontario Consultants on Religious Tolerance, 2000).

Aboriginal Spirituality: Respect Mother Earth

While many Aboriginal peoples (First Nations, Métis, Inuit) are Christian, largely as a result of the conversion of their ancestors by missionaries, many others follow the "old ways." These old ways contain teachings about spirituality and the environment that are followed today, even by many non-traditional Aboriginal people.

Aboriginal peoples have a strong connection to the land. Land is more than geographic territory; it is a sacred, living entity, with its own rhythms and cycles. Aboriginal people are sensitive to these rhythms and heed the signs in nature. The land reflects the people's way of life and their spirituality, and provides sacred places where power, wisdom, and the meaning of life are granted by the spiritual world. In this way, the land is closely linked to the people's destiny. It keeps them strong as nations:

> Without [the land and animals] our spirits will die. Non-Natives sometimes think we are being romantic when we talk about these things. This is not about romance. This is about reality and survival.
> —Norma Kassi, Gwich'in Nation (1989/2006)

Aboriginal peoples have a great respect for the land, and all things of the land have a spiritual significance for them. Aboriginal peoples' "ways of being" are closely linked to the land. It is impossible to separate the foundations of these cultures—their spirituality—from their connections to the land.

In the world view of Aboriginal cultures, all things—organic and living, animate and inanimate—have a spirit. The gifts of the land are to be used and enjoyed. Above all, however, they are to be respected. Understanding this relationship is essential to understanding these cultures. To show their respect, Aboriginal peoples developed many spiritual practices. When a deer was killed for food, for example, the hunter laid down tobacco at the site of the killing as an expression of thanks to the spirit of the deer for giving up its life to nurture the hunter and his family. If the hunter offended the deer's spirit, he would face great challenges in obtaining food in the future. Therefore, the people had to be alert to their spiritual encounters in nature and to heed their messages.

Medicine Wheel teachings help explain the bond between Aboriginal peoples and the land. These teachings provide listeners with a means of understanding and improving themselves and their world from a spiritual perspective.

Medicine Wheel teachings begin with the drawing of a circle. The circle is divided into four directions or teachings. Each of these teachings relates to something in the environment, and all four segments are interconnected. For example, if the spring season is dry, then summer crops may be affected. Without spring rains, crops do not have a chance to grow strong roots. This causes them to wither or die in the summer or to be underdeveloped in the fall. Keeping all four aspects in balance enables nature to be strong and healthy. This balance illustrates the concept of **interdependence**.

Another Medicine Wheel teaching illustrates how balancing the ecosystem, a biological community of interacting organisms in a physical environment, is critical to the health of the environment. The earth comprises four main elements: earth, air, fire, and water. For instance, when large trees are cut down, erosion occurs. Winds blow down the smaller trees, since they no longer have the protection of the mature forest. Fires start easily in the dead foliage, and soil is overexposed to the sun, and dries out.

Aboriginal peoples' connection to the land is illustrated in the Medicine Wheel teaching of the four colours of humans. The Creator has given each group responsibility for different parts of nature:

- White people are responsible for taking care of the air.
- Black people are responsible for taking care of the water.
- Yellow people are responsible for fire.
- Red people are responsible for taking care of the earth.

This teaching is reinforced in many creation stories. As the last to be created, humans were assigned the roles of servants and caretakers for all other creations. This contrasts with the Judaeo-Christian belief that humans have "dominion over the fish of the sea, and over the fowl of the air, and over the cattle, and over all the Earth" (Genesis 1:25).

Table 5.5 illustrates an Aboriginal code of ethics (Roberts, 2006).

interdependence
the state of being influenced by or dependent on one another

TABLE 5.5 An Aboriginal Code of Ethics

Most Aboriginal cultures shared a common code of ethics that was closely connected to their spirituality. The code, which offered guidance for all members of the community, was based on the following principles:

1. Give thanks to the Creator when rising each morning and before retiring each evening for the life within you and for all life and for the good things you experience. Consider your actions and words thoughtfully and seek the courage and strength to be a better person in all things.

2. Respect yourself, others, and the world around you, and show respect as a basic law of life.

3. Respect and listen to those who make decisions about your world, and share your ideas equally with others.

4. Be truthful at all times and in all situations.

5. Treat your guests with honour and consideration, and give the best you have in food, accommodations, and other comforts.

6. Accept the hurt of one as the hurt of all and the honour of one as the honour of all.

7. Welcome strangers and outsiders with kindness and a loving heart because we are all members of the human family.

8. Respect all races as though they are different coloured flowers in a meadow, and acknowledge that each is beautiful and has an important role to play. Understand that the Creator made each race for a special reason and that we must respect one another's gifts.

9. Serve others, because this is the primary reason humans were created. Understand that the secret to true happiness comes to those who dedicate their lives to the service of others.

10. Observe moderation and balance at all times and in all things.

11. Be wise and know the things and actions that will lead to your health and well-being, and those things that will lead to your destruction. Know your heart.

12. Listen and follow the guidance in your heart and expect guidance to come in many forms: in prayer, dreams, quiet reflection, and the actions and deed of the Elders and wise people.

EXERCISE 3

As a continuation of Exercise 2, what images do you have of the following individuals after reading about them in the text? Have your perceptions changed? Discuss.

    a. a Muslim woman wearing a *niqab*

    b. a Chinese Buddhist

    c. a Christian Scientist

    d. a Jehovah's Witness

    e. a traditional Aboriginal man

    f. a Sikh wearing a turban

    g. a Hindu woman wearing a sari

    h. a Muslim man with a beard

    i. a white Protestant woman

    j. a Roman Catholic priest

RELIGIOUS DIVERSITY: POLICE ABILITIES, KNOWLEDGE, AND SKILLS

Police officers need to recognize the role that religious beliefs and practices play in their lives and those of others. Police officers may be involved in conflicts that have religious overtones, and that have the potential to become or be seen as racist, due to the manner in which they are handled. Knowledge of religion can assist police in dealing with issues, properly engaging in effective community policing and police–community relations, communicating efficaciously, and resolving conflict successfully.

The religious group that has assumed the most perceived challenge to policing in the post-9/11 environment is the Muslim faith and by association the Arab/Muslim community. Law enforcement agencies need to know the dynamics of the relationship between Muslims and the host cultures they represent. Police also need to de-homogenize the Muslim people and religion in relation to terrorism, and separate the concept of Islam from terrorism and suicide bombers. To this end, it is important to eliminate racial profiling of Arabs and Muslims as threats to national security so as to build positive and meaningful community relations. There are Muslim terrorists, but very few Muslims and Arabs are terrorists. Muslims themselves see a struggle within Islam between moderates and radicals, the majority identifying and supporting the moderates. Law enforcement agencies need to recognize that fuelling Muslim anti-police sentiment is bad business for law enforcement and the ideals of counterterrorism and peace culture.

Reaching Muslims in the post-9/11 climate and creating dialogue with Muslim communities is a duty. Religious beliefs and practices contribute to the cultural values, moral code, and social conduct of individuals, as do host cultures' perceptions of religious groups. Police may find the beliefs and practices of various religions puzzling or abhorrent. However, labelling religious beliefs and practices as foreign, primitive, or savage is ill conceived. Similarly, religious prejudice is wrong. National and international strategies for intelligence gathering are important, as are cutting-edge technologies applied to border security and counterterrorism. Equally important, however, is focus on the "clash of civilizations" with a view to establishing, re-establishing, or enhancing trust between law enforcement and cultural and religious communities, particularly the Muslim community, as a strategic approach to democratic community policing and protection of civil order (Ewatski, 2006). Police who are dedicated to their profession transcend cultural and religious differences and serve and protect members of all religions and cultures indiscriminately without compromising their mandate to serve and protect.

EXERCISE 4

Police may refer troubled families to their local clergy for help and guidance or may use clergy to calm highly charged emotional situations. Do you believe there is any benefit to police collaborating with clergy or even forming police–clergy teams to respond to crisis situations? Why or why not?

EXERCISE 5

Some religious groups have survived persecution from states and the police of those states. What core values and beliefs contribute to the persecution of these groups? What are the consequences to these groups, the country, and policing?

EXERCISE 6

An important issue for policing in a diverse society is to what extent people of diversity need to adjust their ways to the host culture and to what extent police need to adjust their ways to the diversity of the people they serve and protect. For example, it could be argued that individuals from a religious group have to abide by all the laws of the country (for example, enlisting in the army during a war) even though these laws may be contrary to their religious beliefs and practices.

Debate this topic by dividing the class into two groups. Have one group take the position that religious groups need to adjust their ways to the host culture. Have the second group take the position that the police need to adjust their ways to the religious beliefs and practices of the people. Follow the debate with a general class discussion.

CHAPTER SUMMARY

Pluralistic societies include many religious beliefs and practices. These beliefs and practices may be at odds with those of individual police, different religious groups not from the dominant culture, or the host nation's religious beliefs. An understanding of and respect for various religions, a willingness to respond to religious conflict with effective conflict resolution, and a consideration of proactive approaches to prevent religious conflict and minimize, if not eliminate, the threatening forces of terrorism are important for police credibility and safety, and the ideals of a peace culture. Involving religious leaders and those who understand the religious group in question will assist in reducing conflict and restoring some trust in the community. Further, employing alternative dispute resolution, a practice adopted by many religious groups to solve some internal conflicts, can also be an effective tool in addressing and understanding some of the differences that divide, rather than unite. Alternative dispute resolution involves having the community deal with the dispute rather than going before the courts. One example is the Aboriginal sentencing circle, where the offender may be asked to apologize to the victim and make restitution.

KEY TERMS

religion

religious beliefs

religious practices

interdependence

REFERENCES

Abu-Harb, I.A. (2001). Some basic Islamic beliefs. *A brief illustrated guide to understanding Islam* (ch. 3). Houston, TX: Darussalam. http://www.islam-guide.com/frm-ch3-2.htm.

Bahá'í International Community. (2000). The Bahá'í world. http://www.bahai.org.

Bhattacharya, S. (2006, August 12). Young Muslims worried, frustrated in GTA. *The Toronto Star*, p. A13.

Boeree, C.G. (2000). The basics of Buddhist wisdom. An introduction to Buddhism. http://www.ship.edu/~cgboeree/buddhaintro.html.

Brar, S.S. (1998a). Introduction to Sikhism. http://www.sikhs.org/summary.htm.

Brar, S.S. (1998b). The Khalsa. http://www.sikhs.org/khalsa.htm.

Eddy, M.B. (1994). *Science and health with key to the scriptures.* Boston: The First Church of Christ, Scientist.

Ewatski, J. (2006, April 20). Trust as counterterrorism. Paper presented at the 5th International Counterterrorism Conference, Washington, DC.

The First Church of Christ, Scientist. (2001). Questions and answers. http://www.tfccs.com.

Forman, R.K.C. (Ed.). (1993). *Religions of the world* (3rd ed.). New York: St. Martin's Press.

Himalayan Academy. (2000). Hinduism: The basics. http://www.himalayanacademy.com/basics.

International Shinto Foundation. (2001). What is Shinto in brief. http://shinto.org/isri/eng/brief-e.html.

Islamic City. (2001). Pillars of Islam. http://www.islam.org/Mosque/pillars.htm.

Karma Kagyu Buddhist Network. (2001). Basics on Buddhism. http://www.diamondway-buddhism.org.

Kassi, N. Gwich'in Nation, Speech to the First American Congress of Indigenous Peoples, 1989. Quoted in J. Roberts, *First Nations, Inuit, and Métis peoples: Exploring their past, present, and future.* Toronto: Emond Montgomery, 2006, (p. 27).

Krauthammer, C. (2000, August 14). CNN editorial.

Lawrence, B.B. (2000). *The complete idiot's guide to religions online.* Indianapolis, IN: Alpha Books.

New York City Bahá'í Community. (1999). Beliefs and practices. http://www.bahainyc.

Ontario Consultants on Religious Tolerance. (2000). Taoism. http://www.religioustolerance.org/taoism.htm.

Roberts, J. (2006). *First Nations, Inuit, and Métis peoples.* Toronto: Emond Montgomery.

Shephard, M. (2006, August 12). A friend or foe in the war on terror? *The Toronto Star*, p. A13.

Statistics Canada (2001). Overview: Canada still predominantly Roman Catholic and Protestant. http://www12.statcan.ca/english/census01/Products/Analytic/companion/rel/canada.cfm

The Taoist Restoration Society. (1999). Introduction. http://www.westernreformtaoism.org.

Watch Tower Bible and Tract Society of Pennsylvania. (2001). What Jehovah's Witnesses believe. http://www.watchtower.org/library/br78/index.htm.

Watt, P. (1982). Shinto and Buddhism: Wellsprings of Japanese spirituality. *Asia Society's Focus on Asian Studies, Asian Religions* 2 (1): 21–23.

White, G.C. (1997). *Beliefs and believers.* New York: Berkley Books.

CHAPTER 6

Policing with Diversity Competency

> ## CHAPTER OBJECTIVES
>
> After completing this chapter, you should be able to:
>
> - Describe self-perceptions of police and community perceptions of police.
> - Identify six forms of anti-racism initiatives in pluralistic societies.
> - Understand police training in race relations, cultural sensitivity, and diversity.
> - Develop policing strategies, structures, and skills for cultural competence.

INTRODUCTION

Police and the community share common goals—both want crime-free neighbourhoods and safety, and strive for an improved quality of life. A police officer who is a friend of the people is more effective in fighting crime and apprehending suspects. When people respect the police, they are more prone to assist police officers when required.

The changing face of Canada has been driving police services to rethink how they "competently respond" to the growing diversity, and ensure that the police "organizations are internally welcoming, reflective, and knowledgeable in facing this challenge" (Graham, 2004, as cited in Taylor, 2004, p. 15). This chapter focuses on police–community perceptions, and diversity strategies, structures, and skills in policing that institutionalize cultural inclusivity and responsivity and meet the imperative of public safety.

POLICE–COMMUNITY PERCEPTIONS

The quality of the administration of justice is critical in determining the health of a free society. The police are the one segment of the criminal justice system that has a direct relationship with the community. Understanding the role of the police and the effectiveness of that role requires consideration of two elements: police perception of themselves and community perception of police.

Self-Perception of Police

The three police self-images that have evolved over time can be represented by the acronym ZAC—zookeeper, avenger of the Lord, and champion of the people. The first two images are historical. The zookeeper self-image is a result of police seeing the community as "a large zoo where the ferocious animals must not only be fed and watered but also must be watched every moment and allowed only that limited freedom which the zoo keeper's security can stand" (Steinberg & McEvoy, 1974, p. 149). In describing the image of police as avengers of the Lord, Reverend Billy Graham commented that police are "the sword of the Lord, avenging the wickedness of this world" (Steinberg & McEvoy, 1974, p. 148).

These historical images are not in keeping with contemporary realities. Lewis (1993) indicates that approximately 80 percent of an Ontario police officer's time is spent serving people. These and similar data support the image of police as champion of the people.

Community Perception of Police

Police officers are not in the business of policing to win popularity contests; nevertheless, police officers do care about their public image. A positive public image enhances police self-respect, effectiveness in combatting crime, safety, job satisfaction, and perceived social contribution. While the role of police in society is recognized and honoured, and, in general, most people are satisfied with the police most of the time, issues in relation to community perceptions of police have been raised, particularly in the context of relations between police and people of diversity.

Wortley (1994) assessed community satisfaction with police services in a large Canadian city. His findings are summarized in table 6.1. As you can see, satisfaction rates across all three groups are less than perfect. Satisfaction and dissatisfaction rates are also culturally dependent, with blacks showing the highest dissatisfaction ratings and whites showing the highest satisfaction ratings.

While many variables contribute to the public's perception of the police and satisfaction with their performance, a fundamental factor is the interpersonal encounters between the public and the police. Positive police attitudes toward the public and positive police–public interactions will likely evoke a positive police image in the public, and vice versa. The reciprocal relationship between police–public encounters and perceptions forms a feedback loop that either makes or breaks police–community relations. Negative encounters that generate negative perceptions are self-defeating—negative police perceptions are reciprocated by the community, and vice versa (Coffey, 1990).

TABLE 6.1 Community Satisfaction with Police Services*

	Blacks	Chinese	Whites
Satisfaction	(%)	(%)	(%)
Police enforcing the law	66.9	56.2	80.9
	8.9	**5.7**	**5.7**
Police being approachable/ easy to talk to	33.3	59.3	80.5
	17.5	**10.4**	**5.3**
Police sharing information on ways of reducing crime	57.6	61.4	76.1
	24.5	**17.8**	**11.3**
Police making neighbourhood safe	82.0	76.5	84.6
	9.6	**8.9**	**6.2**

* Non-bold figures represent rates of satisfaction (combined ratings of an average job and a good job). Bold figures represent rates of dissatisfaction (a poor job).

Source: Wortley (1994).

On the other hand, it can be argued that the functions police perform are by necessity coercive (Rodelet & Carter, 1994). This adversarial nature of the police–community relationship creates an inherent conflict and precludes positive encounters. While the view of police and public as adversaries may be justified in certain contexts—for example, when dealing with certain types of criminals or in tough, urban neighbourhoods—Banton (1963; cited in Rodelet & Carter, 1994, p. 229) rejects the view of police and public as adversaries on three grounds:

1. The police officer spends very little time "chasing people or locking people up." The police officer spends most of his or her time helping citizens in distress.

2. It is misleading to describe a police officer's job as law enforcement. An officer's activities "are governed much more by popular morality than they are by the letter of the law."

3. Even criminals recognize the moral authority, as opposed to the power, of the police. When people grumble at the police, they are really "trying to make their violations seem excusable to still their own conscience."

Most people view police as champions rather than as protective zealots. Nevertheless, effective police–community alliances can be tarnished by police conduct that is rude and authoritarian. Rudeness is one of the most common complaints expressed against police officers. Surprisingly, accusations of police rudeness are rarely made by people arrested for serious crimes. Rather, such accusations come from citizens involved in traffic stops, those reporting crimes to police, or those simply seeking directions from police. **Authoritarianism** is "badge-heavy" conduct that demands obedience to authority. While police must be prepared for violence, and while an *authoritative* approach is required in a variety of situations—for ex-

authoritarianism
conduct that demands obedience to authority

ample, interrogating a suspect, handling a crime scene, conducting an investigation, and resolving a domestic dispute—authoritarian conduct is unproductive in situations that require cooperation, compromise, and capitulation and creates an obstacle to police–community alliance.

Visibility, accessibility, client-centredness, ability to solve problems, fairness, and openness to partnership are core values that communities expect from police.

EXERCISE 1

Suppose that police–community relations in your neighbourhood are very poor. The neighbourhood is tense because of incidents of police using excessive force against members of visible minorities and harassing homeless mentally ill people. What actions would you take to ease tensions in the short term? Consider establishing a police–community diversity coalition. What goals would this coalition pursue?

DIVERSITY INITIATIVES IN CANADIAN SOCIETY

Through its Multiculturalism Program, Canadian Heritage lists the following as priority areas (Canadian Heritage, 2006, p. 9):

- Fostering cross-cultural understanding by supporting programs and initiatives that facilitate understanding of cultural differences, fostering an appreciation of the value of diversity, and promoting ties among all sectors of society including urban–rural connections.

- Combatting racism and discrimination by engaging the diverse communities and the broader public in informed dialogue and sustained action to fight racism and discrimination.

- Increasing civic participation by developing among the country's diverse population active citizens with both the opportunity and the capacity to participate in shaping Canadian society.

- Making Canadian institutions more reflective of the country's population by assuming a leadership role to help federal institutions develop policies, programs, and services that are responsive to and reflective of the country's demographic diversity.

POSITIVE DIVERSITY MANAGEMENT IN POLICING

In the past three decades there has been increasing focus on processes, outcomes, and programs related to diversity-based recruitment, promotion, and retention and staff diversity awareness training programs in policing.

Diversity as a Strategic Advantage in Policing

Policing in Canada in the 21st century sees diversity as a strategic advantage. Police service organizations across the country are rethinking diversity as a founding principle and a key component to effective law enforcement rather than a liability. They are increasingly supporting initiatives to ensure that their organizations are reflective of and responsive to the needs of the diverse communities they serve and protect, and are equitable in their recruitment, promotion, and career development strategies (Laws, 2005). In fact, the globalization of business, changing Canadian demographics and market forces, and imperatives of national security and public safety are all combining to make diversity a strategic advantage.

Diversity as a strategic advantage refers to police invoking positive actions that encourage and support a diverse police workforce through two processes: identification and removal of organizational barriers and the development of human resource initiatives to recruit, retain, and promote the most qualified individuals. Diversity as a strategic advantage is different from the traditional employment equity program legislated in federal and provincial jurisdictions. Whereas employment equity recognizes the contribution of just the legislatively designated groups, diversity as a strategic advantage recognizes the contributions that individuals make as individuals (Laws, 2005).

Police Training in Race Relations and Cultural Sensitivity

The traditional model of diversity awareness training in policing followed a stand-alone or an add-on approach in which police officers were exposed to brief race relations, cultural awareness, or cross-cultural training modules, or a combination of such packages. Contemporary diversity awareness training models in policing regard diversity training as integral to the strategic planning of police services rather than piecemeal add-ons.

EXERCISE 2

Role-play situations in which a police officer is questioning a member of the public, using each of the following situations. After your role-plays, have participants describe what happened, how they feel about what happened, and the degree to which they liked or disliked the person with whom they were interacting.

   a. The two participants maintain eye contact at all times.

   b. The two participants avoid eye contact at all times.

   c. One participant follows turn-taking rules while the other does not.

RACE RELATIONS TRAINING

race relations training
training in how to deal more effectively with race-related issues, from the perspective that racism is a social disease that can be eliminated with education

Race relations training is a formal, short-term program designed to prepare police officers to deal more effectively with race-related issues. This approach does not assume that an understanding of cultural heritage offers immediate solutions to or addresses the serious consequences of racism in policing. Instead, this approach considers racism a social disease that requires the antidote of race relations awareness and education.

Early race relations training programs focused on individual attitudes or on raising awareness of race-related beliefs and the requirements of the law in general, and on **employment equity** legislation in particular. These early efforts failed to inspire confidence among police trainees, who viewed them as soft-science or touchy-feely, irrelevant to real police work, confrontational, and ineffective in changing police or institutional attitudes (Rees, 1992; Ungerleider, 1992; Harris & Currie, 1994; Pruegger, 2003).

employment equity
strategy designed to make workplaces reflect society's diversity by encouraging the full participation of people of all diversities

The limitations associated with earlier race relations training programs (see table 6.2) led to a rethinking of the goals of such programs and a new strategic focus on changing police organizations rather than the feelings and behaviours of individual police. Some programs combined both elements—individual and systemic—in their approach to race relations (see table 6.3).

CULTURAL AWARENESS TRAINING

cultural awareness training
training in how to deal more effectively with cultural issues, either in general or in terms of a particular culture

Cultural awareness training is a formal, short-term program designed to prepare police to deal more effectively with cultural issues. Some cultural awareness training programs focus on both culture and race (see, for example, Hennessy, Warring, & Arnott, 1994). Table 6.4 summarizes the important differences between cultural awareness training and race relations. Remember that there is no such thing as a universal cultural awareness training program; such training may be general or focus on a particular culture.

TABLE 6.2 Limitations of Police Race Relations Training Programs

- Use of non-needs-based content (that is, without surveying the needs of police)
- Time-limited training, which precludes meaningful integration and practice
- Passive instructional approach (one-way lectures)
- Confrontational learning environment and teaching style (for example, white bashing and assumption that all white participants are racist)
- Lack of differentiation of training programs from orientation, briefing, and education programs
- Inadequate knowledge and skill of instructors
- Programs not specific to rank in the police organization (for example, new recruits or veterans)
- General programs rather than programs specific to policing structure and functions
- Lack of serious administrative support
- Absence of short- and long-term impact evaluations

TABLE 6.3 Goals of Recent Police Race Relations Training Programs

- Change in the organizational structure of police services to promote employment equity and to eliminate systemic barriers to recruitment, selection, retention, and promotion of visible minorities
- Change in the police organizational climate to reduce racism and race-based conduct
- Change in the behaviour of those who work in police organizations
- Social change—for example, in socio-economic conditions—to eradicate racism

TABLE 6.4 Cultural Awareness Training Versus Race Relations Training

Cultural awareness training	Race relations training
Personal growth	*Personal growth*
Increased understanding of one's own culture	Increased understanding of the dynamics of racism
Interpersonal growth	*Interpersonal growth*
Increased cognitive and emotional understanding of other cultures	Increased competence in combatting racially based discrimination and harassment
Interpersonal effectiveness	*Interpersonal effectiveness*
Increased competence in cross-cultural communication	Ability to effect structural changes in institutions to remove systemic barriers
	Ability to effect social change to eradicate racism

Cultural awareness or sensitivity training for police is justified on several grounds. First, police spend a significant amount of time interacting with people from various cultural groups in the community and in the police services. This extensive contact has the potential for misunderstandings and conflict (Triandis, 2000). Training can give police the necessary tools to deal with intercultural encounters. Second, the most common complaints levelled against police are social in nature rather than specific to law enforcement. Third, police want to be more competent in human relations. Fourth, improved police relations with multicultural groups are associated with police effectiveness and an improved quality of life.

CROSS-CULTURAL TRAINING

Cross-cultural training programs prepare individuals for living in another country or for living in their own country and dealing with people of diverse cultures (Bhawuk & Brislin, 2000). As well, such programs help people to deal with emotional experiences that arise from intercultural encounters, including clashes in cultural values, culture shock, and personal stereotypes and prejudices. Brislin and Horvath (1997) provide a CAB approach to cross-cultural training—cognitive (thinking), affective (emotions), and behavioural (what is actually done). The *cognitive component* focuses on changing people's thinking by increasing their knowledge

cross-cultural training
training in how to deal with other cultures, whether in another country or within one's own country

of culture, cultural differences, and issues that they may face in intercultural encounters. The goal is to increase participants' understanding of people from other cultures so that participants can put themselves in others' shoes. Through cognitive cultural training, police increase the complexity of their thinking using an approach that includes multiple points of view.

The *affective component* focuses on the feelings and emotions generated in intercultural encounters. Cultural differences in habits, customs, and values, and even differences in physical features may draw out negative emotions in police. These negative emotions may in turn contribute to negative attitudes toward people from diverse cultures. Such attitudes can interfere with police functions and contribute to police–community hostilities. The goal of affective cultural training is to help police develop effective strategies to rethink/reframe their negative emotions.

The *behavioural component* focuses on actual behaviours in intercultural encounters. The goal of behavioural cultural training is teaching appropriate behaviours for successful intercultural interaction.

Police Training in Anti-Racism

anti-racism
an action-oriented, educational, and political strategy for institutional and systemic change that addresses issues of racism and the interlocking systems of social oppression

Anti-racism is defined as an action-oriented, educational, and political strategy for institutional and systemic change that addresses the issues of racism and the interlocking systems of social oppression (sexism, classism, heterosexism, ableism) (see Dei, 1996 expanding on formulations of Lee, 1985). Anti-racism in police training should be seen as a pedagogical, academic, and political discourse/practice for culturally sensitive and good policing. Furthermore, police officers need to use a critical anti-racism framework to understand the issues of race, class, gender identity, and equal representation as they relate to institutions other than law enforcement, such as community and educational institutions as well as immigration agencies.

POLICING WITH DIVERSITY COMPETENCY: POLICE ABILITIES, KNOWLEDGE, AND SKILLS

Police play a major role in contributing to their own safety and reputation, and ensuring public safety and order. Their understanding of diversity, their competence in dealing with issues of diversity, and their partnership with people of diversity not only inspire self-satisfaction and positive police–community alliances but also nurture community respect and police protection. On the other hand, a lack of understanding of diversity and collaboration with the community will likely contribute to misunderstandings, miscommunication, tension, and conflict. Negative encounters with people of diversity have the added disadvantage of increasing personal exposure to complaints, lawsuits, and job dissatisfaction—not to mention irate taxpayers and bad press.

In the past two decades, police services have made considerable efforts to change the law enforcement culture so that it is both more inclusive and more responsive to the needs of their communities (MacLeod, as cited in Taylor, 2004). The changes in immigration, globalization, advances in technology, an aging workplace, the *Charter of Rights and Freedoms*, case law decisions, the increased pluralism of the communities that police serve and protect, and events like 9/11 have all contributed to rethinking policing and invoked the imperative of cultural competence—law enforcement organizations that are "internally welcoming, reflective and knowledgeable" (RCMP Assistant Commissioner Steve Graham, as cited in Taylor, 2004). The seeds for sensitivity to diversity training programs planted three decades ago evolved into a view of diversity as a strategic advantage in policing and the consequent initiation of diversity training, establishment of human rights offices and diversity units in police services, participation in the Law Enforcement Aboriginal Diversity (LEAD) network and Data Collection Strategy on Hate-Motivated Crime Initiatives (Canadian Heritage, 2006), drafting of the Bias-Free Policing Policy by the RCMP, and the application of diversity principles to cross-cultural criminal investigations for increased community policing effectiveness and public safety (Pruegger, 2003; Perry, 2004; Taylor, 2004).

Supported by the Multiculturalism Program of Canadian Heritage, the Canadian Association of Chiefs of Police assumed responsibility for LEAD to help law enforcement officers across the country develop better working relationships with the ethnocultural and Aboriginal communities they serve (Dr. William Beahan of the RCMP as cited in Taylor, 2004; Canadian Heritage, 2006), to offer training and information on delivering bias-free policing services, and to help law enforcement institutions become more diverse through recruitment and retention. An important aspect of the LEAD initiative has been development of a website (www.lead-alda.ca) to provide a forum for diversity best practices, and resources in such areas as hate crimes, national crime statistics, community and police partnerships, and issues internal and external to police (Taylor, 2004).

Applying diversity training to community policing recognizes the importance of diversity factors in the conduct of cross-cultural criminal investigations. Cross-cultural criminal investigation entails police understanding of diversity issues in crime, having representative police personnel to interact and gain the confidence of the diverse communities and their leaders to secure critical information as needed, and invoking policing policies that direct investigators or cultural experts to work with community leaders when an investigation is likely to impact the diverse communities (Perry, 2004). An underlying assumption of cross-cultural criminal investigations is that open and honest dialogue with community leaders to identify problems specific to their particular culture and involving them in the process of criminal investigations helps form long-term police–community relationships.

Policing has come a long way in recognizing the value of diversity, changing its traditional "white machismo face" and benefiting both police and society through cultural competence. While there is always room for improvement, it should be acknowledged that police organizations have made strides in diversifying the face of policing.

POLICE SERVICES DIVERSITY AWARENESS TRAINING PROGRAMS

In the past decade, police training in diversity issues has moved from piecemeal training to diversity-based training programs integrated into police training programs and police organizations.

The goal of **diversity awareness training** in policing is to prepare police and police organizations to become culturally competent and deal more effectively

diversity awareness training
training in how to deal more effectively with diversity issues in all their forms

> ### EXERCISE 3
> Some years ago, men selected as field training officers for an American police department were found to have some of the worst complaint and litigation records among their peers. Evidently, these men were using evaluation scores to systematically weed out women and minority recruits. The field training officers were labelling women recruits as "bad drivers," scoring Asian recruits low in radio communication, and unfairly criticizing recruits for their report writing (ACLU, 1991).
> How can Canadian police services learn from this situation?

with the diverse communities they protect and serve. Diversity training programs are different from traditional race- or culture-based training initiatives in four respects. First, diversity training programs are neither piecemeal, as were race relations, cultural awareness, and cross-cultural training approaches, nor are they lip service to diversity in policing. Second, diversity training in policing is integral to policing organizational culture rather than an add-on. Third, diversity in diversity training programs is considered a valuable principle. Finally, diversity training programs are relevant to policing work rather than esoteric.

A best practice police diversity training program is developed as part of a police-sponsored diversity training plan and is based on the following principles: it is grounded in supportive policy, it is integrated into all aspects of policing, it provides targeted training for all levels of service, it allows on-the-job training and mentoring of cross-cultural competence, and it has an anti-racism focus (Pruegger, 2003). Diversity training curriculums and their modules should rely on a variety of instructional approaches, including guest speakers and role-play, to increase police diversity competence.

> ### EXERCISE 4
> Debate the pros and cons of the three approaches to police training in diversity issues: race relations training, cultural awareness training, and diversity awareness training.

CROSS-CULTURAL COMMUNICATION

In addition to integrative approaches to police training in diversity, policing has been focused on cross-cultural training. **Cross-cultural communication** entails understanding the verbal and non-verbal communicative patterns of people from diverse cultures for the purpose of effective intercultural interchange. Communication is a critical issue for police, but especially so in a culturally diverse community. Conflict may occur as a result of misunderstandings over language and cultural behaviours. For example, Middle Eastern people may take time to warm up to and trust people, but North Americans tend to rush right into another person's business. In some cultures, you are expected to wait for an invitation to join others in an activity; in others, you are considered aloof for not joining in.

cross-cultural communication understanding the verbal and non-verbal communicative patterns of people from diverse cultures for the purpose of effective intercultural interchange

Misunderstanding the cultural meaning of rap is an example of **misattribution**—a misinterpretation of a message or behaviour. Fine (1995) explains that rap is a way of communicating a message and establishing reputation. Black and white people's understanding of rap, however, can differ; blacks do not necessarily expect the performer to act on the words.

misattribution
misinterpreting a message or behaviour

Verbal Communication

Police often encounter situations in which a person's accent (or the officer's own accent) or inability to speak or understand a language is a barrier to communication and police performance of duties.

Non-Verbal Communication

Non-verbal communication has been neglected in many cultural awareness training programs even though it is estimated that up to 93 percent of the social meaning of a message is delivered non-verbally (Singelis, 1994).

Paralanguage refers to features of speech, such as tone, loudness, speed, and use of silence. Asians tend to be soft-spoken, Americans loud, and Middle Easterners even louder. Asians and Aboriginal people value silence and interpret the North American rush to butt in and talk as impulsive and rude.

paralanguage
features of speech, such as tone, loudness, speed, and use of silence

Kinesics refers to physical communication: look and appearance, eye contact, facial expressions, posture, body movements, and touching. Some cultures like to touch more than others. Koreans refrain from touching people they do not know as such behaviour is considered rude in their culture. Chinese people do not like to be touched on the head as the action shows a lack of respect. French, Middle Eastern, and Latin-American people touch more than North Americans or Northern Europeans. For example, a Middle Eastern shop owner may take the arm of a customer and lead her or him around the store, explaining the merchandise.

kinesics
physical communication, including look and appearance, eye contact, facial expressions, posture, body movements, and touching

Facial display of emotions is universal. Six facial expressions of emotion are recognizable in all cultures: anger, fear, happiness, sadness, surprise, and disgust. However, the rules associated with displaying emotions are culture-specific. Thus, some cultures prohibit or discourage the public display of emotions whereas others consider it acceptable and normal. For example, Japanese people consider facial expression of emotions bad manners.

While in North America nodding your head up and down signifies agreement, in other cultures (such as Sri Lankan) shaking your head from side to side means the same thing. In North America, direct eye contact is a sign of respect and attentiveness, whereas in other cultures (for example, Laotian) downcast eyes are the norm for showing respect and attentiveness. In some cultures (for example, Japanese), closing the eyes while listening to another, especially a higher-status person, may in some circumstances indicate intense attentiveness rather than disinterest in what is being said.

Proxemics refers to the use of space in terms of physical distance between people. Hall (1966) identified four aspects of use of space:

- Intimate distance, which characterizes comforting, lovemaking, and wrestling.

- Personal distance, in which a comfort zone of about 0.5 to 1 m separates one person from another. A police officer who intrudes on this personal space evokes feelings of discomfort or even threat.

proxemics
use of space, in terms of physical distance between people, as a form of non-verbal communication

EXERCISE 5

Role-play each of the following situations. Have observers watch the verbal and non-verbal communication of the participants. First, role-play the situations according to these scripts. After feedback from the class, re-enact the situations with the "police officers" using culturally competent verbal and non-verbal communication.

Observe the responses of the role players in relation to:

- tone of voice
- facial expression
- eye contact
- body posture and movement
- physical distance
- hand gestures, including touching
- turn-taking rules
- expression of emotions
- empathy
- **persuasive disclosure**

persuasive disclosure
approaches people use to persuade others

Situation 1: Police officer stops a teenager on the street.

Black teenager to police officer: "I was doing nothing wrong."

Police officer: "Listen, boy, with an attitude like yours you're going to be a loser for the rest of your life."

Situation 2: Police officer to white woman involved in an argument with another white woman: "You better shape up, bitch, or else I'm going to lock you in the slammer for good."

Situation 3: Police officer called to school to deal with an incident in which a straight student called a gay student a "fag." Police officer to gay student: "What's the big fuss, boy? You have to stop carrying a chip on your shoulder and learn to get along with all the straight students in school."

Situation 4: A 14-year-old has called police because his father slapped him in the face for getting home after his 2 a.m. curfew. Police officer to father: "You may slap your son in your country, but here in my country we do things differently."

Situation 5: A 13-year-old Arab teenager calls police and complains that her father is not allowing her to go out on a date with a 16-year-old from the neighbourhood. Police officer to father: "This is not the Middle East. When are you going to do things our way?"

Situation 6: A Bosnian family calls police. On arrival, the police officer is told that the family is concerned because the daughter should have been home from school five hours ago. Police officer to distressed mother: "Stop being overprotective. She's probably just having fun with her friends."

- Social distance, in which one person is far enough from another that touching cannot occur.

- Public distance, in which there is a distance of 4 m or more between two people.

Singelis (1994) has identified several functions of non-verbal communication: replacing verbal communication (for example, gesturing instead of using words), modifying verbal communication (for example, raising your voice for emphasis), regulating social intercourse (for example, applying turn-taking and eye-contact rules in social interactions), carrying emotional messages (for example, communicating like or dislike for a person), and conveying attitudes.

Singelis has also described four pitfalls of non-verbal communication: missing signals, confusing context, misattributing, and sending wrong signals. Misattribution, as explained earlier, is the process of misdiagnosing a non-verbal behaviour. Here are some examples of misattribution (Community Policing Consortium, 1996):

- A person's passive facial expression is seen by a police officer as a sign of deceit or obstruction.

- A person's silence is interpreted by a police officer as a sign of disrespect or an admission of guilt.

- Touching by a female police officer is mistaken as sexual by a male police officer.

- A man's loud speech and physical closeness comes across as threatening to a police officer.

- A woman's downcast eyes while being questioned by a police officer is misinterpreted as a sign of deceit and guilt.

CHAPTER SUMMARY

Anti-racism initiatives are required at the societal level and at the policing level. While diversity was once considered a policing issue and a liability, the contemporary view of diversity is one of advantage for policing culture, police–community relations, criminal investigations, and public safety. Traditional piecemeal and stand-alone race relations and cultural awareness police training programs are limited in scope and acceptance. Best practice diversity awareness training programs in policing are part of a police-sponsored diversity awareness training plan and are integral to police culture. The professionalization and diversification of policing are positive developments for police effectiveness and public safety.

KEY TERMS

authoritarianism

race relations training

employment equity

cultural awareness training

cross-cultural training

diversity awareness training

cross-cultural communication

misattribution

paralanguage

kinesics

proxemics

persuasive disclosure

REFERENCES

American Civil Liberties Union (ACLU). (1991, April). *On the line: Police brutality and its remedies.* NY: ACLU Department of Public Education.

Banton, M. (1963, April). Social integration and police. *Police Chief*: 10-12.

Bhawuk, D.P.S., & R.W. Brislin. (2000, January). Cross-cultural training: A review. *Applied Psychology: An International Review* 49 (1): 162–191.

Brislin, R.W., & A.M. Horvath. (1997). Cross-cultural training and multicultural education. In J.W. Berry, M.H. Segal, & C. Kagitcibasi (Eds.), *Handbook of cross-cultural psychology: Social behaviour and applications.* Vol. 3 (pp. 327–369). Needham Heights, MA: Allyn and Bacon.

Calliste, A., & G.S. Dei. (2000). *Anti-racist feminism: Critical race and gender studies.* Halifax: Fernwood.

Canadian Charter of Rights and Freedoms, part I of the *Constitution Act, 1982,* RSC 1985, app. II, no. 44.

Canadian Heritage (2006). Annual Report on the Operation of the *Canadian Multiculturalism Act* 2004–2005. http://www.pch.gc.ca/index_e.cfm.

Coffey, A. (1990). *Law enforcement: A human relations approach.* Englewood Cliffs, NJ: Prentice-Hall.

Community Policing Consortium. (1996, June). *Cultural Diversity* 1. http://www.communitypolicing.org/cultural/index.html.

Dei, G.S. (1996). *Anti-racism: Theory and practice.* Halifax: Fernwood.

DeVito, J.A. (1989). *The nonverbal communication workbook.* Prospect Heights, IL: Waveland Press.

Fine, M.G. (1995). *Building successful multicultural organizations: Challenges and opportunities.* Westport, CT: Quorum Books.

Hall, E.T. (1966). *The hidden dimension.* New York: Doubleday.

Harris, E.V.C., & G.A. Currie. (1994). An integrated anti-racism training model: A framework for positive action. *Crime & Justice: The Americas* 7: 11–14.

Hennessy, S.M., D.F. Warring, & J.S. Arnott. (1994). *A cultural awareness trainer's manual for law enforcement officers.* Scottsdale, AZ: Leadership Inc.

Laws, J. (2005, February 4). Durham Regional Police Service (DRPS): 2005–2010 diversity strategic plan. Graybridge Malkam.

Lee, E. (1985). *Letters to Marcia: A teacher's guide to anti-racist education.* Toronto: Cross-Cultural Communication Centre.

Lewis, C. (1993). The police and the community. In J. Chacko & S.E. Nancoo (Eds.), *Community policing in Canada* (pp. 269–273). Toronto: Canadian Scholars' Press.

MacLeod, E. (2004, Fall). Message from the president. *Canadian Police Chief Magazine*: 7.

Perry, D. (2004, Fall). Complexities of cross-cultural investigations. *Canadian Police Chief Magazine*: 22–24.

Pruegger, V. (2003, February). Community and policing in partnership. Paper developed for Policing in a Multicultural Society Conference, Ottawa.

Rees, T. (1992). Police race relations training. *Currents: Readings in Race Relations* 7: 15–18.

Rodelet, L.A., & D.L. Carter. (1994). *The police and the community.* New York: MacMillan College Publishing.

Singelis, T. (1994). Nonverbal communication in intercultural interactions. In R.W. Brislin & T. Yoshida (Eds.), *Improving international interactions: Modules for cross-cultural training programs* (pp. 268–294). Thousand Oaks, CA: Sage.

Steinberg, J.L., & D.W. McEvoy. (1974). *The police and the behavioural sciences.* Springfield, IL: Charles C. Thomas.

Stephens, B. (2005, February 27). Policing as a career in Ontario. Paper presented at the Hong Kong University Alumni Association. Aylmer: Ontario Police College.

Taylor, N. (2004, Fall). Policing with cultural competency. *Canadian Police Chief Magazine*: 14–19.

Triandis, H.C. (2000). Culture and conflict. *International Journal of Psychology* 35 (2): 145–152.

Ungerleider, C. (1992). *Issues in police intercultural and race relations training in Canada.* Ottawa: Canadian Centre for Police–Race Relations.

Wortley, S. (1994). *Perceptions of bias and racism within the Ontario criminal justice system: Results from a public opinion survey.* Toronto: Commission on Systemic Racism in Ontario Criminal Justice System.

CHAPTER 7

Family Violence and Mental Health Issues

> **CHAPTER OBJECTIVES**
>
> After completing this chapter, you should be able to:
>
> - Discuss diversity issues as they relate to family violence and mental health issues.
> - Identify strategies that enable police to work with diverse groups in the community to address family violence and mental health issues.

INTRODUCTION

Everyone has the right to a safe home environment that is free from neglect and economic, physical, psychological, and spiritual abuse. In the absence of such an ideal, people who are exposed to neglect, intimidation, domination, and physical or sexual assault have the right to protection and assistance, as do people who suffer from mental illness. This chapter discusses family violence and mental illness from the perspective of diversity policing to help police better understand the devastating consequences of these issues, as well as some of the remedies available for people who experience these conditions.

DEFINITION OF FAMILY VIOLENCE

Family violence is a term that includes the many different forms of abuse, mistreatment, or neglect that adults or children may experience in their intimate, kinship, extended, or dependent relationships (Department of Justice Canada, 2006a). While family violence typically involves behaviour that causes one partner in a relationship to be afraid of and controlled by the other, it can also entail abuse of the children by a caregiver or a parent by a child.

Abuse may take a variety of forms, including physical assault, physical neglect, sexual assault, sexual exploitation, emotional and psychological abuse, financial abuse, and spiritual abuse, just to name a few areas. Physical assault may range from bruising to murder. Sexual assault may range from forced participation in an

family violence
caregiver abuse of children or abuse of caregiver by children

unwanted sexual activity to sexual abuse of children to forced rape. Psychological abuse may range from emotional or mental violence (verbal abuse, putdowns, humiliation, threats, property damage, and destruction) to excessive possessiveness, forced isolation from friends and family, and harassment. Spiritual abuse may involve putting a person's religious beliefs and practices down or not allowing that person's spiritual needs to be met. Finally, economic abuse may entail withholding money to buy food or medical treatment, creating a financially dependent relationship, controlling bank accounts, controlling paycheques, making grocery lists and making sure that no money is spent on anything else, checking the gas gauge in the car to ensure that no extra trips are taken, denying access to finances, and preventing a person from working.

FAMILY VIOLENCE AND THE LAW

Family violence is against the law in Canada. Ontario's *Child and Family Services Act* protects the well-being of children and provides for services to children and their families in a manner that respects their "cultural, religious and regional differences" (section 1(a)). Similarly, the *Criminal Code* and the *Canada Evidence Act* include provisions to deter and prevent family violence and are amended periodically to better address family violence issues including rising concerns over child pornography, sexual exploitation of youth, luring children on the Internet, child sex tourism, and testimony of child victims and witnesses (Department of Justice Canada, 2006a).

HOW BIG A PROBLEM IS FAMILY VIOLENCE?

Several studies initiated since the 1980s suggest that family violence in Canada is a pervasive social and policing problem (Committee on Sexual Offences Against Children and Youth, 1984; Rodgers, 1993; Canadian Panel on Violence Against Women, 1993; Statistics Canada, 2000; Health Canada, 2001).

Abuse Among Adults

spousal abuse
behaviour that causes one partner in a relationship to be afraid of and controlled by the other

Spousal abuse is violence or mistreatment that a woman or a man may experience at the hands of a marital, common-law, or same-sex partner. Adult abuse includes spiritual, emotional, psychological, sexual, economic, and physical abuse in intimate relationships (Canadian Panel on Violence Against Women, 1993). The 2004 General Social Survey reports close to 7 percent of Canadian adults (about 653,000 women and 546,000 men) experienced some form of abuse in their marital or common-law relationships in the past five years (Statistics Canada, 2005).

Abuse: Children and Youth

child abuse
physical and psychological maltreatment of children by adults

Child abuse is a generic term for different forms of maltreatment including physical and psychological abuse of children below the age of 14. *Psychological abuse* involves emotionally damaging acts of omission and commission—rejection, isolation, exploitation, and poor socialization. It is important to differentiate between the harm that children experience as a result of acts that are prohibited, deliberate, and preventable and harm that is due to economic disadvantage—for example, poverty.

Child sexual abuse refers to the sexual exploitation of any children under the age of 18 who are made to participate in "sexual activities they do not fully comprehend, are unable to give informed consent to, and that violate the social taboos of family roles" (Schecter & Roberge, 1976). The psychological and behavioural consequences of child sexual abuse include post-traumatic stress disorder and disturbed interpersonal relations.

child sexual abuse
sexual exploitation and maltreatment of dependent and developmentally immature children and adolescents

Abuse: Older Adults

Elder abuse is the physical, sexual, emotional, or psychological abuse or neglect, or the financial exploitation (fraud and theft) of an older person by a caregiver (spouse or partner, adult child, or relative) or institutional staff member, including staff in a nursing home, or crooks. The psychological outcomes of elder abuse include feelings of shame, embarrassment, blame, and inadequacy for the victim. In 1999, 2 percent of all victims of violent crime were 65 years and older (Statistics Canada, 2000).

elder abuse
physical, sexual, emotional, or psychological abuse or neglect, or financial exploitation, of an older person by caregiver

DIVERSITY AND FAMILY VIOLENCE

People of diverse cultural and linguistic backgrounds regardless of their diversity—age, gender, ethnicity, education, cultural identity, socio-economic status, occupation, race, religion, sexual orientation, physical or mental abilities—may be vulnerable to family abuse (MacLeod & Shin, 1990; Green, 1996; Biesenthal et al., 2000; Law Commission of Canada, 2001). Family violence tends to be kept secret in many cultures; people are embarrassed by it and do not want to discuss it. As a result, no one really knows exactly how many people are victims or survivors of this violence. Table 7.1 lists some myths associated with family violence.

> **EXERCISE 1**
>
> What implication does the view that family violence is an issue for only some diversity groups have on police responses to perpetrators and victims?

Sex and Family Violence

While women and men experience similar rates of both violence and emotional abuse in their relationships, violence experienced by women tends to be more severe and more often repeated than the violence directed at men (Statistics Canada, 2005). Women are six times more likely to report being sexually assaulted, five times more likely to report being choked, five times more likely to require medical attention as a result of an assault, and three times more likely to be physically injured by an assault (Statistics Canada, 2005).

TABLE 7.1 Myths About Family Violence

- Family violence is rare.
- Family violence is confined to lower socio-economic classes.
- Family violence happens only in heterosexual relationships.
- People with disabilities are immune to family violence.
- Substance abuse is the real cause of family violence.
- Victims of family violence have masochistic personalities.
- Victims of family violence exaggerate the abuse.
- Abusers have a licence to use violence.
- Abusers cannot control their abusive behaviours.
- Victims of family violence provoke the abuse.
- Victims of family violence consider abuse a sexual turn-on.
- Diversity (for example, culture, disability) is the root cause of family violence.

Immigrants and Refugees and Family Violence

Immigrants and refugees have unique experiences, fears, needs, and hopes that complicate the reality of family violence. Western conceptions of abuse may be different from those of other cultures. Denying girls an education and arranging marriages for both boys and girls can be considered abuse in Western cultures, but are culturally accepted practices in some non-Western cultures. While it is important in all cases to use the legal definitions of abuse and expect all diverse groups to be governed by the rule of law, to ensure objectivity and uniformity it is also important to recognize cultural practices that may mistakenly be perceived as child abuse. Allegations of child abuse because of cultural ignorance may have devastating consequences for parents.

Immigrants and refugees who come from diverse cultures bring attitudes and beliefs that need to be considered in the context of family violence. Immigrants and refugees may come from cultures in which the political, legal, and social positions of women, and women's rights and freedoms, are not as egalitarian as those in the democratic host countries. Similarly, immigrants and refugees may come from cultures or countries where practices such as honour killing, virgin suicides, and female genital mutilation (FGM) may have been sanctioned and considered minor crimes, when in fact such practices constitute serious family crimes in Western countries.

Honour killing is murder of a female family member by a male family member, usually a brother, for allegedly sullying her family's honour. A woman may stain her family's name by engaging in sexual relations out of wedlock, refusing an arranged marriage, or trying to escape an abusive relationship.

Virgin suicides refer to families of disgraced or dishonoured girls locking their daughters in a room for days with lethal weapons—rat poison, a pistol, or a rope—and telling them that death is the only thing resting between their disgrace and redemption ("Virgin Suicides," 2006). Virgin suicides omit the need for honour killings. In honour killings, families lose their daughter to death for disgracing the family and their son to jail for executing the honour killing. In virgin suicides, parents dispense with the daughter to save the son.

Dislocation of families from rural villages to urban cities seems a contributory factor to virgin suicides. Significant tension is created between traditionalist families and young women reared in mostly Middle Eastern countries under protective families and strict familial and religious moral strictures when the family is displaced into a society with secularist and modernist values and practices. The tension between the traditionalist families and their daughters may result in families suspecting their daughters of conduct unbecoming of their family name and resorting to honour restoration ("Virgin Suicides," 2006), familial stress, and family violence.

Settlement support for these families and young women includes raising awareness about human rights generally and women's rights in particular.

> **EXERCISE 2**
>
> List strategies that enable police to help people in a community address family violence in their respective diversity groups.

EXPLANATIONS FOR FAMILY VIOLENCE

Family violence is a complex social issue, with many contributory or vulnerability factors: dislocation from one's culture, language, family, and community; colonization or European subjugation of Aboriginal people; racism; sexism; homophobia; poverty; and isolation.

Explanations for family violence fall into four categories. The *personal view* points the finger at women and suggests that they provoke men into abusing them. The *chemical view* blames abusive behaviour on the use of alcohol and illicit drugs. The *social view* points the finger at several factors: stress, economic hardship, men's hunger for control and power, women's fear of disclosure (which can prolong the abuse) (Champagne, Lapp, & Lee, 1994), and society's lax attitude toward abusers. However, the social view identifies patriarchy as the main culprit, arguing that patriarchal societies institutionalize social control of women and sustain their unequal power status in relation to men. The *divine view* blames abusive behaviour on lack of spirituality or too much spirituality. Some religions may promote the view that gender is destiny and may condone the practice of **gendered apartheid**, which considers women less than human beings and morally unequal to men, and treats women as a subordinate class (Okin, 1999). Gendered apartheid is inconsistent with feminism, which views women and men as equal in morality and human dignity, and promotes a culture in which women have the same advantages as men and the same opportunities to live a fulfilling life (Okin, 1999).

gendered apartheid
viewpoint that considers women unequal to men and treats women as a subordinate class

> **EXERCISE 3**
>
> 1. Identify factors that police should consider when responding to a new immigrant who is in an abusive relationship.
> 2. List factors that need to be considered in creating a safety plan for victims of family violence and their children.

BARRIERS TO LEAVING VIOLENT RELATIONSHIPS

Complex factors contribute to women's silence about and endurance of abuse: the culture of silence, the culture of shame, keeping up appearances, the perceived or false sense of power one has as a result of being in a relationship, fear of reprisal and harm to the children, financial or emotional dependence, social isolation, inadequate response or support from the criminal justice system, and social stigma.

SOCIAL RESPONSES TO FAMILY VIOLENCE

Canada supports a policy of zero tolerance of all types of violence, which dictates that all perpetrators of violence face appropriate consequences from the criminal justice system, victims receive necessary protection from the criminal justice system, and victims and survivors of violence be provided with diversity-sensitive supports and services in their communities.

In the past, community supports and services for victims and survivors of family violence gave little thought to the issue of diversity. This *adiversity* (as in asocial) tradition is changing as programs gradually become more diversity-oriented. Specialized community-based programs are following a support and service philosophy that respects diversity, individual autonomy, and safety; supports a community-wide response to reduce violence against women; and promotes system change at the legal, medical, and social levels and in social responses to victims.

Supports and Services

Community support and services are essential for effective response to family violence. Such organizations need to embrace the value of diversity in the provision of their supports and services. For example, gay and lesbian victims of family violence can feel ill at ease in mainstream shelters because of prevailing homophobia.

Abused immigrant and refugee women have unique vulnerabilities that require special consideration (MacLeod & Shin, 1990, 1994; Kazarian & Kazarian, 1998). Chief among them are worries about their immigration status (for example, their lack of permanent status or the threat of or actual withdrawal of sponsorship by their abuser), their work permits, or deportation; reluctance to relive possible trauma they endured before, during, and following immigration; lack of knowledge of host country laws (for example, that wife assault is a criminal act) and personal rights and freedoms; lack of familiarity with the system and its available community supports and services; and language barriers. MacLeod & Shin (1990) have identified the primary needs of abused immigrant and refugee women, which are listed in table 7.2.

TABLE 7.2 Primary Needs of Abused Immigrant and Refugee Women

- Information about basic rights and freedoms and the laws related to immigration and wife assault
- A supportive network that conveys understanding, caring, a sense of greater freedom, and confirmation that the woman is not alone
- Opportunities to discuss issues of violence with people who understand their language and culture
- Subsidized language training with training allowances and free daycare facilities
- Sensitive, multicultural, multilingual, and multiracial child care facilities to overcome isolation
- Job training
- Affordable housing
- Culture-sensitive and language-specific services to address legal, economic, safety, and support needs

Source: MacLeod & Shin (1990).

POLICE RESPONSE TO FAMILY VIOLENCE

There are three major police response policies regarding family violence. The **mediative policy** invokes a non-arrest approach to family violence calls. Police officers responding to family violence calls take a hands-off approach—that is, they try to get everyone in the household to calm down and leave it to the family to resolve their difficulties or refer the offender or victim to social agencies. Historically, police have not considered violence in intimate relationships a real crime. They have also followed the meditative non-arrest approach because of preoccupation with two major themes: the practical and the patriarchal. Preoccupation with the practical view invoked an attitude of non-arrest for very practical reasons—for example, the victim does not want the offender arrested or cannot afford to have the offender arrested, the offence may be culturally acceptable, the offender may cause harm to the victim once he is released, arrest may ultimately break up the relationship, or the court is likely to dismiss charges when the victim chooses not to prosecute. Police preoccupation with the patriarchal view invoked reluctance to arrest perpetrators of family violence by virtue of police socialization in a patriarchal and hierarchical societal structure in which power, control, and sexist attitudes prevailed. In this man-at-the-top view, police officers displayed little interest in enforcing laws against men who abuse women because they accepted the hierarchical structure of society.

Major changes to police response to family violence calls have occurred since the mid-1970s such that two additional policies have prevailed. The **pro-arrest policy** encourages arrest in family violence cases but leaves the discretion to the officers. The **mandatory arrest policy**, on the other hand, dictates that arrest must take place whenever probable cause exists, even in less serious offences. Police services in many countries, including Canada, have adopted a policy of laying criminal charges in family violence cases, but many police still under-enforce the criminal law in these cases.

mediative policy
a non-arrest approach to family violence calls

pro-arrest policy
encourages arrest in family violence cases but leaves the discretion to the officers

mandatory arrest policy
arrest must take place

> **EXERCISE 4**
>
> As a police officer, what would you do in the following situation? Role-play the scenario, demonstrating a diversity-competent approach to responding to family violence calls. Be aware of your verbal and non-verbal messages.
>
> > I am a physically disabled newcomer to this country. My husband has sponsored me and my three children. I have no one here other than my husband and my children. I have been beaten, as have my children, and I am scared. I finally had the courage to call the police to help me. They are my only hope.

FAMILY VIOLENCE AND MENTAL HEALTH ISSUES: POLICE ABILITIES, KNOWLEDGE, AND SKILLS

Police, Crown attorneys, judges, probation officers, victim-witness assistance personnel, and correctional personnel provide sensitive and appropriate supports and services in the area of family violence, and develop resources on the topic for distribution.

Policing is becoming more responsive to family violence issues. Police executives attend national forums on family violence for self-education on family violence facts and initiatives, approaches, and good practices in police and community responses to family violence, and to develop networks with other police chiefs, professionals, and government agencies (Department of Justice Canada, 2006b).

In addition, police are becoming more effective in responding to family violence calls. Most have shifted from a victim-blaming approach to an abuser-accountability approach. Police officers with traditional victim-blaming attitudes failed the victim by not interceding against the abuser, and also revictimized the victim by giving tacit approval to the abuse.

Police are also recognizing that they can no longer try to fight family violence alone, and that forming alliances with community supports is a more effective strategy. To effect positive changes, some police services have established family-response teams, mapped at-risk households on the beat, and provided family violence training programs.

Finally, police themselves are recognizing that they are not immune to family violence. Police departments are recognizing the vulnerability of their own members to the problem and the need for internal initiatives to address the issue.

MENTAL ILLNESS AND HOMELESSNESS

mental illness
group of disabilities marked by disturbances in thinking, feeling, and relating

homelessness
having no fixed, regular, and adequate address

Mental illness and **homelessness** are two realities that societies tend to hide or avoid discussing. It is estimated that 20 percent of Canadians are likely to experience mental illness during their lifetime, and that the remaining 80 percent are likely to be affected by a family member, friend, or colleague who is mentally ill (Health Canada, 2002). Police contact with people with emotional disturbances is also considerable and on the increase. It is estimated that 7 to 15 percent of police contacts involve people with mental health issues (Stedman, et al., 1996; Cotton, 2003). New psychiatric and psychological treatment approaches to mental illness and deinstitutionalization have contributed to the reintegration of the mentally ill in the community. However, shortcomings in the community mental health services, including insufficient funding, have invoked increased police involvement in mental health calls from the community. This part of the chapter focuses on policing mental illness with a view to increased police understanding of mental illness and effectiveness in responding to mental health calls.

Concept of Mental Illness

Mental illness is a generic term for a variety of disorders. The Police Executive Research Forum (1997) defines mental illness as a group of distinct disabilities marked by disturbances in thinking, feeling, and relating. Mental illness is more common than many people think (Keresztes & Kazarian, 1996; Offord et al., 1994; Health Canada, 2002).

Although mental illness causes disturbances in behaving, feeling, relating, and thinking, such disturbances can also be caused by other factors, including head injury, medical conditions such as diabetes and epilepsy, and substance abuse. For example, people who use cocaine may experience **formication**, a hallucinatory experience in which the users feel that insects or snakes are crawling over or under their skin. Similarly, people in the aftermath of a cocaine high may become irritable and depressed.

formication
hallucination that involves feeling that insects or snakes are crawling over or under one's skin

Mental illness ranges from mild to severe. Severe mental illness includes schizophrenia, mood disorders, organic brain syndrome (a general term referring to physical disorders that negatively affect brain function), and paranoid and other psychoses.

Mental disturbances can be categorized as *psychotic* and *non-psychotic*. Hallucinations and delusions are the two most common psychotic symptoms. Anxiety and depression are the two most common non-psychotic type symptoms.

MENTAL HEALTH LEGISLATION

On December 17, 1991, the international community recognized the fundamental right of mentally ill people to be protected from discrimination when the *UN Principles for the Protection of Persons with Mental Illness and the Improvement of Mental Health Care* were adopted by resolution of the UN General Assembly (Office of the United Nations High Commissioner for Human Rights, 1991). Still, in many countries, mental health legislation allows the removal of the civil liberties of people with mental illness (Persad & Kazarian, 1998). The essential criteria that lead to someone being forcibly confined in a psychiatric hospital are usually the result of illness and are manifested as danger to self, danger to others, and lack of competence to care for self.

Mental Health Act: Ontario

Ontario's *Mental Health Act* was amended and passed as *Brian's Law* on June 23, 2000. Brian Smith was a popular sportscaster and former National Hockey League player who was shot and killed by a man with a history of serious mental illness. *Brian's Law* enables community treatment orders for seriously mentally ill people. These orders allow people to be treated in a community setting that is less restrictive and less intrusive than a psychiatric hospital. Other provinces (for example, Saskatchewan) have similar laws.

Brian's Law also stipulates that a justice of the peace may issue an order authorizing a police officer to take a person in custody to an appropriate place for examination by a physician provided that information grounded on *threat* and *mental disorder* is given under oath. In relation to threat, the statute requires information to the effect that (1) the person has threatened or attempted or is threatening or attempting to cause bodily harm to herself or himself; (2) the person has behaved or is behaving violently toward another person or has caused or is causing another person to fear bodily harm from her or him; and (3) the person has shown or is showing a lack of competence to care for herself or himself. In relation to mental disorder, the statute requires information on reasonable cause or belief that the person is apparently suffering from mental disorder of a nature or quality that will result in (1) serious bodily harm to the person, (2) serious bodily harm to another person, and (3) serious physical impairment of the person.

Finally, *Brian's Law* stipulates that a police officer may take a person into custody provided the police officer has reasonable and probable grounds to believe that disorderly conduct has occurred and has reasonable cause to believe that the person fulfills the conditions of threat and mental disorder described above.

MENTAL DISTURBANCES AND POLICE RESPONSE

Police are most likely to encounter people with substance-related disorders, mood disorders, schizophrenia, and mental retardation. Police are also most likely to deal with the mental disturbances of suicidal behaviour; threatening, destructive, assaultive, or violent behaviour; psychotic thinking and ideation (losing touch with reality); confusion in thought or action; and strange or unusual behaviours that exceed public tolerance.

Substance-Related Disorders

substance-related disorders
mental disorders caused by substance dependence and abuse, and by substance withdrawal

psychosis
form of serious mental disorder in which an actual break with reality occurs

People with **substance-related disorders** may show mental disturbances of both the **psychotic** and non-psychotic types. For example, consuming alcohol can have such serious effects as blackout and aggression. Angel dust (PCP, phencyclidine) is known to produce severe anxiety, depression, disorientation, unpredictable aggression, and paranoid thoughts (Levinthal, 1996). Alcohol and drug abuse are also associated with crime and social violence such as robbery, burglary, shoplifting, pimping, prostitution, and trafficking and distribution of illicit drugs for income.

In responding to a person with a substance-related disorder, police need to

- ensure their own safety and the safety of others,
- recognize the symptoms the person is displaying,
- expect irrational behaviour,
- decide whether the situation is a medical emergency, and
- ensure that an interim use of physical restraint is safe and unlikely to cause the person added harm.

Mood Disorders and Suicidal Behaviour

Mood disorders include depression and bipolar disorder. No one is immune to depression, which affects children as well as adults. More women are diagnosed with depression than men. **Depression** is characterized by extended periods of feelings of despair and hopelessness and lack of interest in life. Contrary to popular belief, it is not simply sadness or feeling down. People who suffer from depression may have trouble simply facing each day. They often experience problems with sleeping (either sleeping too much or too little), eating (overeating or loss of appetite), and feeling alienated or separate from the rest of society.

Bipolar disorder, previously called manic depression, is a condition in which a person has emotional swings between depression and mania. **Mania** is a mood state of emotional high, agitation, and impulsivity. Men and women are diagnosed equally with bipolar disorder. Table 7.3 lists the symptoms of depression and mania.

People with mood disorders may exhibit psychotic and non-psychotic symptoms. The psychotic symptoms tend to be consistent with their mood state. For example, Nathan's belief that his blood type could cure all the sicknesses in the world was consistent with his state of mania. In his elated mood, Nathan insisted that as much blood as possible be drawn from his arm and taken around the world to cure people of their diseases.

Police knowledge of the type of medication a mentally ill person takes may be useful when responding to a mental health call. Table 7.4 lists drugs used frequently to treat depression. Best practices include drug therapy, psychotherapy (cognitive, interpersonal, supportive), psychoeducation for patient and family, and community supports and services.

mood disorders
mental disorders that affect a person's mood, including depression and bipolar disorder

depression
mood disorder characterized by feelings of despair and hopelessness

bipolar disorder
mood disorder that involves emotional swings between depression and mania; formerly called manic depression

mania
mood disorder characterized by feelings of emotional high, agitation, and impulsivity

TABLE 7.3 Symptoms of Depression and Mania

Depression	Mania
■ Feelings of sadness or emptiness	■ Inflated self-esteem or grandiosity
■ Loss of interest or pleasure	■ Talkativeness
■ Sleep disturbance (too much or too little sleep)	■ Extreme irritability
	■ Distractibility
■ Change in eating habits (increase or decrease in appetite)	■ Decreased need for sleep
■ Change in weight (loss or gain)	■ Increased sexual, social, school, and work activities
■ Psychomotor disturbance (agitation or slowness in movement)	■ Increased pleasurable activities (overspending, sexual indiscretion)
■ Fatigue or loss of energy	
■ Loss of self-esteem	
■ Feelings of guilt or self-blame	
■ Cognitive disturbance (poor concentration, indecisiveness)	
■ Suicidal or homicidal thoughts	

TABLE 7.4 Frequently Prescribed Antidepressant Medications

Class	Trade name	Chemical name
Monoamine oxidase inhibitors (MAO-I)	Marplan	Isocarboxazid
	Nardil	Phenelzine
	Parnate	Tranylcypromine
Selective seratonin reuptake inhibitors (SSRIs)	Paxil	Paroxetine
	Prozac	Fluoxetine
	Zoloft	Sertraline hydrochloride
Tricyclic antidepressants (TCA)	Anafranil	Clomipramine
	Elavil, Amitid	Amitriptyline
	Norpramin, Pertofrane	Desipramine
	Pamelor, Aventryl	Nortriptyline
	Sinequan	Doxepin
	Surmontil	Trimipramine
	Tofranil	Imipramine
	Vivactil	Protriptyline
Other	Ascendin	Amoxapine
	Desyrel	Trazodone
	Welbutrin	Bupropion

suicide
symptom of mood disorder that takes the form of ideation, threat, attempt, gesture, and completed suicide

Suicide is a symptom of mood disorder that may take the form of *ideation* (thinking about it), *threat* (expressing the intention to commit a self-destructive act), *gesture* (a self-destructive act with little or no death intent), *attempt* (a self-destructive act with clear death intent), or *completed suicide*. In 2003, 3,764 people in Canada (2,902 male and 862 female) committed suicide (Statistics Canada, 2002–2006). Suicide is blind to diversity. Men succeed in killing themselves more than women, even though women attempt suicide more often than men. According to Statistics Canada (2006), methods of suicide among men and women are as follows: hanging (46 percent for men, 37 percent for women), use of firearms (20 percent for men, 3 percent for women), poisoning (20 percent for men, 42 percent for women), and other (14 percent for men, 18 percent for women). A person's religious beliefs may serve as a protective factor, but they do not provide complete immunity to suicide. Table 7.5 lists risk factors for suicidal behaviour. It is interesting to note that the media rarely report on public suicides such as people jumping in front of trains or jumping off bridges. Even cases with sensational circumstances may not make it into the media. The perceived notoriety gained from such an act is seen as encouraging others who might also want to commit a similar act.

In responding to a depressed and suicidal person, police need to

- avoid telling the person to cheer up or snap out of it;
- assess the risk of suicide by asking direct questions and using the words "kill" or "die" (for example, "Are you thinking of killing yourself?" "Have you made plans to kill yourself?" "Why do you want to die?");
- take suicide threats seriously;

TABLE 7.5 Risk Factors for Suicidal Behaviour

- Suicide plan
- History of past suicide attempts
- Absence of community support
- Recent loss (actual, threatened, or imagined)
- Physical illness, including AIDS or other terminal illness
- Change in lifestyle, behaviour, or personality
- Giving away possessions or valuables
- Putting personal affairs in order (for example, making a will)
- Depression, including feelings of hopelessness and helplessness
- Postpartum depression
- Substance use
- Recent discharge from psychiatric hospital care
- Psychosis
- Anniversaries (birthday, wedding, death of a loved one)

- be empathic (for example, "I would like to help because I know you are in pain");
- avoid swearing secrecy;
- not leave the person alone;
- draw on the person's social support system (family, friends, counsellor); and
- present the person with two options to choose from (for example, "Would you like to go to the hospital with me, or would you rather I called an ambulance?").

In responding to a manic person, police need to

- decrease all extraneous stimulation (for example, noise from a TV);
- avoid arguments;
- allow the person to appropriately discharge energy, such as by pacing;
- be firm, empathic, and direct;
- draw on the person's social support system; and
- present the person with options to choose from.

> **EXERCISE 5**
>
> You receive a call from a family in the Aboriginal community that a 17-year-old male has committed suicide by shooting himself. The surviving family members include a father, mother, and a 7-year-old sister. What would you do to assist the surviving family members in the short and long term?

Schizophrenia

schizophrenia
mental illness described as cancer of the mind that causes psychotic mental disturbances

thought disorder
mental symptom characterized by ideas and speech that are coherent only to the mentally ill person

hallucinations
sensory illusions that are disturbed or disturbing and are real only to the mentally ill person

delusions
ideas that are real only to the mentally ill person

Schizophrenia causes psychotic mental disturbances. It invades men sooner than women. However, in contrast with the symptoms of mood disorders, the psychotic symptoms of schizophrenia tend to be inconsistent with the person's mood state. For example, the person may break into laughter while discussing the death of a parent rather than feel sad or distressed. Table 7.6 lists major symptoms of schizophrenia.

Thought disorders are ideas and speech that make sense to the schizophrenic person but are incoherent to others. **Hallucinations** are sensory experiences that are disturbed and disturbing. Hallucinations can be felt, heard, seen, smelled, or tasted. Hearing voices and seeing things are the more common hallucinations. People who are hallucinating may talk to themselves, show concentration problems, or make head movements toward the source of the voice they hear. A person who is having visual hallucinations may show jerking of the eyes or head. **Delusions** are ideas that are real only to the schizophrenic person. A person with paranoid schizophrenia may believe that he is Jesus and the subject of persecution. Similarly, a person with schizophrenia may believe that dirty thoughts are being inserted into her head or that valuable thoughts are being sucked out of her mind and stolen. A variety of psychotropic drugs are used in the treatment of schizophrenia (for example, clozapine). When schizophrenics discontinue taking their medication, they may become involved with the police. A recent study that focused on police officers' perspectives found that, "By far the strongest theme to emerge was the officer perception that if the person had stayed on their psychiatric medication, the incident might have been prevented" (McAndrew & Sutton, 2004).

In responding to psychotic symptoms, police need to

- be firm, empathic, reassuring, and helpful;
- avoid using deception or humour;
- validate the hallucinatory experience for the person but also communicate that the hallucination does not exist in reality (for example, "I don't see the man, but I understand that you do");

TABLE 7.6 Excess and Deficit Symptoms of Schizophrenia

Excess symptoms	Deficit symptoms
■ Hallucinations	■ Mood disturbances
■ Thought disorders	■ Impaired interpersonal functioning
■ Delusions	■ Lack of motivation

CHAPTER 7 Family Violence and Mental Health Issues

- acknowledge a person's delusion but not agree with, dispute, or attack it, or argue with or try to convince the person that her or his stated belief is not true;

- avoid invading the personal space of a paranoid person or implying special knowledge of the person's paranoidal beliefs;

- employ the Use of Force Continuum if a schizophrenic person presents a threat;

- draw on the person's social support system, if necessary; and

- present the person with two options to choose from.

Mental Retardation

Mental retardation is not the same as mental illness. Three criteria are used to establish **mental retardation**: significantly subaverage intelligence, significant limitation in adaptive functioning, and onset before the age of 18 years. Terms to describe the condition include "intellectually challenged," "developmentally disabled," or "developmentally handicapped." Terms that we now consider derogatory were once acceptable.

The communication development and behavioural development of people who are mentally challenged are varied but limited. They may have a short attention span, speech impairment, or difficulty with understanding or answering questions. They may act inappropriately with peers or the opposite sex, or be easily frustrated, eager to please, or easily influenced by others. Finally, they may show difficulty in carrying out the activities of daily living, including using the telephone and telling time.

In responding to a person with a developmental disability, police need to

- treat the person with respect and dignity,
- use simple language and short sentences,
- be patient but firm, and
- avoid asking confusing or leading questions.

mental retardation
significant subaverage intelligence, significant limitation in adaptive functioning, and onset before the age of 18 years

POLICING MENTAL ILLNESS: POLICE ABILITIES, KNOWLEDGE, AND SKILLS

Policing mental illness is challenging in view of the increasing number of mental health calls received by police services, the importance of successful response to such calls, and the serious consequences of tragic outcomes. Police encounters with people with mental illness may be violent, and incidents of police shootings of mentally ill people are front-page newspaper stories.

Cases of police injury and killings of people with apparent mental illness have made the need for specialized training in mental health important (Commission for Public Complaints Against the RCMP, 2003). The Ontario Ministry of the Solicitor General *Policing Standards Manual* (2000) advises chiefs of police to ensure

> ## EXERCISE 6
>
> Read each of the following situations and indicate what course of action you would take. Options you should consider consist of asking the person to go with you voluntarily to a hospital for assessment; laying a charge and taking the person to hospital; taking the person to hospital without laying a charge; laying a charge and bringing the person before a justice of the peace; diverting the person to a home (family, relatives), a community program, or a community agency for care and safety; and referring the person to a diversion program that involves the criminal justice system and mental health.
>
> 1. A mentally ill man has committed a serious crime and is clearly showing debilitating signs of mental illness.
>
> 2. A homeless man has committed a violent crime and is clearly showing debilitating signs of a mental disorder.
>
> 3. A mentally ill woman has committed a serious crime but has been functioning adequately.
>
> 4. A mentally ill person has committed a minor offence and is clearly showing signs of a serious mental disorder.
>
> 5. A homeless man has committed a non-violent offence and has been functioning adequately.
>
> 6. A mentally ill woman has committed a minor offence but poses no threat to public safety.

that their police service's skills development and learning plans address the training and sharing of information with officers on conflict resolution and the use of force involving individuals who may be emotionally disturbed.

The Commission for Public Complaints Against the RCMP (2003) identified several Canadian police services that have implemented training policy guidelines and/or specialized intervention teams. They include Ottawa-Carleton, Toronto, Niagara, Guelph, Ontario Provincial Police, Hamilton-Wentworth Regional Police Centre, and Chatham-Kent. The specialized approach entails understanding of mental health legislation and mental disturbances, and specific interventions such as tactical communication, crisis resolution, using containment to diffuse potentially volatile situations (for example, a mentally ill person threatening with a gun), and partnership with available community supports and services (Kazarian & Persad, 1999; Kazarian, Persad, Silverson, & O'Flaherty, 1998; Murphy, 1989; Cotton & Coleman, 2003; Commission for Public Complaints Against the RCMP, 2003). These supports and services may include advocacy, consumer and family education, family support, medical and dental services, medication, peer support, police support, and rehabilitation (Fernando & Kazarian, 1995; Kazarian & Joseph, 1994). Community support systems including crisis response services (crisis lines, mental health teams, hospital emergency wards) require adequate funding as the deinstitutionalization movement has resulted in reduction and shortages of hospi-

CHAPTER 7   Family Violence and Mental Health Issues   139

tal beds and acute admissions. Community support systems also require coordination to meet societal needs more effectively and efficiently. Psychologist Dr. Dorothy Cotton states, "Persons experiencing mental illnesses are now more likely to find themselves dealing with the police and the criminal justice system by default, as these individuals and their families, friends and communities find themselves frustrated in their attempts to access mental health services. Police services have gone a long way in developing education and training for their members, as well as trying to coordinate linkages with the mental health system" (Cotton, 2006).

EXERCISE 7

Identify strategies that enable police to work in partnership with the mental health system and diverse groups in the community to deal with mental health calls.

EXERCISE 8

Analyze each of the following scenarios and role-play them. Consider reversing the roles and re-enacting the scenes.

1. A 24-year-old man is threatening his mother with his fists. Your assessment of the situation is that he is unlikely to act out his anger and there is no real possibility that anyone will get hurt. You say, "If you don't stop threatening your mother, you'll have a real battle on your hands. Now what's it going to be?"

What is the problem, what are the issues, what are the solutions?

2. A 28-year-old homeless woman has been drinking and is now threatening passersby with a knife. You decide that she is unlikely to attack anyone or hurt anyone accidentally. You say, "All you homeless people are drunk. What are we going to do with you?"

What is the problem, what are the issues, what are the solutions?

3. A teenager tells you that the dentist put a microchip in his mouth when he went for a filling so now everyone can hear his private thoughts all the time. You say, "You believe people are spying on you. That must be very scary."

What is the problem, what are the issues, what are the solutions?

4. A 65-year-old mentally ill woman tells you that her husband and children are trying to get rid of her by poisoning her food. You tell the family that the woman is "psycho" and you have to take her to the "nuthouse."

What is the problem, what are the issues, what are the solutions?

Finally, police are not immune to having their own mental health issues. It may be difficult for police to accept this reality, since it shatters the image of police invulnerability, formidable emotional strength for dealing with adversity, indestructibility, and emotional impenetrability (Violanti, 1996). Initiatives for promoting the mental well-being of police are consistent with best practices in policing.

CHAPTER SUMMARY

Family violence is a serious problem for society and policing. Family violence affects both men and women. Effective policing requires seeing this violence as the criminal act that it is, understanding the unique experiences and needs of people of diversity, and partnering with community supports and services.

Mentally ill and homeless people come from all walks of life. Police may work in partnership with families, professionals, and community services in response to mental health and homelessness calls.

KEY TERMS

family violence	substance-related disorders
spousal abuse	psychosis
child abuse	mood disorders
child sexual abuse	depression
elder abuse	bipolar disorder
gendered apartheid	mania
mediative policy	suicide
pro-arrest	schizophrenia
mandatory arrest policy	thought disorders
mental illness	hallucinations
homelessness	delusions
formication	mental retardation

FAMILY VIOLENCE REFERENCES

Biesenthal, L., L.D. Sproule, M. Nelder, S. Golton, D. Mann, D. Podovinnikoff, I. Roosendaal, S. Warman, & D. Lunn. (2000). *The Ontario rural woman abuse study: Final report.* Ottawa: Department of Justice Canada.

Canadian Panel on Violence Against Women. (1993). *Changing the landscape: Ending violence—achieving equality.* Ottawa: Minister Responsible for the Status of Women.

Cantin, P. (1998, February 19). Family violence victims face "maze," inquest told. *The London Free Press*, p. A7.

Champagne, C., R. Lapp, & J. Lee. (1994). *Assisting abused lesbians: A guide for health professionals and service providers.* London, ON: London Battered Women's Advocacy Centre.

Child and Family Services Act, RSO 1990, c. C.11, as amended.

Committee on Sexual Offences Against Children and Youth. (1984). *Sexual offences against children in Canada: Report of the committee.* Ottawa: Supply and Services Canada.

Criminal Code, RSC 1985, c. C-46, as amended.

Department of Justice Canada. (2006a). About family violence in Canada. http://canada.justice.gc.ca/en/ps/fm/about.html.

Department of Justice Canada. (2006b). Projects funded by the Department of Justice Canada under the Family Violence Initiative (April 2002–March 2003). http://canada.justice.gc.ca/en/index.html.

Green, K. (1996). *Family violence in aboriginal communities: An aboriginal perspective—Information from the national clearinghouse on family violence.* Ottawa: Health Canada.

Hotton, T. (2001). Spousal violence after marital separation. *Juristat* 21 (7). Ottawa: Canadian Centre for Justice Statistics, Statistics Canada, catalogue no. 85-002-XPE.

Kazarian, S.S., & L.Z. Kazarian. (1998). Cultural aspects of family violence. In S.S. Kazarian & D.R. Evans (Eds.), *Cultural clinical psychology: Theory, research and practice* (pp. 316–347). New York: Oxford University Press.

Kazarian, S.S., & F. Persad. (1999). Mental health plan and police response to a crisis situation involving a mentally ill person: Yu inquest debriefing. London, ON, unpublished manuscript.

Law Commission of Canada. (2001). *Restoring dignity: Responding to child abuse in Canadian institutions.* Ottawa: Minister of Public Works and Government Services.

MacLeod, L., & M. Shin. (1990). *Isolated, afraid and forgotten: The service delivery needs and realities of immigrant and refugee women who are battered.* Ottawa: Health and Welfare Canada.

MacLeod, L., & M. Shin. (1994). *Like a wingless bird: A tribute to the survival and courage of women who are abused and who speak neither English nor French.* Ottawa: Health Canada.

Okin, S.M. (Ed.). (1999). *Is multiculturalism bad for women?* Princeton, NJ: Princeton University Press.

Rodgers, K. (1993). Wife assault: The findings of a national survey. *Juristat* 14 (9). Ottawa: Canadian Centre for Justice Statistics, Statistics Canada, catalogue no. 85-002.

Schecter, M.D., & L. Roberge. (1976). Sexual exploitation. In R.E. Helfer & C.H. Kempe (Eds.), *Child abuse and neglect: The family and the community* (pp. 127–142). Cambridge, MA: Ballinger.

Statistics Canada. (2000). *Family violence in Canada: A statistical profile.* Catalogue no. 85-224-XPE.

"Virgin suicides" take place of "honor killing." (2006, July 13). *International Herald Tribune*, pp. 1, 5.

MENTAL HEALTH ISSUES REFERENCES

Brian's Law (Mental Health Legislative Reform), SO 2000, c. 9.

Commission for Public Complaints Against the RCMP. (2003, October 20). *Report into a complaint concerning RCMP treatment of a person experiencing a mental health crisis.* http://www.cpc-cpp.gc.ca/defaultsite/Reppub/index_e.aspx?articleid=494.

Cotton, D. (2003, March). Top ten reasons for mental illness training. *Blue Line Magazine*: 28.

Cotton, D. (2005, December 8). CACP statement about the Canadian Mental Health Commission. http://www.cmha.ca/data/1/rec_docs/492_Media%20Release%20_2_.pdf.

Cotton, D., & T. Coleman. (2003). Ten years of suggestions: A review of inquest recommendations related to deaths of mentally ill individuals from 1992–2002. Unpublished research. Moose Jaw Police Service.

Fernando, M.L.D., & S.S. Kazarian. (1995, April). Patient education in the drug treatment of psychiatric disorders: Effect on compliance and outcome. CNS Drugs 3: 291–304.

Gendreau, C. (1997). The rights of psychiatric patients in the light of the principles announced by the United Nations: A recognition of the right to consent to treatment. *International Journal of Law and Psychiatry* 20: 259–278.

Heafey, S. (2002, September 30). The relationship between police and the mentally ill. Speech delivered to the First National Conference on Police Mental Health System Liaison. http://www.cpc-cpp.gc.ca/defaultsite/archive/index_e.aspx?articleid=647.

Health Canada. (2002, October). *A report on mental illnesses in Canada*. Ottawa: Author.

Kazarian, S.S., & L.W. Joseph. (1994). A brief scale to help identify outpatients' level of need for community support services. *Hospital and Community Psychiatry* 45: 935–937.

Kazarian, S.S., E. Persad, R. Silverson, & J. O'Flaherty. (1998). Police perceptions of their training and their interactions with mental health institutional supports. London, ON. Unpublished manuscript.

Keresztes, C., & S.S. Kazarian. (1996). Mental health: A developmental perspective. In R. Adler, E. Vingilis, & V. Mai (Eds.), *Community health and well-being in southwestern Ontario: Resource for planning* (pp. 207–216). London, ON: Middlesex Health Unit and Faculty of Medicine.

Levinthal, C.F. (1996). *Drugs, behavior, and modern society*. Needham Heights, MA: Allyn and Bacon.

McAndrew, A., & E. Sutton. (2004). *Searching for solutions: The front line police perspective on mental health interventions in Simcoe County*. Paper for the Research Analyst Program, Georgian College, Barrie, Ontario.

Mental Health Act, RSO 1990, c. M.7, as amended. Amended and passed as *Brian's Law* on June 23, 2000.

Murphy, G.R. (1989). *Managing persons with mental disabilities: A curriculum guide for police trainers*. Washington, DC: Police Executive Research Forum.

Office of the United Nations High Commissioner for Human Rights. (1991, December 17). *Principles for the protection of persons with mental illness and the improvement of mental health care*. http://www.unhchr.ch/html/menu3/b/68.htm.

Offord, D., M. Boyle, D. Campbell, J. Cochrane, P. Goering, E. Lin et al. (1994). *Mental health in Ontario: Selected findings from the Ontario Health Survey*. Toronto: Queen's Printer for Ontario.

Ontario Ministry of the Solicitor General. (2000, February). Police response to persons who are emotionally disturbed or have a mental illness or a development disability, section 29. *Policing Standards Manual*. Toronto: Queen's Printer for Ontario.

Persad, E., & S.S. Kazarian. (1998, November). Physician satisfaction with review boards: The provincial psychiatric hospital perspective. *Canadian Journal of Psychiatry* 43 (9): 905–909.

Police Executive Research Forum. (1997). *The police response to people with mental illnesses*. Washington, DC: Police Executive Research Forum.

Statistics Canada. (2002–2006). Causes of death 1999, 2002, 2003 and Death by causes 2000 and 2001. Ottawa: Author.

Statistics Canada. (2006). Causes of death 2003. Ottawa: Author.

Stedman, H., J. Morrisey, M.W. Deane, & R. Borum. (1996). *Police response to emotionally disturbed persons: Analyzing new models of police interactions with the mental health system.* The National Institute of Justice, p. 14.

Violanti, J.M. (1996). *Police suicide: Epidemic in blue.* Springfield, IL: Charles C. Thomas.

PART II
First Nations Issues in Canada

CHAPTER 8

Pre-Contact

> **CHAPTER OBJECTIVES**
>
> After completing this chapter, you should be able to:
>
> - Identify the differences between the Western European world view and the world view of First Nations people.
>
> - Understand how a people's world view affects all aspects of its culture, from religion to technology.
>
> - Consider how differences in world view will affect the continuing relationship between the mainstream culture and the First Nations culture.

INTRODUCTION

This chapter contrasts pre-contact Europe and pre-contact America to the end of understanding what the two cultures were like before they collided. Identifying the differences between their respective world views is crucial to any such understanding.

We gain insight into a culture's world view by examining its creation story. This first chapter will look at Native creation stories and at Western European creation stories. We will focus on Western creation stories, despite the fact that Canada is widely considered to be a cultural mosaic. Not all Canadians today are familiar with Christian religion. But at the time of colonization and well into the 20th century the majority of Canadians were people of Western European origin. Their European culture was the dominant culture during colonization and arguably remains so today. The fundamental principles of Aboriginal culture have always been quite different from the European principles that underly the mainstream world view in Canada.

WORLD VIEW

> A world view is the set of assumptions and beliefs on which a people's comprehension of the world is based. The stories, symbols, analogies, and metaphors that compose a people's mythology express a world view in coded form. Such expression occurs in informal, formal, unconscious, and conscious ways through family and community, through arts and media, and through economic, spiritual, governmental, and education institutions. (Cajete, 2000, p. 62)

What distinguishes the world view of the dominant culture in Canada? Amid the many cultures that compose Canada there is a dominant, mainstream culture. Members of a mainstream culture are sometimes hardly aware of its existence, but people from outside that culture tend to be acutely aware of it. According to Cajete, our culture gives us a particular world view that affects the way we live and our social and political actions. What are the stories, metaphors, symbols, and myths that express the mainstream Canadian world view?

FOUNDATIONS OF THE MAINSTREAM WORLD VIEW

The foundations of the mainstream Canadian world view include stories of creation, 17th-century philosophy, structures of governance, and capitalist assumptions about land and property.

Religious Creation Story

Our society is still deeply influenced by the Christian religion and its Bible. The Christian belief is that humans are created in the image of God and that humans, alone among the world's creatures, are endowed with a spirit. God has given humans "dominion over the fish of the sea, and over the fowl of the air, and over the cattle, and over all the Earth" (Genesis 1:25). This belief has profoundly shaped the mainstream culture's view of humanity's relationship with the natural world. The Bible's assertion that humans were made to cultivate the earth is in part responsible for the emphasis on agriculture in Western European society while the biblical view that human purpose is to populate the earth was, historically, one of the factors in the high populations of Western European societies.

Our conceptions of justice are rooted in religion. Until very recently, our principles of sentencing for criminal offences were based on notions of retribution and punishment. Although the purpose of sentencing, as expressed in section 718 of the *Criminal Code*, is now more in line with modern thinking, various signs and symbols within mainstream culture (for example, in film, books, and stories) still promote "an eye for an eye" view of justice. This concept of justice or judgment is rooted in biblical notions of punishment.

Finally, the Christian faith is a proselytizing religion, with many factions. This produced religious intolerance in Europe, one of the many reasons Europeans came to settle in new worlds. Proselytizing is based on the belief that there is only one God and one true religion and that others must convert to it or be damned. This way of thinking has affinities with ethnocentrism—the idea that others must live as we do because ours is the best way to live and all other ways are inferior. Not just First Nations people but all people from cultural traditions outside the mainstream one will have come across this ethnocentric propensity in members of the cultural majority.

CHAPTER 8 Pre-Contact

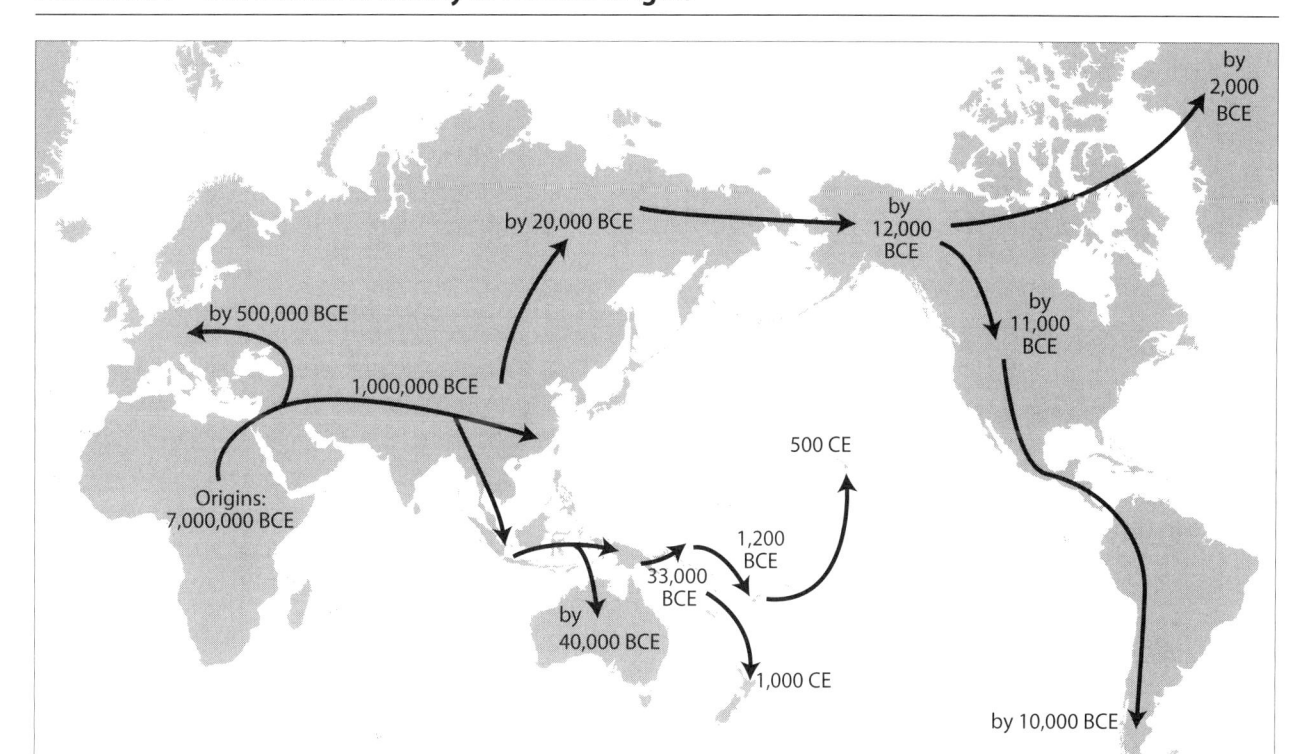

FIGURE 8.1 The Scientific Theory of Human Origins

Scientific Creation Story

Mainstream culture has a second creation story, the scientific one based on Charles Darwin's theory of evolution. This story locates the creation of humanity in the Fertile Crescent of Africa. (According to Christian scientists seeking to validate the biblical story, this is the true site of the Garden of Eden.) It has humans evolving through several stages of development to their final form, then migrating outward to occupy the earth in a gradual process (see figure 8.1).

Darwin's theory has had a huge impact on mainstream culture's world view. That impact is reflected in colloquialisms such as "dog eat dog" and "only the strong survive." The creation story based on Darwin's theory has profoundly affected the way we see both ourselves and life on this planet. It supports our view that life is about competition for resources and survival. For mainstream culture, the scientific view of creation has displaced to some extent the religious view of creation.

Migration Theories

If human life began in the Fertile Crescent of Africa, how did people come to live in the Americas? There are a number of theories as to how the human habitation of the Americas came about.

The first and most commonly held theory is that people came to the Americas over a land bridge called Beringia that once linked Siberia and Alaska. During the last ice age, vast sheets of ice froze 5 percent of the world's oceans. Water levels

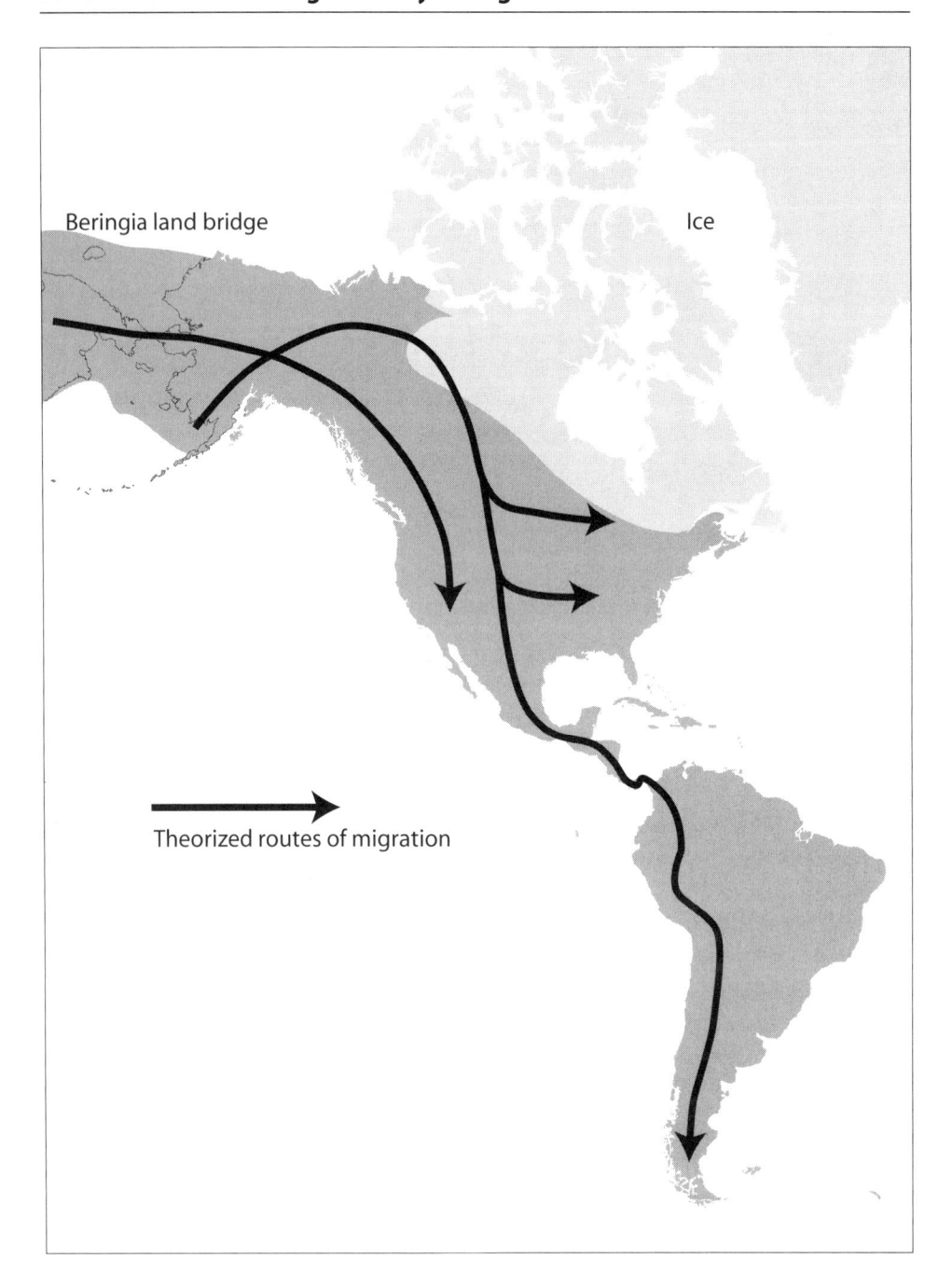

FIGURE 8.2 The Beringia Theory of Migration

dropped, exposing a dry land bridge that facilitated the crossing of people from Siberia to Alaska. There is evidence to support this theory. Alaska and Siberia have similar types of plant and animal life. The peoples who live in these two regions speak similar languages and have similar dental patterns. Tools for hunting and fishing that have been recovered through excavation in both areas are similar as well.

Some experts believe that once the First Peoples crossed over at Beringia, they travelled south down the only passable route—along the present border between Alberta and British Columbia. Other experts disagree and suggest that, according to glacial deposits, ancient pollen, and other organic material found in the area, this corridor was impassable during this period (see figure 8.2).

There are other scientific theories as to how the First Peoples came to be in the Americas. One theory is that these early migrations came by sea, across the Pacific, and then moved down the coast of the Americas. This is the Pacific Route theory. Some of the most persuasive evidence for this theory comes from South America. Ancient artifacts discovered in southern Chile and northeastern Brazil indicate that the First Peoples may have occupied the Americas far earlier than the Beringia theory suggests. Wallace has done DNA research that may support this theory. DNA evidence from some indigenous groups suggests that First Nations and Inuit peoples in the Americas have genetic mutations distinct from peoples in Siberia but common to indigenous peoples in Southeast Asia and the islands of the Pacific. The pattern of ocean currents also lends some support to the Pacific Route theory.

Yet another theory is that the First Peoples came by sea across the Atlantic. A recent excavation in Meadowcroft, Pennsylvania has revealed that hunting tools carbon dated to approximately 18,000 years ago match very closely tools excavated in Northern France and dated to 19,000 years ago. Again, our knowledge of oceanic current patterns lends support to this theory of transatlantic migration.

There is much scientific evidence yet to be uncovered. There are more theories of migration than those mentioned here. A Canadian archeologist states the following in a modern edition of *National Geographic*, in reference to the scientific methods used to trace the origins of First Peoples in America: "We are a discipline, not an exact science. We shouldn't pretend that we are. Everything is subject to interpretation." (Parfit, 2000)

There is one last theory that must be discussed: the theory of American Genesis. An archeologist named Jeffrey Goodman has argued that a unique and separate evolutionary line occurred in the Americas. He cites unconfirmed archeological evidence suggesting that humans occupied the Americas 100,000 years ago. He asserts that a process of reverse migration occurred, with people migrating from the Americas to Asia. This theory is not widely supported in the scientific community at present.

Migration theories or stories are part of what forms mainstream culture's world view. The resources spent on researching theories of migration reflect the importance mainstream culture places on primacy of occupancy. At the heart of migration theories is the notion that we are all immigrants to this land. This notion affects our approach to land rights.

PHILOSOPHY AND GOVERNANCE

Philosopher Thomas Hobbes wrote *Leviathan* in 1660, after the discovery of the Americas but prior to the intense colonizing of the Americas. Thomas Hobbes theorized that life in a state of nature, where there is no strong centralized government with absolute power, is "nasty, brutish, and short." His view of the nature of humans was not a positive one. He presumed that men would kill one another in order to survive. He advocated investing absolute power in a sovereign in order to maintain both structure and peace in society. Hobbes's historical circumstances influenced his opinion. Europe in that period experienced political instability, war, and plagues that wiped out huge portions of the population. There were huge class divisions between the wealthy and the poor, with wealth concentrated in the Church and monarchy. By today's standards, Europe was no democracy. The Church and the sovereign were seen as one concentrated source of power, while ordinary people had very little political control. It was a top-down structure of governance.

Our political structure today is very different. Many academics maintain that our current form of democratic government was to some extent modelled on the forms of government practised by First Nations peoples at the time of their first contact with European explorers.

Locke's Theory of Land Ownership

When we discuss land rights we tend to think in terms of rights to private ownership of property; that is our cultural understanding of people's relationship to land. This understanding is rooted in biblical texts and in political structures that date back to medieval times. Early in European history the division of the "haves" and "have nots" was determined by private land ownership. By the time the Americas were "discovered," most of the land in Europe was already in the hands of private land owners. Those who worked the land for landowners would almost certainly never own land, but would be labourers their entire lives. When the Americas were discovered, philosopher John Locke wrote a theory of land ownership which reinforced the established Western European notion of man's relationship to land. Locke's theory would rationalize the European seizure of land in the Americas. In brief, his theory went like this:

1. All land is owned by all of mankind.

2. Land can be transferred from general to private ownership by mixing one's labour with it.

3. Once converted to private ownership, land requires delineated boundaries (physically represented by fencing).

4. In order to have delineated boundaries, a society must have an established government and laws for enforcing private ownership.

5. Proviso: A man could take as much land as he required, provided he left "enough, and as good" for others. (Bishop, 2003)

Locke's theory is an important one: it will come up again later in this book in connection with the clearing of Native people from the land and our society's justifications for doing so. It is also relevant to our discussion, later in this chapter, of First Nations concepts of land and methods of government.

The concepts we have discussed thus far should be very familiar to all members of mainstream Canadian culture. They are the building blocks of our society's world view. Many other concepts could be discussed, particularly the rise of capitalism, but time will not permit. We must look at another world view, one that is very different from the mainstream one.

FIRST NATIONS

Before Europeans arrived on the shores of what would become Canada, there were self-governing nations of people living in organized groups in all the territories of the land. The land sustained 500,000 to 2,000,000 people in all (archeologists cannot provide more exact numbers) (Dickason, 1997, p. 43). According to archeologists, these nations had been living on the continent for a minimum of 10,000 years and most likely much longer. According to Native people, they have been here since time began. They occupied every space of the continent, using natural resources for sustenance. These nations have rich histories that are tens of thousands of years old. Given conservative archeological estimates of 15,000 years of First Nations occupancy, European history on the continent represents less than one-tenth of the histories of these nations (see figure 8.3).

Across the continents of Central and South America there were an estimated 2,200 languages spoken in the 16th century (Dickason, 2002, p. 5). In what would become Canada, 50 languages were spoken, which have been classified into 11 language families. Not all people who speak the same language can understand each other. Many languages have a number of different dialects—variations of a common language. Since language is the conduit of culture, we know that the cultures are as diverse as their languages. Often we approach Native people across Canada as if they are all part of one homogeneous group. This misconception often damages relationships between Native people and mainstream Canadians.

ORAL TRADITION

Language is used to convey culture from one generation to the next. In Native traditions, storytelling is the means of conveying values, social expectations, history, and knowledge. Through this oral tradition, knowledge passes down from one generation to the next, linking the past with the present and the future. Storytellers hold a special place in Native communities; storytelling is a tremendous responsibility that is taken very seriously. Stories are not passed down in a spontaneous manner; they are told and retold by the storyteller in teaching circles and formal ceremonies. Since few Native cultures traditionally found it necessary to devise any form of writing, these people have always been like living books. The stories they tell have certain characteristics in common:

- They reflect the culture and natural environment in which the people live. Cultures that live near the ocean, such as the Haida, contain elements of the sea, such as water and conch shells, in their stories. Groups that live on the plains include buffalo and prairie grass in their stories.

- They provide answers regarding the meaning and order of the world and regarding how to live a good life. They also provide warnings against breaching cultural values and norms. (See appendix 8.1 for two conservation stories from Alaskan oral tradition.)

FIGURE 8.3   **Cultural and Language Groups Prior to Contact**

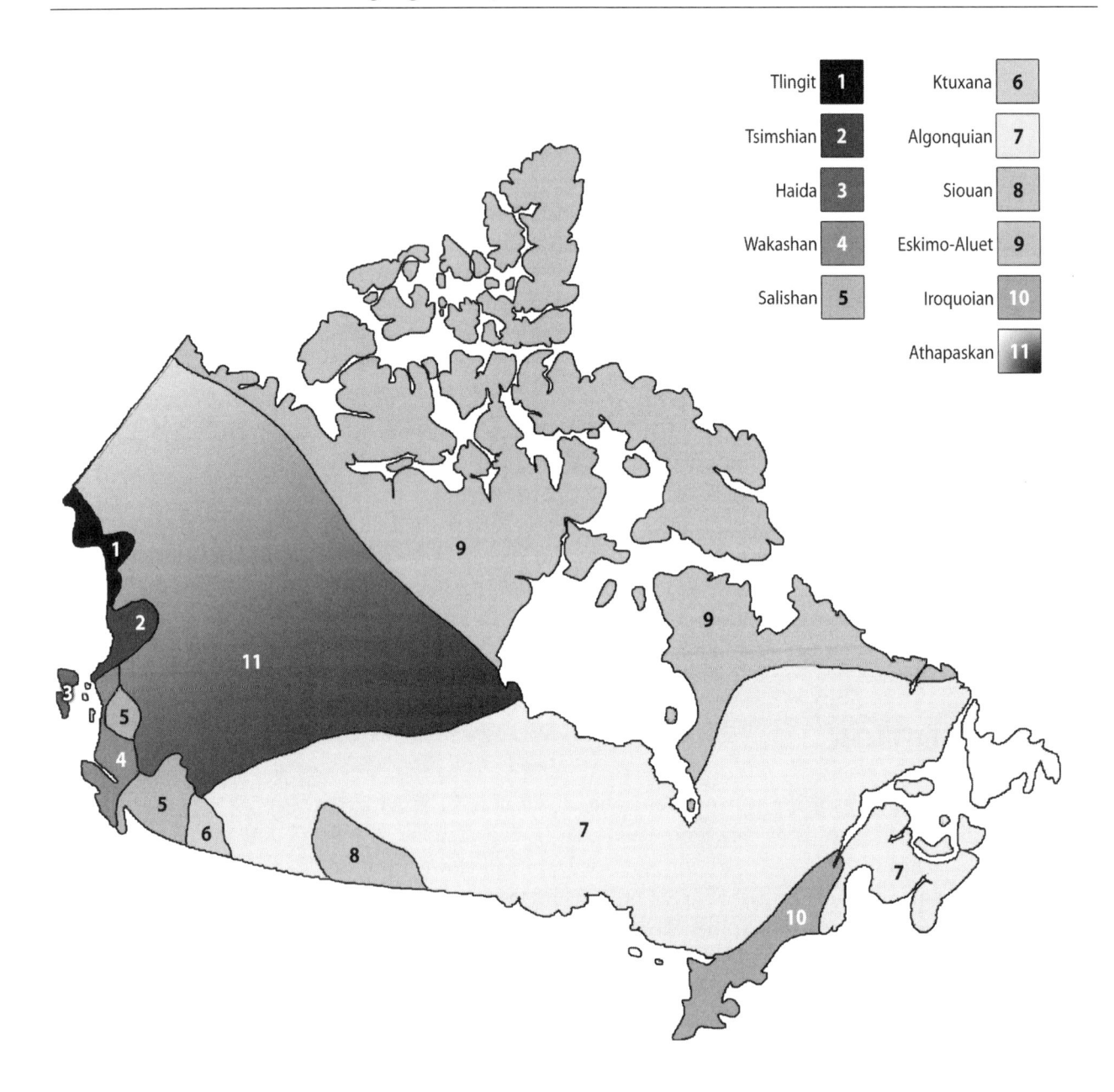

Tlingit	1	Ktuxana	6
Tsimshian	2	Algonquian	7
Haida	3	Siouan	8
Wakashan	4	Eskimo-Aluet	9
Salishan	5	Iroquoian	10
		Athapaskan	11

- They often refer to places that the storyteller's culture deems sacred, such as Dreamer's Rock on Birch Island near Manitoulin Island in Ontario—a sacred place where the Anishnaabe go to fast and receive visions.
- They are rich in symbolism that sheds light on the origin of First Peoples as well as on their world view.

European historians have tended to question the reliability of oral histories, believing that they are susceptible to being embellished, misinterpreted, or misunderstood. But they have found that the earliest recordings of Native stories, compiled by Jesuits in the early 1600s, are identical to the stories being circulated today. This attests to the accuracy and completeness of oral transmission from one generation to the next.

Members of the European tradition need to be reminded that many of their written histories were in fact derived from oral traditions that subsisted for thousands of years before anyone wrote any part of the narrative down. Stories about the Garden of Eden and Noah's ark, and other European creation stories, are, like Native stories, filled with allegory and symbolism.

Written Records of First Nations History

Prior to European contact, few First Nations and Inuit cultures had written records of their histories. In South America, some groups created *hieroglyphics*. These pictures and symbols represented specific words. The Haudenosaunee (Iroquois) recorded laws, teachings, and historical events, such as treaty signings, on *wampum*—shells placed in certain designs to depict meanings. The Anishnaabe (Ojibwe) and Nehiyaw (Cree) wrote symbols and scripts on birch bark to record their historical events and teachings. Many cultures created *pictographs* (drawings and paintings on rock walls) and *petroglyphs* (carvings and inscriptions on rocks). Both methods were used to represent the spiritual experiences, such as dreams, visions, and prophecies, of the chiefs and shamans.

The Europeans who first met the First Nations created most of the written records we have of these societies. In the 1600s, Jesuit priests wrote detailed accounts of their contact with these cultures as they tried to convert them to Christianity. The stories told to the Jesuits by First Nations peoples are consistent with the stories told by the Elders and other storytellers today. In other words, the Jesuits' journals reinforce the idea that these stories are timeless.

CREATION STORIES

One of the most important subjects in First Nations and Inuit stories concerns their origins. Where did the people come from? In all stories, the people were either created from the land in which they have traditionally lived or they came to the land from some other spiritual place. Creation stories are important to a culture because they situate it in the world and shape its world view. Animals figure prominently in Native stories of creation, working collaboratively with humans. (See appendixes 8.2, 8.3, and 8.4 for Ojibwe, Mohawk, and Cree creation stories.) Not only humans but animals and other natural elements are endowed with spirit by the Creator. The Creator gives humans stewardship of the natural world and compels them to live in harmony with it.

Concepts of Land and Spirituality

From these creation stories come foundations for a distinct world view. Intrinsic to this view is the connection to land. Land is more than a geographic territory or a potential source of wealth. It is a sacred living entity, with its own rhythms and cycles. The life and spirituality of the First Nations peoples has always been connected to the land in a close, symbiotic relationship. Because the people were born with the land as part of the common creation, they cannot be separated or differentiated from it.

First Nations peoples' spirituality is connected to the land as well. Their spiritual practices developed to reflect this connection and these practices are as diverse as the nations themselves.

Community Organization

Groups within the First Nations organized themselves in different ways depending on their unique environments and spiritual beliefs. Generally they organized themselves into communal groups that were egalitarian, self-sufficient, and connected to the land and its resources. Often they were connected to other specific nations in cooperative relationships for trade and sharing of resources. These relationships were often set out in treaties which outlined each nation's responsibility to the others and at times delineated territorial boundaries for the purpose of resource management and harvest. Often several nations would be unified in a confederacy.

The Haudenosaunee, for example, were a collection of five nations: the Mohawk, Seneca, Oneida, Onandaga, and Cayuga. Each nation had its own distinctive clan system. The Mohawk were bear, turtle, or wolf clan. The other nations had their respective clans. The Five Nations were united in a "League of Peace" otherwise known as the Iroquois Confederacy. The Confederacy was governed by a council of 50 chiefs representing the participant nations. Decisions were made by consensus among the chiefs and by the chief's consultation with the people whose interests he represented. Women had tremendous influence in the governmental system since they selected the chiefs and had the right also to remove a chief who proved to be unsatisfactory.

> [W]hen decisions had to be made that affected the whole community, each clan would sit around a central fire with all other clans. Decisions the clan made together may include when to move, conservation of the resources of the territories, the striking of alliances and relationships with other nations and how to implement these decisions. Usually after much discussion and further consultation with their clan members, decisions would be made that would respect the interests of all clans and their members. Decisions were not arrived at in the same manner as western society today through majority vote. When decisions had to be made it would be through a consensus process. All people had to agree with the action or no action would be taken. (Clarkson, Morrissette, & Régallet, 1992, p. 16)

These forms of government indicate that cooperation and consensus are among the foundations of the First Nations world view. Their spiritual teachings, by advising that decisions be made in the best interests not only of all living people but of all people of the next seven generations, encourage the long-term continuation of this view. First Nations forms of governments are based on equality and on balancing individual interests against group interests, with group interests always taking precedence.

Because everything is connected in the First Nations world view, spirituality influences land use, and both influence governance structures. There is no separation between these elements as there is in mainstream tradition. The conception of individual rights is not alien to the First Nations system of social organization; it just holds a place of less importance than group or collective rights. Negotiated rights to harvest territories are not individual rights, they are collective rights of the

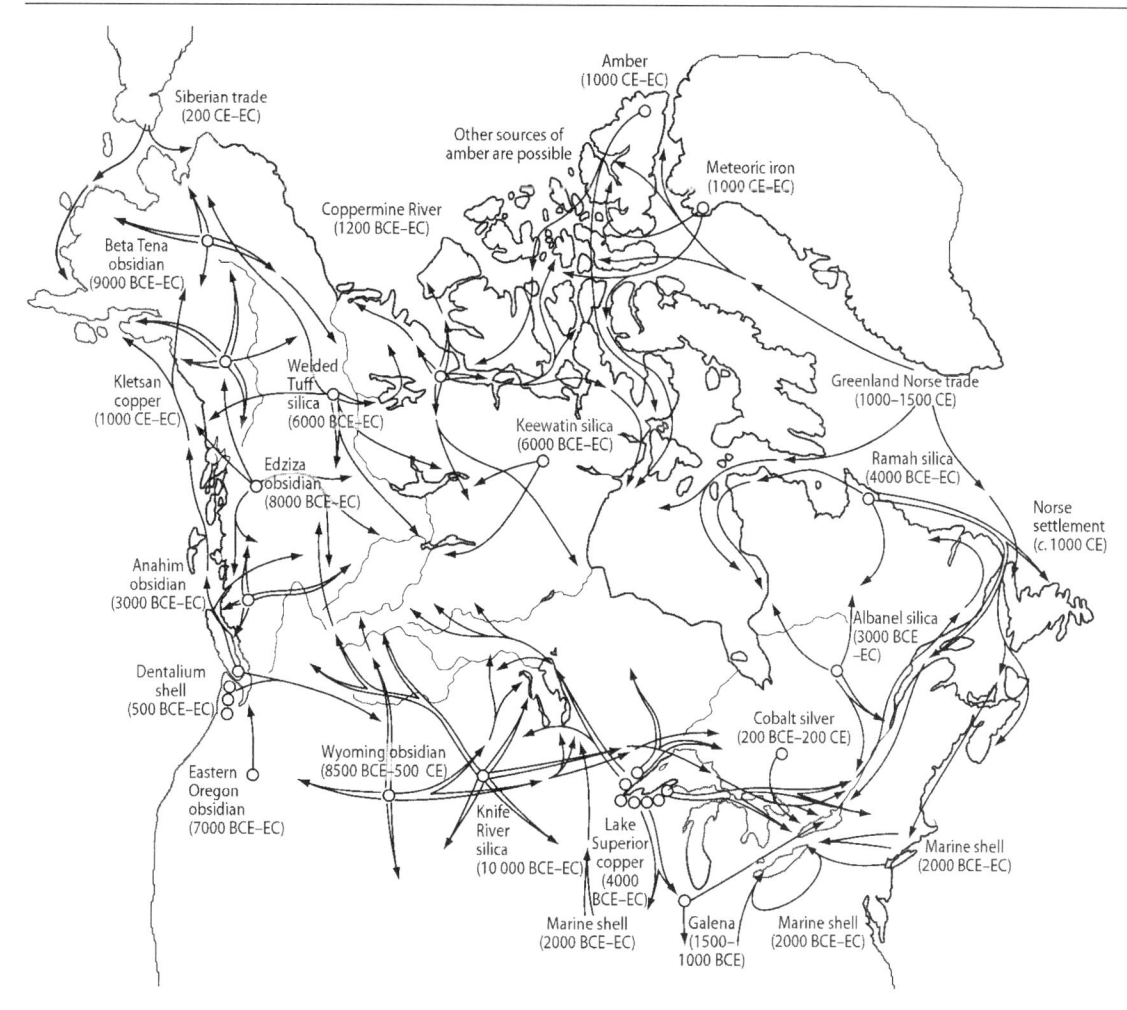

FIGURE 8.4 Trade Patterns Prior to European Contact

Source: Adapted from R.C. Harris (Ed.), *Historical Atlas of Canada: Vol. 1—From the Beginning to 1800* (Toronto: University of Toronto Press, 1987), plate 14.

group. The harvest does not belong to the individual harvester but to the collective group, and is distributed according to subsistence needs. The focus of First Nations teachings is the individual's responsibilities to the group rather than the individual's rights within the group.

International Organization

Individual First Nations did not exist in a vacuum. They were very aware of one another and entered into relationships to exchange knowledge and to trade material goods. In this way, they influenced one another's cultures. Sometimes nations traded for natural resources not available within their own territory. Agricultural societies such as the Iroquois traded their excess agricultural products. Trade took place over vast areas of the Americas (see figure 8.4).

CONCLUSION

When we consider the lifestyle and occupancy patterns of First Nations people in the Americas, we see that they lived in politically organized groups in territories with fluid boundaries. With respect to Locke's theory of land ownership, First Nations peoples certainly did occupy land in the Lockean sense. They managed the resources within their territories and had boundaries negotiated with other nations on this continent. The main cultural difference consists in Locke's emphasis on the individual nature of land ownership. First Nations, by contrast, had a government structure in which individuals were part of a collective whose well-being was primary rather than secondary. These differing emphases on collective rights in one culture and individual rights in the other have complicated the relationship between settler nations and First Nations since first contact. Although the current mainstream political structure in Canada has borrowed heavily from First Nations government structure, the two systems are based on different conceptions of the world. The gulf that separates Native and non-Native world views is where misunderstandings and miscommunications developed long ago and continue in Canadian society today.

REFERENCES

Bishop, J.D. (2003). The Lockean basis of Iroquoian land ownership. In R.B. Anderson & R.M. Bone (Eds.), *Natural resources and Aboriginal people in Canada: Readings, cases, and commentary.* Toronto: Captus Press.

Cajete, G. (2000). Philosophy of native science. In G. Cajete, *Native science: Natural laws of interdependence.* Santa Fe, NM: Clear Light Publishers.

Clarkson, L., Morrissette, V., & Régallet, G. (1992). *Our responsibility to the seventh generation: Indigenous peoples and sustainable development.* Winnipeg: International Institute for Sustainable Development. http://www.iisd.org/pdf/seventh_gen.pdf.

Dickason, O.P. (1997). *Canada's First Nations: A history of founding peoples from earliest times* (2nd ed.). Toronto: Oxford University Press.

Ellis, C.D. (Ed.). (1995). *Cree legends and narratives from the west coast of James Bay.* Winnipeg: University of Manitoba Press.

Frideres, J.S. (1997). *Aboriginal peoples in Canada: Contemporary conflicts* (5th ed.). Scarborough, ON: Prentice Hall.

Parfit, Michael. (2000, December). Hunt for the first Americans. *National Geographic 198*(6).

APPENDIX 8.1

Two Conservation Myths from Alaska

The Indigenous Peoples of Alaska have long known that natural balance, indeed their very subsistence lifestyles, depends much upon how the land is treated. Whereas the Western philosophy of environmental usage was, and still is to an extent, "Take everything and give nothing," the natives of Alaska, like most Native American Indian Peoples, have traditionally regarded the land as both provider and protector. To them, the land and its resources are sacred and the connection between human actions and the Earth's welfare is clear.

From this understanding, numerous taboo myths and legends, didactic in function, exist to illustrate and warn that the land must be treated with respect and stewardship. In these narratives from long-lived oral traditions, the consequences of violating the land and its many resources are portrayed in such horrific accounts that young listeners will remember the lessons throughout their lives and pass on the moralistic message to the next generation.

The following two narratives, "The Ptarmigan Story" from Inupiaq Eskimo and "The Squirrel Shaman" from southeast Alaska Tsimshian, show what happens when nature is destroyed indiscriminately.

The Ptarmigan Story

When young boys are trained to hunt and fish, one of the first lessons they are taught is to respect and care for the game they hunt. If animals are mistreated, then they may no longer allow themselves to be killed for food and clothing, and the Eskimos would certainly die of hunger or freeze to death. Therefore, fathers always tell their children to show respect when they kill an animal.

One day, though, two young brothers left their village to check ptarmigan snares. As they approached the traps, they saw one white bird caught by the leg in one of the snares. The bird was frightened and tried to escape. It jumped up and down and tried to fly away, but the string was very tight around its leg.

The brothers watched the bird and then one spoke to the other.

"I wonder if ptarmigan can fly straight without eyes?" he asked.

The other brother laughed and poked the bird's eyes out with a small branch. Then he threw the blind ptarmigan into the air. It tried to fly but because it could not see, it kept crashing into the hillside and into small bushes. The brothers chased it and they laughed aloud.

Then the other brother asked, "I wonder if ptarmigan can fly without feathers?"

They began to pluck the blind bird while it was still alive! Then they threw it up into the air as before, but each time it just fell to the frozen ground. They did this many times until the bird was nearly dead. When it was time to check the other snares they dropped the poor bird and left it to die without even taking its meat for food.

The next morning both boys awoke feeling very sick. They had the fever and they kept throwing up. The shaman was sent for, but he could do nothing for them. He gave them special medicine, but nothing stopped their suffering. Soon, blood began to pour from their eyes!

The shaman told the parents that the sickness was too great. He said that they must have broken a powerful taboo.

That night the two boys, who had shown such great disrespect to the ptarmigan, died in terrible agony.

The Squirrel Shaman

In a small village upon the Skenna River, three young brothers would hunt and kill squirrels. They hung the tiny furs to dry and collected the tails. Together they had killed so many squirrels that they had to go farther and farther away from home to find more.

One day, one of the boys was hunting alone far from the village when he saw a perfectly white squirrel running along the trunk of a very tall tree. The boy raised his bow to shoot, but he saw that it was so pretty that he could not kill this one.

The white squirrel ran into a hole in the tree and turned around and motioned for the boy to follow. The handsome young man approached and looked inside. He saw that it was a house with a great many empty beds. It was a community house for many people, but there was no one inside. It was entirely empty except for the white squirrel who stood in the middle waving at him to come inside.

"I cannot come in," said the Tsimshian boy. "I am much too big." "Lean your bow against the Great House, and then you will be able to come inside," replied the white squirrel.

The boy did so and to his surprise he became small enough to walk into the empty hall. He saw that the white squirrel was a beautiful young woman who was wearing a white fur coat. She told the boy to follow her up to the top of the Great Tree. When they arrived, an old man who looked like a chief spoke to him.

"I have been waiting for you to come. Why have you killed all of my people? All of my children and grandchildren are gone except for my favorite granddaughter who led you to the Great House. Why have you done this?"

The young man looked around and saw that this room too was empty, and then he answered the old chief, "I have not killed your people. I have never killed a person before. I do not know what you are saying, old father."

"Look around you," said the chief. "See how we are alone here now where once these halls were full of my people."

The boy looked again and replied, "But I did not kill anyone."

The old man came close to the boy and spoke to him again, "I am the chieftain of the Squirrel People. You and your brothers have killed all of my children and now their skins hang outside your house."

Suddenly the boy understood what had happened. He looked at the girl and saw that she was indeed very beautiful. He felt ashamed and saddened.

"We did not know that you live like people. We did not know that you love your children and grandchildren. I am sorry. Forgive me. I will tell my brothers not to hunt your people any longer."

But the chief was still sad. "It is too late to stop killing us. We are all dead now. My granddaughter and I are all that is left."

"But I did not mean to kill you all!" exclaimed the young hunter as a tear filled his eye. "Is there not something I can do?" he asked the old father Squirrel.

"There is a way," said the chief. "I can make you a great shaman and you can return my people."

The young Tsimshian agreed, and so the old man began to work his powerful magic. He took the boy outside and tied his limbs to the tree. Then he pushed sharp needles with string through his skin and pulled them tight in every direction. There was a piercing needle for every dead squirrel. The boy screamed in pain, but the old man said that the pain was part of the power. When he was finished, the chief left the boy hanging for three days. On the third day he returned and sang his magic song for three more days. He did not rest, and he did not eat or drink either. After that, the chief left the boy alone.

One day, the boy's two younger brothers were out hunting squirrels when they came across the carcass of their brother who had been lost for six days. It was hanging in a tall tree just as they had hung the squirrel furs at their house. They cut him down and took his body home.

That night, after they arrived with their dead brother, a magic filled the entire village and all of the dead squirrels came back to life.

They ran back to the Great House and told the chief what had happened. After all of the squirrels were returned, the spirit of the young man flew back into his dead body and returned him to life. From that time on, he was a great and powerful shaman and the Tsimshian did not kill squirrels.

Source: John E. Smelcer, "Two Conservation Myths from Alaska Native Oral Tradition" (Summer 1996) vol. 39, no. 4 *Literary Review* 478-81.

APPENDIX 8.2

The Ojibwe Creation Story

The Creation Story of the Anishinabe is told as the Seven Fires of Creation, each fire being an era of time. How long each one of these are, we don't know. But in the time that the universe knows, they are seen as eons of time: from the place before time even was, when there was only silence and emptiness and darkness and cold, to the time when earth was finally created and life was placed upon its surface.

Creation unfolded in seven stages. At first we are told that there, in the vast unknown, was only darkness, emptiness, silence and cold: forever and without boundaries. And that somewhere in that darkness a sound was heard. It was a sound like the rumbling of the thunder far in the distance. Then there was silence again. And after a long unimaginable silence, the sound was heard again, only this time it seemed closer. This is the way that the very beginning stage of creation is talked about: this sound that rumbled in the distance, which after each long period of silence would be heard again. Each time it would seem closer and closer, until, finally, after an incredible time of emptiness, a blinding flash of light and a deafening sound of thunder broke the long silence. What we are given to understand is that there must have been "Someone" listening in the darkness to that sound; that what was taking place was the first spark of creation, the first explosion of creative activity outward.

And then, it is said, there was a shaking and shimmering sound: a sound like the shaking of seeds in a gourd, that was heard everywhere in the darkness, without end. "What was that sound?" we are given to ask. What was shimmering and shaking? What were the seeds? Were they the thoughts in the Creator's mind? But, it is said, there was another sound. It was a different sound, a "feeling sound." That sound was before the shimmering shaking sound; it was before the rumbling sound that came from the distance. It was before all else. It was the First Thought that ever was. There in the centre of the darkness, that sound, that thought went out into the vast reaches of the unknown. Myriads of thoughts emerged from that first thought. They went on forever in the darkness, there being nothing out there for them to bounce back from. It was known, now, that a "place" had to be created to send the thoughts to.

In the centre there was also a rhythm that was generated from the very heart, the very centre where the Thought first emerged. That heart throb was at the centre of all that was to be. It moved out from the centre in great rhythmic circles, filling the whole empty void. And so it was that even in the beginning, creation could not take place by Thought alone, but by the Heart also. The rhythm of the heartbeat permeated the vastness. The thoughts, touching on the darkness, left a star; the star world was born. By that First Heartbeat and by that First Thought, the universe was created. The First Thought is the first fire of creation.

In the second fire of creation, he created a light. He built, in the darkness, a fire: the first fire, the Creator's fire which is the Sun. He did this to light up a place in the darkness, in order to create. Around that fire, he traced out a great circle and assigned the four directions.

Then he created another light: the Moon whom we know as grandmother, universal woman, the Grand Woman of the sky world. In completing this, he had created Sun and Moon, the twinness of all reality. Without this twinness, nothing else could unfold; so in all things, there must be a twin in order for life to evolve to completion in the created reality. All of wholeness is composed of twinness. In all things we see the twin. Sunrise and sunset, day and night, the two sides of being—even in you there is the twin. The unfolding of twinness is the third stage of creation, and is thus known as the third fire.

Then, in the fourth stage of creation—having created the star world with his thoughts, having built the first fire in the universe (the Sun), and having created the twin (Grandmother Moon)—the whole of the universe was established and he caused the universe to move according to the four directions. This was the fourth fire: the First Movement. And so we know that at the fourth stage in the development of all things, in the unfolding of all life, is the beginning of movement, measured by the principles of the four directions. When you have four, then you can have movement, complete in itself and moving upon itself.

Then he gathered all of what he had created and encapsulated it in a shape and form. It contained the inspiration and the motivation to be. It was possessed of intention and it held in its blueprint the two sides of the whole (the twinness that makes up life itself), and the four quarters of the whole which is the cause of movement. By taking those things and shaping them into a form, he created a Seed, the germ of life. For every form, every shape, every being that would be given life, he shaped a seed, within which was the potential to be. And this was the fifth fire of creation: the First Seed. The Creator took his seed-thoughts and shaped them into the kernels of life essence, to be reflected back to him as creation's every possibility when planted in fertile ground.

Having completed this, he began to make a place to send the seeds of life. And so he created this Earth. Four times he tried, and the fourth time he completed this world, as we know it today. When he had completed the Earth and caused the waters to flow in and around the Earth (being her veins and arteries to carry the force of life itself), then all the birds carried the seeds to spread them over the ground. Then he saw the beauty of the one that he created: the Earth. In this Earth was absolute perfection, absolute wholeness, harmony and balance. All was complete in her, the First Earth, the First Woman. And in having created her, his creation was complete. Then he took from his first fire, the Sun, and placed a heart at the very centre of that first woman, making her first mother: the Mother Earth. She was a mother with a heart, who gave birth to all the seeds of life, her children. This is the sixth fire of creation: the Creation of Earth. Out of his desire to create, to bring into actuality his seed-thoughts, to make them real, to cause his thoughts to bounce back to himself, he therefore created this world. Out of love he created her. Out of his desire to create the most beautiful place to give the finest expression to his thoughts, so he created the Earth. And so it was that out of kindness he created all of creation; that this Earth was made as a place for the highest expression of the Grandfather's desire to manifest and embody his dream: to give shape and form, intention, purpose and meaning to the spirit of life itself.

In the seventh fire of creation, he wished to create "one in his own image." And so he took of the very created world itself: he took four parts of the Earth and he shaped those four parts together, and formed a physical being. Then of his own thoughts, as many as the stars in the universe, he placed within that first being. With this was given the ability and the capacity to hold the very thoughts of the Creator himself. The Creator gave to the first human being his own thoughts. Then he caused to beat in his breast that same heart-throb, that same rhythm that was there at the beginning at the centre of the universe. And so it is said that he caused to beat in the heart of Anishinabe the very rhythm, the very heartbeat, of the creator himself. Then he breathed into him his first breath, the spirit of life itself. And so, being made of this earth, the physical vessel, and being vested with mind, heart and spirit, he was lowered to the Earth: the First Human Being, made of Earth and Sky.

Though knowing that he was formed outside of the created realm, he could see that he belonged to the Earth, being made of the very stuff of the earth. He desired to be a part of this creation, as all other beings of creation were already seen and felt to be, as he saw them moving about on the earth. It was his every desire to be at home in this world, part of that same great harmony and great balance of life.

He wanted to be a part of the great beauty of this creation, seeing how everyone of this creation was kind and was true to the ways that they were created, and shared in the harmony of life. Seeing the strength and the beauty of all that was created on this earth, he too desired to be as this earth and as the creation. And so it is said that, as he approached the earth, he pointed his toes so that somehow, if at all possible, when he touched down on this earth, he would not stamp out or crush even the smallest blade of grass, the tiniest flower, the smallest living creature that crawled upon the earth. Rather, he would come down in and amidst the creation and be a living and loving, harmonious part of all that is.

This is how Original Human Being touched down upon the Earth. That is how the First Human Being, Anishinabe, the red colour of man, met his Mother the Earth for the first time. And from that time, Anishinabe has always known his Mother and has always felt his relationship to the family of creation. Being vested of spirit, the human being comes from the Creator from whom he receives his purpose and intention to be. Through him flows, always, his life force that comes directly from the Creator. But with him also comes his desire to be a part of this life and to give the finest and highest expression to his being in this world. He has within him this desire to reflect back to the Creator the Creator's very intention in making him in his image and lowering him to this earth.

And so, in these seven stages of creation, we see how all things began for Anishinabe, the red colour of the human being. From the first thought, to the final image, the creation unfolded. In the same way, all of creative activity continues to evolve, through those seven stages of unfoldment. It is still reflected in all life activity, even to this day. Everywhere we should be able to see this. From the first thought of bringing new life into this world by couples who come together, bringing about conception itself; to the first division of that first cell, the twinness of life—of man and woman coming together inside the womb; to the first movement within the womb; to the development of that seed to its fullest potential as a human being; so life unfolds according to the original blueprint of creation. It follows that a good and kind and caring place to be in this world is fashioned—the family, the earth-home, and it is completed by the emergence of the first image—the actual human being emerging from the womb to place footsteps for the first time upon the earth. In this natural creative process itself we can see the seven stages of unfoldment. And so it is with all of life.

Even from the first thought in the darkness of our confusion and of our unknowing, to the conception of an idea, we put together the darkness with the light and we create the twinness of our reality. In our thoughts, in our mind, we can cause the idea to move within ourselves and then introduce that idea to others so that they too can be a part of the movement and inspiration it causes. From there we create a seed of change within ourselves and around ourselves. We then make a way; make a place to plant that seed within ourselves and within others, for all to benefit from. The final result is a new being, a realized dream, that is created from this first thought that emerged in the darkness of our own mind. From the idea to the reality is again reflected the process of creation.

And so, Anishinabe can see that if he knows his creation story, if she knows her creation story, they know also how all of life moves. They can know how life comes to be. All of life is a creative process that began in this original way and continues in the same way in all aspects of our life. In all places and all facets of creation, and creative activity, these seven stages are reflected.

Source: Based on the Teaching of the Seven Fires of Creation by Edward Benton-Banai, rendered as a poem entitled "The Seven Fires of the Ojibway Nation" and published in *The Sounding Voice*, Indian Country Press, 1978.

APPENDIX 8.3

The Mohawk Creation Story

In the beginning, Onkweshona, or man-like beings lived in the regions above. They knew not what it was to weep or to cry; sorrow and death were thus unknown to them. And the lodges of the man beings were long, each one belonging to a large family of one clan. In one of these lodges there was a woman who had been born with strong power. People such as this were called down-fended, because they slept on beds of soft down. They were always kept separated from the other people of the lodge, and were cared for in their childhood by an older aunt or uncle.

One day, when the people were out from the lodge, a young man entered and went up to this down-fended woman. She reached out and touched the man, and he died. The woman later became pregnant. She gave birth to a daughter called Aientsik meaning Fertile Earth. Aientsik was a beautiful girl. She grew up in the lodge of her mother, and became a healthy young woman. One day, however, she became ill. Sickness was not known to the man beings, and they did not know what to do.

Aientsik went out one night and sought the spirit of her father, who told her to do the following: "You must travel, my daughter, to the village of Tharonhiawakon, or, He Who Holds Up The Sky. In his village that is lit by the Tree of the Standing Light, you will become his bride. On your way to the village of the Tree of the Standing Light, you must be careful not to touch any man or animal that comes along. When you come to the stream between our village and that of Tharonhiawakon, you will find a maple log. Cross the stream on this log, and accept help from none."

Aientsik left the village of her people and traveled to the east. When she arrived at the stream she found the log, but before she could push the log out into the water, Kahahserine appeared. Kahahserine is the White Dragon of the Fire Body; he sometimes appears in the sky as a falling star or meteor. Kahahserine asked Aientsik if she would like some help. She became frightened and ran back to the village of her people. Just as she left the stream, however, Kahahserine reached out and barely touched her on the shoulder.

When Aientsik arrived back in her village she sought the spirit of her father. He asked if Kahahserine had touched her, and she replied no. He then advised his daughter to return to the stream and to make way for the village of the tree of the Standing Light. Aientsik arrived at the stream's shoreline again, and finding the maple log where she had left it, crossed over to the other side.

When Aientsik arrived at the village of the Tree of Standing Light, she sought out Tharonhiawakon, the chief of the upper world.

She said, "I have come to be your bride."

He said, "Good, make me some supper."

When night time came, Aientsik slept on one side of the lodge, and her new husband slept on the other. They did not really know each other that well, and they did not think that it was such a good idea to start having children right away. Even so, Aientsik became pregnant.

This disturbed the mind of Tharonhiawakon and he had a dream. Tharonhiawakon brought the people of his village together to try to guess the meaning of his dream. None of the people could correctly guess the dream of the Sky Holder.

Finally the White Dragon of the Fire Body stepped forward and said, "Tharonhiawakon, surely your dream means this, that your new wife is pregnant, and you are upset. Therefore, you will take the Tree of the Standing Light by the trunk, you will uproot this tree and place your wife by the abyss. Once done, you will push her through the hole, and cause her to leave the upper world forever."

When Kahahserine had finished speaking, the chief of the upper world said, "Yes, what you have said is true, and by correctly guessing the meaning of my dream, it is as if you have made it come true."

Tharonhiawakon then uplifted the Tree of the Standing Light, he placed his pregnant wife at the edge of the hole, and he pushed her through into the space below.

Aientsik fell. Below her, all of the universe was water. The animals of the water saw her falling, but because the sky was blue, as well as the water, they did not know if she was falling from the sky, or coming up from the bottom of the lake. All of the water animals had an argument about this. The otter said that she was coming up from the bottom of the lake. The beaver agreed, as did the muskrat. The geese and the ducks, however, said that she was falling from the sky. They flew up, and breaking the fall of Aientsik, let her rest upon their backs, and brought her gently down to the surface of the water.

In the meanwhile, a great turtle came up out of the water and volunteered to be a resting place for Aientsik, or Fertile Earth. The beaver, otter and muskrat each dove to the bottom of the lake to try to bring up a mouthful of earth to place on the back of the turtle. The beaver failed and died. The otter failed and also died. But the muskrat was successful. He placed the mud on the back of the turtle and Aientsik was laid down to rest.

When she woke, there was a fire next to her and a pot of corn soup. The back of the turtle had grown in size and it was visibly continuing to grow with every passing minute. Aientsik stood up on the earth, and walked about it, helping in the process of its creation. Every day when she returned to her resting place, there was a fire and a supply of corn, or some beans or squash for her to eat. Corn, beans and squash have been known ever since as the three sister-providers of the Mohawk people.

Aientsik was pregnant and she soon gave birth to a daughter, Tekawerahkhwa, or Gusts of Wind. This daughter grew to maturity, and she soon was a beautiful young woman. One day when Tekawerahkhwa was sleeping in the forest, a man being came up to her and passed two arrows over her stomach. One arrow was tipped with flint, the other was a maple shaft. Tekawerahkhwa became pregnant with twins.

After about nine months, these twins inside the womb of Tekawerahkhwa had an argument. One of the twins, called Thawiskaron, or Flint, said that the best way to leave their mother was by way of the armpit. The other twin, called Okwiraseh, or Young Tree, said that the best way to leave was by between the legs. Before the argument was over, Thawiskaron pierced through his mother's armpit and killed her. Okwiraseh followed, but was blamed for killing his mother by Thawiskaron and his grandmother, Aientsik.

Aientsik asked, "Who is it that killed my daughter?"

Thawiskaron replied, "It was Okwiraseh, my brother."

Okwiraseh was then thrown into the forest by his grandmother and left to die. This was not to be his fate, however. Tharonhiawakon came down from the upper world and taught his grandson how to live in the forest. He taught him how to hunt and to make foods from the things that grew about the earth. He taught him to make the lodges of the Onkweshona and the method of preparing the bark.

Finally, Tharonhiawakon told Okwiraseh to prepare the earth for the coming of man. He told him to make the earth beautiful and to provide growing space for the three sister-providers, corn, beans and squash. Okwiraseh made the Indian corn to grow tall and strong. His brother Thawiskaron took the corn, however, and threw it into the fire, burning the ends and ruining that part of the ear. Okwiraseh rushed to take the corn out from the fire, however, and saved the rest of the ear. Notice today how the end of the corn cob cannot be eaten. Okwiraseh made all of the rivers to run in two directions. This way, men would be able to travel in any direction without having to paddle against the current. Thawiskaron changed the course of the rivers and made them all go just one way. He then threw large boulders in the river in order to prevent river travel. Fortunately, Okwiraseh caught Thawiskaron in time and stopped him, but many of the rivers were made difficult to travel on.

Okwiraseh asked the various animals how they would avoid man in the hunt. When the animals responded, Okwiraseh changed that part of the animal that was going to have a special advantage over man. One day, as Okwiraseh was going about the earth, he noticed that there were no animals about. The animals had all been captured by Thawiskaron and locked into a cave. The season began to grow cold and there was no game. Okwiraseh located the cave where the animals had been confined and he moved back the rock holding them in and freed them.

After this last confrontation with his brother Thawiskaron, Okwiraseh decided to challenge his brother to one last contest of strength. He asked his brother to meet him on top of a mountain deep within the Adirondacks and play a game of dice. The winner was to rule the day, the loser the night.

When Thawiskaron showed up for this contest he brought his own dice. Okwiraseh agreed to use the bowl of Thawiskaron, but not his dice. He called to the sparrows and asked them to give their small heads for dice. The sparrows agreed.

Okwiraseh then called out to all of creation and said, "All you things that are alive, send me your power now so that I may be victorious, and so that all of you may live!"

The animals and the plants, the very earth itself sent power to Okwiraseh and he proved victorious over his brother.

Thawiskaron was banished to the lower world, below the turtle and the earth, only to come out at night when it is dark and cold. Okwiraseh assumed preeminence on the earth during the day, and continued to carry out his grandfather's command to continue the work of making the earth a better place for the coming of man.

One day while traveling about the earth, reviewing all of his work, Okwiraseh came across a man being, Hatowi, blocking the path through the forest.

Hatowi said, "What are you doing here, walking about my creation, as if you had made it?"

Okwiraseh responded that he, Okwiraseh, had done all of this work of creation, and not Hatowi. The two men agreed to a contest of strength. Whoever could make the mountains to move was the agreed upon maker of the earth, and the loser was to serve the winner for all the rest of time. Hatowi went first. He commanded the mountain to move, but of course the mountain stayed in its place.

Then Okwiraseh said, "See, you are not the maker of the earth and all here present that it contains."

Hatowi said, "But you too must try to make the mountain to move."

Okwiraseh replied, "Yes, but first you must turn around and close your eyes."

Then Okwiraseh ordered the mountain to move right up behind Hatowi. The mountain moved, and when Hatowi turned around, he slammed his face right into the side of the mountain. This twisted his face and bent his nose all out of shape.

Hatowi was so surprised that he asked Okwiraseh not to hurt him. Hatowi promised to help mankind for all times. Hatowi said that if men would address him as Grandfather, burn tobacco to him and carve his image in the trunk of a living tree, he would cure men of their sicknesses. Okwiraseh agreed to this and the great curing ceremony of the False Face was born, dedicated to Hatowi, the Great Twisted Face.

Now the earth was ready for the habitation of man. Okwiraseh went to the shore of a great lake and he scooped up a handful of deep red earth.

He said, "Now I make what shall be called Onkwehonwe, or human beings. They will dwell here on this floating island."

So as soon as he had stopped talking he began to make them, and he made the body of the human being. He took up the earth and he said, "This earth that I take up is really alive. It is alive, just as the earth is alive. So too, the body of the human being that I make shall also be alive."

Then at that time he made the flesh of the human being.

As soon as he had completed it he thought for a while then he said, "This will result in a good thing that I have done, and these human beings will continue to have life, just as I myself am alive."

Now at this time he took a portion of his own life and he gave it to the human being; so also he took a portion of his own mind and he enclosed it in the head of the human being; so also he took a portion of his own blood and enclosed it in his flesh; so also did he take a portion of his power to see and enclosed it in the eyes of the human being. Now at the time too, he placed his breath in the body of the human being and man rose and stood on the earth.

Then Okwiraseh said, "Truthfully I have made your body and you now walk on the earth. Look now and see what the earth contains."

At this time, as if by magic, Okwiraseh showed all of the earth to man. He showed him the valleys nestled in between tall gracious mountains. He showed man the clear waters of Iroquoia and the waterways of all the various territories. Okwiraseh showed man the beauty and wealth of the forest, the numerous medicines and foods. Fields of the three sisters growing to maturity were pointed out to man. Large trees bearing nuts and fruits, bushes of berries and the large bounty of game were shown to man. Likewise, the spots where flint could be found, calimite for making pipes and bowls, deposits of clay and sand for pottery, and smooth pebbles for beadwork. All of these things were shown to the first man and he was made very glad.

Then Okwiraseh said, "I have given you all of this that the earth contains. It will continue to give comfort to your mind. I have planted human beings on the earth for the purpose that they shall continue my work of creation by beautifying the earth, cultivating it and making it more pleasing for the habitation of man." Now then man saw his elder brother the Sun come up and cause the daylight on the earth to be warm. And man saw that the earth was beautiful, that the sky was beautiful and he was glad.

Okwiraseh told man that all of this was for man, and all that man had to do was to feel good and to be thankful for all of the gifts of creation. Man must never take the good things of the earth for granted, he was told, or else they would be taken away. Man must always be thankful.

But men forgot these words of the Creator, and they lost respect for the earth and for each other. Because of this the Creator returned to earth, and instituted the four ceremonies of thanksgiving. These four thanksgiving ceremonies would bring the people together at harvests, mid-winter, when the maple runs from the trees, and at the time of green corn. Human beings were told that they had forgotten to be thankful, and so they were ruining the earth. These four ceremonies helped them to remember.

Even with the four ceremonies, however, there was fighting amongst the people. And so the Creator returned to earth again, this time to inspire the formation of the Great Law of Peace and the founding of the Five Nations Confederacy.

Source: http://www.schoolnet.ca/aboriginal/7gen/creation-e.html.

APPENDIX 8.4

The Cree Creation Story

So then, I shall tell another legend. I'll tell a story, the legend about ourselves, the people, as we are called. Also I shall tell the legend about where we came from and why we came … , why we who are living now came to inhabit this land.

Now then, first I shall begin.

The other land was above, it is said. It was like this land which we dwell in, except that the life seems different; also it is different on account of its being cold and mild [here]. So then, this land where we are invariably tends to be cold.

So that is the land above which is talked about from which there came two people, one woman and one man, … they dwelt in that land which was above. But it was certainly known that this world where we live was there.

Now then at one time someone spoke to them, while they were in that land of theirs where they were brought up. He said to them, "Do you want to go see yonder land which is below?"

The very one about which they were spoken to is this one where we dwell.

"Yes," they said, "we will go there."

"That land," they were told, "is different, appears different from this one which we dwell in, which you dwell in now during your lifetime. But you will find it different there, should you go to see that land. It is cold yonder. And sometimes it is hot."

"It fluctuates considerably. If you wish to go there, however, you must go see the spider at the end of this land where you are. That is where he lives."

The spider, as he is called, that is the one who is the net-maker, who never exhausts his twine,—so they went to see him, who is called the spider. So they reached him.

Then he asked them, "Where do you want to go? Do you want to go and see yonder land, the other one which is below?"

"Yes," they said.

"Very well," said the spider. "I shall make a line so that I may lower you."

So then, he made a line up to,—working it around up to, up to the top.

"Not yet, not yet even half done," he said.

Then he spoke to them telling them, better for him to let them down even before he finished it the length it should be.

Then he told them, "That land which you want to go and see is cold and sometimes mild. But there will certainly be someone there who will teach you, where you will find a living once you have reached it. He, he will tell you every thing so you will get along well."

So he made a place for them to sit as he lowered them, the man and the woman.

They got in together, into that thing which looked like a bag.

Then he instructed them what to do during their trip. "Only one must look," he said to them. "But one must not look until you have made contact with the earth. You may both look then."

So, meanwhile as they went along, one looked. At last he caught sight of the land.

The one told the other, "Now the land is in sight."

Again the first told the other, "Now the rivers are in sight."

They had been told however, that "if one, … if they both look together, before they come to the land, they will go into the great eagle-nest and they will never be able to get out and climb down from there."

That's where they will be. That's what they were told.

Then the one told the other, "Now the lakes are in sight. Now the grass."

Then they both looked before they arrived, as they were right at the top of the trees. Then they went sideways for a short while; then they went into the great eagle-nest. That's where they went in, having violated their instructions.

Now then, "Look down!"

They saw all the creatures which live there on earth: the bear, the caribou, the beaver, the otter, the fisher, the mink, the wolverine, the lynx.

Then at one point the caribou walked there right across [from them].

They said to him, "Come and help us. We cannot get down."

The caribou said to them, "No. I never climb up."

He showed them what his hooves looked like.

Then the lynx came by.

So once more they said to him, "Come and help us."

"Never, … not ever am I climbing," said the lynx.

He was not telling the truth. He was deceiving them. Then away he went again past them.

Then the bear arrived.

So he said to them, … they said to him, "Come and help us."

The bear didn't listen for long; but then he started to get up on his hind legs to go and see them. Also another one, the wolverine as he is called. They made one trip each as they brought them down.

But the bear was followed by those people.

That was the very thing which had been said to them, "You will have someone there who will teach you to survive."

This bear, he taught them everything about how to keep alive there.

It was there that these people began to multiply from one couple, the persons who had come from another land. They lived giving birth to their children generation after generation. That is us right up until today. That is why we are in this country.

And by-and-by the White People began to arrive as they began to reach us people, who live in this country.

That is as much as I shall tell.

Source: Ellis (1995).

CHAPTER 9

First Contact

CHAPTER OBJECTIVES

After completing this chapter, you should be able to:

- Identify the similarities and the differences among incursions into the Americas by the Spanish, British, and French.
- Identify the core issues of debate over the legitimacy of claim for land and authority in the Americas.
- Discuss the relationship between the new arrivals in Canada and the First Nations people up to the issuance of the *Royal Proclamation of 1763*.

INTRODUCTION

We begin this chapter with an examination of Europe's first contact in the Americas. First we examine the Spanish incursion into the Caribbean and Central America. We contrast this with the "discovery" of present-day Newfoundland and the British experience with the Beothuk Indians of that area. We investigate the debate that occurred in Valladolid, Spain in 1550 when the champion of Native rights, Las Casas, questioned the validity of the conquest of America and the subjugation and annihilation of the Indians. We find that the foundations of this historically famous argument are still present with us today.

We examine the changing relationship between First Nations people and Europeans. We follow the change in position of First Nations people from partners in trade and allies in war to displaced and subjugated peoples.

LAS CASAS AND THE INDIANS

I am beginning this chapter in an unconventional way by telling a story about the first contact of Europeans in the Americas so that you can draw a comparison of the basic themes involved here to the history of the British and French incursion into present-day Canada. This is an important piece to understand because the themes resonate in Canada and throughout the world today.

When Christopher Columbus set sail in 1492 in the name of Spain, he was looking for a passage to the Orient in order to increase trade and wealth for Spain.

What he found was a continent full of people with complex societies and systems of government, and gold. Lots of gold. The Spanish conquistadors quickly claimed the "New World" in the name of Spain and embarked on a series of campaigns to exterminate the Indians living there. The church assisted in this process by granting the "New World" to the King of Spain and enacting the *Requerimiento*, claiming that Christ was Lord of the Universe and the Indians must convert to Christ, or be killed or enslaved.

In 1502 Spain embarked upon a system of forced labour known as the *encomienda*. In the name of the King of Spain a soldier was granted land and was allotted Indians to work the land. In return, the soldier was required to provide religious training to the Indians, who were in essence his slaves.

The Indians worked and died under inhuman conditions. They laboured extracting gold from the mines and working the land to produce sugar for export. By 1540 the Indians of the Caribbean had been virtually wiped out.

The legitimacy of Spain's acquisition of the new lands has always been questioned. One of the first people to forward this challenge was a man named Las Casas, who came to the New World to seek his fortune and was granted an *encomienda*. He was outraged at the injustice in the Spanish treatment of the Indians and began to petition the King of Spain, conveying the horrors that the Spanish conquistadors were inflicting on the Indians.

Las Casas continued for 30 years to petition the Crown of Spain on behalf of the Indians. During this time, Spain reached the mainland and conquered the Aztec and Inca empires by exploiting the political divisions within the indigenous groups, using some as allies to defeat others. The Spanish used horses and weapons of steel, unknown to the Indians, to overwhelm them. Already weakened by European diseases, the Indians succumbed so swiftly that the Spanish were convinced that their occupation of the Americas and subjugation of the Indians was their manifest destiny, or ordained by God.

Las Casas's voice, along with his supporters', did inspire political reform in Spain. In 1537 Pope Paul III prepared a declaration that the Indians were entitled to retain their property as well as their liberty in the New World. The declaration was designed to protect the Indians from the atrocities experienced at the hands of their masters. However, the conquistadors began to rebel. King Charles had the Pope annul his declaration within a year rather than risk a rebellion in the New World. The Kingdom of Spain, and the church for that matter, had become too dependent upon the wealth flowing from the New World; they could not risk a rebellion.

King Charles himself was moved by the injustices being perpetrated in his name, and in 1542 decreed that no further *encomiendas* would be granted. However, he was powerless to enforce his will on the numerous Spanish colonists who rebelled in Mexico and Peru until the king made it clear that the new laws would not be enforced.

In 1550 King Charles summoned Las Casas and an adviser named Sepulveda to present arguments on how the settlement of the New World could be made in accordance with justice and reason.

Sepulveda argued that the seizure of land and the enslavement of the Indians were justified because the Indians were an inferior race. He provided four proofs to demonstrate this; the absence of technology, the absence of written laws, the absence of the Christian religion, and the absence of the concept of private property.

Las Casas presented his own arguments in turn, insisting that the Pope had no jurisdiction over non-Christians in order to award their lands to Spain and declare them subjects of the Spanish Crown. Furthermore, he insisted that the Indians were rational human beings fit to be called men. He argued that the idea of the equality of man was based in the teachings of Christ, and that all humans have the right to self-determination and basic freedom.

Despite his valiant effort Las Casas was eventually ordered to return to Spain and the conquistadors took full reign over the New World, eventually exterminating up to 95 percent of the original inhabitants of present-day Central and South America and the Caribbean. Two peoples live side by side—one rules and the other is impoverished. Las Casas's words still speak to us of human rights, the rule of law, and the right to self-determination of peoples. His appeals of the legitimacy of Indian culture and ways of being are still heard around the world today (Berger, 1999, pp. 1-25).

CANADA

We leap now to first contact in North America, in the British and French colonies. However, the first people to arrive in Canada were not the British or the French, but the Vikings travelling from Greenland. They arrived in Newfoundland sometime between the 11th and 13th centuries. They settled at L'Anse aux Meadows at the northern tip of Newfoundland, which is today a Canadian World Heritage Site. The Vikings were drawn by the great supply of fish, which later drew many more Europeans, but they arrived just prior to a global shift in weather. As temperatures dropped, they abandoned their settlement and returned to Greenland.

Little is known about the presence of the Vikings in North America; however, they did make record of their encounter with the indigenous people of Newfoundland, whom they referred to as the "Skraelings." Although this indigenous group is known by several names, the most common is the Beothuk Indians. There is very little known about the Beothuk. Historians estimate there were 2,000 to 5,000 members. They were hunter-gatherers, making seasonal movements to the coastline in summer for fishing and sealing, to the interior in winter to hunt game. They were very dependent upon the coastline for fish and seals that would be stored for consumption throughout the winter.

Explorer John Cabot arrived on the coast of Newfoundland in 1497, carrying news of the rich fishing grounds back to Europe. It was said at that time that the fish were so numerous you could walk across the ocean on cod. Many Europeans were drawn by the opportunity to make their fortune exporting fish to Europe. In 1501 Portuguese explorer Gaspar Cortes Real captured 50 Beothuk and took them back to Europe as slaves. Likely due to this incident, the Beothuk generally avoided contact with whites.

By 1578 over 400 European fishing ships came to the region every summer. They began to occupy the coastline to dry fish, limiting the Beothuk's access to the ocean and pushing them further inland. According to European recorded accounts, the Beothuk would help themselves to fishing equipment left behind over the winter when the ships returned to Europe. This caused great hostility among the whites toward the Beothuk. In 1613 a French fisherman shot a Beothuk he believed to be stealing from him. The Beothuk retaliated, killing 37 Frenchmen. As a result, the

French and English began to shoot the Beothuk on sight, believing them to be a threat. The Beothuk were forced inland and, without access to the resources of the sea, they faced great hardship.

The French, British, and Dutch fought over the ownership of the island over the next 100 years. In 1713 the French were expelled and moved to Cape Breton, giving the British title to the island. The British increased their coastal settlements, further limiting the Beothuk's access to the ocean and to the resources that had sustained them for thousands of years. After taking control of the land and the resources, the decision was made to attempt to protect the remaining Beothuk, whose population the British recorded in 1768 as a mere 400. In 1810 the British sent a search party to make contact, but two members of the search party were killed by the Beothuk. The British captured the last few Beothuk a short time later, but the last known Beothuk Indian, Nancy Shanawdithit, died of tuberculosis in 1829. Thus ends the story of the Beothuk Indians in accordance with European recorded history (Dickason, 1997, pp. 73-74).

The first true voyage of discovery into what would become Canada occurred when Jacques Cartier explored the Gulf of St. Lawrence in 1534. He, like Christopher Columbus, was intent on finding a passageway through to the Orient. Failing that, he hoped to find gold for France as the Spanish were busy doing in Central America. Cartier met with the St. Lawrence Iroquois on his journey and engaged in trade with them. He gathered information from them as to the route to the interior of the continent, where he hoped to find gold. The friendship became strained when Cartier took Chief Donnaconna's two sons back to Europe with him at the end of the season. The two survived their trip to Europe and returned the following summer to act as interpreters and guides to assist Cartier in his quest for the route into the heart of the continent.

With the help of his Iroquois guides, Cartier made it all the way to Hochelaga, present-day Montreal. He wrote extensively of his voyage. He counted 14 villages on the north shore, of which Hochelaga was the largest, numbering 50 longhouses with an estimated population of 1,500. Cartier engaged in trade but was forced to return to France as winter set in. He annoyed the Iroquois by setting up a cross to claim the land in the name of France, and then capturing several of the Iroquoian headmen and taking them back to France.

Cartier returned on a third voyage to bring settlers; however, the relationship between the two groups was sufficiently strained that the Iroquois killed the settlers, forcing Cartier to return to France with a ship full of iron pyrite (fool's gold).

The Europeans continued to arrive on Canada's eastern shores, drawn by the opportunity for wealth through the exploitation of Canada's natural resources, in the quest to acquire land, or to escape adverse social and economic conditions or religious persecution. These Europeans continued to make contact with various organized Aboriginal nations, each with its own form of governance and economic system.

Initially, contact involved a spirit of cooperation and respect for one another's sovereignty. The reasons were threefold, and quite practical: (1) the Native nations vastly outnumbered the colonists, who were poorly equipped for the harsh conditions of the land; (2) the economic interests of the newcomers depended on maintaining a good relationship with Native nations, who in turn benefited in terms of trade; and (3) Aboriginal people were desperately needed as military allies by the

French and the English in their wars against one another, and later against the newly independent United States. Aboriginal nations clearly had the upper hand.

This was made most clear in the Two Row Wampum, or the *Guswentha*, the first agreement entered into between the five nations of the Iroquois and the British. To the Iroquois the *Guswentha* was international law, recorded in wampum beads as was their custom. The two coloured rows of wampum represented an English trading ship and an Iroquois canoe. They travel parallel paths along the river of life. These paths never meet as they are bound together in peace and friendship with an agreement for mutual aid and defence; however, neither nation is to interfere with the other or attempt to impose laws over the other.

This agreement is well documented by the British and is referred to in their recorded history as the "**covenant chain**." The covenant chain was a clear recognition by both sides that their political systems would remain separate even as their system of trade and alliance linked them together. There are many references to it through to the early 1800s. One such reference is made in a speech by an Onondaga speaker named Sadakanahtie in 1694 addressing Benjamin Fletcher, governor of New York and Pennsylvania (quoted in Venables, 1992):

covenant chain
first agreement entered into between the five nations of the Iroquois and the British; a clear recognition by both sides that their political systems would remain separate even as their system of trade and alliance linked them together

> When Christians first arrived in this country, we received them kindly. When they were but small people, we entered into a league with them, to guard them from all enemies whatsoever. We were so fond of their society that we tied the great canoe that brought them, not with a rope made of bark to a tree but with strong iron chain fastened to a great mountain. Now before the Christians arrived, the general council of the five nations was held at Onondaga, where there has, from the beginning, a continual fire been burning: it is made of two great logs whose fire never extinguishes. As soon as the hatchet makers (Christians) arrived, this General Council at Onondaga planted this pine tree at Albany (New York), whose roots and branches have spread as far as New England, Connecticut and Pennsylvania; under the shade of this tree all these English colonies have been frequently sheltered.

> Then he renewed the Chain and promised as they likewise expected, mutual assistance in case of any attack by an enemy.

This military alliance with the Iroquois served the British well and led to the defeat of the French in 1760. The French and British continually accused one another of bribing their allies with gifts and also of using Indians on the front lines as "cannon fodder." Native people on both sides of the battle sustained great losses.

Native nations on both sides considered the battle to be between the French and the English. Native nations allied with traditional trade alliances and viewed the outcome as a matter of French or English trade dominance; they had no concept that their lands were at stake. They viewed the land as their sacred territory, which they had allowed Europeans to settle on under certain terms and conditions, such as trade alliances and gift distributions.

Upon the defeat of the French, many Native leaders remarked to the English that it was not the Indians that were conquered but the French. Ojibwa Chief Minweweh, whose warriors had fought on the side of the French, reminded the English: "Although you have conquered the French you have not conquered us. We are not your slaves. These lakes, woods and mountains were left us by our ancestors. They are our inheritance, and we will part with them to none" (Dickason, 1997, p. 155).

To address the fears of the Native nations with regard to loss of their ancestral lands, the British included article 40 in the Capitulation of Montréal between the French and English. This section guaranteed Native nations protection of their lands from the encroachment of new settlers; however, it immediately proved difficult to enforce as settlers began to pour in once peace had been established. Colonial governments displayed little will to enforce the legislation (Dickason, 1997, p. 153).

After the defeat of the French, Native nations found themselves in a worsening position. They had been holding the balance of power between two rivals, but now found themselves slipping into a position of irrelevance to both the British and the French. Gift distributions ended quickly, as did the supply of guns and ammunition. The Europeans no longer respected boundaries that Native nations set out as hunting grounds or sacred territories. Discontent among various nations led to a formidable uprising led by a remarkable man named Pontiac, an Odawa war chief, who was able to unite a number of nations in his quest to defeat the Europeans and drive them from the land. Within the span of two months in 1763 nine British forts fell to Pontiac with almost no casualties sustained by his men. The British feared being overrun and resorted to the first ever recorded case of biological warfare. They distributed smallpox-infected blankets to Native settlements, wiping out entire communities, including women, children, and elders.

In this intense political climate, the British were in the process, as Spain had been in the 1500s, of attempting to justify their acquisition of land in the Americas. It was apparent that the land was in fact occupied by organized nations of people, albeit non-Christians. How would the British acquire this land for resource extraction and for settlement in accordance with principles of justice and reason?

Acquiring the land for these purposes would be impossible without the help of the Native nations. Britain was facing a growing rebellion in the 13 colonies and would require the allegiance of Native nations again in war or would face the loss of the New World altogether. Britain would never be able to secure the allegiance of Native nations if Europeans continued to trespass on territories held by Native nations, causing great animosity toward the British.

THE ROYAL PROCLAMATION

Royal Proclamation of 1763
the cornerstone of Native land claims today; has been called the "Magna Carta of Indian Rights" and has been deemed by the courts to have the force of a statute which has never been repealed

In 1763, the British drew up an important piece of legislation to address the dilemma. The **Royal Proclamation of 1763** would become the cornerstone of Native land claims today. This document has been called the "Magna Carta of Indian Rights" and has been deemed by the courts to have the "force of a statute which has never been repealed."

The first purpose of the *Royal Proclamation* was to reserve a large piece of land for Native occupation and use. The second purpose was to appease Native leaders in order to secure military allegiance and to stop the mounting Native resistance movement. The third purpose was to create a treaty process by which the Crown alone could purchase Indian land for settlement.

Consider the wording of the *Royal Proclamation* itself:

> And We do hereby strictly forbid, on Pain of our Displeasure, all our loving Subjects from making any Purchases or Settlements whatever, or taking Possession of

any of the Lands above reserved [for Indians], without our especial leave and Licence for that Purpose first obtained.

And We do further strictly enjoin and require all Persons whatever who have either wilfully or inadvertently seated themselves upon any Lands within the Countries above described, or upon any other Lands which, not having been ceded to or Purchased by Us, are still reserved to the said Indians as aforesaid, forthwith to remove themselves from such Settlements.

And whereas great Frauds and Abuses have been committed in purchasing Lands of the Indians, to the great Prejudice of our Interests, and to the great Dissatisfaction of the said Indians: In order, therefore, to prevent such Irregularities for the future, and to the end that the Indians may be convinced of our Justice and determined Resolution to remove all reasonable Cause of Discontent, We do, with the Advice of our Privy Council strictly enjoin and require, that no private Person do presume to make any purchase from the said Indians of any Lands reserved to the said Indians, within those parts of our Colonies where We have thought proper to allow Settlement: but that, if at any Time any of the Said Indians should be inclined to dispose of the said Lands, the same shall be Purchased only for Us, in our Name, at some public Meeting or Assembly of the said Indians.

This powerful piece of legislation has never been repealed and therefore is still in effect and legally binding. The 13 colonies were so displeased with the limitations placed upon them by the Proclamation that it became one of the many reasons for their rebellion against the British. The *Royal Proclamation* is legislation drawn up by an imperial power designed to protect the rights of First peoples to their land. As you continue to read, consider whether the British enforced the terms of the Proclamation. Are we honouring these terms today?

The *Royal Proclamation* did accomplish what it set out to do: it drew a line between British territory and Indian land, and convinced Native allies of British "Justice and determined Resolution to remove all reasonable Cause of Discontent" sufficiently so as to secure Native allegiance against the Americans in the War of Independence and later to repel the American invasion of what would become Canada.

The third objective of setting up a treaty process to acquire land had the added benefit that the Crown obtained a monopoly over land sales in Canada, as it set itself as the only legal purchaser of Indian land. This was a source of enormous wealth for the British. In some of the first treaties in Ontario the Crown was able to purchase land for settlement for a mere 3 pence an acre from Indians who could not drive up the prices of their land by selling to any other party. The British then sold the land to private investors for settlement for 6 to 15 pence per acre, making a healthy profit.

Although the *Royal Proclamation* does not refer to Native nations as sovereign nations, neither does it refer to them as subjects of the Crown. We may ask ourselves when the Crown began to assert control or jurisdiction over Native people.

THE FUR TRADE

During early and sparse settlement, the fur trade was well under way. The French allied with the Huron and other East Coast nations, and the English allied with the Iroquois and their Native allies. The division of Native nations existed prior to contact, and the British and the French managed to exploit these divisions both in trade and war.

The British set up the Hudson's Bay Company and the French the Compagnie du Nord. The companies were in direct competition for the harvest and export of furs. Both attempted to extend their trade northward, gaining control over trade routes. As early as 1632 the French were exporting up to 15,000 kilograms of furs a year. The French had 500 to 700 men on the canoe routes travelling to Huronia; in the absence of the discovery of gold, furs were certainly the next best thing (Dickason, 1997, p. 103).

The balance of power at this time was still very much in favour of the Native nations. To give this perspective, in 1633 the French had 3,000 people in their colonies, while the Huron nation alone numbered over 30,000. However, the Huron would shortly experience a rapid population decline as a result of European diseases brought by the missionaries and traders.

seigniorial farms
a system in which a man, usually a soldier, was granted land in the name of France

The French established a system of **seigniorial farms**, in which one man, usually a soldier, was granted land in the name of France. The soldier would bring over his family from France to labour on the farm to produce food for the fledgling colonies. The French did not enact any treaties to acquire this land for farming; they simply considered themselves as sole proprietors of the land by their mere presence. They declared the land to be *terra nullius*—empty land. The French did not recognize indigenous nations as rightful possessors of land since the Native people were not Christian. The French were, however, very cautious to maintain good relationships with Native nations and never made any open assertions to them about the ownership of the land on which they settled. They did not enter any treaties or legal arrangements to clear the land of Aboriginal title. This became problematic later as, upon the defeat of the French, the British also did not enact any legislation to clear the land of Aboriginal title, assuming that the French had already done so.

As the fur trade expanded, forts were erected to house staff and government officials. The fur trade extended into northern Ontario to advance the nation-building intentions of the British Crown, and as a result of the depletion of animal furs elsewhere. The rate of the harvest of furs was not sustainable; beaver were all but extinct south of today's Canada–US border and became near extinct quickly in southern Ontario once the traders moved in.

The trading posts were influential in creating new non-Native communities across the North, and had a tremendous effect on Native people who came to sell their furs. Traditionally migratory peoples began to develop permanent dwellings around the posts, which were often strategically placed near Native summer or winter campsites. For example, Sault Ste. Marie was populated by Native people because of its abundance of fish and access to water travel between Lake Huron and Lake Superior. The place became an early non-Native settlement for the same reasons and to exploit the proximity to Native trappers.

Native people began to trade for objects such as sewing needles, copper pots, knives, and hatchets, which improved their immediate quality of life. (These were items that Native people could not produce themselves, as they did not have the technology.) This barter system did not, however, sustain long-term economic prosperity in Native communities. The real profits were being exported back to Europe in the form of furs, and the resources that had sustained Native people for thousands of years were quickly being depleted beyond recovery.

CHANGES TO NATIVE COMMUNITIES

Fundamental changes began to take place within Native communities due to contact with Europeans. One of these was the development of the notion of wealth. Furs were never a sign of wealth for Native people. Animals were killed for food, shelter, clothing, and tools. Anything that the hunter did not need would be given to another family. The proceeds generated by the hunt were shared among community members. Hunting in excess simply did not make any sense; collecting and storing hides would have been impractical in Native traditional lifestyle.

Selection of leaders began to change as economic power, previously non-existent, influenced the election of leaders within Native communities. The clan system that had previously maintained the groups' cohesiveness by maintaining strict rules, values, and social mores slowly lost its influence.

Natives became increasingly dependent on European traders, and less dependent upon their own natural environment and the traditional web of trade established between Native nations prior to contact. The introduction of alcohol through trade created new societal problems, and its impact continues to reverberate through Native communities today. For many Native nations this dependence on European trade became entrenched; for others it remained nominal. Europeans were eager to foster this dependence as it provided an advantage in trade. For Native people the fur trade did not provide economic stability; prices of furs were dependent upon the whims of fashion, and the harvest of furs depended upon environmental conditions and animal populations. The rate of harvest was unsustainable, and the fur trade was destined to collapse.

Many native animals neared extinction by the early 1800s. As a result, many trading posts closed, bringing extreme hardship to those Native people who had settled around the posts. Many faced starvation and related diseases. The government provided food and other necessities, but could never restore the economy of Native people. Animal resources had been depleted beyond recovery in the first phase of harvest. Native people were later subjected to a second wave of harvest of natural resources (logging and mining), which proved equally or perhaps more devastating.

Along with trade goods, Europeans brought Christian religion—English Protestant and French Catholic—and missionaries to spread the faith. Initially, Native people did not welcome missionaries as willingly as they had traders. It was easy to see value in guns, copper pots, and other tools, whereas the value of new spiritual beliefs was less apparent. Eventually, most Native groups came to respect the spiritual beliefs of their European trade partners, and many began to accept missionaries into their communities. In some instances traders and missionaries assisted one another in their cause; Christian Native trappers were often given better prices for their furs, and at times only Christian Indians could purchase guns and ammunition. However, the missionaries often became frustrated, believing that Native people were converting for convenience rather than genuine adoption of the Christian religion.

Regardless, it is difficult to underestimate the impact of European religion on Native communities. The missionaries chose to restrict or forbid many Native ceremonies, teachings, and cultural practices, deeming them evil. With the elimination of these aspects of culture that were the foundations of values, unity, and governance for thousands of years, communities began to unravel. Differences in religion caused a lack of unity in communities and in families.

In more extreme circumstances the churches or religious orders were given authority to govern reserve land and resources. Resources were extracted and the churches reaped the financial profits, driving the people into poverty.

CONCLUSION

After first contact in Canada, First Nations peoples sustained a huge population decrease as a result of disease and of allegiances in war to European powers. First Nations peoples also quickly moved from a position of power to a position of subservience in trade relationships, which could not ensure long-term economic stability for First Nations communities. The *Royal Proclamation of 1763* was seen as an assurance to guarantee Native rights to land and, therefore, basic subsistence; however, the reluctance of the ruling powers to enforce the provisions of the Proclamation further disadvantaged First Nations peoples.

Spain had enacted legislation in the Caribbean designed to protect First Nations peoples, but was reluctant to enforce such legislation for fear of economic repercussions. The balance of power was now stacked clearly in favour of European colonizing nations.

KEY TERMS

covenant chain

Royal Proclamation of 1763

seigniorial farms

REFERENCES

Berger, T. (1999). *The long and terrible shadow: White values, Native rights.* Vancouver/Toronto: Douglas & McIntyre.

Dickason, O.P. (1997). *Canada's First Nations: A history of founding peoples from earliest times.* Toronto: Oxford University Press.

Royal Proclamation of 1763, RSC 1970, app. II, no. 1.

Venables, R. (1992). *The founding fathers choosing to be the Romans.* Ithaca: NY: Akwekon Press, Cornell University.

CHAPTER 10

Western Expansion and Treaties

CHAPTER OBJECTIVES

After completing this chapter, you should be able to:

- Discuss Western expansion and relate it to the Western European cultural world view.
- Understand the treaty-making process, and the benefits and disadvantages for the British and the First Nations involved.
- Identify the assimilation policies and legislation set out by the Dominion of Canada with regard to First Nations people.
- Discuss the legal, moral, and ethical implications of those policies.

INTRODUCTION

Following the American Revolution, a massive influx of settlers into Upper Canada began. Land was needed for settlement, and in keeping with the *Royal Proclamation of 1763* the British began the tedious process of acquiring Indian land through treaty. Although Native people did not have a full understanding of the treaty-making process, with Canada competing with its US neighbours for occupancy and therefore title over lands and access to resources, the British felt pressure to expand westward.

Once occupancy was established, the "Indian question" remained. What would the colonies do with regard to the Indians with whom they had entered into treaties? The newly formed government of Canada chose to embark upon a journey of forced assimilation by carefully enacting legislation designed to eliminate the Indians as a special group within Canadian society.

TREATIES BACKGROUND

Most **treaties** in Canada were signed between 1800 and the early 1900s. They are non-Native documents that have been approved through the Canadian legislative

treaty
an agreement between two states that has been formally concluded and ratified

process as legally binding. In 1982 the treaties were protected in s. 35 of the *Canadian Charter of Rights and Freedoms,* which reads: "The existing aboriginal and treaty rights of the aboriginal peoples of Canada are hereby recognized and affirmed." Today, the treaties provide a legitimate claim for Native peoples' fight to have the promises of the treaties fulfilled and to have the original spirit of the treaties interpreted by the courts to uphold Aboriginal rights to resources and land.

Treaties were not unknown to First Nations people prior to the arrival of Europeans. Treaties had been made among nations to settle wars, delineate harvest territories, and facilitate trade alliances since time immemorial. The records of these treaties were passed down orally and were honoured by the groups who entered into them. The most frequent subject matter of treaties related to peace and friendship, military alliance, boundaries, or trade.

When Europeans arrived, Native nations entered into treaties with them as well, including the Two Row Wampum treaty between the Iroquois and the British, which we read about in the previous chapter. Another example of a peace and friendship treaty was that between the British and the Mi'kmaq of Nova Scotia in 1725. The British secured military neutrality and assistance from the Mi'kmaq in their war against the French in exchange for facilitating trade and guaranteeing protection of the Mi'kmaq traditional economy of hunting and fishing.

Natives expected the principles that had been established in the creation of treaties of peace and friendship, and military and trade alliances, to carry over into the negotiations over the sharing of the land to facilitate European settlement. To them, mutual respect and understanding were essential components of negotiations. Also for them, the terms negotiated in discussion and recorded by them orally were considered terms of the agreement.

This was not the case for Europeans, as they had a different cultural context for negotiations. In the first place, Natives believed that no one could own the land. The land was a gift from the creator, and they were its guardians, not its owners. To Natives the treaties were intended to lay out the terms of a mutual sharing of resources and their compensation for the sharing of their resources.

Europeans understood the treaties in their own cultural context as land cessation. The intention was to erase Aboriginal title to the land so that it could be parcelled out for ownership. Although both parties had interpreters present, it was difficult to translate this cultural understanding of ownership. In retrospect, one must consider whether the Crown was diligent in its efforts to convey its intended meaning, as a full understanding would have most certainly brought negotiations to an unsuccessful conclusion. Many times it was not until the Europeans began the process of removing Native people from their land that the Native people fully understood what they had signed.

There are three categories of treaties in Canada; pre-Confederation treaties, numbered treaties, and legal claims agreements. The pre-Confederation treaties were entered into before Canada became a country in 1867. Numbered treaties, signed between 1871 and 1921, were intended to provide cohesion to the interior of Canada and to formally recognize these territories as part of Canada. Land claims agreements have existed only since the Land Claims Policy was established in 1973.

All treaties, except the land claims agreements, were initiated by Europeans; at no time did Native nations commence the negotiations to sell their lands. Treaty negotiations increased as more and more colonies were established. Land treaties in southern Ontario started after the American Revolution in 1776. Following their defeat in the United States, the British required land for their displaced Loyalists and their Native military allies, all of whom were at risk if they remained in the United States. The British also needed to reward their military personnel who had fought in the revolution. The Native allies were primarily the six nations (Mohawk, Onondaga, Cayuga, Seneca, Oneida, and Tuscarora) who performed considerable military services for the British and sustained considerable losses for their allegiance to the British. Frederick Haldimand purchased 3 million acres (1.2 million hectares) from the Mississauga in 1784 for £1,180 worth of goods to facilitate the settlement of the Loyalists. The Iroquois loyalists were granted a tract six miles (10 kilometres) wide on either side of the Grand River, a total of almost 1.2 million hectares in what is today southwestern Ontario.

Native groups who were displaced in these early treaties to make way for refugees were given lump-sum payments in money or goods for their land. In return for selling a strip of land 6.5 kilometres wide along the full length of the west bank of the Niagara River from Lake Erie to Lake Ontario, the Mississauga Nation received 300 suits of clothing (Rogers & Smith, 1994). Through to 1798, the government had no problem obtaining Indian land through treaty for about 3 pence per acre in either cash or goods, then selling that land to private investors and settlers for 6 to 15 pence per acre for a healthy profit. By 1912 there were 483 treaties listed for Canada, comprising a considerable body of law (Dickason, 1997, p. 163).

Following the American defeat in the War of 1812, another wave of settlers arrived in Upper Canada (southern Ontario), doubling the non-Native population from 75,000 to 150,000 in a very short time. Land was needed quickly to settle these new arrivals. Because Native military clout and political influence were waning as they were no longer required by Britain in times of relative peace, the government offered Native groups annuities rather than considerably larger one-sum payments. This was a more economical way for the Crown to obtain land through treaty, as the annuities could be paid from the sale of the land, still providing a profit while avoiding the initial lump-sum payout.

There was no uniform practice in treaty making, with the exception that a Crown representative was to be involved in negotiations. For example, in 1790 2 million acres were purchased by the Crown for £1,200 from the Ojibwa and Odawa in southern Ontario. Two years later, 3 million acres (1.2 million hectares) were purchased from the same group for the same amount. Many of these land transactions were not properly recorded or were imprecise in their terms regarding boundaries, giving rise to later disputes. For example, one treaty reads "from the lakeshore to as far back as you can hear a gunshot," aptly nicknamed the "gunshot treaty." Many of the original treaties were lost. By the mid-1830s a sequence of over 30 treaties had been concluded, effectively covering southern Ontario.

NUMBERED TREATIES

After Confederation, treaty negotiations with a large number of Native groups across a vast area of Canada were conducted. Commonly referred to as the numbered treaties, these treaties were made in the interest of nation building for Canada by acquiring land to build a national railway. The Huron Robinson treaty of

1850 set a precedent for the terms of the numbered treaties. The following terms were set out in that treaty:

- Sale of reserved lands and mineral rights was to be conducted by the government for the sole use and benefit of the Indians.

- Negotiations were to be open and accessible to the public.

- Land was to be surrendered only to the Crown.

- Annexed to each treaty, a schedule of reserves was to be held in common by each group affected by the treaty.

- Annuities were to be paid in cash to signing members.

- Natives "retain the full privilege to hunt over territory ceded by them, except such lands as are sold by private individuals."

Most of the agreements included a reserve land based on the number of Native people in the settlement at the time of treaty. These populations were smaller than pre-contact populations as Native peoples had sustained a minimum of 80 percent population loss due to European diseases. Most numbered treaties included agreements for schooling, agricultural equipment, gifts, and annuities.

This brings us to a common misconception among Canadians. Some believe that federally funded education, housing, or taxation exemption is a special provision from the federal government for Indians as an act of generosity. This is not the case; the federal government has frequently tried to alleviate itself of these obligations but has been instructed by the courts that the treaties hold the force of law and must be honoured. These benefits accorded Native people were negotiated in treaties that granted to the Crown the land that is now Canada. In the words of the treaties, these terms are to be upheld "as long as the grass is green, as long as the sun shines and the rivers flow."

There were many problems with the treaty process. First, as discussed previously, was the problem translating concepts such as exclusive possession of property. Second was the unscrupulous interpretation of the oral versus written terms of the treaty. Today, efforts have been made to research the recorded minutes of council meetings before and after the signing of the treaty. This research brings to light new and clearly recorded promises made that were never written into treaty documents that were signed by individuals who could not read. Third was the problem obtaining signatures of a leader of each of the groups affected by the treaty. Many Native nations were left out of the treaty-signing process simply because government officials did not know they were there. With a stroke of a pen, the government seized the land of these people without their permission or signatures. Adhesions had to be made later to the treaties to include some groups who had been overlooked.

> **CLASS ACTIVITY**
>
> Conduct an online search for information on the Lubicon Cree of northern Alberta who were left out when Treaty 8 was signed. Discuss your findings with the class.

WESTERN EXPANSION

The pressure to populate the West with white settlers intensified following the conclusion of the American Revolution in 1783. It was apparent that the Western lands and all the wealth and resources therein would belong to whoever could get there first and be prepared to defend it. The newly independent United States had severed its ties with Britain and therefore was no longer bound by the *Royal Proclamation*. The United States embarked on a series of wars against the original inhabitants of the West in order to clear them from the land. Twice the Americans were defeated, but they managed to break through in the battle of Fallen Timbers in 1794. The British chose not to come to the aid of their former Native allies; in fact, they closed the gates of the forts closest to the battle.

The British colonies created incentives for immigrants and other white settlers to move west, enticing agricultural settlers with 64 hectares of free "Crown land." Rapid work was required to obtain that land from the current occupants by way of treaty. The protection of this western land would be provided in part by the Indians themselves. Recall that the United States concluded terms of independence in 1783; the British then were concerned about the Americans moving west and northward, as well as the possibility of an American attack on the remaining British colonies, which would ultimately happen in 1812. The British had learned a valuable lesson in their wars against the French: the one who has the most Native allies wins. Between 1784 and 1788 the British spent £20,000 on gift distributions to Native people, hoping to secure military allegiance as they moved westward. This was more than the British paid to secure land through most of the treaties to that date. They were successful in securing Tecumseh, who was a powerful Native leader. He sided with the British and united more than 30 nations to lead in the defence of British-held territories. Together they helped the British repel the Americans in the War of 1812. Tecumseh sided with the British not only for the gift distributions but also because he believed them to be the lesser of two evils, as the British continued to make assurances of protecting Indian lands, an assurance that the United States would not make. Consider what Tecumseh said in 1795:

> My heart is a stone. Heavy with sadness for my people; cold with the knowledge that no treaty will keep the whites out of our land; hard with determination to resist as long as I live and breathe. Now we are weak and many of our people are afraid. But hear me; a single twig breaks but the bundle of twigs is strong. Someday I will embrace our brother tribes and draw them into a bundle and together we will win our country back from the whites.

Following the War of 1812, Western expansion accelerated again. Northwestern Indians such as the Sioux, Blackfoot, and Plains Cree, as well as the Métis, had built an economy based on the buffalo. Upon the arrival of traders a market was quickly created for buffalo products. The hides became fashionable to wear, and the bones were exported to create bone china, popular in Europe. Within the span of a century, by 1835, the number of buffalo had been reduced from 70 million to 635. Needless to say, this caused extreme hardship among the Native people of the plains at a time when treaty negotiations were in full swing.

Ultimately, Europeans made it all the way to the West Coast of Canada. In 1785 the first trading ships arrived, drawn by the lucrative trade in sea otter pelts. Contact and trade were done by ship because an overland route was not found until 1804. Within the first 100 years of contact, West Coast peoples suffered an 80 percent population decrease due to European diseases (this was one of the greatest population drops so far seen with first contact) (Dickason, 1997, p. 180).

Sea otter pelt trading was in full swing by 1792, and by 1825 the sea otter population was decimated. One trader, John Kendrick, reported that he traded £100 worth of chisels and iron tools for 200 sea otter pelts. He then received £8,000 for the pelts in Europe (Dickason, 1997, p. 181).

In 1852 Vancouver Island had only 500 settlers; however, the discovery of gold led to the convergence of 25,000 miners on Queen Charlotte Island in 1858. Salish First Nations and miners conflicted regularly, sometimes leading to violence. The destruction of Native territories was rapid, and their land base eroded with the building of roads and mines.

Salmon resources were being exploited for export to European markets. Salmon was a main source of subsistence for many First Nations such as the Nisga'a, and the serious reduction of this resource caused hardship for them.

James Douglas, governor of Vancouver and the British Columbia mainland at this critical time, attempted to acquire land by way of treaty. He had signed 14 treaties with Salish bands on the Island of Vancouver by 1854, but this amounted to only 3 percent of the island's territory. Native people were not eager to enter into treaties, and James Douglas quickly ran out of money. Although the colony was not forthcoming with further finances, Douglas was unhampered and continued to cut reservations for the First Nations people based on their favourite locations and on the number of people in the group. He surveyed 200 acres (91 hectares) per head of family, then simply assumed the rest of Vancouver and British Columbia to be territory of the Crown. He retired in 1864 and was succeeded by Frederick Seymore, who appointed a commissioner of Crown lands, Joseph Trutch. Trutch recognized that the treaties had not been made to secure lands, and compensation had not been provided for the loss thereof. He wrote:

> The Amerindians have no rights to the land as they were of no actual value to them, and I cannot see why they should either retain these lands to the prejudice of the general interests of the colony. Or be allowed to make a market of them to either the government or individuals.

Trutch then reduced the size of the reserves surveyed by Douglas from 81 hectares per head of family to 4, again without compensation.

British Columbia entered Confederation with Canada in 1871 and was allowed to retain control over "Crown land." But the federal government assumed responsibility for Indians and lands reserved for Indians as per the *British North America Act* of 1867. Arguments between provincial and federal governments begin over how much land was to be granted for reserved land for Indians. British Columbia tried to reduce the lands even further to 4 acres (1.6 hectares) per head of family, but the federal government insisted on 80 acres (32 hectares). British Columbia persisted in assigning reserves for Native nations without compensation, and by 1900 there were over 90 reservations established at an average of 75 hectares per reserve.

Note the emerging pattern here with regard to the seizure of land and resources. Most of the resources were exported to Europe; however, much of the wealth produced built what is our very affluent country today. In fact, Canada is still reliant on natural resources such as timber and oil and gas for the production of wealth. Unfortunately, Aboriginal peoples generally do not share in this wealth. As we will see in chapter 12, First Nations people still suffer from higher than average levels of poverty and today live on only one-half of 1 percent of Canada's land mass. Indeed, wealth is often created through the ownership of natural resources in the land, of which Native people in Canada have precious little.

> **CLASS ACTIVITY**
>
> Read appendix 10.1 as a class. Discuss the word "progress" from different cultural world views.

VANISHING RACE

The creation of almost all reserves through the treaty process was done on the basis of the depressed population of the Native group at the time of the treaty, with no provision made for a population increase. This speaks to a strong belief at the time that Native people were vanishing. They were dying at a rapid rate from disease and many were lost in the numerous wars among the colonists. It was believed at the time that within three generations of treaty making there would be no Indians left; they would either die of disease, or be assimilated into mainstream Canada.

The intent of the Canadian government was never made so clear than through the comments of Deputy Superintendent of Indian Affairs Duncan Campbell Scott in 1920 (as cited in Leslie & Maguire):

> I want to get rid of the Indian problem. I do not think as a matter of fact that this country ought to continually protect a class of people who are able to stand alone. That is my whole point. … That has been the whole purpose of Indian Education and advancement since earliest times. One of the very earliest enactments was to provide for the enfranchisement of the Indian. So it is written in our law that the Indian was eventually to become enfranchised. … Our object is to continue until there is not a single Indian in Canada that has not been absorbed into the body politic and there is no Indian question, and no Indian department, that is the whole object of this Bill.

This was also made evident by the actions of Canadians at the time as well. Native graves, often fresh, were dug up so that the remains could be put on display at Wild West shows. Native spiritual and cultural artifacts were taken and sold to collectors and museums at a time when Native people were still using them because collectors anticipated the value of these items to increase as the Native people vanished.

The idea of a vanishing race was appealing to the British for one very important reason: the treaties they had entered into with the Native nations were in perpetuity.

The British could see that the cost of maintaining these promises forever could be high, particularly because the depletion of resources was leaving Native nations in poverty and requiring relief assistance guaranteed by the treaties. Assimilation for those who survived disease and poverty became a paramount concern for the British in the years to come. No treaty Indians meant no obligation to honour treaties as well as free access to reserve lands.

> **CLASS ACTIVITY**
>
> As a class read and discuss appendix 10.2. Consider the author's political position. Consider the meaning of the poem.

THIRST FOR LAND

During the treaty process and later, it proved difficult to keep settlers and resource speculators off reserve land. Several British parliamentary inquiries were undertaken to address this problem. One, in 1830, found that people were circumventing the *Royal Proclamation* and fraudulently purchasing reserve land; furthermore, squatters were settling on the land and, as time passed, laying claim to it. The *Royal Proclamation* contributed to the problem of squatting; it stated that all purchases of Indian land had to go through the Superintendent of Indian Affairs, and there was only one for the colonies, so purchasing was a lengthy process in a system that was desperately underfunded.

To address this problem the Crown drafted the *Crown Lands Protection Act, 1839* declaring Native reserve lands to be Crown lands. This entrenched the emerging idea of wardship and removed authority from Native people to make decisions about their own land use, awarding that authority to the Crown. Still the Crown was unable to stop the encroachment onto Native lands. In 1842 the Bagot Commission resulted in the reaffirmation of the *Royal Proclamation*, asserting that Native people must be compensated for any land lost to settlement or resource harvesting. This commission's work was cited later when new legislation was passed again in 1850 to attempt to control the intrusion of loggers into reserve areas in Temiskaming and the Ottawa Valley.

Ironically, the attempts to protect Indian reserve land resulted in the Crown creating a definition of an Indian. Prior to 1830, Native people were self-defining, as any self-governing body of people are. They determined membership in their group and the transfer of members in and out of the group. When the Crown took on the parental role of controlling the land, it also was required to define an Indian, as it set out clearly that only Indians of the band could reside on the reserve. The following were considered Indians under the definition constructed by the Crown:

- All individuals of Indian blood belonging to a tribe, band, or body of Indians and their descendants.

- All individuals residing among such Indians whose parents were or are descended from either side from Indians and the descendants of such a person.
- All women lawfully married to an Indian and their children. Native women who married non-Native men would not be entitled to be Indian nor would their children.

In 1830, the British began attempts to assimilate Native people into mainstream culture, pushing them to become agriculturalists, set up communities similar to white settlements, and adopt Christian religions and ways of life. Some Native nations accepted this transition and requested assistance with it; they recognized that the industrialization of their lands would make the hunting way of life impossible. Furthermore, they believed that conversion to the "ideal" might help protect their lands. Model villages were set up and overseen by missionaries; many were quite successful. However, regardless of their success, as white communities expanded, the model villages experienced loss of land, and many were relocated. The genius of this plan was that the finances required to set up these communities and begin the "civilization" process would come from the funds generated through the sale of reserve land, or extraction of resources such as lumber from reserve lands. In effect, Native people would pay their own way to "civilization" (Dickason, 1997, p. 199).

In 1836, Upper Canada, under the leadership of Sir Francis Bond Head, intended to move all these settled communities to the isolation of Manitoulin Island. Head managed to secure Manitoulin Island from the Ojibwe on the simple promise that it would be protected by the Crown against settler encroachment; no payment accompanied that promise. He then secured an agreement from the Saugeen Ojibwe from the Bruce Peninsula to trade 1.5 million acres (0.6 million hectares) of the Saugeen tract's fertile land for the northern tip of the Bruce Peninsula. Head advised them that he could not control the squatters settling on their land and therefore they must relocate to Manitoulin Island or the northern tip of the Bruce Peninsula. In effect, they received granite rocks and bog land in exchange for their fertile territory in the Saugeen tract.

CLASS ACTIVITY

As a class, review the legislation, including proclamations and inquiries, made by the Canadian government intended to protect Indian lands. Was the legislation successful? Why or why not?

Compare the Canadian legislation with the treatment of indigenous people by the Spanish government, discussed in chapter 9.

ASSIMILATION LEGISLATION

The Crown passed legislation in 1857 called the *Gradual Civilization Act* to create a process of enfranchisement for Native people to cease being Native. Enfranchisement began as a voluntary process. The legislation set out that if a native male was self-supporting, debt free, and deemed by the superintendent to be a suitable candidate for enfranchisement, he could forfeit his status as an Indian and receive 20 hectares of land cut from his people's reserve. Furthermore, he would thereafter have all the rights of a regular citizen, including the right to vote in provincial and federal elections. This legislation, if it had been successful, would have eroded the reserve land base and Native sovereignty (Dickason, 1997, p. 225).

This enfranchisement plan was less than successful; only one person applied to be enfranchised, Elias Hill from the Six Nations Reserve in southwestern Ontario. He lost his status but never received the promised 20 hectares of land because the Six Nations Council, seeing the legislation for what it was, refused to surrender the tract of land.

In 1869 the *Enfranchisement Act* was introduced to limit blood quantum to one-quarter Indian in order to qualify to remain a status Indian. All others would be removed automatically from treaty entitlements. The purpose of this legislation, in the words of a bureaucrat in 1871, was "to lead the Indian people by degrees to mingle with the white race in the ordinary avocations of life" (Miller, 2004). The result would be fewer treaty Indians. Amazingly, this focus continued to be central to all legislation designed to administer Indian people until 1985.

British North America Act
statute enacted on March 29, 1867 by the British Parliament providing for the confederation of Canada

The **British North America Act** was passed in 1867. It was drawn up during the Confederation of Canada during a time of extensive nation building. The British imperial government transferred responsibility for Indian affairs to the newly formed federal government of the United Canadas. Native people were not consulted in the creation of this Act, a statute that did not recognize the rights of Native people to govern themselves and their land. Section 91(24) of this Act gave authority over Indians and lands reserved for Indians to Canada. Many historians believe this was a turning point in history that marked the beginning of an era of serious oppression of Native people in Canada. With Confederation, the power of Native governments was reduced to less than that of a municipality and, despite the diversity of Native peoples and culture, they would be treated as one homogeneous group. They would no longer have the right to negotiate with the British Crown in regard to legislation affecting them or their lands; rather they had to negotiate with the federal government of Canada that, itself, had a keen interest in the lands occupied by Native people.

THE INDIAN ACT

Indian Act
created in 1876 to consolidate all policies aimed at the administration of Indian populations in Canada

Within nine years of Confederation the legislation regarding Indians was consolidated into one act called the **Indian Act**. The *Indian Act* retained the previous definition of an Indian but continued to broaden its scope of authority to define a band (Dickason, 1997, p. 259). According to the *Indian Act*, a "band" is a body of First Nations for whom the government has set aside lands for their common use and benefit; for whom the government is holding money for their common use and benefit; and who have been declared a band by the governor in council for the purposes of this Act. A member of a band is a person whose name appears on a band list or who is entitled to have his/her name appear on such a list; the process of eligibility is set out by the government. A reserve for the purposes of the *Indian Act* is a tract of land, the legal title to which is vested in the Crown, that has been set aside for the use and benefit of the band. As we learned in our discussion of the Lubicon, many Native groups are still awaiting designation as bands in accordance with this legislation. Without such designation the government does not afford them any benefits or protection. There are currently 633 recognized bands in Canada and 116 in Ontario.

The *Indian Act* did not include the Inuit because there was little contact between Canada and the Inuit at the time. Since the government was intent on reducing the number of Indians and certainly not increasing it, when the question arose in the 1930s, Ottawa's position was that since the Inuit are not culturally Indians, they were not included in the *British North America Act*, s. 91(24), which designated the federal government's responsibility for Indians. In the 1930s the Inuit were hard hit by reduced game, their traditional source of sustenance, and needed relief assistance. Neither level of government wanted to accept any responsibility to provide it, even though fur traders, miners, and whalers had spent decades extracting resources from Inuit land without compensating the Inuit. The Quebec government took the federal government to court, arguing that the Inuit were Indians, in a matter of speaking, and should fall under the authority of the federal government. In 1939 the Supreme Court of Canada ruled that the Inuit, although culturally distinct, would be considered Indians, but would not be included in the *Indian Act*.

Despite their inclusion in legislation the government neglected the Inuit until the need for military expansion into the North arose after World War II. Between 1941 and 1970 the federal government used a disk system to identify the Inuit for which it accepted responsibility. The disk bore the Canadian coat of arms and a number by which the wearer would be recorded; it had a hole punched in it so it could be fastened by a string around the neck. This simplified record keeping since the naming system used by the Inuit was unfamiliar to the government. The disk evolved into proof of status; those who had disks were eligible for government services, those without were not.

Other groups were also left out of the legislation aimed at Indians, including the Innu of Newfoundland and Labrador. When these territories entered Confederation in 1949, the rights of Indians to be defined and dealt with in accordance with Canadian legislation such as the *Indian Act* were originally included in the documents but were penciled out prior to ratification, leaving the Innu with no protection for their territories and no guarantees for any assistance in times of need. We will see in a later chapter how this omission affects the Innu today.

Imposed System of Government

The *Indian Act* quickly provided for the removal of traditional systems of governance of Native peoples and replaced them with a system called the band council. It is similar in nature to municipal governments in that it comprises one chief and several councillors through an election process that is strictly regulated by the Act. This system was implemented for all Native groups in a "one size fits all" fashion with no consideration given to the diverse forms of government and culture across First Nations groups. Furthermore a person called the Indian agent (a white government official set in place to oversee the functions of the reserve) had authority, set out in the Act, to remove the chief or council members for any number of reasons.

Some nations resisted this intrusion in their established systems of government, the Six Nations being one of them. The band managed to resist the transition to an elected band council by agitating for change to the system and petitioning the Queen, insisting they were not subjects of the British Crown, but allies of the British Crown who had not given up their sovereignty at any time in history. In 1924, Deputy Superintendent General of Indian Affairs Duncan Campbell Scott ordered the overthrow of the council by force.

Lt. Col. Morgan was charged with the responsibility of gathering troops provided by the RCMP to overthrow the traditional council and oversee the institution of the first elected band council for the Six Nations.

Gender Discrimination Within the Act

Appeals from Native women who had lost their status and that of their children by marrying non-Native men asserted that this was discrimination under the *Canadian Bill of Rights*, which guaranteed the equality of women in law. Native women argued that Native men who married non-Native women were able to retain their status and their non-Native wives were given status as Indians. Their appeals were unsuccessful in an astonishing 5:4 ruling by the Supreme Court of Canada in the 1974 case *Attorney General of Canada v. Lavell; Isaac v. Bedard*, [1974] SCR 1349, which ruled that the *Indian Act* took precedence over the *Bill of Rights*.

An appeal was made to the United Nations Human Rights Committee, which found Canada was in violation of the *International Covenant on Civil and Political Rights* in denying women their rights to status because of marriage. This was very embarrassing to Canada as the country is renowned for its work and advancement in the area of human rights. The result was the passing of Bill C-31 in 1985, which allowed those women who had lost their treaty rights through marriage to re-apply.

The federal government estimated that there would be about 50,000 people who would qualify for reinstatement and that about 20 percent of those would apply. However, over 100,000 people applied and by 1991 almost 70,000 had been reinstated on application, increasing the number of status Indians dramatically. Nevertheless, a funding increase did not accompany the increase in population. Many people who had regained status through Bill C-31 returned to overcrowded reserves looking for shares in treaty benefits such as housing and education, effectively overwhelming already insufficient resources, and causing division between traditionally status Indians and those newly created through Bill C-31. The Bill left the decision of band membership up to individual bands. Some bands that control their membership have refused to allow Bill C-31 Indians to rejoin the band and therefore refused them residency on the reserve. Under Bill C-31 it is now possible to be a status Indian but not a member of a band. Furthermore, the Bill did not rectify the inequities completely as it limits the passing of status from a Bill C-31–recognized Indian to the third generation, dependent upon the status of their chosen life partner. This is often referred to as the double-grandmother clause.

Another inequity within the Act with regard to women was their exclusion from taking part in decisions regarding the surrender of band land. This was included in the original Act and not changed until 1951 when the Act was overhauled. This is a contrast to many Native societies' understanding that women play a significant role in decisions over land management and are in fact known to be guardians of the land.

Tax Exemption

The *Indian Act* included laws with regard to Indian tax exemption for those Native people living on reserves. Native people had the right to be exempted from any federal tax if they purchased items while living on reserves, in recognition of the special status accorded to the reserves. This tax exemption still exists today and is much maligned by non-Natives as an unfair privilege. Many Native people assert that this is recognition that Native land is sovereign land and not a part of Canada, and that historical tax exemption further supports the fact that Native people have never surrendered their sovereignty and right to self-government. Many non-Native people overestimate the benefits of tax exemption. It is only for people living on the reserve and does not provide exemption for income earned off-reserve. Since on-reserve employment is hard to find, most Native people work off-reserve and are subject to income tax and other taxes that other Canadians pay.

As we will examine later, 47 percent of Native people live off-reserve and therefore work off-reserve. Since tax-exemption status is attached to the territory of a reserve, not to the person, that 47 percent of Native people pay all of the same taxes that all other Canadians pay other than provincial sales tax (PST) on purchases (6 percent). Interestingly, status Indians living off-reserve do not access that tax money to obtain services as other non-Native members of the community do. They are the sole responsibility of the federal government and therefore must access federal funds allocated through Indian Affairs for services. For example, the province funds non-Native education, but the federal government funds Native education.

Changes Through Time

The first change to the *Indian Act* in 1880 was to withdraw "half-breeds" (mixed blood) from treaty agreements. This was to quickly reduce the number of Indians that held status and therefore had treaty rights. At this same time, treaty making was ongoing in the Western plains area. The government could see that the buffalo population was crashing and the Métis, a distinguishable group who had already asserted their right to land, would require assistance in rebuilding their economy. In order to avoid any obligation of assistance the government encouraged them to accept **scrip** (a one-time payment and small land allocation to discharge them from any rights obtained by treaty Indians).

In the same year, the Indian Branch became its own department, with inside staff based in Ottawa including the superintendent general, chief clerk, accountant, and clerical staff, and an outside staff comprising 460 field workers responsible for the implementation of policies directed at Indians. These outside workers were called **Indian agents**, and were invested with tremendous authority over the reservation and the people with whom they worked.

scrip
a one-time payment to discharge treaty rights

Indian agent
federal employee of Indian Affairs in charge of administration on reserves

A 1958 job study lists the authorities of the Indian agent as follows: dealing with the recording of property; registering births, deaths, and marriages; administering band funds; and holding elections. The Indian agent interviewed people who needed farming equipment, those who complained about land encroachments, and those applying for loans. He encouraged people to marry legally and to enlist in the armed forces. He adjusted property when members left or joined the band. He dealt with the estates of the deceased and supervised the building of infrastructure, including schools. He negotiated the surrender of band lands for highways or other purposes, and applied for relief funds to house the needy. He informed the court of matters concerning Indians who were on trial for criminal matters. He was the justice of the peace and the health inspector for the community and, later, for the schools. He presided over band council meetings and could vote to break a tie. Finally, he enforced the *Indian Act* and policies directed at Indians.

In some cases, Indian agents were capable people with integrity; in others, they were not. In all cases, they were non-Indians. This continued for decades. Slowly bands have wrested authority for these matters back from the federal government.

CLASS ACTIVITY

Consider the power of the Indian agent. What power was left to Native governments?

In 1880 the process of unmaking Indians continued with mandatory enfranchisement of a Native person if that person held a university degree, joined the clergy or the armed forces, or voted in a federal election. The new changes in 1880 not only didn't recognize hereditary chiefs, but also only recognized elected band council chiefs. Native people in the West were prohibited from selling their agricultural products because the government did not want them to purchase liquor or other "worthless" things.

In 1884 Native people complained that the government was not fulfilling the treaty agreements that allowed them to use the land; agricultural equipment promised in the treaties was not delivered. The government conceded that this was a legitimate complaint but excused the breach, explaining that the bands were not sufficiently advanced to benefit from the promised tools, livestock, and schools.

The potlatch and other Native ceremonies were banned in 1884, with a two- to six-month jail term for those who contravened this prohibition. This prohibition was included in the Act but was not enforced until the 1920s under the leadership of Deputy Superintendent General of Indian Affairs Duncan Campbell Scott. Cultural practices and ceremonies went underground to avoid the watchful eye of the Indian agent. These practices were critical to the traditions of an oral culture in the passing on of their history, governance, and spirituality to the next generation. Repressing these practices resulted in the beginning of loss of culture.

In 1889 the *Indian Act* was amended to allow the federal government to override a band that did not wish to lease land. By 1894 any Indian lands that were not worked (agriculturally) due to illness or injury could be leased to non-Natives under the authority of the Superintendent. Idle or surplus Indian land was also seen as fair game.

In 1911, s. 46 of the *Indian Act* allowed portions of land to be taken by municipalities or companies for roads or railways without consent of the band but with permission of the superintendent. Section 46(a) permitted the removal of Indians, against their wishes, from any reserve next to or partly within a town of 8,000 inhabitants. For example, a Mi'kmaq reserve in Sydney, Nova Scotia and the Songees reserve in Victoria, British Columbia were moved outside their respective cities to free up urban land for development. In the West between July 1, 1896 and March 31, 1909, Native peoples received $74,343 for surrendered land. The Department of Indian Affairs received $2,156,020 for that land.

The promise of reserved lands through treaty was in some cases not fulfilled; in other cases, the power given to the Indian agent through the *Indian Act* resulted in large sections of reserved lands, coveted by settlers and resource speculators, being carved out—at times without compensation. Railways expropriated reserved lands freely, often splitting communities down the centre. The railway towns that were springing up often grew to displace Native people, and more land was seized, often without compensation, as the towns expanded.

In 1918 enfranchisement was made easier for those who wished to apply; however, the plan still did not meet with success. Subsequently, in 1921, legislation changed to provide the authority to the Indian agent to enfranchise any Indian who was deemed suitable regardless of his or her wishes. In other words, without giving consent, an Indian could lose his or her status with the stroke of a bureaucrat's pen.

You may be wondering why Native people did not rebel against this oppressive legislation and continued seizure of their lands. Native people did respond and organize resistance but it seemed futile. In 1880, in response to political movement in the West to oppose land seizure, a pass system was implemented requiring any Indian leaving the reserve to have a pass issued by the Indian agent. The goal of the system was to inhibit Native people's mobility and discourage a Native alliance that might threaten Canadian authority. Many reserves were impoverished due to the depletion of resources, and any sign of political activism was quickly met with threats of withdrawal of government relief funds.

In 1927, in a heavy-handed response to Six Nations resistance to coming under the authority of the Act and the West Coast Nisga'a's continued appeals to England, the *Indian Act* was again amended to proclaim that no person could raise money to .

1951: CHANGES TO THE ACT

The *Indian Act* was overhauled in 1951 in an attempt to create a more equitable piece of legislation. The ban on potlatches and other traditional dances and ceremonies was lifted. Over the previous 30 years, however, the transference of the culture and oral history that was central to these practices had been seriously disrupted.

The Act established the Indian register as a centralized record of all individuals entitled to be registered. The registrar was given authority to add or delete names from the general band lists. In response to complaints from Indians who were unilaterally removed from the band list, or whose births had never been registered, preventing them from inclusion on the band list, new rules were put in place to require the posting of the band list. An appeal process was instituted for those who were removed from the list, with a limit of six months for appeal.

Despite the overhaul of the Act, there was still no agreement to set up a land claims commission as requested by Native people. Furthermore, the 1951 revisions in section 88 of the Act allowed "all laws of general application in force in any Province to apply as well to Indians on and off reserves." This was undoubtedly a precursor to the federal government's intention to slowly devolve the responsibilities for Indians to the provinces. The problem with this amendment was that provincial laws such as hunting and fishing regulations, if applied to Indians, were in violation of rights accorded under treaty. Today, Canadian courts are attempting to navigate their way through layers of treaty and provincial law to provide an equitable interpretation of that law, and to define Native rights in Canada.

It was not until the early 1960s that Native people were given the right to vote in federal elections. Soon after, Native people would use this right to become politically active in opposing a white paper proposed by then Liberal Indian Affairs Minister Jean Chrétien. This paper proposed the elimination of the *Indian Act*, the elimination of reserved land for Indians, and the elimination of the special legal category of status Indian. It further proposed to transfer all responsibilities for Native people to the provinces and promised to look into land claims. Although assertions were made that the paper was introduced as a path to equality for Native people in Canada, they viewed it as the final stroke of assimilation. The National Indian Brotherhood stated: "We view this as a policy designed to divest us of our aboriginal, residual, and statutory rights. If we accept this policy, and in the process lose our rights and our lands, we become willing partners in culture genocide. This we cannot do" (Dickason, 1997, p. 364).

Once again this policy had been created with little consultation with Aboriginal people. In the words of Dave Courchene, president of the Manitoba Indian Brotherhood from 1967 to 1974: "Once again the future of the Indian people has been dealt with in a high-handed and arbitrary manner. We have not been consulted; we have been advised of decisions already taken. I feel like a man who has been told he must die and am now to be consulted on the methods of implementing that decision" (Dickason, 1997, p. 364).

Cree leader Harold Cardinal stated, "We do not want the Indian Act retained because it is a good piece of legislation. It is not. It's discriminatory from start to finish. But it is a lever in our hands and an embarrassment to the government, as it should be. No just society with even pretensions to being just can long tolerate such a piece of legislation, but we would rather continue to live in bondage under the inequitable Indian Act than surrender our sacred rights. Any time the government wants to honor its obligation to us we are more than ready to help devise new legislation" (Cardinal, 1969, p. 140).

Many treaties originally had been made with the British, and legislation passed the responsibility to honour those treaties to the federal government upon the transfer of power during Confederation. The federal government could not simply exonerate itself of those obligations by passing them on to provincial governments. In 1971 the white paper was abandoned by the federal government, but the idea of devolving responsibilities for Indians to the provinces had not disappeared. It resurfaced in 1986 when the *Nielson Report* recommended that the cost of delivering services to Indians be shared by the provinces. This was motivated by the rising costs of program delivery as Native populations increased dramatically around this time, and Native communities were suffering from the effects of the residential school system, which increased the need for social services. This recommendation was abandoned after much protest from Native people.

A positive change to the *Indian Act* resulted from the fight against the white paper; for the first time the federal government agreed to fund research into land claims and to set up processes by which those claims could be negotiated. We will discuss land claims in chapter 13.

> **QUESTIONS**
>
> The legislated disempowerment of Native people through legislation such as the *Indian Act* has led to the federal government assuming fiduciary responsibility for First Nations in Canada. **Fiduciary responsibility** is a legal term that means the legal duty to act in the best interests of another person, or in this case another group of people. Discuss as a class whether the federal government has fulfilled this duty. Why or why not?

fiduciary responsibility the responsibility to hold something in trust for another

CONCLUSION

The dispossession and disempowerment of Native people in Canada has been a long process that has spanned generations. This dispossession was purposefully conducted by many levels of government to facilitate expansion and economic growth for Canada; however, First Nations people in Canada rarely benefited from the economic growth. Aggressive policies of assimilation were created in Canada to ensure that status Indians with treaty entitlements would slowly disappear. Canada was unsuccessful in accomplishing that goal and so today we struggle to define Native rights in Canada in accordance with treaties. Native people in Canada struggle to reclaim authority over their own affairs, to reclaim lost culture, to rebuild healthy communities, and to create economic growth and prosperity for themselves within Canada.

KEY TERMS

treaty

fiduciary responsibility

British North America Act

Indian Act

scrip

Indian agent

REFERENCES

Armstrong, J.C. (1997). The history lesson. In D.D. Moses and T. Goldie (Eds.), *An anthology of Canadian Native literature in English* (2nd ed.). Toronto: Oxford University Press.

Bill C-31, *An Act to Amend the Indian Act*, April 17, 1985.

British North America Act, 1867, 30 & 31 Vict., c. 3.

Canadian Bill of Rights, SC 1960, c. 44.

Cardinal, H. (1969). *The unjust society: The tragedy of Canada's Indians*. Edmonton: M.G. Hurtig.

Dickason, O.P. (1997). *Canada's First Nations: A history of founding peoples from earliest times*. (2nd ed.). Toronto: Oxford University Press.

Early Canadiana Online. http://www.Canadiana.org.

Indian and Northern Affairs Canada. (1999). *Report of the Royal Commission on Aboriginal Peoples: The Indian Act, chapter 9*. www.ainc-inac.gc.ca/ch/rcap/sg/sgmm_e.html.

Indian Claims Commission. http://www.indianclaims.ca.

Leslie, J., & Maguire, R. (Eds.). (1978). *The historical development of the Indian Act*. (2nd ed.). Ottawa: Indian and Northern Affairs Canada.

Miller, J.R. (2004). *Lethal legacy: Current native controversies in Canada*. Toronto: Macfarlane Walter & Ross.

Scott, D.C. (1926). The Onondaga madonna. In *The poems of Duncan Campbell Scott* (p. 230). Toronto: McClelland & Stewart.

APPENDIX 10.1

The History Lesson

By Jeannette C. Armstrong

> Out of the belly of Christopher's ship
> A mob bursts
> Running in all directions
> Pulling furs off animals
> Shooting buffalo
> Shooting each other
> Left and right
>
> Father mean well
> Waves his makeshift wand
> Forgives saucer eyed Indians
>
> Red coated knights
> Gallop across the prairie
> to get their men
> and to build a new world
>
> Pioneers and traders
> Bring gifts
> Smallpox, Seagrams
> And Rice Krispies
>
> Civilization has reached
> the promised land.
>
> Between the snap crackle pop
> Of smoke stacks and multi-coloured rivers
> Swelling with flower powered zee
> Are farmers sowing skulls and bones
> And miners
> Pulling from gaping holes
> Green paper faces
> Of smiling English lady
>
> The colossi
> In which they trust
> While burying breathing forests and fields beneath concrete and steel
> Stand shaking fists
> Waiting to mutilate
> Whole civilizations
> Ten generations at a blow.
>
> Somewhere among the remains
> Of skinless animals
> Is the termination to a long journcy
> And unholy search
> For power
> Glimpsed in a garden forever closed
> Forever lost.

Source: Armstrong (1997).

APPENDIX 10.2

The Onondaga Madonna

By Duncan Campbell Scott, 1894
Deputy Superintendent of Indian Affairs, Canada

> She stands full-throated and with careless pose,
> This woman of a weird and waning race,
> The tragic savage lurking in her face,
> Where all her pagan passion burns and glows;
> Her blood is mingled with her ancient foes,
> And thrills with war and wildness in her veins;
> Her rebel lips are dabbled with stains
> Of feuds and forays and her father's woes.
>
> And closer in the shawl about her breast,
> The latest promise of her nation's doom,
> Paler than she her baby clings and lies,
> The primal warrior gleaming from his eyes;
> He sulks, and burdened with his infant gloom,
> He draws his heavy brows and will not rest.

Source: Scott (1926, p. 230).

CHAPTER 11

Children and the Residential Schools

CHAPTER OBJECTIVES

After completing this chapter, you should be able to:

- Explain the rationale of the Dominion of Canada for the implementation of residential schools.
- Understand the magnitude of the damage the schools had on the fabric of First Nations societies.
- Connect the seizure of children from First Nations communities through the decades of the 1960s to the 1980s with the residential school experience.
- Discuss the moral, legal, and ethical issues that arise with regard to accountability and healing.

INTRODUCTION

From 1867 to 1945 Native children were not allowed to attend any schools other than those legally recognized as Native schools. Native schools were provided by the Canadian government in conjunction with the Roman Catholic, Anglican, United, and Presbyterian churches. The purpose of the schools was assimilation through the teaching of farming for boys, domestic duties for girls, and religion. The schools were chronically underfunded and the health conditions of the children suffered. Due to poor nutrition and substandard living conditions, many children died of diseases such as typhoid fever and tuberculosis. In these schools many children suffered physical and sexual abuse, and much of Native culture and language was lost. Today, some **residential school** survivors seek to use civil and criminal law to hold the government of Canada and the churches involved accountable for their actions.

The focus of the government on Native children did not end with the residential school system but persisted into the mid-1980s with the removal of thousands of Native children from their communities by well-intentioned social service workers. The workers believed they were rescuing these children from a life of poverty

residential schools
church-run, government-funded residential schools for Native children designed to prepare them for life in white society

and despair so prevalent in Native communities at the time, much of it brought about by the legacy of the residential school system.

Some may question the decision to dedicate an entire chapter of a very limited text to children's issues. However, the results of the final report of the **Royal Commission on Aboriginal Peoples (RCAP)**, released in November 1996, gave society at large a clearer picture of the enormous damage done to Native communities through the assault on the young. Native people who are working to heal their communities believe that the effects of the education system cannot be overestimated. This chapter will discuss the political environment of the time in an effort to show how this could happen in a country that today is renowned for its attention to civil rights. Stories will be borrowed from survivors to help understand the pain suffered.

Royal Commission on Aboriginal Peoples (RCAP)
commission established in 1991 to investigate the issues facing Aboriginal people in Canada

EDUCATION AS A TOOL FOR ASSIMILATION

The appreciation of and the desire for education was shared very early by Indians and non-Indians alike; thus guarantees for state-funded education were set out in some treaties including, for example, the Stone Fort Treaty, which stated, "And further, Her Majesty agrees to maintain a school on each reserve hereby made, whenever the Indians of the reserve should desire it" (Morris, 1971, p. 315). Native leaders recognized the need for new and different education for their children in the rapidly changing environment. It became clear with the depletion of resources and with increasing white settlement that traditional hunting and trapping lifestyles would be severely disrupted, and the resources that had sustained Indian nations since time immemorial would soon no longer be sufficient. Native leaders envisioned state-run schools in partnership with Native nations that would preserve traditional Native life and prepare children for new non-traditional labour markets.

In his biography, John Tootoosis states, "The Indians who at treaty time had asked that their children be educated were asking that they be taught to read and write, to learn to work with figures, to be trained into useful skills to enable them to compete on an equal basis for a way of making a living with the children of the white men. ... Poundmaker (chief at treaty time) had replied very clearly, 'We want to be sure that life will be as good for them (our children) as it will be for your children'" (Goodwill & Sluman, 1982, p. 113).

The federal government had an altogether different vision for the schools; it viewed education as a means of aggressive assimilation, the importance of which was discussed in the previous chapter. Education in Canada was a provincial responsibility at the time and still is. However, the *British North America Act* gave the federal government jurisdiction over Natives and therefore the federal government bore the responsibility for Indian education, which is still the case to this day.

As early as 1830, four mission schools were established in Ontario for the education of the Native populations. A leader in this initiative was an Ojibwa man, Peter Jones, who was also a Methodist missionary. He had founded an agricultural settlement for the Mississaugas on the Credit River (in present-day Toronto) and was providing education through the Credit River School, which was reasonably successful. Jones wished to extend his education provisions to other Native nations by building residential schools for Indian children that would also provide manual training. The Mohawk Institute, established in 1833 by the New England Company for the civilization, Christianization, and instruction of Natives, was a model for Jones, and he asked four different bands in his area to help finance the schools by donating one-quarter of their treaty money. The Methodist church and the federal government also shared in the cost of establishing the schools. Jones had a vision that the schools would eventually be run by Christian Native people. Neither the federal government nor the church shared this vision.

Although Native people supported the schools initially, they soon discovered that the goals of the church and the government were inconsistent with their own. Native leaders soon recognized that schooling meant assimilation and a total rejection of all their own values and traditions. They stopped financial support to the schools and withheld their children from the schools. The experiment was deemed a failure, but the precedent had been set of using partnerships with the church and missionaries in the education of Native children (Grant, 1996).

When the question of education for Native children arose again in 1870, there was no doubt that the churches, for two main reasons, would be recruited in the task of educating Native children. The first was to inculcate Native children with the religious ideals of the day and have them reject all things associated with their own culture. The second reason was merely practical; education would become the most expensive endeavour of the Indian department, and the ability to secure the free labour of missionaries and priests in the running of the schools and the instruction of the children would significantly reduce the cost of education. The federal government would therefore provide funding in the form of land grants, per capita grants, and other material rewards to the four churches that were already involved in Indian education as an act of benevolence. This partnership between church and state would last until 1969.

The decision to make education for Native people "residential" rather than provide day schools on reserves was fuelled by the same two purposes. First, the cost of building a school on each and every reserve, according to the Department of Indian Affairs, was certainly too high (regardless of the wording within the treaty). Second, separating the children from the influence of their families and community was considered necessary for the children to internalize the religious teachings of the church.

PROBLEMS WITHIN THE SYSTEM

One of the first problems to surface in this education system was poor attendance. Health conditions in the schools were not good, and many children died of disease. Rumours of abuse within the schools circulated quickly among parents, who also opposed the curricula designed for assimilation. For these reasons, many Native nations and Native parents chose to withhold their children from residential schools. Poor attendance resulted in a change in the *Indian Act* in 1894 that made school attendance compulsory. Section 119 of the Act gave truant officers authority to enforce attendance by forcible removal of children if necessary for attendance in day schools. In 1920 the Act was amended to extend to residential schools as well and to provide for the conviction of parents of summary offences for withholding children from the schools.

EXERCISE 1

Consider the following quotes taken from records of the time and discuss them as a class:

Sir Hector Langevin, secretary of state for the provinces, argued before Parliament in 1883:

> Industrial schools have succeeded very well in the United States and it is quite likely that they will succeed here as well. The fact is, that if you wish to educate the children you must separate them from their parents during the time they are being taught. If you leave them in the family they may know how to read and write, but they will remain savages, whereas by separating them in the way proposed, they acquire the habits and tastes of civilized people. (Indian Tribes of Manitoba, 1971, p. 113)

The Indian Affairs Annual Report 1889:

> The boarding school dissociates the Indian child from the deleterious home influences to which he would otherwise be subjected. It reclaims him from the uncivilized state in which he has been brought up. ... By precept and example he is taught to endeavor to excel in what will be most useful to him. (Provincial Archives of Manitoba, RG 10, vol. 6040, file #160-4, part 1, C8153)

Hayter Reed, deputy superintendent general for Indian Affairs, quoted in 1894:

> The extension of educational work is chiefly being carried out in the direction of Industrial and semi-Industrial Schools, in which children not only get the positive advantages of instruction superior to what they could be given on reserves, but are removed from the retarding influences of contact with them. ... How can improvement be looked for in a race of children, when out of school they are subject to such a degrading environment? (Provincial Archives of Manitoba, RG 10, vol. 6040, file #160-4, part 1, C8153)

Another problem that surfaced right from the beginning was the disagreement between all agencies involved concerning what type of education should in fact be delivered, by whom, and to whom. Disagreement over age of enrollment in residential school was frequent; some Protestant ministers advocated enrolling students as young as three to "catch them early." Others argued that this would be a waste of money. Some argued the students should be kept until they were 14; some argued for 16, some 18, and some for 21. Enrollment ages did in fact change through the years. Bickering among the Catholic, Presbyterian, Anglican, and Methodist churches over who would get the students was common as each denomination viewed this competition as a battle for souls, or, in some instances, a battle for per capita funding.

As far as curricula, some schools classed as "industrial schools" wished to offer training in what were conceived as more skilled trades such as carpentry, cabinet making, and tailoring. Some of the early schools also produced a well-educated and literate group of graduates. However, two problems followed. The first was that success in acquiring a skilled trade did not guarantee employment; in fact, there were no opportunities for employment. One agent wrote to the Department in December 1907, "Race prejudice is against them and I am afraid that it will take time, under the circumstances, before they can compete with their white brothers in the trades" (quoted in Malloy, 1999, p. 158). Critics of the system insisted that the more costly industrial school training was a waste of resources, since people in mainstream Canada were not prepared to accept working alongside Indians. In response, the industrial schools were phased out.

The second problem with the early success of the schools was most succinctly stated by the Minister of the Interior, Frank Oliver, in 1897: "We are educating these Indians to compete industrially with our own people, which seems to me a very undesirable use of public money" (Hall, 1983, p. 126). The attitudes expressed in these historic records may seem shocking to the average Canadian today, but they reflect the racism and bigotry that was prevalent among many Canadians at the time. The status quo was being threatened by Indians, who could not only learn to read and write but also become great craftsmen on par with non-Indians and could conceivably compete in a labour market for skilled jobs. It had to stop.

As industrial schools were phased out and the number of residential schools increased, the quality of education decreased. By 1932, at the end of Duncan Campbell Scott's career as deputy superintendent general of Indian Affairs, there were 17,163 students enrolled in residential schools. Scott viewed this increase in attendance as proof of his success in the assimilation process; it was more likely due to the compulsory attendance legislation enforced by his government. The flipside of this statistic is that three-quarters of students enrolled were in grades 1 through 3. Only 100 students reached grade 6 (Malloy, 1999, p. 171).

In his autobiography, residential school student Basil Johnston writes about how he had to repeat grades and, much to his dismay, he came to understand that the age of 16 for discharge from the school must coincide with grade 8; thus he and others were destined to repeat grades until they reached 16 and could be released from the school (Johnston, 1989, p. 47).

Harold Cardinal writes, "In plain words, the system was lousy. The curriculum stank, and the teachers were misfits and second raters. Even my own elementary school days, in grade eight I found myself taking over the class because my teacher, a misfit, has-been or never-was sent out by his superiors from Quebec to teach savages in the wilderness school because he had failed utterly in civilization, couldn't speak English well enough to make himself understood. Naturally he knew no Cree. When we protested such inequities we were silenced as 'ungrateful little savages who don't appreciate what is being done for you'" (Cardinal, 1969, p. 54).

Bill Thomas writes of staff in the schools: "The kooky clergy and even kookier staff make a shambles of any potential for effective development. ... For the most part the 'dedicated' staff I knew in the United Church school were old ladies trying to atone for earlier sins and mucking that up. Others were religious zealots or simply strange people who—under ordinary circumstances—could not get a job or fit in anywhere else" (Thomas, 1991, p. 6).

These complaints about the staff from residential school survivors are validated by studies conducted in the early 1960s. The reports indicate that, with few exceptions, staff fell into three categories: first, relatively recent immigrants; second, Canadians from lower socio-economic backgrounds; and finally, a few Indian people. In 1967, researcher Richard King conducted a study of a Yukon Indian School at Mopass. King labelled staff as "generally deviant in the whiteman society." He found that many of the teachers lacked qualifications and many could not even speak English well. It seems that the reasonably attractive pay in comparison with other jobs in society attracted poorly educated and deficient personalities to work in the schools. Letters from the Department of Indian Affairs directed at school administrators as early as 1910 address concerns over the quality of its teachers (Grant, 1996, p. 143).

Besides the quality of the teachers, the labour required to run the schools interfered with the academic achievement of the students. The focus on agriculture and the department's desire that the schools be self-supporting required long hours of manual labour from the students. Half-day classes and half-day labour were to be the rule, but in many cases much more time was spent on labour than in the classroom. Communications from field workers and school inspectors to the department leave us records of these concerns from early times. One letter written in 1916 alerts the department that of a 42-day period, the boys in one school had spent only nine days in class; the rest of their time was spent labouring on the farm to support the school (Malloy, 1999, p. 170). As a result, many students left the school unable to read or even to converse well in English.

HEALTH CONDITIONS

The health of children in the schools was always a source of concern. Unsafe construction, overcrowding, and poor nutrition resulted in health problems and a high death rate. The churches and the administrators at Indian Affairs were well aware of this, but funds were not readily available to make adjustments within the school to provide more sanitary conditions. Dr. P. Bryce was commissioned in 1903 to inspect residential schools and report on the health conditions. His report was scathing, indicating that some schools had a death rate of *50 percent*. He states, "The sight of the ragged, ill-kempt and sickly looking children was enough to make me sick at heart." Indian Agent MacArthur in 1910 reports that the Duck Lake residential school had suffered a death rate of 50 percent as well. S.H. Blake, a lawyer, conducted a review of the Anglican missions and reported to Minister of Indian Affairs Frank Oliver, "The appalling number of deaths among the younger children appeals loudly to the guardians of our Indians. In doing nothing to obviate the preventable causes of death, brings the department within unpleasant nearness to the charge of manslaughter" (Malloy, 1999, p. 77).

In many of the schools nutrition was certainly lacking, which left the children vulnerable to disease. Dr. Simes conducted an inquiry into Elkhorn School in 1943 in response to complaints from the Indians at The Pas, Manitoba. He reported that the children were dirty and their clothes were disgraceful; furthermore, he reported that 28 percent of the girls and 69 percent of the boys were underweight, and the menu as forwarded to the Ministry had many omissions and few substitutions (Malloy, 1999, p. 114). Today, many residential school survivors remark about never having had enough to eat.

Dr. Bryce found at File Hills Boarding school that 75 percent of the students on the discharge roll were dead. Of the 31 students on the roll, 15 had died in the school, and 7 died at home within three years of discharge. All these students reported that their health at the time of enrollment was good. File Hills was certainly the worst account, but if its statistics were factored in with the other schools, the death rate would be 42 percent in the 35 schools included in Dr. Bryce's study. To project those figures throughout the system in 1907 would indicate that of the 3,755 children in the schools, 1,614 would die prematurely (Malloy, 1999, p. 90).

This information was not restricted to government officials. Dr. Bryce's report made headlines in the newspapers, informing the public of the horrific conditions in the schools, as well as the unacceptable death rate. One reporter wrote that the death rate would be unacceptable even in war. Other efforts were made to attract public attention to the appalling conditions of the schools, but to no avail. It seems that the Canadian public was content to be complicit in the brutality of this process of forced assimilation. Dr. Bryce would continue to criticize the ministry of doing nothing to improve sanitation even up to 1922. Bryce was successful only in ensuring that he did not secure a position in Duncan Campbell Scott's administration as the department's minister of health.

Ultimately, there were modest measures taken to improve the conditions, but the communications between school administrators and Indian Affairs indicate that high death rates and poor sanitary conditions were constant problems throughout the decades that the schools were operated. Four decades later, in 1948, Neil Walker, Indian Affairs superintendent, wrote: "If I were appointed by the Dominion Government for the express purpose of spreading tuberculosis, there is nothing finer in existence than the average Indian residential school." (Malloy, 1999, p. 262)

EXERCISE 2

Read appendix 11.1 together as a class and discuss the guardianship position of the government for Indian children as well as the treaty obligation to provide education.
  Discuss the value that mainstream society placed on Aboriginal children.
  Consider the mandatory attendance legislation instituted by government.
How would you feel as a parent of an Indian child in this era?

ABUSE WITHIN RESIDENTIAL SCHOOLS

Abuse within residential schools has generally been divided into four categories by most authors who write about it: sexual, physical, mental, and spiritual/cultural. Each will be examined in turn, followed by an examination of the aftermath of this abuse and the efforts to reach some agreement on liability and possible compensation.

In 1964, 10-year-old Willie Blackwater was removed from his family home on Kisiox Reserve in British Columbia and taken to Port Alberni Indian residential school on Vancouver Island, 1,600 kilometres away. Immediately, Blackwater was singled out by dorm supervisor Henry Plint, who sexually abused Blackwater during his years at the school. Blackwater revealed the abuse to several authorities, including a government official, none of whom believed him. Furthermore, when news reached Plint that the boy had accused him of abuse, he beat the child so severely that Blackwater ended up in the infirmary. Blackwater suffered as an adult trying to cope with his childhood, but came forward again to begin an investigation into his abuse at the school. Thirty other adult men came forward in attempt to make Plint accountable years later, and in 1995 and 1997 Plint, at the age of 72, was convicted and sentenced to 12 years in prison; he showed no remorse. In his judgment Supreme Court Justice Douglas Hogarth referred to Plint as a sexual predator and a sexual terrorist whose activities were allowed to go on unchecked: "As far as the victims are concerned, the Indian residential school system was nothing more than institutionalized pedophilia" (quoted in Fournier & Crey, 1997, p. 72).

This is only one of thousands of incidents of sexual abuse endured in residential schools across Canada that came to light in the 1990s. In 1990, the Manitoba Grand Chief of the National Assembly of First Nations talked publicly of his experience of sexual abuse while in residential schools in Manitoba. The Native community was divided in its response to sudden public scrutiny. Some felt these experiences were so painful and shameful that they should not be brought forward by causing victims to relive their pain; others felt that the only way to begin the healing process was to openly face the harsh reality of what had been suffered.

The RCMP and other policing agencies became involved in uncovering information on historic sexual assaults within the schools. They quickly uncovered thousands of victims. Investigations were difficult because many of the perpetrators had died or could not be located. In some circumstances, victims who made disclosures to police were unable to cope with dredging up the past; some have committed suicide, and some have turned to alcohol and drugs in order to deal with their pain.

No one can know for certain how widespread the sexual abuse was, as we can count only those who have come forward voluntarily. In 1990, *The Globe and Mail* reported that Rix Rogers, the special adviser to the minister of national health and welfare on child sexual abuse, discussed during a meeting of the Canadian Psychological Association that the abuse revealed to that date was believed to be just the tip of the iceberg. He believed that "a closer scrutiny of the past treatment of native children at Indian residential schools would show 100% of children at some schools were sexually abused" (*The Globe and Mail*, June 1, 1990).

Physical abuse also was rampant within the schools, as the application of corporal punishment was difficult to contain. Stories abound from across the country of children being forced to eat their own vomit, having their faces rubbed in human feces, and being beaten for minor infractions of school rules. Many incidents of abuse are imbedded within the Department of Indian Affairs files. Reports from empathetic teachers describing the assaults on children were answered with the teachers' dismissal for disloyalty. One such letter states:

> Children's faces are slapped, [they are] hit on the head, struck across the nose causing nose bleeds. ... One teacher said a boy in her classroom had a swollen face for two days from being slapped. Another teacher reported that one of her pupils was slapped because he couldn't read the small print in the hymn books. One of my grade 8 boys was slapped on the head until he was pale, he staggered, complained of feeling dizzy and his nose bled profusely. This was witnessed by most of the school boys. He fainted five days later in prayers and again in my classroom. (Indian and Northern Affairs Canada, file 956/1-13, vol. 1, August 8, 1958, and attached correspondence; quoted in Malloy, 1999, p. 282)

Eventually, the Department of Indian Affairs issued a number of regulations to address the use of corporal punishment in response to both allegations and the children's injuries that were observed when the schools were inspected. It seems these regulations resulted in little change, as school administrators continued on a course of physical punishments that had been set as policy when the schools were established.

In 1965, in response to the widespread allegations of physical abuse, the department solicited an evaluation of the residential school system to be presented at the first Residential Principal's Conference. The department handpicked six residential school graduates who were of "impeccable authority and character" as witnesses, each successful in public service, education, or church service. One respondent was a graduate of the Mohawk Institute in Brantford, Ontario, and he described the conditions there as follows: 90 percent of the children suffered from dietary deficiency, evidenced by boils, warts, and general ill health. He reported seeing children eating from the garbage and the bin intended to feed the pigs. Lice infestations were common and so children's heads were frequently shaved. Runaways retrieved were brought back to run a gauntlet where they were hit with anything found on hand. He reports he had "seen boys crying in the most abject misery and pain with not a soul to care—the dignity of man!" (Indian and Northern Affairs Canada, file 1/25-20, vol. 1, as quoted in Malloy, 1999, p. 284). The appraisal of the schools resulted in some positive comments, but most were overall unfavourable and difficult to ignore.

Emotional abuse is perhaps the most damaging of all. Students were made to endure humiliation and ridicule by staff. As a punishment for bedwetting at one school, children were made to wear the wet sheet draped over their heads. In another school, female students were stripped of their underwear and struck on the bare buttocks in front of the class. This disclosure came from the principal of a northern school who believed the punishment to be reasonable. Children report being locked in a room in only their underwear and restricted to a bread-and-milk diet as a punishment for running away. Two female runaways were forced to attend meals in the dining room in only their underwear. Children were ridiculed and taunted by staff and called derogatory names specifically targeting their race.

The department was aware of the persistent problem of children running away. Many died while trying to escape, mainly due to exposure. The department also had to deal with the problem of children attempting suicide within the schools. These two problems were further indicators of real problems within the school itself and the system at large. In 1920, nine boys attempted suicide by eating water hemlock; one died. In 1981, at Muscowequan school, five girls between the ages of eight and ten tied socks and towels together in an attempt to hang themselves.

Finally, spiritual and cultural abuse was evidenced in the very purpose of the schools: assimilation. The express purpose of the schools was to eliminate the Indian way of life for the next generation. Duncan Campbell Scott believed that within three generations the Indian race would no longer exist as a result of the government's assimilation policies; residential schools were to be one of the most effective means to this end. Ultimately Scott was mistaken; even though three generations of Native children did attend residential schools, and in many areas of the country four or five generations were victims of these schools, Native nations are alive and persevering in Canada today.

Residential schools attacked with a vengeance the ambitious goal of eliminating Native culture. Many survivors report that the most severe punishments meted out by school staff were reserved for children who spoke their Native language or attempted to carry on any Native tradition. As children arrived at the schools, their birth name was replaced with an identification number and a new Christian name. Many of the children spoke little or no English and so could not communicate with staff. A few schools would assign an interpreter from the older student population, but most schools simply expected the child to stop speaking in his or her Native tongue until the child could acquire sufficient English to communicate. Isabelle Knockwood writes of her experiences at Shubenacadie residential school in Nova Scotia: "When little children first arrived at the school we would see bruises on their throats and cheeks that told us that they had been caught speaking Mi'kmaw. Once we saw the bruises begin to fade, knew they'd stopped talking" (Knockwood, with Thomas, 1992, p. 81).

The idea for such a forcible attack on language was borrowed from the United States in that country's approach to Indian education. In 1867 President Grant called strongly for linguistic genocide: "Through sameness of language is produced sameness of sentiment, and thought. ... In difference of language today lies two-thirds of our trouble. ... Schools should be established, which children should be required to attend; their barbarous dialect should be blotted out and the English language substituted" (Reyhner & Eder, 2004).

The psychological effects of the suppression of language were severe. Erasing the language meant erasing an identity, the child's concept of self, and how the child viewed the world and his or her place in it. A saying from this era expresses this destruction of identity: "Kill the Indian and save the child/man." The systematic destruction of everything Indian in the child's life was not replaced with any new values or world view. The intent was for Christianity to take the place of Native culture and values, but the coercive way in which Christianity was taught belied its own values and few children internalized these new ideals.

For many children, acquiring a new language under such stressful circumstances was difficult. Many children simply stopped speaking and ceased to express emotions such as frustration, fear, and anger; therefore, children learned to internalize emotion rather than express it. These obstacles to communication continued after the child was discharged from the school. As the children returned to their home communities, the first generation of survivors could not communicate with any members of their community, even their own families. They had lost their language and spoke only English, not widely spoken by members of their community. The emotional isolation thus continued.

Other issues have impacted on the decline of Native languages after the closure of residential schools—for example, the move of Natives to large urban centres. However, in 1941 less than 10 percent of Natives claimed English as their first language; in 1971, when the schools had mostly been phased out after the third generation of children attended, 54 percent of Canadian Natives reported English as their first language. By 1996, 75 percent of Canada's Native population listed English as their mother tongue.

We know that language is both the construct of a culture and the conduit of culture, and if languages are at risk of being lost forever, as many Native languages are, aspects of culture are also lost.

> **EXERCISE 3**
>
> Read appendix 11.2 and discuss the reading as a class.
> Conduct an online search on Aboriginal languages in Canada to see how many languages still exist today and how many of them are at risk of being lost.

AFTERMATH OF SCHOOLS

The federal government undertook a review of Indian residential schools in 1948. The government found that the schools were a dismal failure and proposed the phasing out of residential schools in favour of integrating Indian students into mainstream schools. The review of the schools found that a Native graduate from the residential school system was less prepared for life than a Native who had never attended any formal education institution. The federal government began to provide per capita funding to provincial schools to include Indian children. Nevertheless, many of the schools were kept open until the 1960s and the last school did not close until 1988.

The effect of the schools on Native communities has been devastating. As many studies in social issues have proven, those who are abused often become abusers; this is particularly so when it comes to sexual abuse. Native leaders report that sexual abuse is like a disease ripping through their communities. A 1989 study commissioned by the Native Women's Association of the Northwest Territories found that 80 percent of girls under the age of eight and 50 percent of boys under the age of eight had been victims of sexual abuse.

Families have also been torn apart by violence, as residential school survivors have learned that adults exert power and control over children by physical punishment. The cycle of child abuse has been put in motion in Native communities, where long ago few would have ever thought to raise a hand to a child for punishment or discipline. The cycle is difficult to stop. Positive parenting practices such as nurturance and respect have never been experienced by residential school survivors, and many have faced difficulties raising their own children. These struggles are being passed to another generation, and without intervention, this cycle will continue.

In 1990 one First Nations leader wrote to Minister of Indian Affairs Tom Siddon:

> Social maladjustment, abuse of self and others and family breakdown are some of the symptoms prevalent among First Nations baby boomers. The graduates of Ste. Anne's Residential school are now trying and often failing to come to grips with life as adults after being raised as children in an atmosphere of fear, loneliness and self loathing. Fear of caretakers. Loneliness in knowing that elders and family were far away. Loathing from learning to hate oneself, because of repeated physical, verbal or sexual abuse suffered at the hands of various adult caretakers. This is only a small part of the story. (Indian and Northern Affairs Canada, file E6575-18-2, vol. 4, letter to Tom Siddon, November 15, 1990)

Native leaders have called for a public inquiry into the residential school system to determine the breadth and depth of the damage it has caused and to suggest resolutions for their communities on how to deal with healing. The federal government will not agree to such an inquiry. In 1992, the Royal Commission on Aboriginal Peoples (RCAP) was called by the federal government in response to a land claims issue that erupted into violence. A considerable amount of the commission's efforts were dedicated to the residential school issue. The final report given by the commission contains the following recommendation (at p. 338):

> Our research and hearings indicate that a full investigation into Canada's residential schools system, in the form of a public inquiry ... is necessary to bring light and begin to heal the grievous harms suffered by countless children, families, and communities as a result of the residential school system. The inquiry should conduct public hearings across the country, with sufficient funding to enable those affected to testify. The inquiry should be empowered to commission research and analysis to assist in gaining an understanding of the nature and effect of residential school policies. It should be authorized to recommend whatever remedial action it believes necessary for governments and churches to ameliorate the conditions created by the residential school experience. Where appropriate, such remedies should include apologies from those responsible, compensation on a collective basis to enable Aboriginal communities to design and administer programs that assist the healing process and rebuild community life, and funding for the treatment of affected people and their families.

To date there has been no public inquiry.

ATTEMPTS AT RESOLUTION

How can the residential school legacy be resolved? First and foremost, Native communities and leaders agree that no amount of money can ever compensate Native people for the suffering they have endured. The issue then is, how do Canadians reconcile themselves with the past and partner in the healing process for Native people? It becomes a question of justice. What is the fair and just thing to do considering all that has taken place?

As discussed earlier in the chapter, Henry Plint was convicted of sexually assaulting Willie Blackwater and many other boys at Port Alberni Residential School during the 1960s. In 1995 and 1997 he was sentenced to 12 years in prison. In 1998 Blackwater and 30 other residential school survivors embarked on a civil suit against Plint, that also named the federal government, which organized the residential school system, and the United Church of Canada, which ran the Port Alberni school. The trial was difficult for survivors to endure, as they faced hard questioning by government and church lawyers. In 2001, the complainants chose to take an out-of-court settlement for a reported $180,000 to $290,000 apiece in order to end the trial. But the questions remain: who is responsible for these atrocities? Is it Henry Plint alone or is it the entire Indian Affairs Department that appears to have turned a blind eye to the abuse of children? Is the government to be held fully responsible for setting up an education system with very few formal accountability processes, thereby creating a situation that was destined to foster abuse? As historic files of Indian Affairs are examined, the department's attempt to document complaints of abuse is clear. It chose to institute modest—failed—attempts to stop the abuse. Should churches share in the responsibility because they supplied unqualified staff who were the abusers?

Survivors have used a variety of methods to seek redress for their suffering. The first method is the criminal prosecution of offenders. But, as in the Blackwater case, victims are revictimized during the investigative and trial processes and the investigation is often hampered by the fact that police are frequently unable to locate the offenders, many of whom are now deceased.

The second and most popular method to seek redress has been civil litigation. There are several reasons for choosing this process, aside from financial reparation. The first is the recognition of the legitimacy of the mainstream judicial system in Canada. A victory in the public forum of the court system is a recognition that wrong has occurred and that a victim deserves compensation. The second is that this type of public recognition satisfies those who seek vindication on a matter of principle. The third is that the court system is perceived as levelling the playing field between the plaintiff and the accused. Although it cannot be perfectly even, as the defendants (government and churches) in all cases have more financial resources for the litigation process, the plaintiff can be assured that there is no back door, high-pressure negotiation, with the powerful being pitted against the powerless, as often is the perception in the alternative dispute resolution process. The justice system, although imperfect, aspires to autonomy from unequal distributions of power. The fourth is that a court decision establishes precedents that other courts are bound to follow, thereby helping to ensure that victims will be treated equally.

The fifth and final reason victims choose the civil litigation process is that they want their stories heard. This desire was clear in the findings of the RCAP. Its recommendation was for a cross-country inquiry into the damage done by the residential schools, a recommendation that the federal government adamantly refuses to follow. The victims want to be heard and understood, and they want to become a part of the consciousness of mainstream Canadian society. This will happen only if a resolution is sought in a public forum such as the court system where the transcripts and outcome are part of the public record. It is startling that many young adults are only vaguely aware that Indian children until comparatively recently were forced to attend residential schools. Non-Natives have not been taught, or simply have not chosen to inquire about the residential school legacy. Seeking just resolutions to all issues involving Aboriginal people in Canada can happen only if Aboriginal and non-Aboriginal Canadians have the same awareness of the past and present, and can become partners in shaping the future.

There are drawbacks to the civil litigation process. The most obvious is the cost to the victim. Some victims have resolved this through the use of contingency fees, although victims have been charged up to half of the financial settlement in legal fees (Tibbetts, 2000).

Another drawback to this method of resolution is that the recognition of harm done is limited only to the individual victim; there is no recognition of harm on a broader scope for the victim's family, for subsequent generations, and for the community. This recognition is particularly important to Native people and to their communities.

Despite these drawbacks, there are a growing number of cases. As of July 2003 there were 12,000 claims filed, very few of which had been resolved. Many more potential claimants were waiting to see what resolutions would be reached before filing their own claims. It is possible that the number of claims could reach 30,000. At its height, the residential schools numbered 88 across Canada, and the 1991 Census reported that there were 105,000 residential school survivors alive at that time. It was estimated that, if it continues at its present pace, the pursuit of civil litigation could stretch the time frame for settlement to over 50 years, in which time almost all the plaintiffs would be dead.

In order to address these drawbacks the government has embarked upon an Alternative Dispute Resolution process commonly known as ADR. This process has been slow as many matters had to be settled, not the least of which was the division of the responsibility between church and state. The federal government announced, after negotiations stalled, that it would accept a division of responsibility for 70 percent of the claim amount, leaving the churches responsible for the remaining 30 percent. The churches insist that this amount could in fact leave them bankrupt. Another issue faced in this process is the refusal of the government to address loss of culture and language. The government insists it will address these losses through government-funded initiatives for Aboriginal language and cultural renewal, and will provide compensation to victims only for sexual and physical abuse suffered in the schools.

A major flaw in the ADR system is that it moves the resolution of these matters from the public to the private forum, where only those directly involved are included in the negotiations. The system thereby reduces accountability to the public and brings into question whether justice has in fact been served. However, as long as the parties are happy with the settlement, is it relevant whether or not the interests of justice have been served? The ADR system, started in June of 2001. In 2003, a lawyer representing some former students pointed out that of the $1.2 billion dedicated to the ADR process, $540 million was earmarked for legal costs rather than compensation (Frank, 2003).The survivors of residential schools grow older each year and many pass away without closure to this most life-altering experience. On May 10, 2006, through the ADR process, an Indian residential schools settlement agreement (IRSSA) was reached. Under the agreement, Aboriginal people who can prove their attendance in the schools will be eligible to receive a "common experience payout" of $10,000 for the first year of atendance and $3,000 for each subsequent year. An estimated 79,000 living former students will qualify (www.anglican.ca/Residental-Schools).

RECOGNITION OF WRONG

In 1998 the government issued a carefully worded apology delivered by then Minister of Indian Affairs Jane Stewart, apologizing specifically to those who had suffered physical and sexual abuse at the schools. At the time, an announcement was made that a new initiative would support community-based healing for people affected by residential schools, including those suffering the intergenerational impacts. This Aboriginal Healing Fund provided $350 million for use over 10 years for counselling programs and culture recovery initiatives. Native people were divided in their sentiment regarding both the apology and the Aboriginal Healing Fund initiative. Many felt that the apology was a step forward; others felt that the healing fund was incapable of even scratching the surface of the social problems inflicted on Native nations by the schools. Others believed that neither the healing fund nor the apology was sufficient. As one former Native professor at Mohawk College in Hamilton, Ontario stated, if there were only one million Aboriginal people in Canada (there are many more), the fund would amount to $350 for each person, paid out over 10 years, to seek professional counselling for social problems suffered as a result of cultural genocide. To underscore the inadequacy of the amount, he pointed out that in the same month the federal government announced it would pay $500 million in penalties to cancel the order for new helicopters for Canada's military.

Despite the sentiment on either side of this debate over the sufficiency of the apology or healing fund, this was an historic occasion in Canada, since it was the first time the government publicly recognized that harm had come as a result of its former policies with regard to Native people.

THE SIXTIES SCOOP

A discussion of the government's historic mistreatment of the youngest generation of Aboriginal people cannot be complete without addressing a more recent phenomenon that occurred as the schools were phased out between the 1960s and 1980s. It has been dubbed the "**Sixties Scoop**" by sociologists, referring to the practice of removing Indian children from Native communities and placing them in foster care or out for adoption in non-Native homes. As the schools closed, the question of what to do with the children remained. After three or four generations of Native people had been raised in schools rather than in family homes, the ability of residential school survivors to raise their own children was severely handicapped. The prevalence of poverty, alcoholism, and other social problems on reserves left many children in need of protection or, at the very least, intervention. After generations of the schools' efforts to break and destroy family ties, the communities had difficulty in rebuilding harmonious family lives.

Sixties Scoop
the practice of removing Native children from Native communities and placing them in foster care or for adoption in non-Native homes

In 1947 the Canadian Welfare Council and the Canadian Association of Social Workers presented a brief to a federal Special Committee proposing that Indian children who were neglected lacked the protection afforded under provincial social legislation available to white children. This was true, because Native children fell under the authority of the federal government, which was in the process of dismantling the school system. Child welfare services were provided to the mainstream population through provincial funds and under provincial legislation. The concerns expressed by social workers were addressed with new changes to the *Indian Act* in 1951, which allowed for all laws in application in the province to apply to Indians as well, effectively bringing child welfare services under the authority of provincial child welfare workers. The problem then arose: who would fund the provision of these services to the Indian reserves and Indian children? There was considerable debate over this issue, which resulted in postponing intervention for Indian children. When the federal and provincial governments finally agreed to a cost-sharing process to finance these services, well-intentioned social workers quickly sprang into action. Although only 1 percent of all children in care in 1959 were Native, by the end of the 1960s, 30 to 40 percent of all children in care were Native, even though they comprised only 4 percent of the population.

Reasons cited for the removal of children included inadequate housing, unsafe drinking water, no running water, no available school, poor health conditions—none of which the federal government chose to address. Rather, the decision was to remove the children to white communities. Services such as counselling and child care were not made available to intact Aboriginal families; these services could be funded only if the child became a ward of the state. "The caseloads in social service agencies were so high that workers did not have time to properly screen homes, nor was monitoring of either foster or adoptive homes usually feasible. But most social workers, none of whom were aboriginal, felt little harm could befall an aboriginal child rescued from poverty and placed with a nice, middle-class, white family. Yet behind the closed doors of their foster and adoptive homes, aboriginal children were even more isolated and vulnerable than they had been in residential school. … In many cases, children were taken from parents whose only crime was poverty and being aboriginal" (Fournier & Crey, 1997, p. 85). In a holdover from the residential school days, siblings were separated due to not only the large sizes of families but also the belief that they would adjust more quickly to their new homes and new environments without the influence of siblings.

Bridget Moran, a social worker in British Columbia at the height of the Sixties Scoop, writes in *A Little Rebellion* that social service workers had no resources available that might have helped keep Aboriginal families together. They had no family support workers, treatment centres, or transitional housing. Moran reports that when they found a child at risk, they had no alternative but to place the child in foster care. Ernie Klassen, former district superintendent for Indian Affairs, recalls that on one weekend a social worker chartered a bus to apprehend 38 children on the Spallumcheen reserve in British Columbia and was asking for 38 different foster homes to accommodate the apprehension (Fournier & Crey, 1997).

One result of the apprehension of the children was the intensification of social problems on reserves that were experiencing the loss of their young. Native leaders spoke out against the practice with vehemence, but their voices were rarely heard.

By the end of the 1970s, one in every four status Indian children could expect to be separated from his or her parents for all or part of childhood. In British Columbia in 1997 one in three legal wards was of Aboriginal heritage. Many Aboriginal children were shipped out of province and many went to families in the United States. Some private adoption agencies, mostly of a religious nature, sprang up to secure Canadian Indian children for adoption to US families. In all, Manitoba lost the greatest number of Aboriginal children, an estimated 20,000, of which 55 percent were sent out of province, in comparison with 7 percent of non-Aboriginal adoptions going out of province. In 1982, Manitoba judge Edwin Kimmelman was called in to investigate the apprehension of Manitoba's Native children at the insistence of Native leaders. He conducted his investigation and concluded that the child welfare services were well intentioned but misguided, and guilty of cultural genocide. In response to his findings, a moratorium was placed on out-of-province adoptions, and the wholesale removal of children was stopped in the mid-1980s.

Tragically, many of these adoptions failed, as many of the children suffered from an identity crisis in their teens. Many had to endure racism in schools and from society at large without the support of the Native community. Many had been subjected to abuse while they were in the foster system prior to adoption, and were unable to overcome that legacy. Others were suffering from health complications such as fetal alcohol syndrome and fetal alcohol effects that were not diagnosed prior to adoption, and newly adoptive parents were unable to cope with the challenges of raising such a child. Today our court system and our jails are filled with these tragic figures.

CULTURAL GENOCIDE

The term "**cultural genocide**" has been used widely by academics studying the history of the relationship between Canada and First Nations peoples. "Cultural genocide" can be defined as the deliberate and systematic destruction of the culture, traditions, language, and ways of being of a specific cultural group. More recently, the term "genocide" has been used by academics writing about the experiences of First Nations people in Canada and around the world. In response to the discovery of the atrocities committed against Jews during World War II, the international community rallied together through the United Nations to create the *Convention on the Prevention and Punishment of the Crime of Genocide*. Canada participated in this Convention in 1948, more than 50 years after the establishment of residential schools and prior to the proposed closure of the schools. The Convention reads:

cultural genocide
the deliberate and systematic destruction of the culture, tradition, language, and ways of being of a specific cultural group

Article 1: The Contracting Parties confirm that genocide, whether committed in time of peace or in time of war, is a crime under international law which they undertake to prevent and to punish.

Article 2: In the present Convention, genocide means any of the following acts committed with intent to destroy, in whole or in part, a national, ethnical, racial or religious group, as such:
   (a) Killing members of the group;
   (b) Causing serious bodily or mental harm to members of the group;
   (c) Deliberately inflicting on the group conditions of life calculated to bring about its physical destruction in whole or in part;
   (d) Imposing measures intended to prevent births within the group;
   (e) Forcibly transferring children of the group to another group.

Article 3: The following acts shall be punishable:
   (a) Genocide;
   (b) Conspiracy to commit genocide;
   (c) Direct and public incitement to commit genocide;
   (d) Attempt to commit genocide;
   (e) Complicity in genocide.

Article 4: Persons committing genocide or any of the other acts enumerated in Article 3 shall be punished, whether they are constitutionally responsible rulers, public officials or private individuals.

> ### EXERCISE 4
>
> Using information from chapters 9, 10, and 11, discuss as a class whether the UN Convention's definition of genocide fits the experiences of previous generations of Native peoples in Canada.
>
> If you conclude that the definition does fit, discuss who should be held accountable and how. If you believe that the definition doesn't fit, give reasons.

CONCLUSION

All aspects of the assimilation process have been devastating to Native communities: the suppression of culture through aspects of the *Indian Act*; the seizure of resources and territory forcing economic dependence; the influence of missionaries to undermine Native traditional values and force an agricultural way of life. However, none have been so devastating as the harm done to First Nations' youngest, most vulnerable members through the residential school system. The social consequences of this system wreak havoc in Native communities today in the form of broken families, violence, substance dependency, and ill health.

In British Columbia, research was recently conducted on one reserve to determine the health status and quality of life of Native residential school survivors compared with those Native people who did not attend residential school. The results were not surprising; there was little difference between the studied populations. However, as a whole both groups suffered from poorer health and a lower quality of life than non-Native people. Researchers concluded that the effects of residential schools are distributed throughout the community as the trauma of the residential school experience was transferred to collateral victims and from generation to generation (Benton et al., 2005, pp. 295-312).

Where do we go from here? What are the obligations of mainstream Canadians toward Native people? Native leaders are forging ahead, making every effort possible to heal their communities and come to a fair and just settlement with mainstream Canada. Furthermore, they are looking to redefine their relationship with the Crown, one that is freshly rooted in equality and justice.

KEY TERMS

residential school

Royal Commission on Aboriginal Peoples (RCAP)

Sixties Scoop

cultural genocide

REFERENCES

Benton, S. et al. (2005, August). *Social Indicators Research, 73*(2), 295–312.

Cardinal, H. (1969). *The unjust society: The tragedy of Canada's Indians.* Edmonton: Hurtig.

Fournier, S., & E. Crey. (1997). *Stolen from our Embrace: The abduction of First Nations children and the restoration of Aboriginal communities.* Vancouver: Douglas and McIntyre.

Frank, S. (2003, July). *Time Canada, 162*(4), 30.

The Globe and Mail. (1990, June 1). Reports of sexual abuse may be low, expert says.

Goodwill, J., & N. Sluman. (1982). *John Tootoosis: A biography of a Cree leader.* Winnipeg: Pemmican Publications.

Grant, A. (1996). *No end of grief: Indian residential schools in Canada.* Winnipeg: Pemmican Publications.

Hall, D.J. (1983). Clifford Sifton and the Canadian Indian Administration 1896–1905. In Ian A.L. Getty & Antoine S. Lussier (Eds.), *As long as the sun shines and the water flows: A reader in Canadian native studies.* Vancouver: UBC Press.

Indian and Northern Affairs Canada. (1958, August 8). File 956/1-13, vol. 1 and attached correspondence. Quoted in Malloy (1999).

Indian and Northern Affairs Canada. (1990, November 15). Letter to Tom Siddon, file E6575-18-2, vol. 4.

Indian and Northern Affairs Canada. File 1/25-20, vol. 1.

Indian Tribes of Manitoba. (1971). *Wahbung: Our tomorrows.* Manitoba: Manitoba Indian Brotherhood.

Johnston, B.H. (1989). *Indian school days.* Norman, OK: University of Oklahoma Press.

King, A.R. (1967). Case study of a Yukon Indian School: How education fails. *The school at Mopass: A problem of identity.* New York: Holt, Rinehart, & Winston.

Knockwood, I., with Thomas, G. (1992). *Out of the depths: The experiences of Mi'kmaw children at the Indian residential school at Shubenacadie, Nova Scotia* (p. 81). Lockport, NS: Roseway.

Malloy, J.S. (1999). *A national crime: The Canadian government and the residential school system 1879–1969.* Winnipeg: University of Manitoba Press.

Moran, B. (2002). *A little rebellion.* Vancouver: Arsenal Pulp Press.

Morris, A. (1971). *The treaties of Canada with the Indians of Manitoba and the North West Territories.* Toronto: Coles Publishing.

Native Women's Association of the Northwest Territories. (1989).

Provincial Archives of Manitoba. RG 10, vol. 6040, file #160-4, part 1, C8153.

Reyhner, J., & Eder, J. (2004). *American Indian education: A history*. Norman, OK: University of Oklahoma Press.

Thomas, W.C. (1991, January 7). Letter, *Western Report*, p. 6.

Tibbetts, J. (2000, August). Lawyers agree to stop swooping in on victims. *The Ottawa Citizen*.

United Nations. (1948, December 9). *Convention on the Prevention and Punishment of the Crime of Genocide*, adopted by Resolution 260(III) A of the United Nations General Assembly.

APPENDIX 11.1

Inhumane Conditions at Residential School

MEMO

TO: Mr. R.S. Davis
The Department of Citizenship and Immigration
Indian Affairs Branch
Norlyn Bldg.
Winnipeg Manitoba

FROM: G.H. Marcoux
Regional Inspector of Indian Schools

DATE: October 21, 1953

RE: Situation at Residential School

I visited the school on October 19th and 20th and found the following situation:

From the front entrance to the corridor of the basement one was subjected to an unbearable odor. The floor of the boiler room was covered with liquid from the sewage system to a depth of 6 to 8 inches, some of the liquid was seeping into the boys' recreation room. At the other end of the building, in the girls' recreation room there are a number of trap openings on the floor. Upon opening these traps one could see the same kind of liquid containing raw sewage, direct from toilets, almost to the level of the floor.

It looks as if the entire sewage piping under the floor had collapsed and that the sewage piping leading to the outside has been blocked by some obstruction.

On Monday, October 19, the smell in the building was unbearable and no human being should be asked to live under such conditions. There is no doubt in my mind that such drastic action must be taken to remedy the situation and make sure it does not re-occur in the future. I, therefore, strongly recommend that the school be closed until such time as the necessary repairs are made. Should this condition continue or happen again at a later date, the health of the pupils and the members of the staff can be seriously affected. Furthermore, should there be an outbreak of disease in a school like this one, the Indian parents would blame the school and refuse to send their children there. This would be a ten year set back in the education plan.

This is respectfully submitted in the hope that the department be advised of the situation and that immediate appropriate action be taken.

Source: INAC File 501/25-1-019, vol. 1. (1999). G.H. Marcoux Memorandum to Mr. R.S. Davis, October 21, 1953. Reprinted in John Malloy, *A national crime: The Canadian government and the residential school system 1879 to 1986*. Winnipeg: University of Manitoba Press, pp. 259-260.

APPENDIX 11.2

I Lost My Talk

I lost my talk
The talk you took away.
When I was a little girl
At Shubenacadie school.

You snatched it away;
I speak like you
I think like you
I create like you
The scrambled ballad, about my word.

Two ways I talk
Both ways I say,
Your way is more powerful.

So gently I offer my hand and ask,
Let me find my talk
So I can teach you about me.

Rita Joe, Mi'kmaq

Source: Rita Joe, "I Lost My Talk," in D.D. Moses & T. Goldie (Eds.), *An Anthology of Canadian Native Literature in English* (Toronto: Oxford University Press, 1998).

CHAPTER 12

Lingering Socio-economic Issues

> ### CHAPTER OBJECTIVES
>
> After completing this chapter, you should be able to:
>
> - Connect colonization, assimilation policies and legislation, and the residential school experience to current socio-economic issues facing First Nations people in Canada.
>
> - Discuss the future with regard to socio-economic issues, economic development, and self-government.

INTRODUCTION

The socio-economic issues facing First Nations people today are connected to the experiences of colonization and forced assimilation. We have journeyed here together as mainstream Canada and First Nations people. As one speaker so eloquently put it, "We were not standing on the shores of Eastern Canada waiting for the white man to arrive in his sailing ship carrying a welfare check." (Geddes et al., 1997) Native populations are increasing rapidly, but economic growth is slow for First Nations communities. In this chapter we look at obstacles to that growth and the ultimate goal of self-sufficiency and self-government.

CASE STUDY

Prior to beginning a discussion on demographics I would like to look closely at a northern Ontario reserve and its journey to the present socio-economic condition. The community I've chosen to examine is the Ojibwa community of Grassy Narrows. It is important to understand that although we are looking at one community, every Native community in Canada has its own history, its own journey, to the present. Space constraints will not permit an in-depth investigation into more than one community within this text, but, as a class, consider reviewing other communities in crisis to see how their crisis came to be.

Grassy Narrows is located 80 kilometres north of Kenora, Ontario, near the Manitoba border. Today the population is 1,000, with 700 members living on the reserve; 70 percent are children or youth.

The reserved area for the Grassy Narrows people had been set aside in 1873 in the signing of Treaty No. 3, which relinquished 14 million hectares to the government. As part of the agreement the Native people of the area were to retain their right to pursue their traditional occupations such as hunting and fishing on the surrendered tract of land, except such areas as may "from time to time" be required for settlement, mining, or forestry. The government was to maintain schools for instruction, and pay annuities to the band at $5 per person per year.

Missionaries began work in the Grassy Narrows area in the 1840s, accessing the area by canoe, but most Native people were out on the land, far from the reach of the missionaries, following a traditional hunting and trapping way of life. The people would return from the traplines in May to their summer grounds where they would plant gardens and live in their well-spaced summer cabins. Those who were taken to the residential schools at McIntosh or Kenora were most influenced by the missions.

Land development came with the building of a railway to access forestry products, but few Native people left the community. There was no welfare or social services; the Indian agent came to the reserve once a year to distribute treaty money. The isolation allowed Native people to preserve their culture, way of life, self-sufficiency, and freedom until 1963. That summer, Indian Affairs began the process of relocating the people of Grassy Narrows to a new community on the Jones logging road, which was linked to both the railway and the city of Kenora. Indian Affairs intended to provide the Native people with the benefits of modern life, and to break the isolation that had facilitated their resistance to assimilation.

The new community was built 8 kilometres from the old one, on the English Wabigoon River. The river was to supply their water needs, as the promise of running water was not initially fulfilled. The housing provided on the new reserve was crowded and of poor quality. The hunting and trapping way of life became difficult to maintain as the government insisted that the children remain on the reserve and attend school, making the parents reluctant to leave for the traplines through the fall and winter.

Prior to the move, the traditional economic system of the Ojibwa people was systematically being dismantled by the government. Wild rice harvesting had been an activity of Ojibwa people since time immemorial; however, in the 1950s the government began a process of issuing licences for that harvest as the price of wild rice had increased, making it a possible source of income rather than sustenance. Initially, the Ojibwa people were issued licences for harvest but in the 1970s non-Native wild rice farmers took over many of those licences as their mechanical harvesting could produce a greater quantity.

Access to the new reserve from Kenora made it easier for government officials to enforce fishing regulations over the Grassy Narrows people. Changes in the *Indian Act* making all laws of the province applicable also to Aboriginal people made the Ojibwa subject to fishing regulation even though this was in direct violation of their treaty rights. Commercial fishing licences were issued to some Grassy

CHAPTER 12 Lingering Socio-economic Issues

Narrows people, but sport fishing licences were given priority because they brought more revenue to the area, predominately in white communities.

With limited access to paid employment and the severely reduced ability to use traditional forms of sustenance, the community began to sink into despair. The Jones logging road, intended to bring to the people of Grassy Narrows the benefits of modern life, brought an unregulated flow of alcohol at this time of great social upheaval in the community. Alcoholism, violence, and suicide spiralled out of control, as is shown in figure 12.1.

Studies conducted at Grassy Narrows in 1977–1978 concluded that 70 percent of adults in their child-bearing years and 80 percent in their child-rearing years were heavy drinkers. Alcohol has been, and continues to be, a disruptive influence on Native communities in crisis. The drinking of the child-rearing population is reflected in the substance abuse by the children and the subsequent failure of children to achieve academically. Gas sniffing is a very real problem among young people who live in these communities.

The extensive development of the North by the Department of Indian Affairs and Northern Development (DIAND) in the form of forestry and mining brought more bad news for Grassy Narrows. In the early 1920s, a pulp and paper mill was opened in Dryden, Ontario, 130 kilometres upstream from the Grassy Narrows traditional area. Between 1962 and 1970, Dryden Chemicals Limited pulp and paper mill, with the sanction of the Ontario government, dumped over 20,0000 pounds of mercury into the river system, resulting in its poisoning. The commercial fisheries on the reserve had to be shut down, and the people were advised not to eat the fish. Those who held fishing licences were issued $300 in compensation for the loss of their livelihood. In the 1970s and after, health officials conducted tests on the population and found that their mercury levels were 40 to 150 times

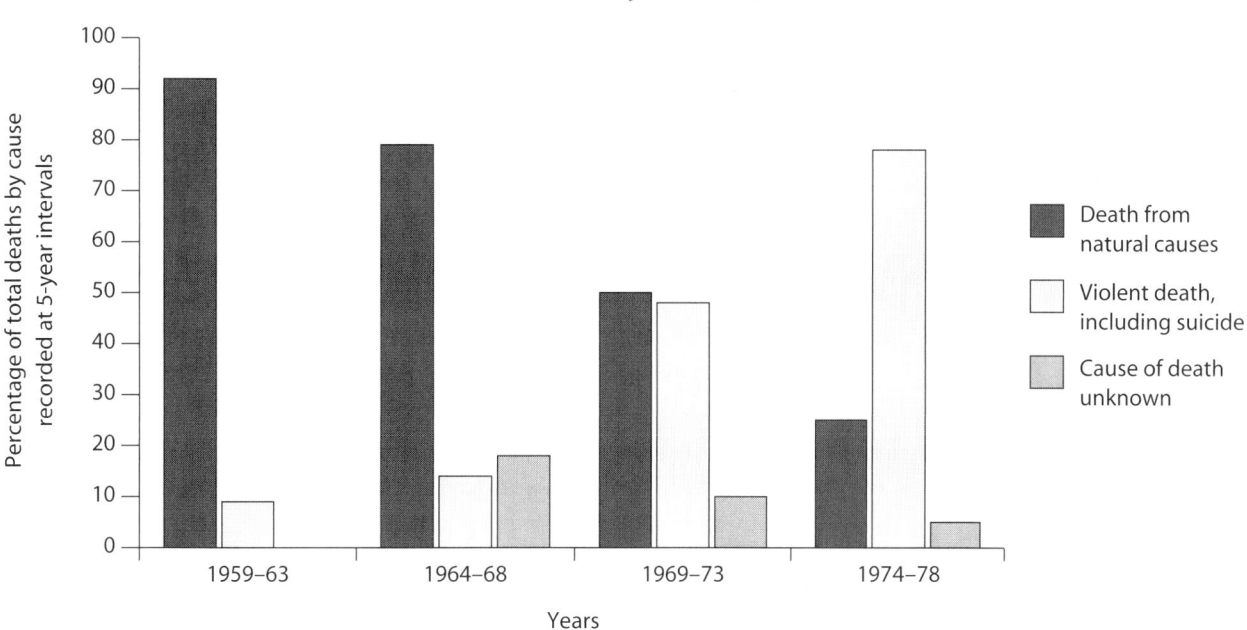

FIGURE 12.1 Incidence of Violent Death at Grassy Narrows, 1959–1978

Source: Shkilnyk (1985).

TABLE 12.1   School Dropout Rate at Grassy Narrows, 1977–1978

Grade	Number of Dropouts	Class Size	Percentage of Class
Kindergarten	10	20	50
1	3	16	18
2	7	24	29
3	9	17	53
4	7	17	41
5–8	10	24	42
4–6 (special class)	10	25	40

Source: Based on the records of attendance at the Grassy Narrows Federal Elementary School.

Source: Shkilnyk (1985).

TABLE 12.2   DIAND Expenditures at Grassy Narrows, 1969–1977

Fiscal Year	Amount ($)
1969–70	37,600
1970–71	106,400
1971–72	143,100
1972–73	356,800
1973–74	413,300
1974–75	377,600
1975–76	442,135
1976–77	708,970
1977–78	950,900

Source: The data from 1969–70 to 1972–73 were provided by the Kenora district office of DIAND and correspond to band financial records. Data for 1973–74 on came from the band's audited financial statements.

Source: Shkilnyk (1985).

higher than the average Canadian's, likely due to consumption of not only fish but also animals higher in the food chain.

The government's expenditures at Grassy Narrows quickly skyrocketed. In a community that had been visited once a year by an Indian agent and received limited health care, within 15 years of relocation DIAND was spending almost $1 million annually to address community needs for health, food, and housing.

There were conflicts between the provincial government and the mill as to who was responsible for the environmental disaster; neither wished to accept accountability. The mill had followed acceptable environmental practices as outlined in provincial law and therefore ultimately the band was unable to hold any agency accountable.

The band continued to appeal to the government for assistance in alleviating its severe social problems. In 1977, the federal government held a Royal Commission on the Northern Environment. The commission heard cited the following reasons for the severe physical, mental, and spiritual breakdown in the community (Shkilnyk, 1985):

1. The intentional undermining of religion and way of life.
2. Loss of income from trapping due to flooding and hydroelectric development.
3. Jones logging road breaking isolation of the community upon relocation.
4. Alcohol accessible to community.
5. Introduction of a foreign value system.
6. Loss of commercial fishing due to mercury poisoning.
7. Availability of welfare but no work.
8. Inability to hold any agency accountable for mercury disaster.

It was not until 1985 that the Grassy Narrows community received a negotiated settlement for the poisoning of their environment and their exposure to mercury; by then the community had already hit rock bottom and was in the process of finding a way upward. The situation at Grassy Narrows improved through the 1990s, and today the people are moving forward and taking control over many aspects of their community life. Currently, they are addressing logging issues in their traditional territories with some success. (The Crown sold logging rights to Grassy Narrows traditional territory and 50 percent has been clear-cut.) The band continues to blockade roads and negotiate for the preservation of their environment.

This is a very brief look at Grassy Narrows; I challenge you to research the past 50 years of Grassy Narrows history. My purpose is to demonstrate the recent influences that place First Nations communities at risk for severe social and economic problems. Almost every First Nations community in Ontario has been relocated at some point from its original and traditional area. Some have been relocated hundreds of kilometres from their territory for reasons that differ by community, but usually for access to resources that government and private interests wish to exploit. In almost every experience of relocation the aftermath for the Native people has included severe social problems and economic hardship. The Canadian government had known this from the very first relocations in the 19th century, but, until recently, continued to make the same decisions. It would take volumes of books to chronicle the destruction of Aboriginal communities across Canada; nevertheless, every one of those communities is moving forward, with Native leaders forging the path to recovery and health.

Many Native communities face social problems at a rate that far exceeds that of the average Canadian non-Native community. Sociologists are divided in their views regarding alcoholism in Native communities. Some consider alcohol and substance dependency to be a result of social chaos that includes poverty, hopelessness, and trauma. Others argue that alcoholism brings about social chaos, poverty, and hopelessness.

CLASS ACTIVITY

There are compelling arguments on both sides of this debate about alcoholism in Native communities. Discuss as a class.

> **CLASS ACTIVITY**
>
> Through its treaties, the federal government of Canada undertook the fiduciary responsibility for Native people. Discuss as a class whether you think the government fulfilled that duty in the case of Grassy Narrows.
>
> Discuss as a class the name of the branch of the government charged with this duty during the 1970s: Department of Indian Affairs and Northern Development. Separate that title into two distinct interests: "Indian Affairs" and "Northern Development." Discuss what these two had in common and the conflicts between the two.
>
> In groups, research the past 50 years of other Native communities in crisis; for example, Natuashish, Pikangikun, Sayisi Dene, Sheshatshiu, and the Lubicon Cree. Look for the common threads that run through the past in each of these communities.
>
> View the National Film Board documentary *The Mushuau Innu: Surviving Canada* and as a class discuss the film.

NATIVE DEMOGRAPHICS

Before discussing the socio-economic issues relating to Canada's Native people, it is important to look at the context for the figures that will be discussed.

According to Statistics Canada, the 2001 census shows that Aboriginal people's share of the total Canadian population is on the rise, with 1.3 million people reporting some Aboriginal ancestry in 2001, comprising 4.4 percent of the total Canadian population, compared with 3.8 percent in the 1996 census.

Of the 1,319,890 persons who claimed some Aboriginal ancestry in 2001, a total of 976 305 of them claimed Aboriginal identity (343,585 persons had some Aboriginal ancestry but did not identify as Aboriginal), up from 799,010 in 1996. North American Indians accounted for 608,850 (529,040 in 1996) persons, Métis were at 292,310 (204,115), and Inuit at 45,070 (40,220).

Aboriginal Growth Rates

The population of those reporting an Aboriginal identity (North American Indian, Métis, Inuit) grew 22.2 percent since 1996, with a 15.1 percent growth rate among North American Indians, according to Statistics Canada (see table 12.3). This figure marks a tenfold increase since 1901 in the number of people who claimed Aboriginal ancestry, while the total population rose by only a factor of six.

One of the main reasons for this increased growth rate among Aboriginal peoples was an improved level of health care, which considerably reduced the infant mortality rate after 1960. During the first 50 years of the 20th century, the Aboriginal population grew only 29 percent, while the population of Canada increased by 161 percent. However, after 1960, the Aboriginal population increased sevenfold, while the Canadian population only doubled.

Another important reason for the dramatic increase in those persons who claimed Aboriginal ancestry was a decrease in racism after 1960 and an awareness of Aboriginal issues in this country. Before the 1960s, it was not "popular" to be

TABLE 12.3 Size and Growth of the Population Reporting Aboriginal Ancestry and Aboriginal Identity, Canada, 1996–2001

	1996	2001	Percentage growth 1996–2001
Total: Aboriginal ancestry[a]	1 101 960	1 319 890	19.8
Total: Aboriginal identity	799 010	976 305	22.2
North American Indian[b]	529 040	608 850	15.1
Métis[b]	204 115	292 310	43.2
Inuit[b]	40 220	45 070	12.1
Multiple and other Aboriginal responses[c]	25 640	30 080	17.3

[a] Also known as Aboriginal origin. [b] Includes persons who reported a North American Indian, Métis, or Inuit identity only. [c] Includes persons who reported more than one Aboriginal identity group (North American Indian, Métis, or Inuit) and those who reported being a registered Indian and/or band member without reporting an Aboriginal identity.

Source: Adapted from Statistics Canada (2003, p. 20).

Aboriginal, and therefore many people who could have claimed Aboriginal ancestry did not do so. After the 1982 **constitution** enshrined Métis as Aboriginal people, the number of people claiming Métis ancestry grew dramatically, and continues to do so. For example, the number of persons claiming to be Métis in the Hamilton, Ontario census area grew by 87 percent between 1996 and 2001.

Statistics Canada also reports that an increased reporting of Aboriginal issues since 1986, such as the Oka crisis, the Royal Commission on Aboriginal Peoples, the creation of Nunavut, and reporting on Aboriginal land claims, human rights issues, and residential schools has increased an awareness and pride among Canadians in their Aboriginal roots and has encouraged them to acknowledge their Aboriginal ancestry.

constitution
the core system of rules and principles by which a nation or group is governed

Decrease in Birth Rate

The birth rate for Native peoples has been declining over the past 30 years. Native women, on average, tended to have 6.2 children 30 years ago. In 1986, the average Native woman had 3.2 children, while the average non-Native Canadian woman had 1.67 children. In 1999, the First Nations birth rate was 23.0 births per 1,000 population, two times the comparable rate for Canada, according to Health Canada. Over one-half (58 percent) of First Nations women who gave birth in 1999 were under 25 years of age. Native peoples consistently have more children than the average Canadian and the trend continues today. Overall, the size of Native families contributes to a steadily increasing Native population, both on-reserve and off-reserve.

Increase in Life Expectancy

From 1956 to 1986, Native life expectancy increased by 10 years. For an Aboriginal male, life expectancy increased from an average of 53.8 years to 63.8 years. In comparison, on average, a non-Native male lives for 73 years. Within this same period, Aboriginal women increased their life expectancy from 61 years to 71 years, compared

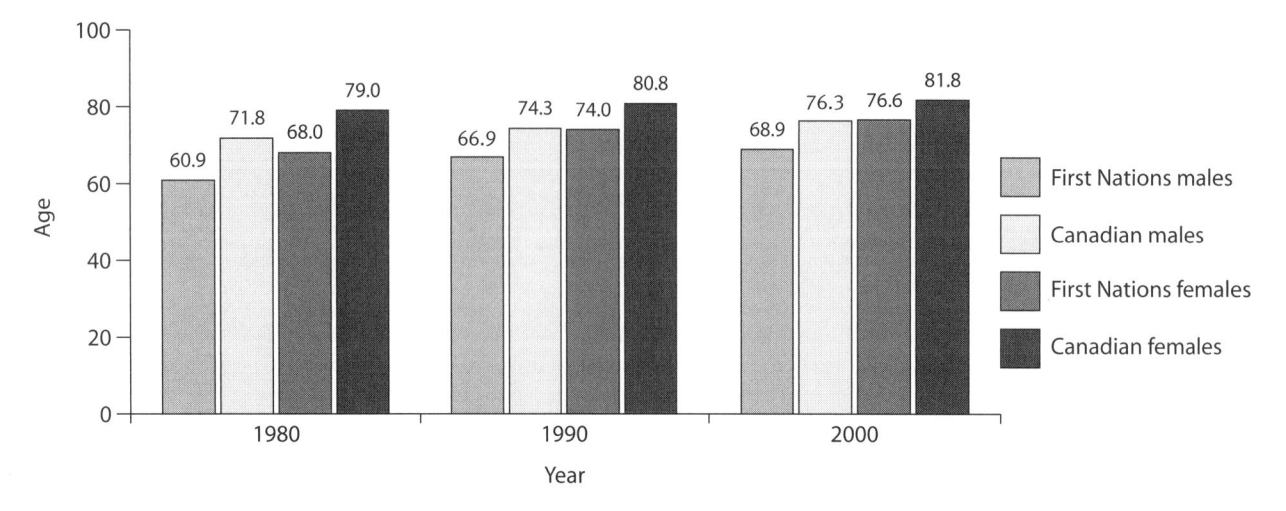

FIGURE 12.2 Life Expectancy at Birth, First Nations and Canada

Year	First Nations males	Canadian males	First Nations females	Canadian females
1980	60.9	71.8	68.0	79.0
1990	66.9	74.3	74.0	80.8
2000	68.9	76.3	76.6	81.8

Source: Indian and Northern Affairs Canada (2001).

with 79.7 years for non-Native females (Indian and Northern Affairs Canada, 1990). Life expectancy continues to improve among the First Nations population. In 2000, it rose to 68.9 years for males and 76.6 years for females, an increase from 1980 of 13.1 percent and 12.6 percent, respectively, according to Health Canada (see figure 12.2). Mortality rates for Aboriginal peoples also remained high, which continues to have an adverse impact on their ability to maintain a cross-section that represents all age groups equally within their populations. The reasons for high mortality rates will be discussed later in this chapter.

Aboriginal Youth and Median Age

The 2001 census showed that the median age of the North American Indian population was 23.5 years, compared with 37.7 years in the non-Aboriginal population. This means that 50 percent of the North American Indian population in 2001 was under 23.5 years of age. On a province-to-province basis, the median age for Natives in Saskatchewan was 18.4 years, in Manitoba 20.4 years, and in Alberta 21.2 years.

Census figures show that more than one-third of the North American Indian population in Canada was under 14 years of age in 2001, compared with 19 percent of the total non-Aboriginal population. When these figures are compared with the median ages documented in the previous paragraph, and when noting that there will be four times more Native youth entering the workforce than are leaving due to retirements, it is clear that employment opportunities will have to be created, training programs established, and other social services made available to help the youth find employment.

North American Indian Seniors

According to Statistics Canada, while the North American Indian population is relatively young, there is a significant increase in those over 65 years of age. The 2001 census enumerated 24,170 North American Indians aged 65 and over, an increase of 31 percent since 1996. Over half of these people (53 percent) lived on-reserve, a five-year increase of 34 percent. These figures indicate growing pressures on housing, social services, and health care.

Reinstatement of Native Status Through Bill C-31

The biggest factor for the significant population growth of Natives is primarily the result of the reinstatement of Native peoples who had lost their Native status before 1985. After Bill C-31 was passed in 1985, these Natives could reapply to have their status returned. Those who were most affected by Bill C-31 were Native women and their children who lost their status when they married non-Native men before 1985.

Those Natives who lost their status through enfranchisement could also regain it after the passage of Bill C-31. Before 1985, if the paternity of children born out of wedlock was identified as non-Native, they were removed from the registry. With the passage of Bill C-31, these children had the right to apply for reinstatement of their Indian status. Between 1955 and 1982, 13,502 adults and children (and their descendants) were enfranchised (Frideres, 1997).

A 1999 court decision giving off-reserve band members a vote in band elections particularly affected reinstated women, many of whom live off-reserve. Bands were given until November 2000 to implement the court decision.

Provincial Distributions of North American Native Populations

Ontario has the highest Native population (21.6 percent) at 131,560 persons, up from 17.7 percent in 1996, followed by British Columbia at 19.4 percent, or 118,295 persons. Nunavut has the smallest population of North American Native people with 95, followed by Prince Edward Island with 1,035 persons, or 0.2 percent of the total Native population in Canada of 608,850 persons.

Native Migration to Cities

Increasingly, Natives are leaving the reserves, either for economic reasons or to access social and education services. In 2001, less than half (47 percent) of the North American Indian population lived on reserves, while a total of 151,770 of them lived in one of the 27 major census metropolitan areas. Winnipeg had the largest North American Indian population at 22,955 persons, followed by Vancouver (22,700), Edmonton (18,260), Toronto (13,785), and Saskatoon (11,290), according to Statistics Canada.

These figures mirror the overall Aboriginal identity population (see table 12.4). Winnipeg had the highest Aboriginal identity (Indian, Métis, Inuit) population at 55,755 persons, an increase of 6.9 percent over the 1996 census, followed by Edmonton (40,930) and Vancouver (36,860). Winnipeg had a significant increase in its Aboriginal population of over 10,000 people in the five years between 1996 and 2001. This Aboriginal population formed 8 percent of Winnipeg's total population.

Census figures indicate a slow but steady growth among Aboriginal people living in Canada's cities. Almost one-half (49 percent) of people who identified themselves

TABLE 12.4 Population Reporting Aboriginal Identity in Selected Census Metropolitan Areas (CMA) and Census Agglomerations (CA) with an Aboriginal Population of 5,000 or More, 1996 and 2001

	1996[a]		2001	
	Number in CMA or CA	Percentage of total population	Number in CMA or CA	Percentage of total population
Winnipeg	45,750	6.9	55,755	8.4
Edmonton	32,825	3.8	40,930	4.4
Vancouver	31,140	1.7	36,860	1.9
Calgary	15,200	1.9	21,915	2.3
Toronto	16,100	0.4	20,300	0.4
Saskatoon	16,165	7.5	20,275	9.1
Regina	13,610	7.1	15,685	8.3
Ottawa-Hull[b]	11,500	1.2	13,485	1.3
Prince Albert	10,090	24.9	11,640	29.2
Montréal	9,965	0.3	11,085	0.3
Victoria	6,570	2.2	8,695	2.8
Thunder Bay	7,355	5.9	8,200	6.8
Prince George	5,810	6.7	7,980	9.4
Greater Sudbury	4,815	2.9	7,385	4.8
Hamilton	5,460	0.9	7,270	1.1
Wood Buffalo	5,460	15.1	6,220	14.6
London	4,490	1.1	5,640	1.3
Sault Ste. Marie	3,580	4.3	5,610	7.2
Kamloops	4,425	5.2	5,470	6.4

[a] In order to facilitate data comparisons, the 1996 CMA and CA data have been adjusted to reflect as closely as possible the 2001 CMA and CA boundaries. [b] Now known as Ottawa-Gatineau.
Source: Adapted from Statistics Canada (2003).

as Aboriginal lived in urban areas. The on-reserve Aboriginal population dropped from 33 percent in 1996 to 31 percent in 2001.

Aboriginal people showed consistently more mobility than did other Canadians. Overall, in the 12 months prior to the 2001 census, held in May 2001, 22 percent of Aboriginal people moved their place of residence, compared with 14 percent of non-Aboriginals, although approximately 66 percent of those Aboriginals who did move did so within their own communities.

Elementary and Secondary Education

Forty years ago, the majority of Native children attended residential schools set up by the government. Today, they can attend either provincially funded schools or federal schools, at the elementary and secondary levels (Frideres, 1997). Provincial schools are funded by each provincial government. Native cultural or language programs are offered in provincial schools with high Native student enrollment rates. When a Native child attends such an institution, the federal government pays the local school board a per diem fee.

Federal schools consist primarily of band schools and boarding schools. A band school is located on-reserve and the band administers the school, providing a culturally relevant education for its children, within federal government curriculum guidelines. The children often receive their instruction in their Native language, are taught language-specific courses, and receive cultural teachings in addition to the standard curriculum.

Boarding schools are generally for Aboriginal children who live in isolated communities and, because of their small populations, have no schools within their vicinity. The children are housed with other families within the community where the school exists. Boarding school students are either integrated into the existing school system off-reserve or receive their education from an off-reserve school created specifically for their benefit. At the elementary level, the majority of Native children attend federal schools as opposed to provincial schools (Frideres, 1997).

Aboriginal-controlled education aims to impart skills to Aboriginal children that will enable them to succeed in the outside world, and to immerse Native children in a supportive environment that is culturally relevant in content, style, and outcome. Native people believe that only an educational system that is completely managed and implemented by Native direction will eradicate the injustices of the formerly imposed educational system. Native-run schools have implemented a number of strategies: greater reliance on Native learning and teaching styles, increased exposure to and use of the Aboriginal languages, greater awareness and sensitivity of teachers and staff to Native customs and experiences, and the removal of any biased or distorted texts or educational materials (Fleras & Elliott, 1996).

In the years since the creation of band schools, Native student enrollment has increased. For example, in 1991, of the Aboriginal people who were 15 years or older, 18 percent had less than grade 9 education compared with the 1981 figure, where 37 percent had less than grade 9. Educational standards are steadily improving for Native peoples. Reasons that contributed to increased Native participation in secondary-level education include the introduction of language and cultural classes into schools with large Native student populations, greater awareness and promotion of education by the bands themselves, and the development of Native-run secondary schools. In the 1996–97 school year, there were 112,060 Native students enrolled in kindergarten, elementary, and secondary schools. The percentage of students remaining in school until grade 12 increased to 71 percent in 1996–97 from just 31 percent in 1981 (Indian and Northern Affairs Canada, 1997).

According to Indian and Northern Affairs Canada, other reasons for Native student retention might be the fact that band-operated schools increased by 54 percent from 1990–91 to 1999–2000, federal funding for postsecondary education rose from $109 million in 1987–88 to $280 million in 2000–1, and Aboriginal studies programs have expanded to more than 13 Canadian universities.

The figures in the 2001 census of educational characteristics for those claiming Aboriginal identity are quite revealing:

Total North American Indian population 15 years of age and older by school attendance	395,325
Not attending school	311,130
Attending school full time	65,715
Attending school part time	18,485

Total North American Indian population 15 years of age
and older by highest level of schooling 395,325
Less than high school graduation certificate. 200,070
High school graduation certificate only 35,470

Postsecondary Education for Natives

Natives recognize the importance of providing postsecondary education for their populations. More and more Native students are enrolling in, attending, and graduating from college and/or university. In 1996, an estimated 27,487 Native students enrolled in postsecondary education compared with 5,467 in 1981. In 1995–96, 3,929 Native students graduated from either colleges or universities across Canada (Indian and Northern Affairs Canada, 1997).

The following figures from the 2001 census reveal the state of Native postsecondary education:

Total North American Indian population 15 years of age
and older by highest level of schooling 395,325
Some postsecondary education 50,355
Trades certificate or diploma 45,425
College certificate or diploma 42,165
University certificate or diploma 5,660
University degree. 16,165
   Bachelor's degree 12,515
   University certificate above bachelor's degree 1,570
   Master's degree 3,425
   Earned doctorate. 280

Total North American Indian population 15 years of age
and over by major field of study. 395,325
No postsecondary qualifications 285,895
Educational, recreational, and counselling services 13,280
Fine and applied arts. 5,330
Humanities and related fields. 3,870
Social sciences and related fields 17,430
Commerce, management, and business administration 20,605
Agricultural, biological, nutritional, and food sciences. 5,265
Engineering and applied sciences 1,310
Applied science, technology and trades. 29,585
Health professions and related technologies. 11,410
Mathematics, computer, and physical sciences. 970
No specialization. 370

Despite these improvements, however, Native enrollment and participation in education continue to lag behind the average Canadian rate (see figure 12.3). Native students' graduation rates are also behind the national average. Non-Native students are 2.4 times more likely to earn a degree than Native students. Language and cultural differences often account for these discrepancies and have not been adequately addressed. Since 1992, the Ministry of Education and Training through Strategy funding has provided funds to develop and implement initiatives to enhance Native student success at the postsecondary level.

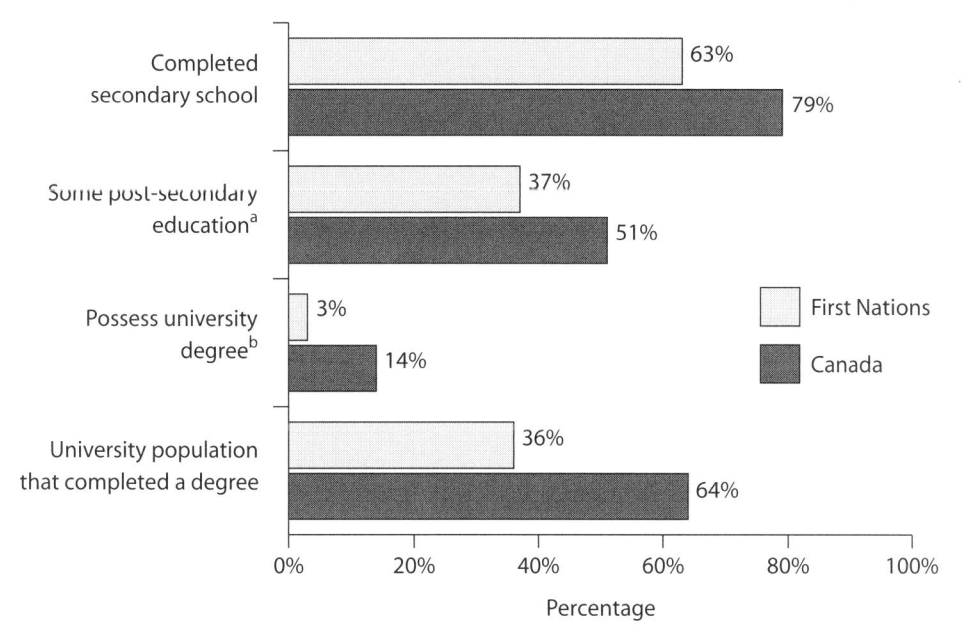

FIGURE 12.3 Educational Attainment in First Nations and Canada, 1996

Category	First Nations	Canada
Completed secondary school	63%	79%
Some post-secondary education[a]	37%	51%
Possess university degree[b]	3%	14%
University population that completed a degree	36%	64%

[a] This includes university, trades schools, and other non-university post-secondary education. [b] Population 15 years and older not attending school.

Source: Hull (2000).

PHYSICAL HEALTH

Compared with the average Canadian, the average Native experiences a lower standard of health. We will examine a number of factors that reflect this reality in the following pages.

Infant and Child Mortality

Statistics Canada reports that in 1999, the First Nations infant mortality rate was 8.0 deaths per 1,000 live births, or 1.5 times higher than the Canadian infant mortality rate of 5.5. By contrast, the 1979 First Nations infant mortality rate was 27.6 deaths per 1,000 live births, a rate that has been steadily declining. The First Nations and the Canadian population had similar proportions of births with low birth weight in 1999; however, almost twice as many First Nations births were classified as high birth weight in the same year. However, the most recent figures indicate that Native babies still have almost twice the chance of dying as newborns, compared with the rest of the Canadian population. Infant deaths are primarily the result of infectious diseases, respiratory illnesses, sudden infant death syndrome (SIDS), and injuries.

A number of socio-economic factors—for example, depression, alcoholism, and lack of employment opportunities—and other health factors contribute to this problem. Native living conditions remain below the national average. If a newborn is returned to a reserve, he or she has a greater chance of being raised in a poorly made reserve house, with little or no heat, inferior bathroom facilities (many northern Natives still use outdoor toilets), etc. In addition, many northern Native communities are far from medical facilities. When infants from these reserves become ill, by the time they are taken to the nearest hospital, their situations have become critical. Another factor contributing to the poor health of some children is the lack of parenting skills of a number of Native mothers and fathers. This can be linked to the residential schools where the grandparents and parents of today as children were not raised in an environment that enabled them to observe parenting skills and behaviours first hand.

The high rate of adolescent pregnancies among Native mothers may also be related to infant ill health and mortality rates. Native mothers on-reserve tend to be younger than the average Canadian mother. Nine percent of Native mothers, as opposed to 1 percent of non-Native mothers, are under the age of 18. The maturity, knowledge, and personal supports that each young mother possesses contribute to her overall ability to raise her child in a healthy and happy environment.

Native communities are working to combat these problems by providing parenting classes and other programs to support parents and their children. For example, in pre-natal classes, mothers-to-be learn about the effects of smoking, alcohol drinking, and caffeine consumption, and how these factors may affect fetal growth and birth weight. In addition, Native health services promote the positive effects of breast feeding. In 1998, a survey conducted for the national Database on Breastfeeding Among Indian and Inuit Women found that 60.7 percent of infants were breast fed at birth, and the rate dropped to 31.1 percent by the time the infants were 6 months old. Breast-feeding rates were the lowest among the mothers younger than 18 (MacMillan, 1996). Further efforts are being made to promote better health and care of Native children of all ages by Native services both on- and off-reserve.

Native children are four times more likely to die from an injury compared with the average Canadian child (63 compared with 15 per 100,000). The potential for more mature Native children dying of their injuries was also higher than the national average. For preschoolers, the rate increased to more than five times the national average (83 compared with 15 per 100,000). Teenagers between the ages of 15 and 19 were three times more likely to die from their injuries when compared with non-Native teenagers (176 compared with 48 per 100,000).

In addition, Native children have an increased risk of contracting an infectious disease, such as bronchitis, pneumonia, and croup, compared with non-Native children. It has also been suggested that the infections that are acquired by Native peoples (both children and adults) tend to occur more frequently and are also more severe in nature (Statistics Canada 1996, *Aboriginal Peoples Survey*, "Health Status"). Although the reasons why Native peoples of all ages tend to have an increased risk for some infectious diseases are unknown, potential factors include nutritional deficiencies, genetics, poverty, overcrowded living conditions, and environmental pollutants such as tobacco and wood smoke.

Adult Mortality and Morbidity

According to Statistics Canada, the crude mortality rate for First Nations in 1999 was 354.2 deaths per 100,000 population. The four leading causes of death were injury and poisoning, circulatory diseases, cancer, and respiratory diseases. For each of the causes of death, the rate has decreased when compared with the 1991 to

1993 period, to 22.4 percent for cancer and 40.9 percent for respiratory diseases such as pneumonia and bronchitis.

The crude mortality rate for First Nations males was 1.3 times higher than the rate for First Nations females in 1999. The rate difference is largely attributable to higher rates among males for injury and poisoning (146.7 deaths among males per 100,000 and 67.6 among females) and to circulatory disease (97.5 deaths per 100,000 among males and 72.2 among females). Age-specific death rates in 1999 were higher in First Nations males than in females for almost all age groups. The largest difference between the sexes occurs in the 5–9 and 20–24 age groups.

The most common cause of death for First Nations people aged 1 to 44 was injury and poisoning. Among children under 10, deaths were primarily unintentional (accidents). Suicide and self-injury were the leading causes of death for youth and adults up to age 44. For First Nations people aged 45 and older, circulatory diseases were the most common cause of death. These trends parallel the Canadian population as a whole. Motor vehicle collisions were the leading cause of death in all age groups.

In 1999, according to Statistics Canada, First Nations people experienced a disproportionate number of infectious diseases. These include pertussis (3 times higher than the Canadian population as a whole), chlamydia (7 times higher), hepatitis A (5.3 times higher), and shigellosis (almost 20 times higher). The proportion of Canada's total AIDS cases contracted by Aboriginal people climbed from 1.0 percent in 1990 to 7.2 percent in 2001, according to Health Canada. Over that same period, the tuberculosis rate among First Nations people remained 8 to 10 times higher than that of the Canadian population.

Dental decay rates for Aboriginal children in Ontario are 2 to 5 times higher than rates for non-Aboriginal children.

Common Health Problems

Natives have a higher rate of certain types of health problems than the rest of the population. In 1994, the Canadian Medical Association published a paper that revealed the increasing incidence and prevalence of certain types of chronic illness within Native populations. These included diabetes, cardiovascular disease, cancer, and end-stage renal disease. In addition, infectious diseases such as tuberculosis, otitis media, sexually transmitted diseases, and hepatitis have increased (Canadian Medical Association, 1994).

Various groups of Aboriginal people are also at a greater than normal risk of developing infectious diseases (such as tuberculosis and AIDS), injuries, respiratory diseases, nutritional problems (such as obesity and diabetes), and substance abuse. As a preventive measure, Native communities and Indian Friendship Centres across Canada are attempting to provide awareness and eating style changes through nutrition programs. Let's now look at some of these diseases.

Various forms of diabetes are prevalent among Aboriginal populations at critically high rates. For example, diabetes mellitus affects 6 percent of Aboriginal adults, compared with 2 percent of all Canadian adults (MacMillan et al., 1996). Young and Sevenhuysen (1989) evaluated the distribution of diabetes mellitus in Natives across Canada and found that the highest rates of Native diabetes were among Native peoples from the Atlantic region (8.7 percent) and the lowest rates were found among Native peoples in the north (Yukon, Northwest Territories, and British Columbia). It appeared to be lower in Native groups who are continuing to eat a more traditional diet. Native people living in urban areas, women, and particularly Native people living in southern Canada have an increased risk of diabetes (MacMillan et al., 1996). Native diabetes is solidly linked to poor diets; however, this disease (not proven to have existed prior to introduction of European foods) may also be the result of dietary changes—from a diet consisting primarily of meat and vegetables to one that now includes many starches, sugars, and fried foods.

Obesity is another major nutrition-related problem among Canadian Native peoples today. In a study by Young and Sevenhuysen (1989), 704 Cree and Ojibwe adults who lived in northwestern Ontario and northeastern Manitoba were surveyed. Their findings showed that over 90 percent of those surveyed had a body mass index in the overweight or obese range within specific age and gender groups—that is, more Native women between 45 and 54 years old tend to be overweight.

Another nutritional problem is the lack of vitamins and minerals within Native groups. Some of the vitamin and mineral deficiencies include iron (this problem may occur with a low immune system) and a low intake of vitamin D (required for energy) among pregnant women and infants. Native children living in Winnipeg who were originally from Manitoba reserves were found to have iron deficiency anemia. As well, Native children tend to suffer from cavities because of poor dental care habits and, in some communities, because of the unavailability of fluoride supplementation (unfluoridated water supplies) (MacMillan et al., 1996).

The Native rate of cardiovascular disease (excluding heart problems related to smoking) and some forms of cancers are lower than the national average. For example, both Native men and women were found to have a lower incidence of cancer of the colon, lung, prostate, breast, uterus, lymphoma, and leukemia (MacMillan et al., 1996). However, Natives experienced a higher rate of kidney cancer and Native women had a higher incidence of cancers of the gallbladder, cervix, and kidney. Death due to cervical cancer was five times higher among Native women than non-Natives.

MENTAL HEALTH PROBLEMS

Many social issues that are reported as problems by Native peoples are closely tied to mental health problems. High rates of stress, anomie, low self-esteem, poverty, and so on contribute to problems such as suicide, alcoholism, and other substance abuse.

Suicides

Suicide was among the leading causes of death in First Nations for those aged 10 to 44, according to Health Canada. In 1999, suicide accounted for 38 percent of all deaths in youth (aged 10 to 19) and 23 percent of all deaths in early adults (aged 20 to 44) in First Nations. That year, the First Nations suicide rate was 27.9 deaths per 100,000 population. This rate has not declined from the years 1973–1999. Notably, the 1999 rate was 2.1 times the Canadian population's suicide rate, which was 13.2 deaths per 100,000 population.

In 1999, suicide accounted for approximately 1,315.4 potential years of life lost per 100,000 First Nations people. This is greater premature mortality than for all cancers combined and 50 percent more potential years of life lost than for all circulatory diseases.

All First Nations age groups up to 65 years are at increased suicide risk when compared with the Canadian population. First Nations males are at higher risk than females. Using data for the period 1989–1993, the highest First Nations suicide rates were among males aged 15 to 24 and 25 to 34, at approximately five times and four times the Canadian rates. The widest gap with the Canadian rates was seen in females aged 15 to 24 and 25 to 39—approximately eight and five times the Canadian rates, respectively.

Compared with youths in the general population, suicides of Aboriginal youth are more likely to occur in groupings or clusters within a specific time and location. Malchy et al. (1997) found that suicide clusters were similar. Most likely, the youth had attempted suicide previously, had damaged himself or herself physically, was known to someone who had died violently, had recently broken up with someone with whom he or she had a relationship, had a history of moving often and attending more schools, and/or had lived with more parent figures. The study also reported that the choice of method, time, and place of the suicide correlated with previous suicides of youths known to them. Suicide clusters are extremely traumatic and have the potential to be even more so within Native communities because of their small size. Most of the youths know each other and/or may be related. A shared sense of predicament may put Aboriginal youths at greater risk of committing suicide; hence, a cluster of suicides may be the result. One suicide often has a profound impact on the community; the effect of two or more is devastating.

Native suicides occur for a number of reasons and are linked very strongly to sociocultural factors. Carson, Butcher, and Coleman (1988, p. 142) identify Native peoples as a high-risk group for suicides because they are from socially disorganized areas. Native peoples are a group undergoing severe societal pressures and find themselves trapped in "a sort of no-man's-land between their past culture and assimilation into the white world." In a conference on suicide held by the Canadian Psychiatric Association Section on Native Mental Health in 1985, a number of issues were linked to Native suicides, including anomie or feelings of powerlessness and hopelessness, breakdown of social roles, norms and responsibilities, community disaster, alcoholism, criminal behaviour, troubled personal relationships, poverty, and low self-esteem (Malchy et al., 1997).

Alcoholism

There is a debate over alcohol misuse among Natives (see appendix 12.1). There are, however, facts that are indisputable. Alcohol and substance abuse is considered a major problem in many Aboriginal communities. In 1996–97, according to First Nations and Inuit Health Programs, 46 percent of people in detoxification and treatment facilities in the Regina Health District were of First Nations or Métis descent. Health Canada claims that Native youths are at two to six times greater risk for every alcohol-related problem than youth in the general Canadian population.

Why is there a problem with alcoholism for Native populations? Natives had no access to alcohol until 300 years ago. Their vulnerability to alcoholism may be related to the unavailability of the drug in traditional times. In addition, Adrian, Layne, and Williams (1991) found that factors such as general economic conditions contributed to the levels of alcohol consumption. Sixty percent of the variation in alcohol consumption among non-Native counties was accounted for by such social factors as income, rate of employment, northern isolation, amount of tourism, size of households, and level of industrial activity. Improving the economic situation tended to reduce the amount of alcohol consumption.

Alcoholism or alcohol abuse also leads to other problems including violence, suicides, criminal behaviour, and fetal alcohol syndrome. Fetal alcohol syndrome (FAS) or fetal alcohol effects (FAE) is a major problem in Native communities. According to one study, researchers have found that FAS has reached epidemic proportions in a First Nations reserve in Manitoba. One in 10 children was found to be a product of alcohol teratogenesis. In addition, the researchers estimated that two to three other children out of the 10 demonstrated behavioural and learning difficulties that were caused by exposure to alcohol in utero (Square, 1997). The study recommended that more studies, intervention, and programs were needed to reduce the problems and to identify children who were experiencing academic and behavioural problems as a result of FAS.

The future is not all bleak. Health Canada's National Native Alcohol and Drug Abuse Program (NNADAP) reported in Statistics Canada's Aboriginal Peoples Survey that while in-patient admissions to treatment centres fluctuated between 4,500 and 4,700 annually through the mid-1990s, and reached a peak of 4,987 in 1996–97, the admissions rate dropped 30 percent in 1999–2000. The recidivism rate also dropped 40 percent between 1996–97 and 1999–2000, and the percentage of clients seeking treatment for alcohol abuse had dropped to 43 percent, an 11-year low.

Other Substance Abuse

Substance abuse, including alcohol, is cited by Native communities across Canada as a major issue. A recent survey found that between 1990 and 1993, more Native youths were using psychoactive substances than their non-Native counterparts. These substances included lysergic acid diethylamide (LSD), marijuana, solvents, and other hallucinogens. Native communities cite inhalants as a cause of major health problems and inhaled intoxicants use is increasingly reported throughout isolated Native communities. The median age of children using solvents is between 9 and 13 years of age (Levinthal, 1999). According to a report on Aboriginal health, the median age of children using solvents was 12, and sniffing was reported among Native children as young as 4 years old (MacMillan et al., 1996). Native youths who admitted to using solvents also reported that they came from communities where financial hardship, neglect, family conflict, or child abuse exists (Canadian Medical Association, 1994).

Statistics Canada reports that in 1985–86, use of alcohol and drug treatment centres by Aboriginal people in Ontario was six times higher than what would have been predicted based on the number of Aboriginal persons in the province or based on equal per-capita use between Aboriginal and non-Aboriginal people. In the 1991 Aboriginal Peoples Survey, 73 percent of First Nations respondents said that alcohol abuse was a problem in their communities, and 59 percent said that drug use was a problem. In the 1996 Northwest Territories Alcohol and Drug Survey, Aboriginal people 15 years and older living in the Northwest Territories were almost three times more likely than non-Aboriginal residents to have used marijuana or hashish in the previous year. They were three-and-a-half times more likely to have used LSD, speed, cocaine, crack, or heroin.

As well, this population was about 11 times more likely to have ever sniffed solvents or aerosols than the survey's non-Aboriginal respondents, and almost 24 times more likely than the general population to have done so. In fact, one in five Aboriginal youth reported that they had used solvents. One in three solvent users was under the age of 15. Over half of these youth began using solvents before reaching the age of 11. No progress was reported in reducing drug and alcohol abuse between 1995 and 1997, according to the First Nations and Inuit Regional Survey, 1999.

The percentage of National Native Alcohol and Drug Abuse Program's clients who reported using hallucinogens and other non-narcotic drugs as the primary substance abused has been on an upward trend since the mid-1990s, rising to 10 percent and 14 percent respectively in 1999–2000. Meanwhile, the percentage abusing narcotics has dropped off after reaching 27 percent in 1995–96. However, data from 1999–2000 suggest that narcotic abuse has been rising again in recent years.

Living Conditions

As a result of their poverty, Aboriginal peoples generally live in poorer housing and living conditions than non-Natives. Many northern communities still have inadequate water supplies and proper waste disposal. Between the years 1989–90 and 1996–97, the total number of housing units on reserves increased from 60,509 units to 80,443 units. Overcrowded living conditions are known to contribute to escalating tensions and, ultimately, disintegration of relationships and a higher risk of violence. (Note: An indicator for quality of living is one person per room. If there are more people than rooms in a house, the occupants are considered to be living in overcrowded conditions.) Fifteen years ago, one-third of on-reserve houses were overcrowded compared with about 20 percent today (Indian and Northern Affairs Canada, 1997). Despite the increase in the number of Native homes built in the past 15 years, Aboriginal peoples, both on-reserve and off-reserve, experience greater overcrowded living conditions compared with the average Canadian (at 1 percent).

Water supplies and sewage disposal in Native communities have improved dramatically. For instance, from 1977 to 1989, only 53 percent of reserve houses had adequate water supplies and 47 percent had adequate sewage disposal. By 1996–97, these services increased to 96 percent of band homes receiving a water supply and 92 percent benefiting from a proper sewage system (Indian and Northern Affairs Canada, 1997). Although "outhouses" can still be found in many northern reserves, the government has assumed responsibility for installing both water and sewage systems in reserves across Canada.

Shelter is a significant issue among First Nations communities, according to Statistics Canada, because only 56.9 percent of homes were considered adequate in 1999–2000. (Adequate shelter is defined as not needing minor or major repairs or replacement.) During those same years, 41.4 percent of the First Nations communities south of 60 degrees latitude reported that at least 90 percent of homes were connected to centralized water treatment plants. Similarly, 33.6 percent of First Nations communities had at least 90 percent of their homes connected to a community sewage disposal system.

This, of course, isn't saying much. These figures indicate that 43.1 percent of homes were inadequate, that 58.6 percent of homes were not connected to centralized water treatment plants, and that 66.4 percent of homes were not connected to a community sewage system.

While some living conditions have improved, Natives find that their environment is becoming more polluted. For example, Natives who still include traditional foods in their diets have found significant levels of mercury in their circulatory systems due to eating mercury-poisoned fish. In some northern Native communities in Ontario and Quebec, for example, catching and eating the fish within their traditional areas has become greatly reduced because of the fear of mercury poisoning. The Cree from northern Ontario and Quebec were exposed to levels of mercury by eating fish near sites of industrial contamination. Scientists have concluded that these adverse effects to mercury poisoning are only present after a life-long exposure to the substance (Clarkson, 1992). Since mercury poisoning was first brought to the public's attention, mercury levels have decreased in the fish populations and, consequently, the Cree of James Bay have also experienced lower levels of mercury. In other areas and as another issue, polychlorinated biphenyls (PCBs) are commonly detected in northern communities. The breast milk of Inuit women in northern Quebec has been found to contain a total PCB concentration seven times greater than that of non-Native women within southern Quebec (MacMillan et al., 1996). Again, since the publication of these results, these figures have been reduced in recent years. However, Cree and other Native leaders caution that these decreases may not be permanent (industrial activity is ongoing) and, therefore, the issue is not necessarily resolved.

Living Arrangements: Children Under 15

A disturbing trend is seen in statistics in the 2001 census relating to living arrangements for Aboriginal children under the age of 15 years. Only 60.5 percent of Aboriginal children in all areas of residence live in a two-parent family, compared with 82.5 percent of non-Aboriginal children. This figure increases to 65.0 percent of on-reserve children under 15 living in two-parent families, but the figure still does not come close to the figure for the non-Aboriginal population. Further, 35.4 percent of Aboriginal children live in single-parent families compared with only 16.9 percent of non-Aboriginal children.

These figures do not improve significantly when examining the situations of children under 15 in rural non-reserve areas, urban non-census metropolitan areas, and urban census metropolitan areas. The reasons for the differences between the Aboriginal and non-Aboriginal statistics are not examined in this book, but they are worthy of future study. Possibly income or health considerations may be behind the reasons why fewer Aboriginal children live in two-parent families than do non-Aboriginal children. Could there be a higher incidence of marital failure among Aboriginals, and what are the effects of living in single-parent situations for Aboriginal children? How might these figures affect situations such as the need for day care, the incidence of single parents needing social assistance, or mental health issues that may be attributed to these living arrangements? We may be creating problems that don't exist. Whatever the implications of these statistics, further study needs to be initiated.

Administration of Health Services

The federal government assumed jurisdiction for the health of Native peoples after the creation of the *Indian Act* in 1876. Since the 1970s and after the white paper, the government has been slowly transferring the administration of services to the band level. Native peoples within the communities have developed such programs as the NNADAP, the Community Health Worker Program, the Mental Health Worker Program, and Child and Family Services, to name a few. Under these programs, Native peoples have hired their own community members and/or other trained Native professionals to administer and deliver these services. Off-reserve Native populations were often excluded from any such services until the mid-1980s when Indian Friendship Centres began to provide urban Natives with similar health services. As an example, in 1982, the government helped to create the Brighter Futures Program that provides community mental health services in Aboriginal communities.

Despite an increase in the number of health-related services provided to Native communities, Aboriginal peoples continue to have less access to health care services compared with other Canadians. Generally, this is a result of such factors as geographic isolation, inadequate allocation of federal funding for Aboriginal services, and a lack of personnel trained to meet the needs of Native populations. Since approximately 30 to 50 percent of Aboriginal communities are in remote regions, Native health care will continue to experience problems, contributing to an overall lower standard of health for Native peoples. Federal funding for Native health services continues to lag behind the funding given to provincial coffers. In addition, there is a shortage of Aboriginal people within the Canadian health care workforce. An increase in the number of Native health care professionals would contribute positively to Native health because of their cultural understanding of Native health issues.

The 1996 report of the Royal Commission on Aboriginal Peoples provided a comprehensive review of a number of issues of Canada's Aboriginals. While the commission did not focus specifically on health, it highlighted and confirmed the more serious health issues facing Native peoples today and made some recommendations. The most important recommendation dealt with providing justice and fairness in a renewed relationship between Aboriginal and non-Aboriginal peoples. It determined that the only way that justice and fairness could occur was to provide Native peoples with a guarantee to practise Native self-determination. If what was said is accurate—that health and economic status go hand in hand—then unless the government settles land claim agreements and provides Natives with greater autonomy over their communities, economic viability, cultural integrity, and improved health for Aboriginal peoples will not be achieved. The report also called for a refocus on family supports as opposed to apprehension of Native children by child welfare authorities. As well, it recommended that steps be taken to provide adequate housing, water, and sewage systems within Native communities; the administration of Native education to be totally in the hands of Native peoples; and the creation of Aboriginal health centres and healing lodges. These recommendations are based on the premise that, if all of these areas are addressed, then ultimately Native peoples can experience the same quality of life as that experienced by their non-Native neighbours.

SOCIO-ECONOMIC STATUS

As the 1996 report of the Royal Commission on Aboriginal Peoples mentioned, unfavourable economic, social, and health conditions are inextricably linked to Native peoples' issues and oppression. Poverty has a profoundly debilitating effect on health status. Poverty creates dependency, limits self-expression and self-determination, and contributes to the demoralizing and often passive acceptance of substandard community infrastructures. In this section, we will look at Native employment, income, and social assistance.

Employment

The 1996 labour force participation rate for the total Canadian population (68 percent), according to Statistics Canada, was 1.2 times higher than it was for the First Nations on-reserve population. The gap between the First Nations and Canada was widest among the 15–24 age group, at 30 percentage points. Labour force participation includes both those who are employed and those who are looking for work.

The gap between the employment rates of First Nations people (43 percent) and Canadians (62 percent) was considerably wider, at 19 percentage points, than the gap between labour force participation rates, at 9 percentage points. However, this gap has closed slightly since 1991. The 25–44 age group had the highest employment rate among First Nations people in 1996.

The 1996 First Nations unemployment rate was almost three times higher than the Canadian rate. For all age groups and sexes, the First Nations rates were at least two times higher. The highest unemployment rate was seen in the 15–24 age group, at 41 percent. For both populations, greater educational attainment is correlated with lower unemployment rates. Education may also help to narrow the gap between First Nations and Canadian unemployment levels.

First Nations unemployment data reported by Indian and Northern Affairs Canada for 1997–98 show little change from the 1996 rates; the unemployment rate on First Nations reserves stood at 29 percent, compared with a rate of 10 percent for Canada as a whole. In 2000–1, the employment-to-population ratios of First Nations reserves were substantially higher for postsecondary graduates (64 percent) than for high school graduates (45 percent), according to Indian and Northern Affairs Canada.

The following labour force characteristics are taken from the 2001 census:

Total North American Indian population 15 years of age and over by labour force activity	395,325
In the labour force	226,670
Employed	176,345
Unemployed	50,320
Not in the labour force	168,645
Participation rate	57.3
Employment rate	44.6
Unemployment rate	22.2

CHAPTER 12   Lingering Socio-economic Issues

Total North American Indian labour force 15 years of age and over by industry	226,665
Industry—not applicable	15,730
All industries	210,930
Agriculture, forestry, fishing, hunting	12,095
Mining and oil and gas extraction	3,735
Utilities	1,605
Construction	16,900
Manufacturing	17,230
Wholesale trade	3,890
Retail trade	17,305
Transportation and warehousing	9,705
Information and cultural industries	2,755
Finance and insurance	2,835
Real estate and rental and leasing	1,930
Professional, scientific, and technical services	4,740
Management of companies and enterprises	55
Administrative and support, waste management, and remediation services	10,165
Educational services	15,680
Health care and social assistance	25,480
Arts, entertainment, and recreation	6,250
Accommodation and food services	15,755
Other services (except public administration)	8,410
Public administration	34,415
Total North American Indian labour force 15 years of age and over by occupation	226,665
Occupation—not applicable	15,730
All occupations	210,935
Management occupations	14,275
Business, finance, and administration	28,315
Natural and applied sciences and related	6,225
Health	6,360
Social science, education, government service, and religion	23,960
Art, culture, recreation, and sport	4,890
Sales and service	59,280
Trades, transport, equipment operators, and related	39,455
Primary industry	16,055
Processing, manufacturing, and utilities	12,120
Total North American Indian experienced labour force by class of worker	210,935
Paid workers	200,210
Employees	197,870
Self-employed (incorporated)	2,335
Self-employed (unincorporated)	10,290
Unpaid family workers	435

Income

Statistics Canada reports that, like unemployment rates, average income for First Nations people is also below that of the Canadian population as a whole, at any age or education level. On reserves, the First Nations income levels in the 1996 census were only half that of Canadians. First Nations income levels are increasing over time, however. Between 1990 and 1995, average individual income among all registered Indians rose from $11,941 to $14,833, according to Indian and Northern Affairs Canada in 2000. For registered Indians on reserves, average individual income over the same period climbed 31.5 percent, compared with a 17.2 percent rise for the Canadian population as a whole. Although education and gender may play a significant role in an individual's labour market participation and income level, many other geographic, social, institutional, and cultural factors are likely to be important, such as regional labour markets, discrimination, and differing social contexts.

Based on the unemployment figures seen in the next section of this book, which shows that approximately 1 in every 5 Natives over 15 years of age was unemployed in 2001, compared with approximately 1 in 14 of the total non-Aboriginal Canadian population, income for Natives was considerably below average. The average employment income for Natives was $32,176 according to the 2001 census, compared with $43,486 for the total Canadian non-Aboriginal population. One in 15 Native people reported being without income in the census data, compared with 1 in 23 non-Aboriginals. In relation to low income statistics, 37.3 percent of North American Indians 15 years and over reported having a low income, compared with only 12.4 percent of the non-Aboriginal population. Of unattached individuals over 15 years of age, 59.8 percent of North American Indians reported having a low income, compared with only 37.6 percent of the non-Aboriginal population.

The following income-related statistics are taken from the 2001 census:

Total North American Indian population 15 years of age and over by employment income work activity	395,325
Did not work in 2000	59,750
Worked full year full time	90,375
Average employment income	$32,176
Standard of error average employment income	$75
Worked part year or part time	142,290
Average employment income	$12,837
Standard error of average employment income	$38
Total North American Indian population 15 years of age and over by composition of total income in 2000	100.0%
Employment income	72.0%
Government transfer payments	24.3%
Other	3.6%

Total North American Indian population 15 years of age and older by total income groups	395,325
Without income	26,950
With income	368,375
Under $5000	94,595
$5000–$9999	60,485
$10 000–$19 999	93,315
$20 000–$29 999	49,740
$30 000–$39 999	32,440
$40 000–$49 999	17,000
$50 000–$59 999	9,595
$60 000 and over	11,200
Average income	$17,376
Median income	$12,263
Standard error of average income	$26
Total population in private households by economic family status and incidence of low income in 2000	325,450
Number of economic family persons	285,980
Low income	106,785
Other	187,130
Incidence of low income in 2000	37.3%
Number of unattached individuals 15 years and over	39,475
Low income	23,595
Other	15 880
Incidence of low income in 2000	59.8%

GROUP DISCUSSION

1. What strategies could you propose that may economically benefit bands and Native peoples both now and with the increased populations in the near future?

2. What will happen if the present status of Native employment is maintained?

Social Assistance

Not only do Aboriginal peoples rely on social assistance more than any other group in Canada, but there is evidence that this reliance is increasing. Government expenditures have doubled over the past two decades (Frideres, 1997). To put this into perspective, however, the expenditure of social assistance on Natives represents about 3 percent of the overall total Canadian social assistance payments. Today, most bands administer the delivery of their own social assistance payments; 78 percent is spent on child and family services and 22 percent is spent on adult care. The funds provide for the basic levels of health, safety, and family unity, as well as for food, clothing and shelter, and counselling to assist them in becoming independent. Despite the high rates of social assistance for Native peoples, figures also indicate that the rate of poverty remains twice as high as that of the general population. Since employment opportunities are not present in many Native communities, social assistance is often offered as an alternative.

Social assistance has created serious problems for Native peoples as a whole. Factors such as a lack of employment opportunities have created a cycle of dependence that is difficult to break. Frideres (1997) cites that many Canadians feel that Aboriginal peoples are responsible for their need for social assistance. The possible danger in this assumption is that this draws attention away from more critical issues, and to lay blame on those needing social assistance is to ignore such realities as a lack of education, discrimination, poverty, lack of employment opportunities, and low self-esteem. According to Frideres (1997), these issues prevent Aboriginal peoples, as well as other Canadians on social assistance, from fully participating in Canadian society.

The Department of Indian Affairs and Northern Development (DIAND) has been involved in on-reserve social assistance activities to provide individuals and families with the means to meet basic needs of food, clothing, and shelter. DIAND also funds special needs allowances for goods and services that are essential to the physical or social well-being of individuals, and include items such as basic furniture needs and physician-recommended diets. DIAND funds First Nations who in turn deliver programs and services to community members.

DELIVERY OF SERVICES AND PROGRAMS

To understand the programs and services that are provided to address Native concerns, it is important to become familiar with the source of their funding. In general, the majority of Native funding comes from the federal government. To be more specific, four departments, the Department of Indian Affairs and Northern Development (DIAND), Health Canada, Canada Mortgage Housing Corporation (CMHC), and Human Resources Development Canada (HRDC), are collectively responsible for 97 percent of the total federal funding directed at Aboriginal peoples. The DIAND's expenditures represent 71 percent of all federal funding directed almost exclusively to Status Indians living on-reserve. At the present time, and as a result of the **devolution** process, 82 percent of DIAND's funding for programs is administered by the First Nations peoples themselves. The funding from the other departments is directed at the Aboriginal populations both on-reserve and off-

devolution
the return of control of programs and services to Native peoples

TABLE 12.5 DIAND's Expenditures on First Nations Communities, 1997–98

Programs/services	Expenditures %	$ million
Schools, infrastructure, housing	23	1,011
Elementary/secondary education	19	858
Social assistance	13	592
Claims	14	616
Social support services	7	329
Indian government support	7	335
Post-secondary education	6	274
Administration/regional direction/funding services	3	174
Lands and trust services	2	92
Northern affairs	2	95
Economic development	1	61
Self-government	1	33
Total	100	4,471

Source: Indian and Northern Affairs Canada and Canadian Polar Commission (1998).

reserve. The most important aspect to note is that 80 percent of DIAND's programming expenditures are for basic services provided to other Canadians through provincial, municipal, and territorial governments (see table 12.5).

OFF-RESERVE ABORIGINAL POPULATIONS

The off-reserve Aboriginal population needs to be examined separately, since there are numerous issues relating specifically to this group that need to be addressed. According to the 2001 census, 713,000 Aboriginal people lived off-reserve, accounting for 70 percent of those persons who identified themselves as Aboriginal. This figure includes approximately 46 000 Inuit and 295,000 Métis, leaving the approximate off-reserve First Nations population at 358,000 persons, with approximately 43 percent of these in metropolitan areas.

Consider the Hamilton, Ontario urban area as a typical model. Approximately 1,000 Aboriginal people have moved into this area since 1996, bringing the total Aboriginal population to 7,270 persons. According to the article by Cheryl Stepan found in appendix 12.2, this group is characterized by poverty, high unemployment, and low educational achievement.

Health concerns are one of the most pressing issues among non-reserve Aboriginals. Generally, off-reserve Aboriginals rated their health status as poorer than that of the general population. For every age group between 25 and 64, the proportion of Aboriginal people reporting fair or poor health is about double that of the total population, according to O'Donnell and Tait (2003), in their analysis of the 2001 census as it relates to off-reserve Aboriginal people. The health of Aboriginal women aged 55–64 is of particular concern, with 40 percent reporting fair or poor health, compared with 19 percent of women in the same age groups in the total Canadian population.

Arthritis, rheumatism, high blood pressure, asthma, and diabetes are the most commonly reported chronic health problems in the Aboriginal off-reserve population. According to O'Donnell and Tait (2003):

> Among the adult population, 19.3 percent of the non-reserve aboriginal population reported arthritis or rheumatism, nearly twice the proportion of 11 percent among the total Canadian population. Similarly, 12 percent of the aboriginal population reported high blood pressure, compared with 8.7 percent among the total population.

Diabetes is of particular concern, especially among the North American Indian population, where 8.3 percent of the population age 15 and over was diagnosed with diabetes. This figure is somewhat higher than the figure for off-reserve Aboriginals, according to Health Canada.

In the area of education, 40 percent of the Aboriginal people in the Hamilton, Ontario area, according to Stepan (2003), have not completed high school. This compares with 48 percent of the national Aboriginal population, as opposed to 26 percent of the total Canadian population. While the figure for the Hamilton area looks marginally brighter, it is an undeniable fact that twice as many off-reserve Aboriginals fail to complete secondary school compared with the general Canadian population.

In every category under consideration, off-reserve Aboriginal people fared poorly compared with the total Canadian population. Quality of housing, income, health care, and employment rates all fall well below the Canadian average.

CONCLUSION

As so eloquently stated above, Native people were not waiting on the shores of Canada for the white man to arrive with a welfare cheque; the process of dispossession has been a long one. Native people have been an administrated people over the last 150 years. The power of the state over the communities and lives of Native people has been almost absolute and has led Native people to this place. Low educational achievement, high unemployment rates, poor physical and mental health, substance abuse, and poverty continue to be prevalent in First Nations communities at a rate far greater than that of the general population of Canada. The suicide rate among Aboriginal people is at least twice that of the general population of Canada and, in some locations, ten fold that of the general population. The past focus of treatment of the individual has not met with success. New comprehensive interventions must include treatment of communities and families.

Since the 1970s white paper, which proposed eliminating the status of First Nations and reserves, Canada seems prepared to relinquish some of its control over Native people, and they have quickly seized this opportunity to assert control over community infrastructure such as education, housing, delivery of social services, policing, and other areas of community life. Statistics indicate that quality of life is improving with this new control but much work needs to be done. Former Chief of the National Assembly of First Nations Matthew Coon Come explained in his April 8, 2003, speech that many Native people in Canada live in developing-third world conditions. Native people in Canada rate 63rd on the United Nations standard of

CHAPTER 12 Lingering Socio-economic Issues

> ## GROUP DISCUSSION
>
> Read the following summary and answer the questions below:
>
> In his book Surviving as Indians, Boldt (1993, p. 214) proposes an interesting premise. He believes that Natives have fallen into a complacent mode of thought, which stems from Native survival as distinctive cultures, despite the aggressive attempts of the Canadian government to assimilate Native peoples. He argues that instead of boasting cultural survival, Native cultures are in essence in a state of crisis, "traditional values, norms, customs and social systems have lost their relevance, their legitimacy, and hence their capacity for maintaining social order within their communities." He proposes that for Native cultures to transform into positive forces, they must not become victims of cultural isolation but carry their traditional, fundamental philosophies and principles, and develop a clear vision of what they want to be in the future.
>
> 1. Based on everything we have examined thus far, how accurate is Boldt in capturing Native issues? Explain your answers to the group.
>
> 2. What strategies would you suggest to reduce the problems Natives are facing so that they can enjoy a quality of life similar to that of other Canadians?

living scale, which is lower than the standard of living in Botswana, Vietnam, and El Salvador. The Native population is also the fastest growing segment of the Canadian population, which speaks to the urgency of taking action now.

Native people have been legislated into dependence on government, and the cycle of dependency is difficult to break. With very little economic development on reserves, social assistance is the only alternative. With no employment the community becomes demoralized and lacks purpose. Social problems such as alcohol and substance abuse, poor mental/physical health, and suicide follow such demoralization—and the cycle repeats. Without economic development and the creation of employment the future appears bleak. Many Native people leave their territories looking for employment in large urban centres only to find themselves trapped in the ranks of the working poor or the marginally employed.

One of the greatest obstacles to economic development is lack of land. Native people in Canada are striving to boost their economies; however, in a country whose economy is based on natural resources it is difficult for First Nations to enter that economy when they have less than one-half of 1 percent of Canada's land mass. Resources that had supported First Nations people for thousands of years are now in the control and possession of private industry and governments that are not willing to allow First Nations people a share of those resources. In 2005 a decision by the Supreme Court of Canada denied Native people in eastern Canada the right to access Crown land for logging to increase their presence in the logging industry. First Nations people have logging privileges for 3 percent of Crown land, with the remainder leased by the Crown to private interests. First Nations people were fighting to press for rights to access a greater percentage of the forestry industry, but the Supreme Court ruled that logging for profit was not part of pre-contact

Native societies' activities and therefore they had no right to access the industry.

Separation from land and resources means that Native people have neither land nor capital, which leads to demoralization and secures their position in Canada's economy as solely wage labourers for the dominant culture of Canada's businesses and private interests. Therefore, access to land and resources continues to be a focus for Native leaders to secure a brighter future for Native people. Land issues are the main focus of the June 29, 2008 planned day of action for Canada's First Nations.

> **CLASS ACTIVITY**
>
> As a class, connect four social conditions in which Native people experience lower quality of life to historical events that may be contributing factors to these conditions.
>
> Discuss opportunities for economic development on reserves that could create jobs and reduce social assistance dependency. Consider the obstacles and determine ways to overcome them.
>
> Discuss the potential benefits and possible pitfalls of building casinos on reserves.

KEY TERMS

constitution

devolution

REFERENCES

Aboriginal Youth Network. Addictions. www.ayn.ca/health/addictionsalcohol.aspx.

Adrian, M., Layne, N., & Williams, R.T. (1991). Estimating the effect of native Indian population on county alcohol consumption: The example of Ontario. *International Journal of Addiction, 25,* 731–765.

Berger, T. (1999). *A long and terrible shadow: White values, Native rights in the Americas since 1492.* Vancouver/Toronto: Douglas & McIntyre.

Boldt, M. (1993). *Surviving as Indians: The challenge of self-government.* Toronto: University of Toronto Press.

Canadian Medical Association (CMA). (1994). *Bridging the gap: promotion of health and healing for Aboriginal peoples in Canada.* Ottawa: CMA. www.cma.ca.

Canadian Psychiatric Association. (1985, October). *Suicide in the North American Indian: Causes and prevention.* Transcribed and edited proceedings of the 1985 meeting of the Canadian Psychiatric Association section on Native Mental Health. Shannonville, ON.

Carson, C.C., Butcher, J.N., & Coleman, J.C. (1988). *Abnormal psychology and modern life* (8th ed.). Glenview, IL: Scott Foresman.

Chaimowitz, G. (2000, September). Aboriginal mental health moving forward. *Canadian Journal of Psychiatry, 45*(7).

Clarkson, L. (1992). *Our responsibility to the seventh generation: Indigenous people and sustainable development.* Winnipeg: International Institute for Sustainable Development.

Constitution Act, 1982, RSC 1985, app. II, no. 44.

First Nations and Inuit Health Branch, Health Canada. (2004). *In-house statistics.* Ottawa: Public Works and Government Services Canada.

Fleras, A., & Elliott, J.L. (1996). *Unequal relations: An introduction to race, ethnic and Aboriginal dynamics in Canada.* Scarborough, ON: Prentice Hall.

Frideres, J.S. (1997). *Aboriginal peoples in Canada: Contemporary conflicts* (5th ed.). Scarborough, ON: Prentice Hall.

Friends of Grassy Narrows. www.friendsofgrassynarrows.com.

Geddes, C., Doxtater, M., & Krepakevich, M. (1997). *No turning back: Royal Commission on Aboriginal People.* National Film Board of Canada.

Hull. J. (2000). *Aboriginal post-secondary education and labour market outcomes: Canada 1996.* Ottawa: Indian and Northern Affairs Canada.

Indian and Northern Affairs Canada. (1990). *Highlights of Aboriginal conditions.* Ottawa: Supply and Services Canada.

Indian and Northern Affairs Canada. (1997). *Basic departmental data 1997.* http://www.ainc-inac.gc.ca/pr/sts/bdd00/bdd00_e.pdf.

Indian and Northern Affairs Canada. (2001). *Basic departmental data 2000.* Catalogue no. R12-7/2000E. http://www.ainc-inac.gc.ca.

Indian and Northern Affairs Canada and Canadian Polar Commission. (1998). *Performance report for the period ending March 31, 1998.* http://www.ainc-inac.gc.ca/pr/est/perrep.pdf.

Kirmayer, L.J. (2000, September). The mental health of Aboriginal peoples: Transformations of identity and community. *Canadian Journal of Psychiatry, 45*(7).

Kirmayer, L., Simpson, C., & Cargo, M. (2003, October). Healing traditions: Culture, community, and mental health promotion with Canadian Aboriginal peoples. *Australasian Psychiatry, 11*(S1), S15.

Levinthal, C.F. (1999). *Drugs, behavior, and modern society.* Needham Heights, MA: Allyn & Bacon.

MacMillan, H.L., et al. (1996). Aboriginal health. *Canadian Medical Association Journal, 155,* 1569–1598.

Malchy, V., et al. (1997). Suicide among Manitoba's Aboriginal people: 1988 to 1994. *Canadian Medical Association Journal, 157,* 1133–1138.

McGregor, G. (2001). Debate rages over native alcoholism. *First Nations Drum.* http://www.firstnationsdrum.com/Sum2001/Cult-debate.htm.

O'Donnell, V., & Tait, H. (2003). Aboriginal peoples survey 2001: Initial findings—Well-being of non-reserve Aboriginal population. Statistics Canada. Housing, Famly, and Social Statistics Divisions. Catalogue no. 89-589-XIE, pp. 13-15. Ottawa: Industry Canada.

Postl, B. (1997). It's time for action. *Canadian Medical Association Journal, 157,* 1665-1666.

Reserves rack up 300 million in deficits, Native leaders blame underfunding. (2004, February 18). *Turtle Island News,* p. 1.

Royal Commission on Aboriginal Peoples (RCAP). (1996). *Report.* Ottawa: Supply and Services Canada.

Shkilnyk, A. (1985). *A poison stronger than love: The destruction of an Ojibwa community.* New Haven, CT: Yale University Press.

Square, D. (1997). Fetal alcohol syndrome epidemic on Manitoba reserve. *Canadian Medical Association Journal, 157,* 59–60.

Statistics Canada. (1996). *Aboriginal peoples survey.* Ottawa: Supply and Services Canada.

Statistics Canada. (2001). *Aboriginal peoples of Canada: A demographic profile.* Catalogue no. 96F0030XIE2001007. Ottawa: Supply and Services Canada.

Statistics Canada. (2001). *Aboriginal peoples survey.* Ottawa: Supply and Services Canada.

Statistics Canada. (2001). *Canadian community health survey, 2000-1.* Ottawa: Supply and Services Canada.

Statistics Canada. (2001). Selected educational characteristics. www12.statcan.ca/english/census01.

Statistics Canada. (2003, January 31). *Aboriginal peoples of Canada: A demographic profile, 2001 census (analysis series, 2001 census).* Catalogue no. 96F0030. Ottawa: Supply and Services Canada.

Statistics Canada. (2003, September). *Aboriginal peoples survey 2001—Initial findings: Well-being of the non-reserve Aboriginal populations, 2001.* Catalogue no. 89-589. Ottawa: Supply and Services Canada.

Stepan, C. (2003, October 11). Aboriginals: Now I know who I am. *The Hamilton Spectator,* p. F5.

Williamson, P., & Roberts, J. (2004). *First Nations Peoples.* (2nd ed.). Toronto: Emond Montgomery.

APPENDIX 12.1

Debate Rages Over Native Alcoholism

Some argue that a chief's warning to sober up is welcome recognition of a major problem. Others call it unfair stereotyping.

When Assembly of First Nations Chief Matthew Coon Come warned that native leaders must sober up, he was drawing on a long standing and persistent stereotype of native alcoholism that has never been proven conclusively.

"Our people smoke too much and drink too much," said Mr. Coon Come, Canada's top elected Native. "I think it does not give a good signal if a chief and council and anyone who is in Indian leadership is denying that he has alcohol problems."

To many, Mr. Coon Come's recent [2001] remarks came as a welcome recognition of a health problem endemic to Canada's aboriginal communities.

But to others, it was an endorsement of an unfair stereotype that natives have tried to shake for years.

Had it been anyone but Mr. Coon Come who said it, they suggest, the remarks would be vilified as bigoted and uninformed.

Indeed, former Newfoundland premier Brian Tobin was publicly castigated last year [2000] for saying pretty much the same thing as Mr. Coon Come when he suggested many aboriginal leaders in Labrador are "themselves abusers of alcohol and themselves in need of help."

His remarks set off a rage of controversy, with Phil Fontaine, Mr. Coon Come's predecessor at the AFN, denouncing the comments as "a stereotypical image of our people that's so completely wrong."

Today, the idea that natives are more susceptible to the mind-bending effects of alcohol remains so tenacious that even some natives believe it.

In her book *Firewater Myths* [1976], anthropologist Joy Leland reported that many American Indians believe they have a physiological weakness to the effects of alcohol and that alcoholism is "in the blood."

Ms. Leland concluded that young natives used the hereditary explanation as an excuse for their own abuse of alcohol, even though studies show aboriginals do not metabolize alcohol much differently than people of other races.

In Canada, social-scientific data suggest that aboriginal communities are hit harder by substance abuse than non-aboriginal communities. But the data is far from conclusive.

In a major study of existing research, Health Canada admitted it is difficult to measure alcohol and drug abuse on reserves because of poor response rates and cultural differences that complicate surveys. This makes direct comparison to non-aboriginal populations difficult.

Instead, epidemiologists who study native alcoholism rely on data that show why natives get sick or die.

Injury and poisoning are leading causes of mortality and morbidity in aboriginal communities, both of which are consistent with alcohol abuse.

Few would argue, however, that alcohol is not a problem in Canada's aboriginal communities.

A 1984 survey of First Nations communities in Manitoba found that 86 per cent rated alcohol as either a "serious problem" or "major problem."

A study in Ontario the following year found that alcohol consumption was as much as 35 per cent higher in counties that have native reserves than in those which don't.

But other data assembled by Health Canada show that a lower proportion of aboriginals drink daily (two per cent versus three per cent of non-natives) and fewer drink weekly (35 per cent versus 46 per cent) than non-aboriginals. Also, almost twice as many aboriginals count themselves as teetotallers. About 15 per cent of aboriginals say they abstain from drinking, compared with eight per cent of other Canadians.

"There are indications that drinking is more tenacious among young people on reserves," said Gary Roberts of the Canadian Centre on Substance Abuse. "But there's not a lot of good information."

He says figures show that aboriginal youth are between twice and six times as likely to have alcohol problems as non-natives of the same age.

Mr. Roberts says another test of drinking problems, the rate of fetal alcohol syndrome, has also been tested in aboriginal communities, but it is difficult to compare to non-native rates because of a lack of data.

The perception of high rates of native alcoholism is partly grounded in reality, but has been embellished by non-aboriginals who have limited exposure to reserves.

Non-natives are likely to form their opinion on native drinking from the people they encounter on city streets, he said. "It comes from people's perceptions, noticing that particularly off reserves in Western Canada you will find individuals of aboriginal descent living on the street."

Off-reserve natives are believed to have a much higher rate of alcohol and drug dependency, but again, there is little reliable information to back up this theory. Data collection in urban centres has been even less rigorous than on the reserves.

Mr. Roberts said there is nothing but anecdotal evidence to support Mr. Coon Come's assertion that there is an alcohol problem among the aboriginal political leadership.

"But if it does occur, it is going to limit their effectiveness to become active on the alcohol abuse problems in their communities," he said.

Source: McGregor (2001). Reprinted with permission.

APPENDIX 12.2

Aboriginals: Now I Know Who I Am

More than 7,000 people in the Hamilton area told census takers they are native—a 33 percent jump. The city's native people express pride in their ancestry. But their legacy of struggle continues as almost half of them live in poverty.

The family hid the secret for decades. It was one of those things no one dared talk about, at least not while their mother was alive.

Yet, there was a part of Jean Beauchamp that always knew. There was something special about her, and she could feel it growing up.

So it didn't come as a surprise to her when her aunt called her a few months after her mother died and revealed what her mother never would. Her father was an Indian. That meant she, too, had aboriginal blood in her veins.

"In my heart, I knew. But you didn't talk about things like that," Beauchamp said. Her mother was white, French Canadian and living in northern Ontario in the '60s, a time she wasn't comfortable publicly acknowledging she was with an aboriginal man.

"It just hurt my mom too much … because of the stigma of being with an aboriginal. You didn't go out with Indians if you were white."

Beauchamp is part of a tidal wave of people recently discovering and embracing their aboriginal ancestry, including status Indian, Inuit, and Métis—or mixed aboriginal and European—people.

In the Hamilton–Burlington–Grimsby Census Metropolitan Area (CMA) between 1996 [and] 2001, there was a 33 per cent growth in the aboriginal population.

The 2001 census reports that 7,270 people identified themselves as aboriginal in 2001, up from 5,460. By comparison, the population on Six Nations, Canada's most populous reserve, is around 11,000.

Province-wide, the aboriginal population also increased by 33 per cent, much higher than the growth rate of 6.1 per cent for the entire population. …

No one can say for sure what's driving the surge in numbers of people who state they are aboriginal because the census doesn't take into account the reasons people claim a certain identity. …

It's perhaps not surprising that aboriginal people would try to hide behind a white mask [previously]. Decades of oppression and racism, and such government policies as residential schools and adoptions into white families took their toll on a population that was struggling with a changing way of life.

The legacy of that struggle is seen to this day as 48 per cent of aboriginal people in Hamilton live in poverty, according to the Social Planning and Research Council. By rough comparison, slightly more than 16 per cent of the city's overall population are living below the low-income cut-off set by Statistics Canada.

Another factor, according to Sherry Lewis, executive director of Hamilton's Native Women's Centre, a women's shelter, is that aboriginal community leaders are encouraging people to come forward so social and government agencies can get a more accurate picture of the population and its needs.

She said mainstream programs often don't work for aboriginal people because they don't address specific problems—such as residential school syndrome—or take into account aboriginal spiritual and cultural needs.

The 2001 census shows that much of the [aboriginal] community is concentrated in low-income neighbourhoods in the lower city.

The aboriginal population in the CMA has a median income 33 per cent lower than that of the overall population—$16,554 compared to $24,987.

Aboriginals' median income has improved since 1996 when it was just $14,366, but the gap between their income and that of the overall population—which rose too—is not closing.

In 2001, the unemployment rate was 12.3 per cent for aboriginal people, compared to a rate of 5.7 per cent in the overall population.

They also have less formal education—40 per cent of aboriginal people over age 25 do not have a high school diploma. In the overall [Canadian] population, just 27 per cent of those over 20 years have not graduated.

Aboriginal people also have a disproportionate number of kids in Children's Aid Society custody. Planning and Research Council reports that 43 per cent of children in foster care are aboriginal.

Source: Stepan (2003). Reprinted with the permission of the *Hamilton Spectator*.

Note: While the statistics cited in this article apply to the Hamilton, Ontario region, they do not differ significantly from figures in other parts of the province. The 2001 Census shows that Aboriginal people across the province have a long way to go to catch up with the economic and social conditions enjoyed by the larger population.

CHAPTER 13

Current Issues Over Land

CHAPTER OBJECTIVES

After completing this chapter, you should be able to:

- Connect historical treaties and case law to present day land claims.
- Connect access to land and resources to Aboriginal self-determination and independence.
- Understand the present-day process of defining Aboriginal rights to land and resources.

INTRODUCTION

On Thursday, November 27, 2003, the *National Post* printed an article disclosing that 50 percent of Canadians believe that land claims made by Aboriginal people in Canada are not valid (Curry, 2003). The source was the Centre for Research and Information on Canada, which conducted a poll to gauge the public's readiness to move forward on recommendations made by the Royal Commission on Aboriginal Peoples to begin implementing increases in Aboriginal land base. Aboriginal-held territory at the time comprised less than one-half of 1 percent of the Canadian land mass (Coon Come, 2003).

Since police services across the country are composed of members of the public, we can assume that 50 percent of police officers in this country share this opinion. The police in this country, however, are tasked with the responsibility of keeping the peace when issues involving Aboriginal claims to land manifest themselves in the form of roadblocks or peaceful (and sometimes not so peaceful) occupations. The police have at times, particularly in the case of the Ipperwash incident (see appendix 13.1), been used as an enforcement arm of provincial and federal governments in resolving both land and resource disputes with disastrous results for both officers and First Nations populations. Undoubtedly, it would be difficult to maintain an objective and unbiased approach to peacekeeping if an officer believed that Native protestors had no rights under the law for their actions and no justification in law for their grievances. Nevertheless, I believe that this is the current state of affairs in Canada, and so I will attempt to relay the legal history of land and resources claims in Canada by reviewing constitutional rights afforded to Aboriginal people and the case law that has attempted to define those rights. In this way I will show Native peoples' justification for their land claims.

BACKGROUND

The *British North America Act* of 1867 established the legislative powers of the government in Canada, and divided those powers between the federal government and the provinces. Under s. 91(24) of the Act, jurisdiction and governance over territories reserved for Indians was given to the federal government of Canada. Aboriginal nations were not party to the creation of this Act, nor were they consulted. Nine years after the implementation of this Act, previous policies regarding Indians were consolidated into the *Indian Act*, an oppressive Act designed to strip away the governing rights of Indian nations. The *Indian Act* was also used to suppress any resistance to the continuation of forced relocations and land seizures by the federal government. As the land base of Aboriginal peoples dwindled, their level of poverty increased and their dependence on the government for survival was set. In a country whose economy was, and is, based on the harvest and export of natural resources, Aboriginal people divested of land would become the poorest group in the country.

Most Aboriginal communities in Canada today are economically dependent on the federal government for support, much to the dismay of those communities. The hope of becoming economically independent and economically viable is inextricably tied to access to the harvest of natural resources on areas outside the small reserves assigned to them, areas that are part of their traditional territory and areas to which they possess rights under the constitution to access. Until recently, the government of Canada, in collusion with large corporations, had been successful through legislation in shutting out Aboriginal people from those lucrative harvests, trapping them in a position of dependency.

HISTORICAL CASE LAW

One of the first cases on the rights of Aboriginal people in Canada with reference to land issues was the case of *St. Catherine's Milling & Lumber Company v. The Queen* (1888). It set a precedent establishing the status of the rights of Aboriginal people to the land for all Aboriginal nations in Canada. Ironically, Aboriginal people were not represented and were not even involved in this litigation process. The case unfolded such that the Ojibwa people in northern Ontario entered into Treaty No. 3 with the federal government of Canada in 1873. Shortly thereafter, Sir John A. Macdonald, acting in capacity as prime minister of Canada and superintendent of Indian Affairs, issued a timbering licence to St. Catherine's Milling and Lumber Company with which he was alleged to have been closely connected (Monture-Angus, 1999, p. 68). The company had cut two million feet of lumber when Ontario filed for an injunction to prevent further lumbering and the removal of the lumber. Ontario asserted that the province, as opposed to the federal government, was entitled to licensing fees and royalties for timber since Treaty No. 3 areas fell within the boundaries of Ontario. The province cited s. 109 of the *British North America Act* as the source of entitlement. It reads:

> All Lands, Mines, Minerals, and Royalties belonging to the several Provinces of Canada, Nova Scotia, and New Brunswick at the Union, and all Sums then due or payable for such Lands, Mines, Minerals, or Royalties, shall belong to the several Provinces of Ontario, Quebec, Nova Scotia, and New Brunswick in which the same are situate or arise, subject to any Trusts existing in respect thereof, and to any Interest other than that of the Province in the same.

The federal government therefore became the defendant in this case. It argued that the Indians had owned the land and had passed that ownership on to the federal government through Treaty No. 3; therefore, the federal government owned the land and the resources within it despite the fact that it lay within Ontario's provincial boundaries. The federal government cited s. 91(24) of the *British North America Act*, which states that the responsibility for "Indians, and Lands reserved for the Indians" falls to the federal government. Ontario argued successfully that Indian title to land was not full ownership since Indians had no concept of property rights as recognized in British law. Ontario argued that the title to all lands of North America was vested in the Crown and any rights to land asserted by Indians were granted by the generosity of the Crown. This, of course, is inconsistent with both the *Royal Proclamation of 1763* and the treaties. Nevertheless, the decision resulted in the definition of Indian title in the land being less than full title. It was held that Indian interest in the land was mere "personal and usufructuary right," which translates as the right to use the land at the pleasure of the Crown and gives the power to the Crown to take that right away at any time.

Since this case was decided by the Judicial Committee of the Privy Council in England, the highest court in the land, the decision became binding on all future land issues involving Indian title to land. This system of precedents in the Canadian court structure acts as a huge obstacle to anyone attempting to move forward in Aboriginal rights cases (Monture-Angus, 1999, p. 67). This precedent was followed for almost a century until the *Calder* case in 1973. The movement toward Native land and resource rights was also hindered during this time by the provisions placed in the *Indian Act* in 1927, which prevented Indian nations from hiring lawyers or pursuing claims to land. This provision was not repealed until 1951.

The *Calder* case began in 1971 when four Nisga'a communities in British Columbia's Nass Valley brought their case to the Supreme Court of Canada, asserting rights over traditional territory outside the reserve created by the federal government. The communities based their assertion on the fact that they had never entered into any treaties and had never relinquished their lands to either the federal government or the province of British Columbia. They and their ancestors had in fact occupied the land since time immemorial, and they had never agreed to any relinquishment of land or resources. The Supreme Court was split in its decision in this case three to three. In his rendered decision Justice Judson stated:

> [T]he fact is that when the settlers came, the Indians were there, organized in societies and occupying the land as their forefathers had done for centuries. This is what Indian title means and it does not help one in the solution of this problem to call it a "personal or usufructuary right." What they are asserting in this action is that they had a right to continue to live on their lands as their forefathers had

lived and that this right has never been lawfully extinguished. (*Calder*, 1973, p. 328; quoted in Monture-Angus, 1999, pp. 75–76)

Justice Hall went further to discuss the process of extinguishment. He stated that should the Crown claim to extinguish Aboriginal title to land the Crown must do so in a clear and plain manner; the Crown cannot rely on implied extinguishment. The most significant part of this judgment is that all six of the judges agreed that Aboriginal title to land existed, as defined by British law, at the time of colonization and, furthermore, that the Crown must act in a clear and plain way to extinguish that title (Nisga'a Lisims Government, 1997–2000).

Although the *Calder* case does not accomplish the provision for the court of a clear test of extinguishment (this test arises later as a result of the case of *Sparrow* in 1990), it did achieve the long-desired response from the federal government to work toward settling Native claims in regions of the country where treaties had not extinguished Aboriginal title. Native activists had been pressing the government, to no avail, to create a process by which to settle land claims since the repeal of the prohibition against the pursuit of land claims in the 1951 revision of the *Indian Act*.

Another case that significantly impacted Aboriginal land and resource claims in Canada was *Guerin v. The Queen* (1984). Prior to the verdict in *Guerin* the Department of Indian Affairs had a moral duty to act in the best interest of Aboriginal nations in the administration of reserve lands and resources but this duty, known as a fiduciary duty, was not recognized in law. Subsequently, there was limited accountability of the department to the Indian people it administrated; the department was accountable only to the federal government.

In *Guerin*, the Musqueam Indian Reserve had agreed to lease 66 hectares of reserve land in the City of Vancouver to the Shaugnessy Golf Club in 1955. In keeping with the *Royal Proclamation of 1763*, providing that Indian land can be surrendered or leased—that is, is alienable—only to the Crown, the band was required to surrender the land first to the Crown in order that the lease of the 66 hectares could take place. A meeting was held in which the band and the Indian agent agreed upon the terms of the lease to be acquired with the golf club. These terms were misrepresented to the band. The land was surrendered and the Crown entered into a lease agreement with the golf club on terms that were unfavourable to the band and outside of what was agreed upon by the band. The band attempted to grieve this action to no avail. The band was unsuccessful in even procuring a copy of the lease agreement, which it had never received at the time of surrender, until 1970. When the band obtained a copy of the lease, it attempted to sue the Crown for damages. The case made its way to the Supreme Court of Canada, which issued its decision in 1984. At the heart of the argument was the Crown's responsibility to act in the best interest of the band. The Crown argued that the responsibility amounted to a "political trust" enforceable by Parliament but not to a "true trust" enforceable by the courts. The Crown was unsuccessful in its argument, and ruled in the final verdict:

> An Indian Band is prohibited from directly transferring its interest to a third party. Any sale or lease of land can only be carried out after a surrender has taken place, with the Crown then acting on the Band's behalf. The Crown first took this responsibility upon itself in the Royal Proclamation of 1763. It is still recognized in the surrender provisions of the *Indian Act*. The surrender requirement, and the

responsibility it entails, are the source of a distinct fiduciary obligation owed by the Crown to the Indians. (*Guerin*, 1984, p. 376)

Furthermore, Justice Dickson stated:

After the Crown's agents had induced the Band to surrender its land on the understanding that the land would be leased on certain terms, it would be unconscionable to permit the Crown simply to ignore these terms. Equity will not countenance unconscionable behaviour in a fiduciary whose duty is that of utmost loyalty to his principal. (*Guerin*, 1984, pp. 336–337)

There have been many cases of this nature that question the responsible administration by the Crown of band resources and band land. *Guerin* set a precedent that the mismanagement of band land actions by the government will result in the government's being held responsible. In the *Guerin* case the band was awarded $10 million in restitution. The sum of the settlement was based on the lease value of the land to date had the band never entered into the agreement to alienate the land to facilitate the unfavourable lease (Henderson, 1996). This is a long and slow process, as you can see; after a number of appeals the decision was rendered a full 14 years after the discovery of the extent of the misdealings of the Crown when the copy of the lease was obtained, and 29 years after the original proposed lease.

CONSTITUTION

During the *Guerin* case's litigation, the Canadian constitution was patriated. Prior to the patriation of the constitution Native activists appealed to international powers and to governments in Canada and Europe for the inclusion of Aboriginal rights within the constitution. Their work culminated in the inclusion of s. 35 of the *Constitution Act, 1982*, which states:

> 35(1) The existing aboriginal and treaty rights of the aboriginal peoples of Canada are hereby recognized and affirmed.
> (2) In this Act, "aboriginal peoples of Canada" includes the Indian, Inuit and Métis peoples of Canada.
> (3) For greater certainty, in subsection (1) "treaty rights" includes rights that now exist by way of land claims agreements or may be so acquired.
> (4) Notwithstanding any other provision of this Act, the aboriginal and treaty rights referred to in subsection (1) are guaranteed equally to male and female persons.

Since this inclusion in 1982, Canadian courts have been trying to clarify the extent of Aboriginal rights in this country. It is important to note the wording of the section; the *existing* rights of Aboriginal people are *recognized and affirmed*. This section does not provide any new rights for Aboriginal people in Canada. Of course, Aboriginal rights existed in common law in Canada prior to the enactment of the constitution. The source of those common law rights was the occupation of land and Indian social and political organization that existed prior to Canada's assertion of sovereignty. Some of those rights were expressly terminated by the Crown through treaty but many were not. Some Aboriginal rights were also laid out through the treaty process. Section 35 of the constitution, rather than creating new rights, elevates the rights that existed already, through common law and treaty, to a constitutional status. This restricts the right of the Crown to modify or extinguish Aboriginal rights (Bell & Patterson, 2003, p. 108).

The inclusion of s. 35 provided protection for Aboriginal rights but did not simplify the process of defining what an Aboriginal right is and what it is not. So what is protected under s. 35 of the constitution? Aboriginal people have been taking their cases to court steadily over the years to have the courts define these constitutionally entrenched Aboriginal rights.

It is important to understand that Aboriginal people have a somewhat different conception of the purpose of this battle for rights. I do not suppose to speak for Aboriginal people and so quote Native activist, author, and lawyer Ardith Walkem:

> When Indigenous Peoples speak of Aboriginal Title and Rights, it is a much broader conception than that which has evolved under Canadian Law. Indigenous Peoples are not seeking to have distinct practices protected, nor title recognized to small parcels of land. The reason that Indigenous Peoples engage in the court process stems from a simple desire and imperative: Our continued existence as peoples and maintenance of our ability to continue to exist and thrive on the territories on which the Creator placed us and according to the laws which bind us to the lands and waters and govern the relationships between all living things and the spiritual beings that also live within and through the lands and waters. These elements, at a minimum, embrace the fundamental aspects of Indigenous Peoples aspirations:
>
> 1. Territory (both land and water) and recognition of our responsibility to manage, protect and benefit from that territory.
>
> 2. Recognition of the laws, traditions, languages and cultures of Indigenous peoples which flow, and are intricately tied to, our territories, and
>
> 3. Recognition of a right to self determination which ensures that we are able to survive into the future governed by, and accountable to, our own laws.

(Walkem, 2003, p. 198)

Certainly, as previously discussed, the will to be self-determining requires a certain degree of independence from the control of the Canadian government. This independence will require a degree of economic independence, meaning that Aboriginal people must rebuild their economies to thrive in today's world. This will require both land and the control over resources of the land.

Therefore, many of the cases that have been brought before the Supreme Court involve rights to the harvest of natural resources; in short, hunting and fishing rights, such as those in *R v. Sparrow* (1990). Mr. Sparrow is a Salish and lives on the Musqueam Indian Reserve, which is located within Vancouver's city limits. He fishes commercially and for food. In May 1984 he was charged with using a drift net that was longer than British Columbia fishing regulations allowed. Mr. Sparrow did not dispute the facts in issue in the case but argued that he had an Aboriginal right to fish in the area as his forefathers had for generations, and that this right was protected under s. 35 of the constitution. Therefore, he could not be bound by the British Columbia fishing regulations. Mr. Sparrow did not embark upon this case lightly and was aware that the outcome of this case would affect Aboriginal fishing rights across Canada. His decision to assert this right was supported by the band whose members were being increasingly charged under the fishing regulations. Relations between the band and the Department of Fisheries were growing hostile and the decision to embark on the case was in the interest of the community not simply one fisherman (Monture-Angus, 1999, pp. 88–89).

Mr. Sparrow's case was decided by the Supreme Court of Canada in 1990. In reviewing the case, the court recognized that the main issue was whether Parliament had the right to regulate Aboriginal fishing in light of s. 35 of the constitution. The first matter to be decided was whether the rights of the Salish to fish were "recognized and affirmed" in the constitution. The right would have to be determined to be an existing right at the time of the patriation of the constitution in 1982. The Crown's position was that the right was extinguished prior to 1982 as a result of the myriad of provincially enacted fishing regulations over time in British Columbia. The Crown was unsuccessful in its argument due to the finding in the *Calder* case in 1973, which stated that the Crown must articulate in a plain and clear manner its intent to extinguish an Aboriginal right and cannot rely on implied extinguishment. Justices Dickson and La Forest stated in the *Sparrow* case:

> The test of extinguishment to be adopted, in our opinion, is that the Sovereign's intention must be clear and plain if it is to extinguish an aboriginal right. (*Sparrow*, 1990, p. 1099)

The Supreme Court found that enactment of provincial regulations is implied extinguishment only and does not meet the test for extinguishment. Therefore, Mr. Sparrow's right to fish was constitutionally entrenched in 1982.

Since the constitution is the supreme law of the land, statutes cannot be enacted to alter rights guaranteed in it. However, the Supreme Court in *Sparrow* recognized that the rights of Aboriginal people to the fisheries are not absolute. In *Sparrow* the Supreme Court set out a two-part test for infringement on the Aboriginal constitutional right to fish. The first part is that any infringement on the right must be justifiable by the Crown's having "compelling and substantial objectives," one of those being the protection of the resources in order to ensure the continuation of the right. The second test is that any legislation with the objective of limiting Aboriginal constitutional rights to fisheries must be consistent with the Crown's fiduciary obligation to Aboriginal peoples. Other compelling objectives may involve balancing the constitutional rights of Aboriginal peoples to the fisheries with the rights of non-Aboriginal peoples to the fisheries. In the latter circumstance the test of fiduciary obligation would come first.

The judgment rendered in *Sparrow* was seen as a victory for Aboriginal people. They did not intend to seize a right to the resource that would ultimately exclude non-Aboriginal access; rather, they sought increased access to the resource in order to increase economic self-sufficiency. Ultimately, the victory was significantly limited when power was vested in the Crown to limit access by using the two-part test. However, the onus was placed on the Crown to justify infringement, including minimal infringement. If the rights were infringed for justifiable reasons, consultation for the infringement must occur through a process of negotiation. Bell and Patterson (2003, p. 107) offer a concise summary of the framework of the litigation process to determine Aboriginal rights that are constitutionally protected:

1. identification of the nature and content of the right;
2. determining whether the right is an "existing right" recognized and affirmed by section 35 (or whether it has been lawfully extinguished prior to the enactment of Section 35);
3. determination of whether federal or provincial legislation constitutes a prima facie infringement with the exercising of an existing Aboriginal right; and
4. analysis of the legitimacy of justification for government interference.

The *Sparrow* decision shows how a common law Aboriginal right to fish becomes protected under the constitution. Later, in *R v. Badger* (1996), the Supreme Court clarified that rights set out in treaties must be protected in the same manner. This will have far-reaching consequences, as many of the over 500 treaties include the right to hunt and fish without interference by the Crown, and many treaties include hunting and fishing rights over territories ceded in the treaties that are now Crown land or interest has been vested in third parties due to grants by the Crown. The same two-part test set out in *Sparrow* must be applied to infringement of an Aboriginal right that is sourced in treaty.

There have been a number of cases since *Sparrow* that expound upon the two-part test. The *Van der Peet* case settled by the Supreme Court of Canada in 1996 offers a new aspect to the *Sparrow* two-part test. Dorothy Van der Peet was charged for violating the British Columbia fishing regulations, which prohibited the sale and barter of fish. Van der Peet was a member of the Sto:lo First Nation. She sold 10 salmon for $50 to a non-Aboriginal person. In this case the Supreme Court set new criteria for characterizing and interpreting Aboriginal rights. It narrowed what could be an Aboriginal right to that which existed pre-contact. It held that a right is not an Aboriginal right if it exists because of European influence. In this case it held that the activity of exchanging fish among nations or people at the time of contact did not translate in a contemporary form to an unlimited commercial right to fish, but a right to fish for livelihood. Therefore, Aboriginal rights must owe their origin to pre-contact activities. This decision will set a precedent for the battle over the right to access the forestry industry, Canada's greatest export and source of wealth. The Supreme Court will later rely on the *Van der Peet* decision to disallow increased commercial access to the forestry industry because it is not an activity in which Aboriginal people engaged pre-contact.

ABORIGINAL TITLE TO LAND

The *Delgamuukw* case (1997) began its journey through the Canadian court system in the early 1980s. The Gitksan and Wet'suwet'en people brought their case forward with the intention of forcing the province of British Columbia to recognize Aboriginal title over bands' traditional territory, which they had never ceded to the province or federal government through treaty or any other means. The area encompasses approximately 58,000 square kilometres in north-central British Columbia. The province asserted that Aboriginal title to land in British Columbia had been extinguished in 1871 as a result of the province's incorporation into the Dominion of Canada. This case was decided by the Supreme Court in 1998.

CHAPTER 13 Current Issues Over Land

This case set precedents for Aboriginal rights including title to land, and Crown sovereignty, which the courts assert can coexist with Aboriginal rights.

In sharing details of this case I must share the arguments put forward by the Crown to assert that there was no Aboriginal title over the land of British Columbia. I do this because these are the very same arguments I hear from students at the beginning of this course every time I deliver it. It is important that students understand that their arguments have been expressed by the Crown in regard to the matters of Aboriginal title and have been rejected by the Supreme Court.

The BC Crown argued the following:

1. Aboriginal peoples were so low on the scale of social organization that their lands can be treated as vacant and unoccupied for the purpose of issuing Crown grants pursuant to laws enacted by settler governments without regard to the prior occupation of Aboriginal peoples (Mandell, 2003, p. 166).

2. Colonial land legislation before Confederation extinguished Aboriginal peoples' relations to the land; once the colony (soon to become a province) enacted legislation regulating Aboriginal peoples' rights to the land and resources, their rights were extinguished by implied extinguishment and by the powers vested in the colony/province (Youngblood Henderson, 1999).

3. The creation of land grants by British Columbia to settlers extinguished the Aboriginal tenure because Aboriginal people were precluded from sustaining their relationship with the land; once settlers were granted land and began occupying it Aboriginal peoples' relationship to the land was broken. The existence of third-party interests displaces Aboriginal use, right, and title (Youngblood Henderson, 1999; Mandell, 2003).

4. The establishment of federal Indian reserves in British Columbia extinguished Aboriginal tenure because Aboriginal people "abandoned" their territory (Youngblood Henderson, 1999). (An underlying assertion of this argument is that the benefits of colonization, such as "civilization" and "Christianity" were compensation enough for voluntarily vacating traditional lands [Mandell, 2003].)

5. Section 88 of the *Indian Act* allowed provincial laws of general application to apply as well to Indians, extinguishing Aboriginal title and rights (Youngblood Henderson, 1999).

6. Aboriginal title and rights vanish with the passage of time (Mandell, 2003, p. 169).

All of these Crown arguments were rejected by the Supreme Court in the *Delgamuukw* decision. Arguments 2 to 5 inclusive rely on the power of the colony or province of British Columbia to extinguish Aboriginal title to land. Whether this power manifested itself through legislation that implied extinguishment or not, the court ruled that the province never had the constitutional authority to extinguish Aboriginal title, and since that title has never been extinguished it is protected under s. 35 of the constitution.

The court did not recognize the passage of time as extinguishing title or rights nor the argument that Aboriginal people were not a people capable of holding territory because they were "uncivilized."

In its decision the court identified three components of Aboriginal title:

1. That it encompassed the right to exclusive use and occupancy.

2. That it includes the right to choose to what uses the land can be put with the limitation that it cannot be altered to destroy the capacity to sustain future generations of Aboriginal people.

3. That the lands held pursuant to Aboriginal title have an economic component.

The first component displaced the *St. Catherine's* ruling of 1888, which stated that Aboriginal interest in the land was merely "personal and usufructuary" at the benevolence of the Crown. It elevates the interest in the land to exclusive use and occupancy. The second component suggests that Aboriginal people must be consulted over decisions pertaining to the uses of the land held under Aboriginal title. The title includes mineral rights and rights to modern exploitation of natural resources. This translates to having rights to make decisions over resource harvesting and development. Finally, recognizing the economic component of the value of the land suggests that the fiduciary responsibility of the Crown must be scrutinized in the dealings with Aboriginal land, and that Aboriginal people must benefit from the lands and resources. The Supreme Court also established a test for infringement on the rights inherent in Aboriginal title. It specified that infringements must be justified by the Crown and compensation must be paid for the infringement based on the nature of the infringement, in recognition of the economic component of Aboriginal land title.

As in all cases involving Aboriginal rights a move forward would not be complete without a limitation placed on it. The *Delgamuukw* decision set a two-part test for infringement on Aboriginal title. The first part is that the infringement must be for a valid legislative directive. The Supreme Court held these directives to be very broad:

1. The development of agricultural, forestry, mining, and hydroelectric power;

2. The general economic development of the province;

3. The protection of the environment or endangered species;

4. The building of infrastructure; and

5. The settlement of foreign populations to support those aims (McDonald, 2003, p. 231).

The second part of the test is that the infringement must be consistent with the fiduciary responsibility of the Crown to Aboriginal people. Because of this second part of the components of Aboriginal title (the right to choose to what uses the land can be put), Aboriginal people *must* be consulted in reaching a decision about infringement and compensation. This consultation process has not always gone smoothly, and the breakdowns can lead to serious and sometimes dangerous confrontations. For an example of a breakdown we will look briefly at the East Coast lobster fisheries dispute between the Crown and the Mi'kmaq.

> **CLASS ACTIVITY**
>
> Did you know that there are currently 800 land claims in backlog? Conduct an online search for claims entered.

RECENT CASE STUDY

Originally, the Mi'kmaq were partners in the Wabanaki confederacy, which comprised five nations; the Mi'kmaq, the Passamaquoddy, the Penobscot, the Maliseet, and the Abenaki. The traditional territory of this group covered Atlantic Canada, Maine, and parts of Quebec. The Mi'kmaq were aligned with the French post-contact but made treaties with the British after France was forced to cede its territories in Acadia to the British. A series of treaties, beginning in 1725, were signed to establish peace between settlers and the original inhabitants of the territory. This series included, among other things, the right to fish and hunt as had been done always. The treaty did not contain any land cession provisions. This treaty was renewed in 1749, 1752, 1760, 1761, and 1794 and was characterized as a covenant chain, with each treaty connected and linked to the others. The highlights of those treaties were as follows:

> British laws would be a great hedge about the Mi'kmaq property and rights. Mi'kmaq could traffic and barter or exchange commodities in any manner with managers of truckhouses (trading posts). Mi'kmaq would receive gifts in the form of goods on the First day of each October and the nation to nation relationship between the British and the Mi'kmaq would be respected and the Mi'kmaq way of life would be preserved. (Knockwood, 2003, p. 47)

Following this chain of treaties the *British North America Act* was instated, then shortly thereafter the *Indian Act*, which essentially denied the treaty rights of the Mi'kmaq. Following this, a myriad of federal and provincial laws were enacted to regulate and limit the Mi'kmaq rights to fish and hunt. Nevertheless, the Mi'kmaq continued to press for the recognition of the treaties and continued to hunt and fish outside the regulations that were unilaterally imposed. In 1928 Gabriel Sylliboy was charged for hunting out of season. He was found guilty when the trial judge asserted that the treaty protection did not extend to Mi'kmaq outside the small band of the Shubenacadie, as he interpreted that the treaty was applicable only to that one small band. Since Sylliboy was not a member of that specific band he had no protection under the treaty. Furthermore, the judge ruled that even if Sylliboy were a member of that small band he would still be found guilty because when the treaty was signed in 1752 the Mi'kmaq were not an independent power legally capable of entering into a treaty. One must question the logic of this statement; why would the British negotiate a treaty with a group whom they did not recognize as having the legal capacity to enter into a treaty?

The precedent was set; in a subsequent case, *The Queen v. Francis* in 1968, Justice Richard of the New Brunswick Magistrate's Court ruled for the conviction of

Martin Francis for fishing without a licence. (Knockwood, 2003, p. 52) Francis also asserted that the treaties set out his right to fish. Although the judge was sympathetic to the issues, he found it his "painful duty" to convict because the law did not provide for the treaty to be recognized as a result of previous case law.

A number of cases ensued involving the Mi'kmaq who, seemingly undaunted, continued to battle in the courts to assert their rights. The first case that followed the constitutional provisions enshrined in s. 35 came in 1985 in the case of *Simon v. The Queen*. The *Sylliboy* decision, stating that the Mi'kmaq were not capable of entering into treaties, was overturned. Mr. Simon, charged with hunting infractions, was not convicted on the basis that the treaty of 1752 was a valid treaty to which the Mi'kmaq had the capacity to enter into and constituted a source of protection against infringements on hunting rights. The Supreme Court found that the right was not an "absolute right" and was subject to federal regulation. Nevertheless, this was a victory, as it was the first time the Mi'kmaq treaties had been recognized, affording them protection under s. 35.

The last related decision of the Supreme Court came in 1999 in the case of *R v. Marshall*. Donald Marshall Jr., a Mi'kmaq fisherman, was charged for violating federal fishing regulations by selling eels without a licence, fishing without a licence, and fishing during the closed season with the use of illegal nets. Marshall had caught 463 pounds of eels that he sold for $787.10 (*Marshall*, 1999, para. 4; Donham, 2003, p. 366). Entered into evidence for the defence were minutes from the treaty negotiations from 1760–61. Those minutes included requests from the Mi'kmaq for truckhouses in which to sell their peltries and agreements on behalf of the Mi'kmaq to barter and trade their catches and hunts with the managers of the truckhouses for "necessaries." In 1999 the Supreme Court interpreted this as the Mi'kmaq having retained not only their right to harvest resources but also the right to sell and trade to their best advantage. The court interpreted "necessaries" to mean "a modest livelihood." The court, as in other cases previously discussed, did not give the right to an unlimited commercial harvest, but rather provided that federal regulations could be used to contain the right to protect the resource. In keeping with the *Delgamuukw* decision, the agreements on containing the right would happen through negotiation with the Mi'kmaq with a close eye on the fiduciary duty of the Crown.

Approximately 40 Mi'kmaq boats took to the water to celebrate the recognition of their rights and began to fish lobster. The same waters were home to some 2,893 non-Native lobster boats. The backlash by non-Native fishers, particularly commercial fishers, was fierce. They lobbied the government to re-open the *Marshall* case and insisted that the conservation of lobster fisheries was at stake. Violence broke out in some communities between Native and non-Native fishers. The Department of Fisheries quickly applied pressure for Mi'kmaq and other bands to sign agreements limiting their newly recognized rights to fish. Twenty-seven bands did sign agreements with the department within a year. Bands at Indian Brook and Burnt Church refused to sign, and continued to fish and develop their own conservation plan. They were portrayed in the media as renegade bands unwilling to reason, and persistent in their determination to fish illegally. The media failed to point out that the quantity of Native traps was in fact less than 0.2 percent of the non-Native traps (Donham, 2003, p. 371).

As Native traps were destroyed by angry non-Native fishers, and violence broke out, the RCMP was called upon to keep the peace and the Department of Fisheries was sent in to save the lobsters from Native fishers who, according to the media, were about to drive the lobsters to the brink of extinction. The Department of Fisheries arrested Mi'kmaq fishers and participated in sinking several of their vessels (Obomsawin, 2002). The RCMP did what it could to keep the peace. By 2002, the Mi'kmaq acquiesced and signed agreements to severely limit their take of the resource. Ten Mi'kmaq fishers had been arrested for fishing violations and further criminal offences relating to resisting Department of Fisheries officers' arrests. The conflict is not over as the Mi'kmaq attempt to inch their way into the commercial fishing business. One of the poorest groups on the East Coast, with the greatest right, according to the Supreme Court of Canada, to resource harvesting, has been assigned the smallest amount of the harvest. The Supreme Court decision rendered in *Marshall* was intended to increase Mi'kmaq access to the fishery to provide economic hope for the community. It would appear that non-Native commercial fishers are not prepared to share the resource (New Brunswick Environmental Network, 2002).

> **CLASS ACTIVITY**
>
> View the film *Honour of the Crown*, which follows François Paulette's 25-year battle to reclaim 9 tracts of land dating back to an 1899 treaty.

WORKING TOGETHER

Thus far we have examined the litigious and adversarial nature of defining Aboriginal rights to land and resources. Because our system is based in Western European legal structures it is adversarial in nature. However, there are other ways of defining rights and reaching mutually acceptable agreements to resource sharing and management. Because the claims process through litigation is so costly and takes so long, frequently development continues quickly on contested lands. By the time settlements are reached, often the resources of the land are already harvested or the land is permanently altered by developments such as mining and oil and gas exploration. Co-management has been implemented in some areas where Aboriginal rights to lands have not been extinguished. These processes are successful predominantly in more remote areas where settlement is beginning to occur and resources are beginning to be harvested. Co-management is a more inclusive and consensus-based approach to resource harvest and development through sharing of decision-making power with non-traditional actors in the process of resource management. Non-traditional actors include non-government and non-industry interests such as environmental groups, Aboriginal groups, and local users of the resources. Co-management stresses negotiation rather than litigation to resolve conflict (Tracy Campbell).

As discussed earlier in this chapter, particularly in the *St. Catherine's Milling* case, the protection of treaty rights such as hunting and fishing is seen as the responsibility of the federal government. However, management of natural resources is seen as a provincial responsibility. Confusion may result when Aboriginal people exercise their treaty rights on provincial Crown land. The scale of development of that provincial land determines whether it is possible to exercise those rights.

Concepts of co-management fit well with the Supreme Court ruling in *Delgamuukw*, particularly the second component, which set out the right of Aboriginal people to determine the uses to which the land can be put. This process of co-management fulfills that component of the ruling, which set out an obligation for sincere negotiations over land usage.

Current co-management schemes differ in the degree of control Aboriginal people have in the management of resources. Provincial governments will sometimes call their proposals co-management when instead informing Aboriginal people about decisions already made with regard to the contested territories, and not consulting with them on how to minimize the harmful effects to their communities. This is inconsistent with the true spirit of co-management. Degrees of co-management range from cooperation to communication to advisory committees to participation on management boards all the way to partnership and community control. Ideally, the co-management process culminates in a partnership of equals and absolute joint decision making. This requires commitment and a delicate balance of interests.

LAND CLAIMS

comprehensive land claims
claims to territory that are not covered by treaty or land cessation agreements

Land claims are divided into two categories, comprehensive land claims and specific land claims. **Comprehensive land claims** affect land that has not been covered by treaty, meaning approximately 50 percent of Canada's land mass. Since a treaty involving that land was not entered into, Aboriginal people have an interest in any land that, as per *Delgamuukw*, has a distinct economic nature. Treaties are not a thing of the past, as the process through which the claim over these areas is settled results in a modern-day treaty. Settlement of these claims comprises a variety of terms, including money, land, forms of local government, rights to wildlife, rights protecting Native language and culture, and joint management of lands and resources. These modern treaties set out terms that include resource allocations, governmental structures for self-government, and many other details related to economic interests in the land. The government often negotiates for an increase in Aboriginal land base in return for the extinguishment of title over an even larger portion of land. This is highly controversial for Aboriginal people since the extinguishment of rights over territory is contrary to what they are fighting for. Furthermore, as previously discussed, Aboriginal people have a special relationship to the land from which they are required to be alienated from.

specific land claims
claims that relate to specific misdealings of the Crown with relation to land or resources

Specific land claims are based on lawful obligation and involve claims that relate to the management of Indian lands and assets. The main issues addressed in specific claims are the loss by bands of established band lands and natural resources in the band's territory as a result of unilateral action on behalf of the Crown. The *Guerin* case discussed earlier in this chapter is an example of a specific land claim.

Each claim is distinct, with individual differences reflecting the needs and history of each area. Take, for example, the claim put forward in 1988 by the Golden Lake Algonquin (Steckley & Cummins, 2001a). This claim is still in the process of negotiation and is a long way from settlement yet even though it is nearing 30 years in the process. The Golden Lake Algonquin live 140 kilometres west of Algonquin

CHAPTER 13   Current Issues Over Land

Park, Ontario. They have never surrendered their rights to the land and have never signed a treaty. The government signed a treaty with a band of Ottawa Natives who spent a few years in the area around 1680 but did not hold the area to be their traditional territory. The Algonquin were overlooked in the treaty process. This is not unusual and has happened to different Aboriginal groups in Canada; for example, the Lubicon Cree in Alberta and the Temagami Anicinabe in northern Ontario. The Golden Lake Algonquin have been attempting to assert their claim to the land since 1772 when they petitioned government to recognize their title to the land. The Algonquin were assured by Sir William Johnson that they were protected under the *Royal Proclamation* to title to their lands, in spite of the fact that they were being overwhelmed by white settlement. The government made several promises to keep settlers off the land until 1836 when it asserted that the Algonquin had already surrendered the land to the Crown under treaty and had been compensated accordingly. The 1845 Bagot Commission, which investigated the uncompensated alienation of Natives from their lands, looked at the Algonquin situation and recommended that the Algonquin be compensated for their land and that a tract of land be set aside for them. This recommendation was not followed.

In 1857, hemmed in on all sides by settlers, five Algonquin families petitioned the government for reserve land. Six years later they were granted 631 hectares of land on which to live. Soon other families joined the group and the population grew to the point that the established acreage could not sustain them. Algonquin Provincial Park was created in 1893 from Crown land for sale for settlement. Other groups of Algonquin were living in the area that would become the provincial park, and they petitioned the government to set aside lands for them in light of their displacement due to the creation of the park. They were advised by the government to join the Golden Lake group on the area already set aside. The government wished to avoid the creation of more reserves because it believed that real estate would drop if there were too many Indians in the area. The Algonquin continued to petition the government, insisting that they had neither surrendered their land nor been compensated for its loss; furthermore, they believed they had protection under the *Royal Proclamation*. Their petitions were ignored.

In the mid-1980s a Provincial Court judge agreed with the Algonquin that they had not ceded their traditional land and therefore had protection through the *Royal Proclamation*. The Supreme Court of Ontario overturned that decision; regardless, the Algonquin entered a claim covering 8.8 million hectares, which included most of the park and much of the surrounding area, including small municipalities.

The Algonquin wished to reclaim unoccupied Crown land only, not private commercial or municipal lands. Four issues were brought forward in this claim: land, natural resources, self-government, and compensation for the loss. The province began the negotiation process in response to the claim but the public was outraged. The loss of the park and Crown land meant no capacity to expand white communities.

An interim agreement was reached by 1991 outlining hunting and fishing rights in the area, which included the park for the Algonquin, much to the dismay of non-Native hunters. No resolution has been reached with regard to the land or other resources; however, negotiations are ongoing, although a quarter century has passed since the claim was entered.

The government has set out the following as objectives in the negotiation of the Algonquin claim:

> We are committed to achieving a just and equitable settlement of the longstanding claim of the Algonquins of Golden Lake First Nation, and in doing so, we intend:
>
> - To avoid creating injustices for anyone in the settlement of the claim.
> - To establish certainty and finality with respect to title, rights and interests in the land and natural resources with the intention of promoting stability within the area and increasing investor confidence.
> - To identify and protect Algonquin rights.
> - To protect the rights of private landowners, including their rights of access to and use of their land.
> - To enhance the economic opportunities of the Algonquins with the intention of also benefiting and promoting general economic and commercial opportunities in the area.
> - To ensure that Algonquin Park remains a park for the appropriate use and enjoyment of all peoples.
> - To establish effective and appropriate methods and mechanisms for managing the lands and natural resources affected by the settlement, consistent with the principles of environmental sustainability.
> - To continue to consult with interested parties throughout the negotiation process and to keep the public informed on the progress of negotiations.

(Ontario Secretariat for Aboriginal Affairs, 2005)

The length of time it takes to negotiate a claim is obviously a major problem. Proposals have been put forward to speed the process along but it remains painfully slow. Many claims wait much longer than the Algonquin's. Most claims are negotiated in the absence of protests or violence; however, when the negotiation process breaks down, Aboriginal people may take action in the form of protests and/or setting up blockades. This most frequently occurs when resource harvesting or development is happening at a rapid rate on contested land. Aboriginal groups cannot afford to wait 20, 30, or even 50 years while their claim makes its way through stages of research and negotiation. If they did, there would be nothing remaining to negotiate for. These protests and/or blockades have the potential for violence as investors and construction or forestry crews become angry with the work stoppage, and Native people become frustrated believing that their petitions are being ignored.

ONTARIO

Generally, there are three kinds of land claims in Ontario.

(1) **Claims relating to the fulfillment of terms of treaties**. These claims are usually the result of disagreements between the Crown and First Nations about the size and location of the reserves that were set aside in accordance with the treaties. These claims may also involve the wording of treaties and the understanding of the parties at the time of treaty signing. Claims can also arise as a result of events that occurred after the treaty signing such as the flooding of reserve land for hydroelectric power and the expropriation of reserve land for public purposes such as high-

claims relating to the fulfillment of terms of treaties
claims that are usually a result of disagreement between the Crown and First Nations about the size and location of reserves set aside by treaties

CHAPTER 13 Current Issues Over Land

ways, infrastructure, or military building without compensation. The Ipperwash land dispute falls into this category. (See appendix 13.1 for details.)

(2) **Claims arising from the surrender for sale of reserve land**. These occur when a First Nation seeks compensation for, or the return of, land that had been surrendered to the Crown for sale for the benefit of the band. Although these surrenders did take place, the funds generated from the sale of land were to be set aside for the sole benefit of the band. However, on many occasions the band did not receive these funds, or the land remained unsold and the band was not compensated.

(3) **Claims arising from Aboriginal title**. There are few of these claims in Ontario since most of the province is covered by treaty; however, other large areas of Canada are not covered by treaty. These claims are based on the allegation that lands traditionally used and occupied by Aboriginal people were never surrendered to the Crown by Aboriginal people. The Golden Lake Algonquin claim is an example of this type of claim in Ontario.

claims arising from the surrender for sale of reserve land
claims occurring when First Nations seek compensation for, or the return of, land that had been surrendered to the Crown for sale for the benefit of the band

claims arising from Aboriginal title
claims based on the allegation that lands traditionally used and occupied by Aboriginal people were never surrendered to the Crown by Aboriginal people

CONCLUSION

The Mi'kmaq fishing crisis on the East Coast is only one of the many conflicts that have escalated to violence in Canada. Whenever these situations occur (and there are at least three ongoing in Ontario with serious potential for violence), the police are called to the front line to keep the peace. The importance of maintaining a neutral position cannot be overstated. It is critical that each officer present at the front line understands the issues. Of course, we all carry biases; to state otherwise would be deceiving ourselves. We carry these biases in all that we do, and they may become transparent under stressful conditions. When it comes to Native land and resources disputes, these biases are increasingly fed by the media. It is important to look behind the press coverage, behind the events that are unfolding moment by moment, and outside the traditional tactical box of policing. It is crucial to see the issue in its historical context to understand how emotionally charged these situations can be. It is the responsibility of police to ensure the safety of all persons involved and to maintain a neutral position.

After reading this chapter it should be clear that Aboriginal land and resource claims have their foundations in law. The Supreme Court has clearly laid out the obligations of all parties with regard to negotiating claims to both resources and land. Problems arise, however, when these legal obligations are not followed by governments, developers, and commercial industry.

KEY TERMS

comprehensive land claims

specific land claims

claims relating to the fulfillment of terms of treaties

claims arising from the surrender for sale of reserve land

claims arising from Aboriginal title

REFERENCES

Amnesty International. (2005, December 19). *It is time to comply: Canada's record of unimplemented UN human rights recommendations.* http://www.amnesty.ca/resource_centre/reports/view.php?load=arcview&article=3131&c=Resource+Centre+Reports.

Badger, R v., [1996] 1 SCR 771.

Bell, C., & Paterson, R. (2003). Aboriginal rights to repatriation of cultural property in Canada. In A. Walkem & H. Bruce (Eds.), *Box of treasures or empty box? Twenty years of section 35.* Penticton, BC: Theytus Books, pp. 104-154.

Calder v. Attorney-General of British Columbia, [1973] SCR 313.

Churchill, W. (1992). *Last stand at Lubicon Lake: Struggle for the land.* Toronto, ON: Between the Lines.

Coon Come, M. (2003, April 18). Remarks of National Chief Matthew Coon Come, Commonwealth Policy Studies Unit London. http://www.cpsu.org.uk/downloads/MatthewC.pdf.

Curry, B. (2003, November 27). Half of Canadians disbelieve land claims, National survey: Atlantic Canada most opposed to special rights for aboriginals. CanWest News Service.

Delgamuukw v. British Columbia, [1997] 3 SCR 1010.

Donham, P.B. (2003). Fishery: Lobster wars. In R. Anderson & R. Bone (Eds.), *Natural resources and Aboriginal people in Canada: Readings, cases and commentary.* Concord, ON: Captus Press.

Friends of the Lubicon. (2006). United nations holds Canada in continuing violation of Lubicon human rights. http://www.tao.ca/~fol/pa/humanr.htm.

Gibson, G., Higgs, E., & Hrudey, S. (1998). Sour gas, bitter relations. *Alternatives Journal: Environmental Thought, Policy and Action, 24*(2).

Guerin v. The Queen, [1984] 2 SCR 335.

Henderson, B. (1996). http://www.bloorstreet.com/200block/rguerin.htm.

Goldi, J., & Goldi, J. (Producers). (2004). *Ipperwash: A Canadian tragedy.* [Motion picture].

Knockwood, C. (2003). The Mi'kmaq-Canadian treaty relationship: A 277-year journey of rediscovery. In A. Walkem & H. Bruce (Eds.), *Box of treasures or empty box? Twenty years of section 35.* Penticton, BC: Theytus Books, pp. 43-60.

Mandell, L. (2003). Offerings to an emerging future. In A. Walkem & H. Bruce (Eds.), *Box of treasures or empty box? Twenty years of section 35.* Penticton, BC: Theytus Books.

Marshall, R v., [1999] 3 SCR 533.

McDonald, M. (2003). Aboriginal forestry in Canada. In R. Anderson & R. Bone (Eds.), *Natural resources and Aboriginal people in Canada. Readings, cases and commentary.* Concord, ON: Captus Press.

Monture-Angus, P. (1999). Journeying forward: Dreaming First Nations independence. Halifax: Fernwood Publishing.

Nisga'a Lisims Government. (1997–2000). http://www.kermode.net/nisgaa/story/calder.html.

Obomsawin, A. (2002). *Is the Crown at war with us?* National Film Board of Canada.

Ontario Secretariat for Aboriginal Affairs. (2005). *Statement of shared objectives.* http://www.aboriginalaffairs.osaa.gov.on.ca/english/negotiate/algonquin/objectives.htm.

Radford, T., & Krepakevich, J. (2001). *Honour of the Crown.* National Film Board of Canada.

Royal Proclamation of 1763. RSC 1970, App. II, No. 1.

Simon v. The Queen, [1985] 2 SCR 387.

Sparrow, R v., [1990] 1 SCR 1075.

St. Catherine's Milling & Lumber Company v. The Queen (1888), 14 App. Cas. 46 (PC).

Steckley, J., & Cummins, B. (2001a). The Golden Lake Algonquin and Algonquin Park: Missed by treaty. In *Full Circle: Canada's First Nations.* Toronto: Prentice Hall, chapter 14.

Steckley, J., & Cummins, B. (2001b). Social issues: The Dudley George story. In *Full Circle: Canada's First Nations.* Toronto: Prentice Hall, chapter 20.

Sylliboy, R v., [1929] 1 DLR 307.

Van der Peet, R v., [1996] 2 SCR 507.

Walkem, A. (2003). Constructing the constitutional box: The Supreme Court's section 35(1) reasoning. In A. Walkem & H. Bruce (Eds.), *Box of treasures or empty box? Twenty years of section 35.* Penticton, BC: Theytus Books, pp. 196-222.

Youngblood Henderson, J. (1999). *Impact of Delgamuukw guidelines in Atlantic Canada.* http://mrc.uccb.ns.ca/impactdelgamuukw.html.

APPENDIX 13.1

The Dudley George Story

During the American revolution and the war of 1812 the Anicinabe, originally from northern Ontario, were allies with the British. They settled in southern Ontario following the wars and became known as the Chippewa. The government of the Chippewa signed a treaty in 1825 that created four reserves: Sarnia, Walpole Island, Kettle Point, and Stoney Point. In 1928, the provincial government pressured the Stoney Point people to sell 152 hectares of prime waterfront land to private interests. Although they were against the idea of sale of their land, the band had little control. Indian Affairs, through the oppressive *Indian Act*, sold the land without the band's permission. A large part of that land was reserved to create the Ipperwash Provincial Park in 1936. The Stoney Point people were unhappy about the sale and unhappier still when their burial site was disturbed in the creation of the park.

In 1942 the federal government asked the Stoney Point people to relinquish what remained of their land so that a military base could be built to support the war efforts. (Many of the Stoney Point men were, in fact, overseas serving as soldiers.) The federal government offered $23 per acre for 2,211 acres of land (895 hectares). The Stoney Point people voted on the offer and declined. Invoking the *War Measures Act*, the federal government expropriated the land regardless. The Stoney Point people were paid the said amount and were promised that the land would be returned to them at the end of the war, provided the military had no further need for it. The Stoney Point people were forced to leave and live with their neighbors at Kettle Point.

At the end of the war the Stoney Point people requested to enter into negotiations for the return of their land. The armed forces continued, however, to make peacetime use of the land as a cadet training camp and therefore did not return the land. In 1981, 36 years after the end of the war, the federal government agreed to pay the Stoney Point band $2.4 million in compensation for the 40-year use of the land and agreed to return the land pending an environmental assessment. The cost to clean the area environmentally was expected to be high because of the way it was used by the military. The Department of National Defence then decided that it did not want to relinquish the land. The department promised to review the requirements for the training camp every three years; if the training camp was deemed unnecessary, the department would turn it over to the Stoney Point people.

A recommendation was put forward in 1992 by the Standing Committee on Aboriginal People that the federal government return the land. The committee insisted that the government's reasons for failing to relinquish the land were "without substance." The recommendation was not followed. In May 1993, the Stoney Point people, bringing tents and trailers, moved onto the military property. They maintained a tenuous relationship with the military, alongside whom they were living. In September of that same year, they walked for three weeks to Ottawa to insist that action be taken to return the land. No action was forthcoming.

On September 4, 1995, Native protestors moved into the adjacent provincial park after it had closed for the season. One of the contentious issues about the park was the burial ground, which the Stoney Point people had requested be protected and fenced off. This had never occurred despite clear archeological records of the existence and location of the burial ground. The Harris government would deny that a burial ground was even located in the park; the government was subsequently proven wrong.

Newly elected Premier Mike Harris held an emergency meeting the day following the occupation. OPP Inspector Ron Fox was at that meeting. It was alleged that Premier Mike Harris insisted that the protestors be removed from the park. This allegation appears to have been substantiated: years later at the 2006 inquiry of the incident, in a conversation between Fox and OPP Inspector John Carson that was tape-recorded directly following the emergency meeting, Fox can be heard saying, "No question they don't give a shit about Indians," and "They just want us to kick ass." During the course of the inquiry Mike Harris would deny saying, "Get the fucking Indians out of the park." Various members who were present at the meeting would testify that they heard Mike Harris say this; others would testify that he did not. Regardless, after four days of testimony at the inquiry, Harris stated that he would not make any changes in the way he handled the Ipperwash incident.

Following the September 5, 1995 meeting the OPP prepared themselves for the altercation they expected. They ordered night-vision goggles, gas masks, and helicopters, and brought in 250 officers from across the province. The OPP had received intelligence information that the protestors were unarmed.

On September 6, the order was given to the OPP to get the protestors out of the park. After dark, the OPP advanced on the 30 unarmed protestors in the park. Sergeant Kenneth Deane, a sniper for the Tactics and Rescue unit, then shot Native protestor Dudley George, who later died from his injuries. Deane would testify that he witnessed a muzzle flash and saw George with a rifle. The investigation would reveal that there was no rifle, and George was unarmed at the time of the shooting. The police did not call an ambulance for George; the protestors attempted to call for one but were arrested. George was driven to the hospital by family members; a car breakdown en route delayed medical treatment even further. George's family members were arrested at the hospital; it was too late to save George, who died from his wound.

Kenneth Deane was charged and found guilty of criminal negligence causing death. He was sentenced to two years less a day to be served in the community plus 180 community service hours. He appealed his conviction unsuccessfully. Deane did not testify at the 2006 inquiry because he died in a car accident before it took place.

The Native protestors were arrested and faced 62 charges, most of which were dropped. Charges that stemmed from their entry into the park were dismissed because it was decided that they had colour of right to the park—that is, interest in the property—because the burial ground, previously assessed as non-existent, was within it.

Native rights groups immediately demanded an inquiry into the incident. The Conservative government refused, and it was not until the election of a new government in 2003 that an announcement was made that an inquiry would begin.

Following the announcement of the inquiry, the CBC received OPP surveillance tapes that were aired on the news. The tapes show OPP officers at the scene just prior to the shooting making racist comments about the protestors. These tapes brought the OPP's actions and motives into question.

Today, there is still no resolution with regard to the land issues. The inquiry's report, released May 31, 2007, ruled that the OPP, the government of former Ontario premier Mike Harris, and the federal government all bear responsibility for events that led to Dudley George's death. Both federal and provincial governments had more than 50 years to resolve these issues and chose not to. This choice led to a violent confrontation between police and Native protestors that culminated in the death of Dudley George. This tragedy could certainly have been avoided. Police services in Canada would be wise to study and learn from these events to ensure that they are not repeated in the future, as confrontations involving Native land and resources are likely to occur for decades to come.

Sources: Goldi & Goldi (1991); Steckley & Cummins (2001b).

APPENDIX 13.2

The Lubicon Cree

The Lubicon Cree were traditionally hunters and gatherers. They lived in a 10,000 square kilometre area surrounding Lubicon Lake in northern Alberta since time immemorial. In 1899 a delegation from the Canadian government travelled through northern Alberta to secure the signatures of bands occupying the area to Treaty No. 8. However, treaty commissioners failed to contact a number of small bands scattered throughout the vast territory covered by the treaty. The Lubicon was one of those bands; members did not hear of the treaty until 1912. The band never signed a treaty, nor did they ever cede or relinquish rights to their traditional territory.

Under the provisions of Treaty No. 8, each band was to receive a "reserved" land, the acreage depending on the population of the band, and each member was to receive an annuity in payment for the alienation of the land. Bands that were not notified of the treaty could go to designated locations and be added to the pay list for annuities. When the Lubicon band members were notified of the treaty by other bands, they made their way to Whitefish Lake and received an annuity there. Government officials then added the Lubicon names to the band list at Whitefish Lake, although the Lubicon group had no connection to that band and were a separate and individual band as they had always been.

In 1935 the Indian Department sent notice to the Lubicon band that they were living off their designated reserve, and must relocate to live at Whitefish Lake. The Lubicon protested that they had never lived there as they were a separate and distinct band that resided at Lubicon Lake; they requested that they be declared a band by the Indian Department. The department investigated, concluded that the Lubicon were indeed a separate and distinct band, and approved the creation of a new reserve at Lubicon Lake. In 1940 that reserve was surveyed by the department according to the population of the band at the time, which was set by the Indian agent at 127 members. At 52 hectares per person, the reserve was surveyed for 6,500 hectares.

Prior to the completion of the deal in 1942, Indian Affairs official Malcolm McCrimmon was sent to northern Alberta to see that the pay lists for annuities for Indians were in order. Because World War II expenses were mounting, the federal government was looking to reduce expenditures elsewhere and the Indian Department seemed a logical place to cut costs. McCrimmon rewrote the rules for addition to treaty annuity lists and eliminated all members who joined after 1912. He insisted that birth records be provided to prove that only pure-blood Indians were on the lists—and this was in a remote area where children were born at home and it was common to have no birth record. McCrimmon eliminated 700 names from the annuity pay list, including 90 members of the Lubicon Cree band. He then argued against the establishment of a reserve for the Lubicon, saying that there were insufficient members of the band to warrant a reserve. As a result, the Indian Department postponed the creation of a reserve indefinitely.

The Lubicon continued to live at Lubicon Lake, but a renewed interest in the area occurred in 1950 when Alberta Lands and Forest Division received inquiries from a large mining corporation regarding the Lubicon area. The company wanted the provincial government to open it for exploration. The province of Alberta requested that the Indian Department relocate the proposed reserve for the Lubicon to a "less isolated area." However, the federal government failed to respond to the province, which was anxious to lease the land. The province eventually sent a letter with an ultimatum, that the federal government respond within 30 days or the province would deem the proposed reserve not to exist. The federal government failed to respond. Alberta then requested that Indian Affairs strike the band from the record as an official band. The federal government could not comply with this request because it had declared the Lubicon a distinct band in 1939 even though it had failed to finalize a reserve for the band. Alberta insisted that the Lubicon band be reduced through enfranchisement where possible, and the remainder of the band relocated to live with the Whitefish band. The two levels of government could not come to an agreement on how to resolve this issue.

In 1971 Alberta secured oil company financing to build an all-weather road into Lubicon territory for the purposes of exploration. The Lubicon lobbied the government to stop the encroachment of corporations and insist that they have a right to their traditional territory. The Alberta government insisted that the Lubicon were squatters on provincial Crown lands with no land rights to negotiate. In 1975, as developers began exploration, the Lubicon filed a caveat under provincial law to place would-be developers on notice that title to the land was contested. The provincial government asked for a postponement of the caveat and rewrote legislation under Bill 29 to end grounds for Lubicon legal action.

In 1979 the all-weather road was completed and people poured into the area, severely disrupting the Lubicon way of life. In 1980 the Lubicon appealed to the federal government to provide them with financial assistance to seek an injunction to stop development until a resolution could be reached over the land title issues. The federal government denied the request. In 1981 Alberta declared the main settlement area of the Lubicon a hamlet, subdivided the area into 0.8 hectare lots, and proposed to lease or gift the lots to individual band members. The Lubicon were very concerned about how this "land tenure program" would affect their land claim and petitioned the federal government to look into the matter.

The minister of Indian Affairs discovered that the land in question could no longer be subject to a land claim because as a hamlet it was no longer classed as provincial Crown land.

In 1982, with the federal and provincial governments still unable to reach an agreement over the land allocation, the Lubicon filed a second legal action before the Alberta Court of Queen's Bench requesting the retention of Aboriginal rights over their traditional area, which would void the leases provided by the province to oil companies. The band requested an immediate injunction to stop development until the land issues could be resolved. The concluding arguments in the case were heard on December 2, 1982 but the court postponed the delivery of its verdict until March 1983. At that time an injunction to stop development was received—too late. The companies had simply accelerated their exploration through the winter, and the area became irredeemably altered environmentally.

By 1983, 400 oil wells had been drilled within 15 kilometres of the Lubicon's main settlement. Trapper income was reduced from $5,000 per year to $400, and moose killed for food plummeted from 200 to 19. The Lubicon experienced a rash of suicides and rising alcoholism within the community. Welfare dependence in the community increased from 5 percent to 90 percent. The community's extreme poverty and a tuberculosis outbreak affecting one-third of the community demoralized the band even further.

Following the injunction, the companies returned to court to argue that the injunction is unnecessary since the drilling was already complete and the pumping process remaining would not cause any further environmental degradation. By 1987 it was estimated conservatively that oil and gas revenues from the area were in excess of $500 million per year.

In 1984 the Lubicon appealed to the United Nations Human Rights Commission after the Supreme Court of Canada refused to hear their case. The United Nations conducted a study of the situation and concluded in 1987 that the Lubicon could not possibly achieve political redress in Canada. The United Nations appealed to Canada to do no further harm to Lubicon territory until a hearing could be held on human rights violations. However, in 1988 Alberta announced that it had granted timber rights to the Lubicon territory to a Japanese company, Daishowa, which planned to cut 4,500 hectares of timber per day to produce 1,000 tonnes of pulp per day.

In response to the news of the lease, the Lubicon toured Europe prior to the 1988 Olympics seeking support from other countries. European nations refused to lend Native artifacts to "The Spirit Sings" Native art exhibition at the Olympics. Also in 1988, the Lubicon, fed up with the system, withdrew all cases from Canadian courts, declared themselves a sovereign nation, and blockaded all roads leading into their territory. The RCMP arrested 27 people involved in the blockades, and the province refused to negotiate with the Lubicon until the blockades were removed.

Concerned that the situation could escalate into violence, Alberta returned to the negotiating table. Alberta negotiated the Grimshaw Accord, which included the creation of a reserved land base for the Lubicon people that included subsurface rights to the land. The federal government disagreed, offering a reserved land base with no subsurface rights. The subsurface rights were critical for the Lubicon since mining and drilling are the only ways they can now sustain their people—the degradation of the land made their traditional economy impossible. The subsurface rights are not forthcoming.

In 1989 the federal government exploited divisions within the band. Faced with extreme poverty with no resolution in sight, some members of the band wavered in their support of the band governance body. The federal government met with a dissident group and agreed to create a new band called the Woodland Cree, insisting that they have rights to the contested area. The federal government presented the rejected offer from the Lubicon band to the Woodland band, offering them an additional $1,000 each to sign the agreement absent of subsurface rights. The federal government offered the same deal to the Loon Lake Cree, and subsequently pressured the Lubicon to sign the same agreement absent of subsurface rights. The chief of the Lubicon band, Bernard Omniyak, says the agreement is "deficient in the area of providing economic stability for the future. In essence the Canadian Government has offered to build houses for the Lubicon and support us forever on welfare like animals in the zoo who are cared for and fed at an appointed time."

In 1990 the United Nations charged Canada with human rights violations under article 27 of the *International Covenant on Civil and Political Rights*. Canada did not answer to the charges, which stand today.

In 1991 the Lubicon organized an international boycott of Daishowa. In response, Daishowa agreed to stay out of Lubicon territory until the land issue was resolved; however, in 1994 Daishowa sued the organizers of the boycott for $5 million in compensation for lost business. The suit was unsuccessful.

In 1994 the Lubicon protested oil and gas corporation Unocal's plans to build a sour gas processing plant within 4 kilometres of the proposed reserve. Alberta's energy board failed to convene a hearing on the matter until after the plant was built. The plant went into operation in 1995.

Following the opening of the sour gas plant, Alberta proposed that the size of the proposed reserve be reduced from the original 243 square kilometres stated in the Grimshaw Accord because the population of the Lubicon band had decreased due to the creation of the Woodland Cree band and the transference of members to that group (Gibson, Higgs, & Hrudey, 1998).

In 2002 an agreement was finally reached between the federal and provincial governments and the Lubicon Cree over the construction of a new reserve for the Lubicon Cree, although subsurface rights were still undetermined. On November 1, 2005, the United Nations Human Rights Committee reaffirmed its earlier conclusion that Canada is violating article 1 of the *International Covenant on Civil and Political Rights* with regard to the Lubicon in so far as Canada is denying basic subsistence due to destruction of the traditional economy and way of life. Furthermore, Canada is in violation of article 27 of the Covenant insofar as it is participating in the destruction of culture, language rights, and way of life of the Lubicon by refusing to negotiate a reasonable resolution to their claim to land. The committee reiterated its 1987 recommendation (for which there is support in Canadian case law set in the 1997 *Delgamuukw* decision) that Canada should consult with the band before granting licences for economic exploitation of the disputed land and ensure that in no case such exploitation jeopardizes the rights recognized under the Covenant. Canada has not responded to the committee's findings. However, Amnesty International provided the following statement:

> One of the most glaring failures to implement UN level human rights recommendations is the situation of the Lubicon Cree in Alberta. In 1990, the Human Rights Committee issued a detailed report documenting serious violations of the rights of the Lubicon, stemming from a decades-old failure to enter into an

agreement with the Lubicon regarding their land rights. The Committee called on the government to ensure a prompt and just settlement of the dispute. Fifteen years later the dispute remains unresolved, the ability of the Lubicon to provide for themselves remains under threat, and there have been no negotiations between the government and the Lubicon for over two years. (Amnesty International, 2005; also see Friends of the Lubicon, 2007)

The issues regarding land rights have still not been resolved. The Lubicon band suffers economically and socially and the resource that has brought economic wealth to the province of Alberta and Canada has led to economic collapse for the Lubicon. Negotiations are still ongoing.

CHAPTER 14

Aboriginal People and the Criminal Justice System

CHAPTER OBJECTIVES

After completing this chapter, you should be able to:

- Connect Native concepts of justice to First Nations people's world view.
- Discuss Native people's overrepresentation in the criminal justice system.
- Critically analyze the relationship between the police and First Nations people in Canada.
- Critically analyze the role of police in land and resource claims between Canada and First Nations people.

INTRODUCTION

The incarceration rate for Native people in Canada is high. It has been linked to socio-economic issues and institutionalized racism. In this chapter we will examine the relationship between the police and Aboriginal people in Canada, the advent of Aboriginal policing and alternative justice, and the role of police in conflicts between the government of Canada and First Nations people. This chapter contains issues for analysis and should prompt discussion on how to improve the relationship between Native people and police.

NATIVE OVERREPRESENTATION IN THE CRIMINAL JUSTICE SYSTEM

Aboriginal people are overrepresented in the criminal justice system and in the corrections system. Aboriginal men comprise 18 percent of federally sentenced offenders and Aboriginal women represent 28 percent of federally sentenced women

(Correctional Service Canada, 2005). Nearly one-third of provincially sentenced offenders are Aboriginal. The rate of recidivism is higher for Aboriginal women than for their non-Aboriginal counterparts. A recent survey in Saskatchewan found that 58 percent of Aboriginal people released from custody between April 1999 and March 31, 2000 were readmitted within four years (Statistics Canada). This was twice the proportion of non-Aboriginal people. It appears that our traditional criminal justice and corrections system is unable to adequately meet the needs of Aboriginal offenders. Some of the strategies used to address issues of overrepresentation will be discussed in this chapter. I would like to begin, however, by quoting Aristotle, who said that "poverty is the mother of crime." If he is correct, then the overrepresentation of Aboriginal people in the criminal justice system is a natural representation of the poverty and marginalization of Aboriginal people in Canada today. The failure of the system to address this overrepresentation is rooted in the vast difference in Aboriginal concepts of justice and European concepts of justice, Canada's system being constructed on the latter.

To examine overrepresentation of Aboriginal people within the criminal justice system we must consider colonization. Crime, violence, and rates of incarceration are higher for Aboriginal populations within all colonized countries. Many Aboriginal people are poor and marginalized. Due to the residential school system, family dysfunction is common; this dysfunction manifests itself through family violence or a culture of violence in some Native communities.

Aboriginal people see the family as a central part of the social health of their communities. Other marginalized groups recognize this importance as well. The assimilation processes enforced by the federal government severely disrupted family relationships in First Nations communities. Residential schools are blamed for causing the greatest amount of damage; the abuse endured within the schools left the children with serious emotional scars. Those who did not complain of abuse still suffered loss of both language and family relationships. Some were unable to develop healthy relationships with even their own children.

As the residential school system wound down in the 1960s, a new form of family dislocation occurred, that of the child welfare system. Cross-cultural adoptions and foster placements were so common that many communities lost almost an entire generation of children. Those adoptions rarely worked out; adoptive parents were often unprepared for the challenges of rearing an already troubled child who would face discrimination (Wagamese, 1996). Communities reeling from the loss of their children continued to unravel (Fournier & Crey, 1997). In some penitentiaries, 95 percent of First Nations prisoners are victims of the child welfare system, having been separated from family, culture, and community through adoption, foster care, and, eventually, custody (Royal Commission on Aboriginal Peoples [RCAP], 1996, p. 129).

Loss of land through the colonization process and economic collapse in Aboriginal communities led to extreme poverty and economic reliance on the Canadian government. At the conclusion of the era of colonization (some academics argue that this era continues today), Aboriginal people endured "ill health, run-down and overcrowded housing, polluted water, inadequate schools, poverty and family breakdown/violence at rates found more often in developing countries than in Canada" (RCAP, 1996, p. 129). These problems reinforce one another to create a circle of disadvantage for Aboriginal people; swirling amidst this circle is the prevalence of alcohol and substance abuse.

Joan Sangster examined the historical overrepresentation of Aboriginal women in custody at the Mercer Reformatory between 1920 and 1960. Her study of admissions records at the Mercer Reformatory in the 1950s indicated that 70 percent of Aboriginal women's admissions were for alcohol-related offences. Sangster writes, "When a middle aged woman, who lost all her eight siblings to disease and her father to alcoholism, told the Mercer doctor that her drinking is 'unfortunate but unchangeable' one can perhaps understand her tone of resignation" (Sangster, 1999). Sangster attributes three factors to the overrepresentation of Aboriginal women in the criminal justice system. The first is material and social dislocation due to colonization. The second is gender and **race paternalism**, which translates into loss of autonomy and therefore agency over one's own actions. The third is the cultural gap between indigenous ideas of justice rooted in healing and restoration and European ideas of justice rooted in crime and punishment. Sangster's ideas are supported in academic material and her three attributes rely heavily on the experience of colonization.

race paternalism
a system under which the dominant group take authority to supply needs and regulate conduct of a minority group

ALCOHOL AND CRIMINALITY IN NATIVE COMMUNITIES

In the past, alcohol problems in Aboriginal communities were examined from a biological perspective; problem drinking was seen as a weakness of race and Aboriginal people were believed to have a genetic predisposition to alcoholism. Several studies in the 1970s disproved this theory but its rumours reverberate today. The disease model of alcoholism gained popularity after the demise of genetic- or race-based theories. First Nations addiction workers quickly embraced this model as it not only offered a reprieve from the victim blaming and racial bias intrinsic in the prior theory, but also held out hope for treatment and recovery. More recent examinations of the disease model question its validity as well; the most recent examination indicates that many problem drinkers are not alcoholics but binge drinkers who engage in violent behaviour (Thatcher, 2004, p. 21).

I address the issues of alcohol in this chapter since the correlation to crime and violence, particularly family violence, is very strong. There are two theories on the prevalence of alcoholism in Aboriginal communities. The first is that alcohol abuse is a symptom of social problems such as poverty, ill health, and family breakdown; the second is the reverse, that alcoholism is the primary factor and ill health, family breakdown, and violence are the result (Whitehead & Hayes, 1998, pp. 6-7). I would present that the foundation of colonization and the social upheaval it caused in Aboriginal communities supports the first theory of alcohol abuse (and more recently substance abuse for urban Natives) as a symptom of social problems rather than the primary cause.

In some Aboriginal communities, alcohol-related crime and family violence (which is also related to alcohol and substance abuse) has become the norm. In her examination of the Grassy Narrows reservation in 1984, Shkilnyk records that "they reject the concept of guilt and punishment for behavior influenced by alcohol ... they are not condemned by members of their own community" (Shkilnyk, 1985, p. 25). In their examination of family violence, Anne McGillivray and Brenda

Comaskey note that 75 to 80 percent of northern Ontario adult Aboriginal women are assaulted in an intimate relationship (McGillivray & Comaskey, 1999, p. 13). Domestic violence is accepted as a normative state for many Aboriginal communities: "In the reserve just, like, everybody had black eyes, walking around, all the ladies, all black. I thought that's the life … nobody don't say nothing" (McGillivray & Comaskey, 1999, p. 8).

Crimes committed under the influence of alcohol are deemed by consensus in some communities not to be criminal. Domestic violence is not seen as criminal or deviant because it is the norm. This normative state creates a situation where denunciation and deterrence (s. 718 of the *Criminal Code*) as a function of sentencing in criminal law are irrelevant. There is a strong correlation intergenerationally within domestic violence; children who witness or experience abuse become abusers. The intergenerational correlation exists as well with alcohol abuse and exhibits its onset with gas sniffing, as seen particularly in more isolated and economically desperate regions. This cycle is almost impossible to stop.

Shkilnyk (1985) and McGillivray and Comaskey (1999) direct their research at reserves; however, the relatively recent migration of First Nations people to large urban centres has resulted in high crime statistics amidst urban Aboriginals. Today only 47 percent of Aboriginal people live on reserves. A 1992 study revealed that only 19 percent of federally sentenced Aboriginal offenders were from a reserve. In 1992, the Edmonton Inner City Violent Crime Task Force found that 50 to 60 percent of incarcerated Aboriginal offenders in Alberta come from urban areas (LaPrairie, 2002). Enforcement directives differ greatly between reserve policing and urban policing. In urban policing, resolutions for incidents of criminal behaviour outside of laying criminal charges are less frequently considered.

Effects of colonization have occupied theories around Aboriginal criminality for good reason. Colonization has led to poverty and marginalization. Carole LaPrairie asserts that if colonization and culture conflict are the central matters, there should be no variation in levels of overrepresentation of Aboriginal people across the country since all Aboriginal people suffered colonization.

LaPrairie uses a report from the Canadian Centre for Justice Statistics (2000) to illustrate the variation in Aboriginal admissions to custody. The greatest overrepresentation she notes is Alberta at 9 times the rate of incarceration for non-Aboriginals, Saskatchewan at 10 times, and Manitoba at 7 times. The rate of Aboriginal incarceration in federal institutions had increased from 11 to 17 percent in 2002, and the numbers have increased since, according to Correctional Service Canada's 2004 report. According to McGillivray and Comaskey (1999), the highest enrollment rates at residential schools were also in these provinces, which would lead one to link overrepresentation to assimilation and colonialism as primary factors rather than contributing factors.

As well, many urban Aboriginal people suffer from low socio-economic status and marginalization, and are isolated in high-crime urban communities that result in a criminogenic environment. This places urban Aboriginal people in a position of double risk.

CHAPTER 14 Aboriginal People and the Criminal Justice System

FIGURE 14.1 Victims of Crime, 1999

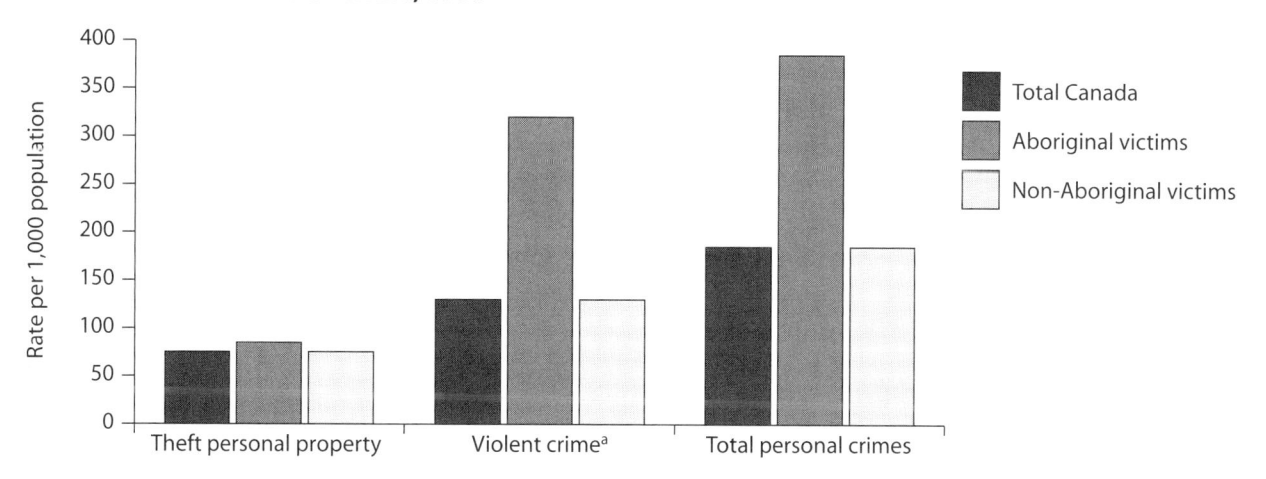

[Bar chart showing rate per 1,000 population for Theft personal property, Violent crime[a], and Total personal crimes, comparing Total Canada, Aboriginal victims, and Non-Aboriginal victims. Aboriginal victims show substantially higher rates for violent crime (~320) and total personal crimes (~380).]

[a] Includes sexual assault, assault, and robbery.

Source: Adapted from Statistics Canada (2001, June 14; 1999 data).

FIGURE 14.2 Aboriginal Adults in Custody, 1999

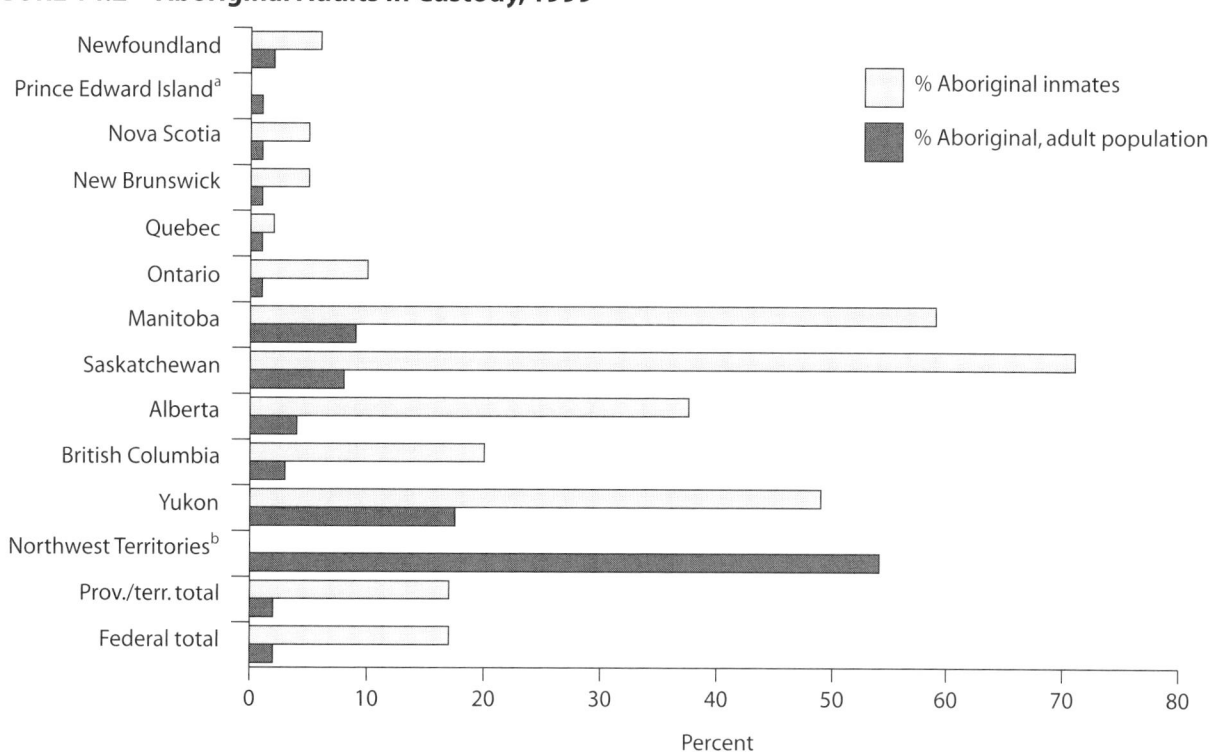

[Horizontal bar chart showing % Aboriginal inmates vs % Aboriginal adult population by province/territory: Newfoundland, Prince Edward Island[a], Nova Scotia, New Brunswick, Quebec, Ontario, Manitoba, Saskatchewan, Alberta, British Columbia, Yukon, Northwest Territories[b], Prov./terr. total, Federal total. Saskatchewan shows ~71% Aboriginal inmates; Manitoba ~59%; Yukon ~49%; Alberta ~37%.]

[a] Amount too small to be expressed for Aboriginal inmates. [b] Figures not available for Aboriginal inmates.

Source: Adapted from Statistics Canada (2001, June 14; 1999 data).

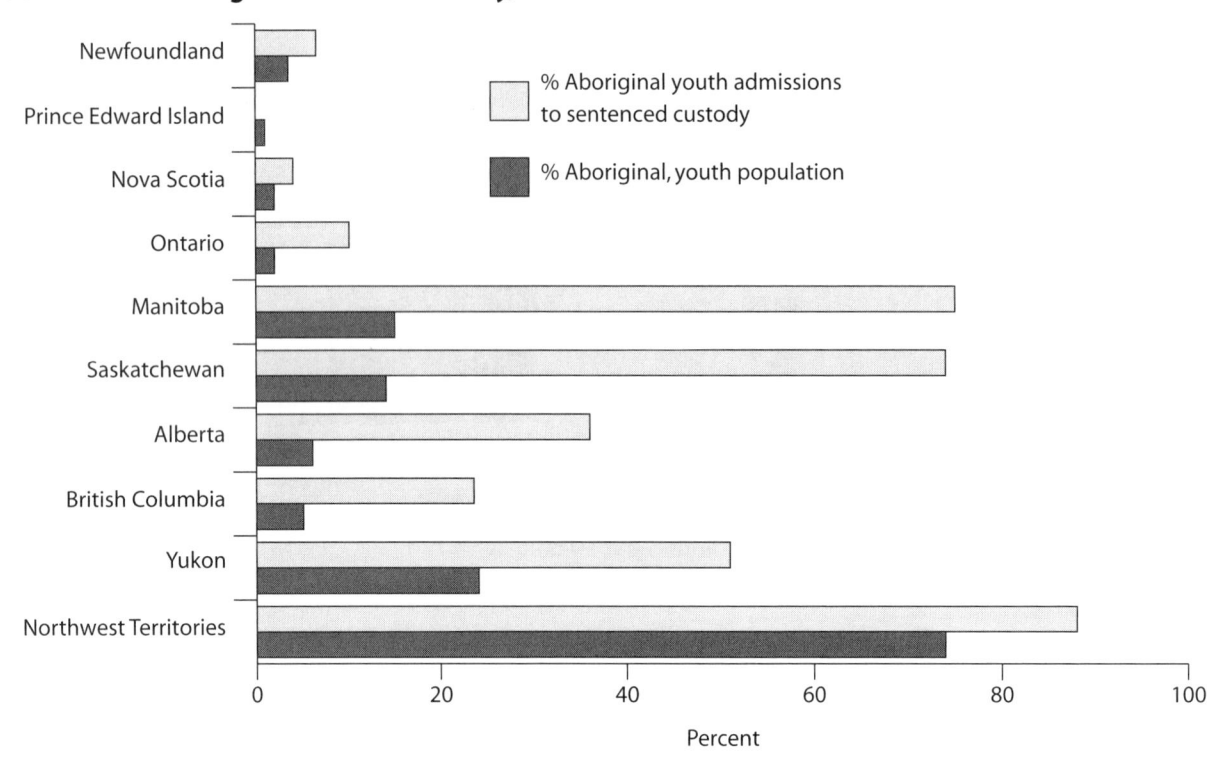

FIGURE 14.3 Aboriginal Youth in Custody, 1999

Province/Territory	% Aboriginal youth admissions to sentenced custody	% Aboriginal, youth population
Newfoundland	~6	~3
Prince Edward Island	0	~1
Nova Scotia	~4	~2
Ontario	~9	~2
Manitoba	~75	~15
Saskatchewan	~74	~14
Alberta	~36	~6
British Columbia	~23	~5
Yukon	~51	~25
Northwest Territories	~88	~74

Note: New Brunswick and Quebec were unable to report sentenced custody admissions by Aboriginal status. Figure excludes unknown numbers.

Source: Adapted from Statistics Canada (2001, June 14; 1999 data).

SYSTEMIC PROBLEMS

Much attention has been paid in the last two decades to the overrepresentation of Aboriginal people both in the criminal justice system and in correctional facilities. Of grave concern are the matters of justice and economics. The Native population is increasing at double the rate of the non-Aboriginal population in Canada. The demographics for Native communities show an average age much younger than that of non-Aboriginal Canadians. These two factors indicate that the overrepresentation of Aboriginal people in the system will increase unless significant interventions occur. At a federal incarceration rate of $199 per day for males and $315 per day for females, there are serious financial repercussions for inaction.

A number of studies have been undertaken in order to direct policy and action for intervention. The 1991 Report of the Aboriginal Justice Inquiry of Manitoba was one such study, and occurred in 1986. It found (vol. 1, p. 86):

- More than half of the inmates of Manitoba's jails are Aboriginal.

- Aboriginal accused are more likely to be denied bail than non-Aboriginal accused.

- Aboriginal people spend more time in pre-trial detention than non-Aboriginal people.

- Aboriginal accused are more likely to be charged with multiple offences than non-Aboriginal accused.

- Lawyers spend less time with their Aboriginal clients than with their non-Aboriginal clients.

- Aboriginal offenders are more than twice as likely to be incarcerated than non-Aboriginal offenders.

These findings supported the concept of systemic discrimination in criminal justice. **Systemic discrimination** is the enforcement of laws and the creation of policies that are inherently prejudicial to a group or culture. Sometimes treating all people as equals does not amount to justice. The clearest example of this inequality is in the sentencing process. Factors that judges must consider in providing custodial or non-custodial sentences include socio-economic factors such as education level, family situation, having a fixed address, and employment or prospects of employment. On the surface these appear to be neutral factors; however, if you consider your reading from chapter 12, Aboriginal people are most often the unemployed, the transient, and the poorly educated, making them prime candidates for custodial sentences. Consider the following quote from the Report of the Aboriginal Justice Inquiry of Manitoba, quoted in the 1996 Royal Commission on Aboriginal Peoples (RCAP) report:

systemic discrimination the enforcement of laws and the enforcement of policies that are inherently prejudicial to a group or culture

> Historically, the Justice system has discriminated against Aboriginal people by providing legal sanction for their oppression. This oppression of previous generations forced aboriginal people into their current state of social and economic distress. Now a seemingly neutral justice system discriminates against current generations of aboriginal people of lower socio-economic status. This is no less racial discrimination; it is merely laundered racial discrimination. It is untenable to say that discrimination which builds upon the effects of racial discrimination is not racial discrimination itself. Past injustices cannot be ignored or built upon. ... These statistics [of overincarceration] are dramatic. There is something inherently wrong with a system that takes such harsh measures against an identifiable minority. It is improbable that systemic discrimination has not played a major role in bringing this state of affairs into being.

Racial profiling in policing is a problem faced by many minority groups in Canada, and Aboriginal people are no exception. Overpolicing of their populations also leads to more charges against Aboriginal people. Aboriginal people are also over-represented as victims of crime; nevertheless, in the past police have at times given less consideration to Aboriginal victims of crime than non-Aboriginal victims.

Consider also the conclusions of the Royal Commission on the Donald Marshall Jr. prosecution in 1989. Donald Marshall was falsely accused and convicted of murder, and spent 11 years in jail until witnesses heard the real murderer bragging about his deeds. The case was re-opened and Marshall was acquitted after witnesses in the original trial admitted giving false evidence. The commission of inquiry into the wrongful conviction came to the following conclusion:

> Donald Marshall, Jr.'s status as a Native contributed to the miscarriage of justice that has plagued him since 1971. We believe that certain persons within the system would have been more rigorous in their duties, more careful, or more conscious of fairness if Marshall had been White.

> **CLASS ACTIVITY**
>
> Read appendixes 14.1 and 14.2. Discuss them as a class.

CULTURE CONFLICT AND ALTERNATIVE JUSTICE

Besides systemic discrimination, the differing concepts of justice between Aboriginal people and the dominant system are considered to be another cause of over-representation. The current system of law is inconsistent with Aboriginal people's original conceptions of law. Before European contact Aboriginal people did not have jails, police officers, or courts. Each group had its own methods of social control and its own manner of dealing with people who behaved outside what was accepted in the community. Disputes were resolved through mediation, with elders playing a primary role. The focus was on restoring the harmony within the community. Offenders were encouraged to accept responsibility for their offence and make amends to the victim and the community. All community members played a role in the offender's restoration to harmonious relationship within the community.

Once again I stress that each different group had distinct ways of handling justice; the former are just commonalities. Herein lies one of the complexities of changing the structure of justice. Do we allow each group to structure its own independent system based on traditional justice systems that predate colonization? Can and should pre-colonial systems be resurrected, and would they be successful in today's environment? Mary Ellen Turpel both poses and answers this same question in the RCAP report on justice issues (RCAP, 1996, p. 65):

> Can the pre-colonial regime ever be reconstructed? In my own view no, not except as a relic of the past. It cannot be resurrected because we have all been touched by imperialism and colonialism, and there is no simplistic escape to some pre-colonial history except a rhetorical one. In my view, we [aboriginal people] need to regain control over criminal justice, indeed all justice matter, but in a thoroughly post-colonial fashion. ... One cannot erase the history of colonialism, but we must, as an imperative, undo it in a contemporary context. ... We have to accept that there are profound social and economic problems in Aboriginal communities today that never existed pre-colonization and even in the first few hundred years of interaction. Problems of alcohol and solvent abuse, family violence and sexual abuse, and youth crime—these are indications of fundamental breakdown in the social order in Aboriginal communities of a magnitude never known before. A reform dialogue or proposals in the criminal justice field have to come to grips with this contemporary reality and not just retreat into a pre-colonial situation.

Aboriginal people are infusing specific differences of approach into criminal justice programs directed at their communities. First, decision making is dispersed among many people in a search for consensus rather than having the sole sentencing authority resting on one individual such as a justice or judge, or limited to the Crown, defence attorney, and the justice. Second, Aboriginal women play a primary role in all stages of the process, in keeping with the traditional role of women in Aboriginal societies as integral in all decision making. Finally, considerations with regard to mediation or sentencing are expanded to consider a large web of relation-

Canadian versus Traditional Native Justice

Anglo-Canadian Justice	Traditional Indian Justice
Laws formulated by elected representatives	Laws formulated by the community through tradition and consensus
Laws tied to man-made economy	Laws tied to the natural environment, only a few universally condemned actions
Protestant ethic and Christianity the moral foundation of law	Traditional Indian religions the foundations of codes of behavior
Personal offences seen as transgressions against the state as represented by the monarch	Personal offences seen as transgressions against the victim and his/her family; community threatened only when the public peace is threatened
Law administered by representatives of the state in the form of officially recognized or operated social institutions	Laws usually administered by the offended party, i.e., family, clan
Force and punishment used as methods of social control	Arbitration and ostracism usual peacekeeping methods
Individualistic basis for society and the use of the law to protect private property	Communal basis for society; no legal protection for private property; land held in trust by an individual and protected by the group

Source: Frideres & Gadacz (2005, p. 136).

ships far beyond the victims and offenders. This is a reflection of an Aboriginal world view that espouses that all things are connected and nothing can be addressed in isolation (RCAP, 1996). For a comparison of Canadian versus traditional Native justice, see the table at the top of this page.

CLASS ACTIVITY

Read appendix 14.3. Discuss as a class the different conceptions of justice displayed in this community program.

PROPOSED SOLUTIONS

There are a number of proposed solutions to address the failure of Canada's mainstream criminal justice system. Patricia Monture-Angus suggests creating one autonomous indigenous system. This has been recommended in most comprehensive studies and inquiries. Another option involves creating autonomous but government-funded Aboriginal agencies to work within the dominant system or, preferably, integrating Aboriginal ideas and people into the dominant system (Monture-Angus, 2000, p. 167).

Creating an autonomous indigenous system has been recommended by academics, policy advisers, and both the Royal Commission and the Manitoba Inquiry on Justice. Visions for programs similar to that used in the Hollow Water community (see appendix 14.3) hold great promise but they must have points of contact with the mainstream criminal justice system. For this reason a two-track approach is recommended: reform of the non-Aboriginal system and creation of an Aboriginal system. These two efforts must occur simultaneously, with close attention to how they will work in partnership.

Autonomous government-funded agencies have been created to work within the dominant system. Examples of this include Aboriginal court liaison officers and corrections inmate liaison officers. These agencies will be discussed in the following sections.

The integration of Aboriginal ideas and people into the dominant system is happening currently as Aboriginal people gain entry into all levels of the system, as police officers, justices, lawyers, and correctional officers. Currently, however, Aboriginal people are underrepresented in all these areas. Only 1 percent of all police officers in Canada are Aboriginal. Only 2.7 percent of people working in provincial correctional services are Aboriginal; federally that number is 4 percent. The number of Aboriginal justices of the peace and judges is also extremely low.

The solutions generated in the past 15 years have been developed in consultation with First Nations political organizations. Some solutions are listed below; each is addressed in the following paragraphs.

- Indigenizing existing criminal justice structures by increasing Aboriginal representation within the system. This includes the creation of a First Nations policing policy for Aboriginal-run police agencies on reserves, and other initiatives.

- Sentencing reforms, including the creation of new sentencing directives, including s. 718.2(e) of the *Criminal Code* and subsequent creation of alternative measures, sentencing circles, and diversion programs.

- Amendments to the *Corrections and Conditional Release Act* including ss. 79 to 84, which recognize the needs of Aboriginal offenders.

- Incorporating Correctional Service Canada's National Aboriginal strategy, which provides for culturally appropriate rehabilitation programs in custody facilities (Canadian Criminal Justice Association).

Indigenization

indigenization
the incorporation of indigenous people into the justice system

Indigenization in the present system presents a number of challenges. First, as some academics argue, the incorporation of indigenous people does not guarantee the incorporation of indigenous values and thought. The incorporation of Aboriginal police officers, court workers, lawyers, and judges does not change the adversarial nature of the judicial system, which is intrinsically opposite to indigenous values.

POLICING

The evolution of First Nations policing began in 1969 when the Department of Indian Affairs and Northern Development (DIAND) encouraged bands to hire "band constables" to enforce band bylaws. In 1971 the department increased this authority to the hiring of "special constables." The authority of these officers was limited; they did not carry firearms and received very low pay. In 1973 a study by DIAND resulted in a focus on the employment of Aboriginal people in a comprehensive policing role. One option was to establish autonomous police forces on reserves; another was to develop a special constable contingent within existing police forces. The latter was the most common choice, with larger forces hosting Aboriginal contingents.

In 1991 the federal government announced a new on-reserve policing policy, making policing increasingly autonomous. First Nations reserve policing would now come under the authority of the Solicitor General. With the assistance of the Solicitor General's office, provincial, federal, and First Nations governments now come together to partner in agreements over police services that will meet the needs of each community. Agreements must be reached regarding cost sharing for the creation and maintenance of police services.

Under the federal government's First Nations policing policy, a number of forms of policing can exist. One is the First Nations–administered police service; for example, the Nishnawbe-Aski Police Service, which serves 46 Ojibwe and Cree communities. Another form is having Native officers employed within a provincial or municipal service with dedicated responsibilities to Native communities, which can include urban Native communities since nearly 50 percent of Aboriginal people live in urban centres. A third model is a "developmental policing arrangement" where the special branch of Native officers within a non-Native-run police service work and train toward the creation of a First Nations–administered service.

The First Nations policing policy generally has been deemed a success; however, there have been some criticisms. In 2000 a study was commissioned by the First Nations Chiefs of Police Association to survey police chiefs, police officers, civilian staff, and community stakeholders regarding a number of issues affecting their First Nations Self-Administered Police Service. Ninety percent of community stakeholders felt that their local police service should have further Aboriginal awareness training, and 75 percent felt that recruit training did not reflect First Nations community values (Cummins & Steckley, 2003, p. 171). If this is the case in Aboriginal policing services, one can only imagine the inadequacies in non-Native policing agencies.

The Royal Commission on Aboriginal Peoples identified part of the problem as Aboriginal police agencies often being structured after mainstream police agencies. Aboriginal communities must have more input into the structure, the function, and the mission statements of their police services. This can be accomplished only by connecting control over policing and justice to self-government. As discussed in chapter 13, self-government requires an economic base.

ABORIGINAL COURT WORKERS

Recently there has been an emphasis on recruiting Aboriginal people into all levels of the court system, including the appointment of Aboriginal justices of the peace and Aboriginal judges, particularly in areas of the country where there is a large Aboriginal population.

Most provinces also have a Native Criminal Courtworker Program funded through a cost-sharing initiative between the province and the federal government. The need for the program was identified in a number of studies into Aboriginal people in the justice system. One such inquiry in Toronto in 1989 quoted a judge as saying, "Unfortunately, Indians are the ideal accused in the courts. They are quick to accept blame for their offences and they accept their punishment very passively. In many ways they appear to be the victims of the system" (RCAP, 1996, p. 97). Whether such easy admissions of guilt are culturally based or based on an unfamiliarity with the criminal justice system is unclear; however, the courtworker program was initiated to address these specific issues. The program's purpose is to have the system feel less alienating for Aboriginal accused and to ensure they have a clear understanding of their rights as well as a person to advocate on their behalf as they make their way through the system. Low socio-economic status among Aboriginal people has, in the past, forced offenders to rely almost solely on the legal aid process, which may partly explain why Aboriginal accused spend less time with a lawyer and more time in pre-trial detention. Furthermore, if they spend less time with legal counsel, they are less likely to be informed of available alternative justice programs.

Aboriginal court workers are intimately familiar with the issues that are likely to bring Aboriginal offenders into court; they have a unique perspective on both cultures and can advocate for their clients to try to make the justice system work to the benefit of their clients and communities.

CULTURAL AWARENESS TRAINING

Lately there has been a focus on the delivery of Aboriginal awareness training to non-Aboriginal employees of the criminal justice system. Studies in Aboriginal issues have been included in college courses that lead to employment as police officers and correctional workers. Staff already in the field have received training in issues that bring Aboriginal people into the system and in the difference in world views to prevent miscommunications. This training is ongoing in most provinces and territories, although much work has yet to be done.

Recommendations for this training were put forward in the 1996 RCAP report and reiterated by the First Nations Chiefs of Police Association's 2000 study.

Sentencing Reforms

In 1996 Bill C-41 on sentencing reforms added s. 718.2(e) to the *Criminal Code*. This section states that "all available sanctions other than imprisonment that are reasonable in the circumstances should be considered for all offenders, with particular attention to the circumstances of aboriginal offenders."

(This addition was intended to reduce the overincarceration of Aboriginal people. This is a noble purpose; however, I offer one observation that reflects the beginning of this chapter. If those who study the issues agree that colonization, which cannot be undone, and poverty, low academic achievement, marginalization, and substance abuse are the root causes of the crimes that lead to overincarceration, perhaps we are addressing the matters in reverse order.)

The wording of s. 718.2(e) states that sanctions other than incarceration must be available, including sentencing circles, alternative measures, and diversion programs. Since many offenders are in large urban centres, programs are required both on- and off-reserve. This is supported by the Supreme Court's decision in *R v. Gladue* in 1999, which states that urban Aboriginal people must be considered in accordance with this section even if they are not connected to a particular Aboriginal community. The alternatives created for sentencing have been used widely by both Aboriginal and non-Aboriginal offenders, allowing for a more individualized and restorative approach to justice. There is concern, however, that these sentencing options, particularly conditional sentences, are being used more often as an extension of punitive power rather than as a diversion to incarceration. Twenty-eight thousand conditional sentences were ordered in the first two years of their existence, and prison populations have not been reduced to close to the same degree (Roach & Rudin, 2000).

ALTERNATIVE MEASURES

The alternative sentencing options under s. 718.2(e) include options other than conditional sentences. Diversion programs are common for both Aboriginal and non-Aboriginal offenders, either pre-charge or post-charge. Diversion programs are used in a variety of criminal offences, particularly minor thefts. Often in a non-Aboriginal setting the offender will be required to attend an education session, write letters of apology, and the like. In an Aboriginal setting, more serious cases may be subject to diversion at the discretion of the Crown. The Crown may suspend the disposition of the case until the Aboriginal panel or deliberative body has settled on an appropriate resolution for the case. In the case of minor and non-violent offences, charges against the accused are then generally withdrawn, having been adequately dealt with by the community.

Sentencing circles and elders' panels are common forms of alternative sentencing options. They are based on traditional Aboriginal justice structures and allow communities to have control over rehabilitation efforts for offenders. (Sentencing circles have become commonplace for non-Aboriginal youth offenders under the *Youth Criminal Justice Act*, although they are known as "youth justice committees.") The problem of having an outside person pass sentence over an Aboriginal person in an Aboriginal community is addressed in this initiative; people who know the accused and have relationships with both the accused and his/her family as well as the victim and the victim's family have insight that an outsider may not possess and that may be difficult to translate into a pre-sentence report.

An elders' panel consists of elders or clan leaders who sit with the judge and provide advice regarding an appropriate sentence. In a sentencing circle, community members are invited to sit in a circle with the accused and a judge to decide the sentence. There are prerequisites for the availability of a sentencing circle as an option. First, the accused must recognize his guilt and have a clear intention to rehabilitate to become a good citizen of his community. Second, the community must have a desire to intercede on behalf of one of its members. Third, the victim must also support the initiative.

YOUTH

All of these options are also available for youth sentencing. As figure 14.3 indicates, Aboriginal youth are also overrepresented in the justice system. They are also more likely than their non-Aboriginal counterparts to receive custodial sentences and to receive longer periods of probation. Without intervention, these youth will make their way into the adult system. To combat this, family group conferencing is available to all youth, particularly Aboriginal youth. It is a process by which the youth and members of his or her family, a youth advocate, a police officer, a social worker, and other community members meet to decide what types of intervention are available to the youth and what strategies can assist the youth to become a productive member of the community. Family group conferencing can happen pre-charge or post-charge.

Corrections and Conditional Release Act

Amendments to the *Corrections and Conditional Release Act* including ss. 79 to 84, which recognize the needs of Aboriginal offenders, provide for early release considerations by parole boards. This would reduce the cost of incarceration, but the processes must be in place within the community to assist the offender in successful readjustment. Considering the high rate of recidivism for Aboriginal offenders this has not been an area of strength for our corrections system and efforts are currently under way to partner with Aboriginal communities to allow their input into the release process.

Recent revisions to the *Corrections and Conditional Release Act* include s. 81, which provides for the transfer of a First Nations offender from a correctional facility to a First Nations community in a non-institutional setting with supervision, treatment, and programming provided under 24-hour supervision of community members for the term of sentence. Other types of arrangements can also be made under this section; an offender may be transferred to a spiritual or healing lodge, or a treatment facility in an urban centre.

Section 84 of the Act gives First Nations communities the opportunity to participate in an offender's release plan from custody at the time of parole. The release plan balances the needs of the community as well as the needs of the offender. Successful reintegration is the primary goal for all parties: the victim, the offender, and the community.

First Nations community involvement is the beginning of the devolution of control over justice issues. However, it is only the beginning. Money is required to accompany the additional responsibility the communities are accepting for their members.

Culturally Appropriate Programs in Custody

The Correctional Service Canada Aboriginal Strategy involves providing culturally appropriate rehabilitation programs in custody. Under s. 80 of the *Corrections and Conditional Release Act*, Correctional Service Canada is required to provide programs designed to address particularly the needs of Aboriginal offenders. This section authorizes the Solicitor General to enter into agreements with Aboriginal communities to provide services such as traditional healers and elders to work with offenders. Furthermore, it mandates the establishment of a national Aboriginal advisory committee to advise Correctional Service Canada on how best to provide services to Aboriginal inmates.

This is an important strategy for Aboriginal inmates since the chaplaincy program funded by Correctional Service Canada and other counselling programs are

FIGURE 14.4

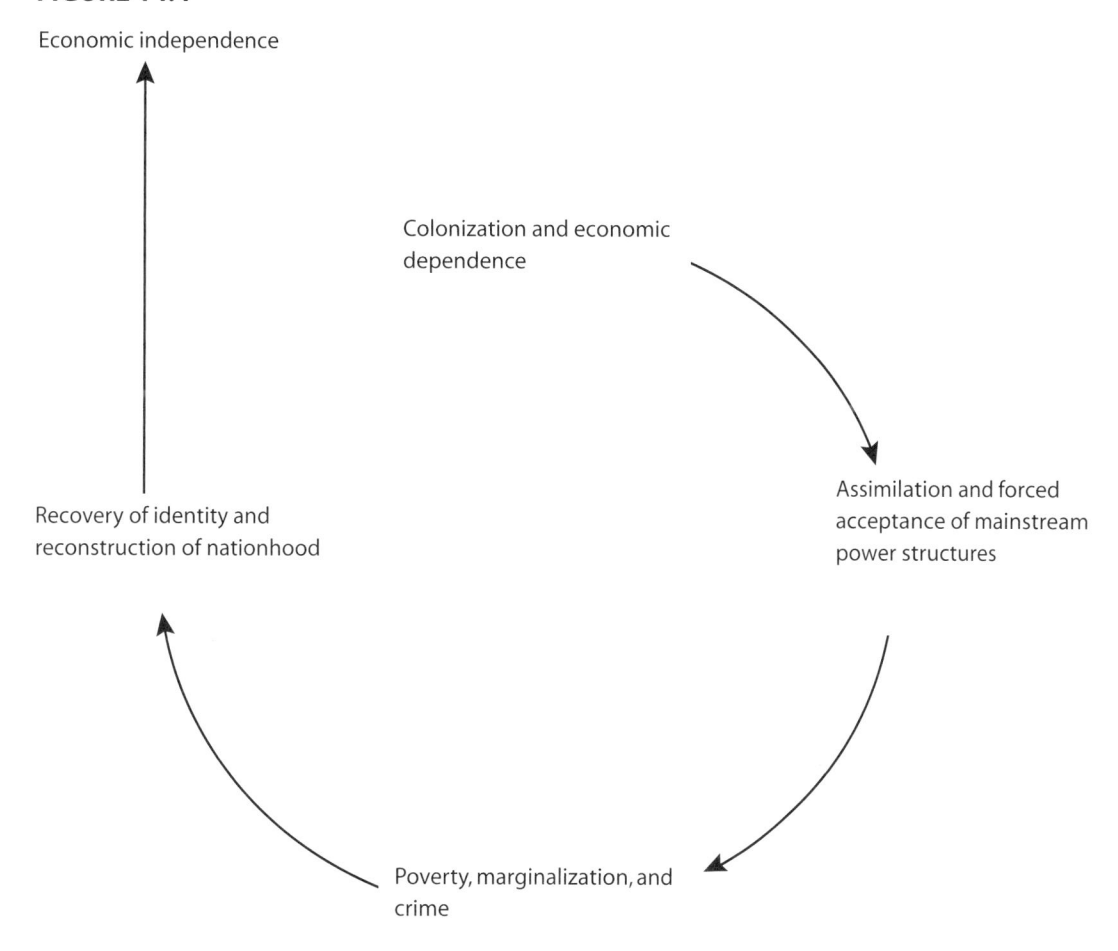

Economic independence

Colonization and economic dependence

Assimilation and forced acceptance of mainstream power structures

Recovery of identity and reconstruction of nationhood

Poverty, marginalization, and crime

ill equipped to deal with issues distinct to Aboriginal experiences. Furthermore, some evidence supports the fact that exposure to Aboriginal spirituality and connection to culture has been effective in the healing and rehabilitation of Aboriginal offenders. In the Cawsey Report, which was studied by the Royal Commission, Justice Cawsey noted that "Everything that has worked for Aboriginal people has come from Aboriginal people" (RCAP, 1996).

CONCLUSION

In conclusion, I return to Monture-Angus's three options discussed above. Her second option addresses the creation of a separate but government-funded Aboriginal justice system. Monture-Angus supports giving the responsibility for community crime back to the community because First Nations people have the right to be responsible. I agree that First Nations people must be given the power to find solutions independent of government interference. They must be given the freedom to take responsibility for their own populations. The mainstream government does not easily relinquish control of its criminal justice system; although the current move to adapt the existing system to accommodate Aboriginal people provides some forward movement, it is not fast enough for those experiencing the negative effects of crime in First Nations communities or those who are languishing in prison. Duplicating colonial structures with an indigenous flair to be administrated by indigenous people will not take First Nations people to healthy communities. Although this approach is cost effective, the logic behind it is seriously flawed.

Aboriginal efforts to create new programs for treatment of offenders and community are often hindered by lack of funding. The federal government should provide funding; however, if Aboriginal communities could finance those efforts that are turned down for federal funding, they would have more autonomy and power to be creative in community problem solving.

A separate Aboriginal-run justice system cannot be created without serious attention to the pursuit of economic independence of Aboriginal nations. As long as the federal government is funding justice initiatives in Canada for Aboriginal peoples, there cannot be complete independence. Freedom from marginalization and poverty, the key causes of crime, cannot be achieved in the absence of economic independence.

Legislative reforms in justice have shown some positive results but are not the only answer. First Nations communities in Canada are complex; many obstacles are interconnected and one issue cannot be addressed in isolation from the others. Native people are working on all fronts to improve the situation of Aboriginal people in Canada. They cannot be successful without a sincere partnership with mainstream Canadians willing to follow Native peoples' lead. Up to this point, mainstream Canada has held the lead in guiding Aboriginal people in terms of justice initiatives. This is **paternalism**. Aboriginal people need to be leading when they are the subjects of concern.

paternalism
a system under which an authority undertakes to supply the needs and regulate the conduct of those under its control

KEY TERMS

race paternalism

systemic discrimination

indigenization

paternalism

REFERENCES

Alfred, T. (1999). *Peace, power, and righteousness: An indigenous manifesto.* Don Mills, ON: Oxford University Press.

Canadian Criminal Justice Association. (2006, March 3). Changes within the present system. www.ccja-acjp.ca.

CBC.ca. (2005, November 22). Racist e-mail spurs probes among RCMP, police. www.cbc.ca/canada/story/2005/11/22/native-song-051122.html.

Corrections and Services Canada. (2005). Basic facts about Corections Service of Canada. Public Works and Government Services Canada.

Cote, H., & Schissel, W. (2002). Damaged children and broken spirits. In B. Schissel & C. Brooks (Eds.) *Marginality and condemnation: An introduction to critical criminology.* Halifax: Fernwood Publishing.

Cummins, B.D., & Steckley, J.L. (2003). *Aboriginal policing: A Canadian perspective.* Toronto: Pearson Education.

Dickie, B., & Macdonald, J. (2000). *Hollow water.* National Film Board of Canada.

Fournier, S., & Crey, E. (1997). *Stolen from our embrace: The abduction of First Nations children and the restoration of Aboriginal communities.* Vancouver: Douglas & McIntyre.

Frideres, J.S., & Gadacz, R.R. (2005). *Aboriginal peoples in Canada: Contemporary conflicts* (7th ed.). Toronto: Prentice Hall Canada (Pearson Education).

LaPrairie, C. (2002). Aboriginal over-representation in the criminal justice system: A tale of nine cities. *Canadian Journal of Criminology, 44*(2).

McGillivary, A., & Comasky, B. (1999). *Black eyes all of the time: Intimate violence, Aboriginal women, and the justice system.* Toronto: University of Toronto Press.

Monture, A.P. (1995). *Thunder in my soul: A Mohawk woman speaks.* Halifax: Fernwood Publishing.

Monture, A.P. (1999). *Journeying forward: Dreaming First Nations independence.* Halifax: Fernwood Publishing.

Monture-Angus, A.P. (2000). Lessons in decolonization: Aboriginal overrepresesntation in the Canadian criminal justice system. In D. Long & O.P. Dickason (Eds.), *Visions of the heart: Canadian Aboriginal issues.* Toronto: Harcourt Canada.

Prison Justice. (2006, March 2). Facts and statistics for 2001-2002. www.prisonjustice.ca.

Report of the Aboriginal Justice Inquiry of Manitoba. (1991). *Volume I: The justice system and Aboriginal people.* Winnipeg.

Roach, K., & Rudin, J. (2000). Gladue: The judicial and political reception of a promising decision. *Canadian Journal of Criminology, 42*(3).

Royal Commission on Aboriginal Peoples (RCAP). (1989). *Gathering strength.* Vol. 3. www.ainc-inac.gc.ca/ch/rcap/sg/sgmm_e.html.

Royal Commission on Aboriginal Peoples (RCAP). (1996). *Bridging the cultural divide: A report on Aboriginal people and criminal justice in Canada.* Ottawa: Supply and Services Canada.

Royal Commission on the Donald Marshall Jr. Prosecution. (1989). *Commissioner's report, findings, and recommendations.* Vol. 1. Halifax. www.aboriginallegal.ca/docs/hill_factum.htm.

Samuelson, L., & Angus, P.M. (2002). Aboriginal people and social control: The state, law, and policing. In B. Schissel & C. Brooks (Eds.), *Marginality and condemnation: An introduction to critical criminology.* Halifax: Fernwood Publishing.

Sangster, J. (1999, March). Criminalizing the colonized: Ontario Native women confront the criminal justice system, 1920-1960. *Canadian Historical Review, 80*(1).

Schissel, B., & Brooks, C. (Eds.). (2002). *Marginality and condemnation: An introduction to critical criminology.* Halifax: Fernwood.

Shkilnyk, A. (1985). *A poison stronger than love: The destruction of an Ojibwa community.* New Haven, CT: Yale University Press.

Statistics Canada. (2001, June 14). Aboriginal Peoples in Canada— Profile Series. Catalogue no. 85F0033MIE2001001.

Thatcher, R. (2004). *Fighting firewater fictions: Moving beyond the disease model of alcoholism in First Nations.* Toronto: University of Toronto Press.

Wagamese, R. (1996). *The terrible summer: The national newspaper award-winning writings of Richard Wagamese.* Toronto: Warwick Publishing.

Whitehead, P.C. & Hayes, J.J. (1998). *The insanity of alcohol: Social problems in Canadian First Nations communities.* Toronto: Canadian Scholars' Press.

APPENDIX 14.1

Racist E-mail Spurs Probes Among RCMP, Police

Several police forces across the country are investigating after some officers circulated an e-mail containing a profanity-laced song that refers to native people drinking, sniffing gas and committing crimes.

It contains a song called the *Native Rap* that includes the lyrics, "The RCMP is always chasing me/'Cause I'm a smelly f***ing native and I can't even see."

It continues to talk about natives robbing liquor stores, punching old ladies, "curb-stomping Whities," slapping women and shaking babies.

The audio file was obtained by CBC News, which tracked it to one officer at Peel Regional Police in Brampton, Ont.

When the CBC told the force about the e-mail, it immediately started a professional standards investigation.

But the e-mail had already been forwarded to nearly two dozen people, including an Ontario government employee, seven Peel police employees and seven RCMP officers.

Eventually, it landed in the in-boxes of several First Nations RCMP officers and one of them complained.

Dean Fontaine, who recently retired from the RCMP after 22 years, said he received a copy of the e-mail at his current workplace, the Assembly of First Nations.

Fontaine, who was a decorated RCMP officer, said most officers were "very dedicated" but he still had to silently endure racist remarks early in his career.

"Unfortunately, there are racist police officers out there and unfortunately, it just takes a handful of these police officers to make everybody look bad."

An RCMP spokesperson, Staff Sgt. Paul Marsh, said the force has been investigating the offensive e-mail since July.

"There's no doubt, though, that the audio clip is reprehensible," Marsh said.

"We're determined to get to the bottom of it, to make sure where did this come from and if it is from within the RCMP, that people be disciplined for those improper actions."

Peel Regional Police also launched an investigation.

The complainant in the case declined to speak to CBC News, concerned about repercussions.

The RCMP says it encourages its employees to come forward with any complaints of racial harassment.

However, a number of RCMP officers told CBC News, on the condition of anonymity, that such complaints often lead to being ostracized by co-workers and can ruin any chance of promotion within the force.

Source: CBC.ca (2005).

APPENDIX 14.2

Natives in Fear of Police

Here's an unpalatable fact: If you were a Native living in Saskatoon, you would almost certainly be afraid of the police.

Rightly or wrongly, you would be afraid, if you were a young man, that you might die if the police took you into custody. If you were a parent of that young man, you would be afraid for him.

Neil Stonechild was a 17-year-old aboriginal kid in November 1990 who had too much to drink, as 17-year-olds will, and created a disturbance. When two police officers took him away in handcuffs in the back of their patrol car (a fact they later denied), Stonechild screamed to a friend that they were going to kill him. Four days later, his body was found in an industrial area of the city. Stonechild had frozen to death.

Friends and family said the boy was the victim of a police practice of dumping Native trouble makers on the outskirts of the city.

A report released by the Saskatchewan justice minister this week is damning in its indictment of the police department's involvement in the case, from beginning to end. Justice David Wright, who headed the inquiry and wrote the report, rejected the officers' testimony and found that Stonechild was in their custody the night he froze to death and that those officers did have the opportunity and time to dump him in the subzero cold. (Wright stops short of accusing the officers of actually doing so.)

The report accuses the Saskatoon police department of systemic denial and/or coverup of what happened to Stonechild.

This issue is not about one Native youth, or about two police officers. It is about, as one Native leader said, "Ugly stains on the fabric of policing."

What the report doesn't include is the stories of Rodney Naistus, 25, a Native found inexplicably frozen to death outside Saskatoon on Jan. 29, 2000; Lawrence Wegner, 30, a Native found inexplicably frozen to death in the same area five days later; Darrell Night, a Native dumped in the same area by two police officers the night before Naistus was found. He survived to complain and those officers were jailed and fired. The report didn't of course, cite Dudley George, an unarmed Native man killed by a police officer (later convicted of criminal negligence causing death) during a 1995 standoff at Ontario's Ipperwash Provincial Park.

But we had better believe that many members of the Native communities in this country connect those dots. We had better understand that Native people, particularly in Canada's western provinces, believe police and the broader "white" community that they represent see them as second-class citizens. Some of them see police as the enemy.

The recommendations of the Stonechild inquiry report should be reviewed by every province. They call for aboriginal recruiting into police services; for Native involvement in policing issues at advisory and liaison levels. They call for new complaint procedures and for regular race relations training.

The report calls for major, significant efforts to bridge the chasm between police departments and aboriginal communities. We should listen, and governments across the country must act. The lonely, cold death of a frightened teenage boy deserves that.

APPENDIX 14.3

The following is an excerpt from Rupert Ross's discussion paper *Duelling Paradigms? Western Criminal Justice versus Aboriginal Community Healing*. This article was published in *Justice as Healing: A Newsletter on Aboriginal Concepts of Justice* (Native Law Centre, Spring 1995).

Hollow Water is an Ojibway community of some 600 people located on the east side of Lake Winnipeg, some 200 kms north of Winnipeg.

In 1984, a group of social service providers, concerned with the future of their young people, looked into the issues of youth substance abuse, vandalism, truancy and suicide. Their focus shifted to the children's home life and, upon closer examination, inter-generational sexual abuse was identified as the root problem. By 1987, they tackled sexual abuse head-on, creating their Community Holistic Circle Healing Program (CHCH). They presently estimate 75% of Hollow Water residents are victims of sexual abuse, and 35% are "victimizers."

They formed a broad-based team to promote and respond to disclosure. It includes the child protection worker, Community Health Representative, the Nurse In Charge and the NADAP worker, together with others from the RCMP, school division and community churches. The majority of team members are women, many of whom are volunteers.

They broke down the professional barriers between them, including separate chains of reporting and confidentiality, to create a coordinated response. They believed that if each "helper" worked in isolation on separate aspects of each troubled person or family the result would be a further splintering, exactly opposite the goal of creating "whole" people. Outside professionals were seen from the outset as necessary to the project's success but were required to "sign on" to a coordinated team approach. They also had to permit a "lay" member of the team be with them at all times, so their skills could be learned by community members and so they could learn the community approach to healing. Partnership was, and remains, the model.

They evolved a detailed protocol of 13 steps, from initial disclosure to the Healing Contract to the Cleansing Ceremony. The Healing Contract, designed by people involved in or personally touched by the offence, requires each person to "sign on" to bring certain changes or additions to their relationships with the others. Such contracts are expected to last more than 2 years, given the challenges in bringing true healing. One is still being adhered to 5 years after its creation. If and when the Healing Contract is successfully completed, the Cleansing Ceremony is held to "mark a new beginning for all involved" and to "honour the victimizer for completing the healing contract/process."

Criminal charges are laid as soon as possible after disclosure. The victimizer can either proceed on his/her own through the criminal process, or with the healing support of the team. For the latter, they must accept full responsibility for their acts and enter a guilty plea at the earliest opportunity. Virtually all accused have requested the team's support, with the result that trials are rare.

The team requests to delay sentencing so they can begin their healing work and prepare a Pre-Sentence Report. The Report analyzes everything from the offender's state of mind, level of effort, and chance of full rehabilitation, to the reactions, feelings, plans and suggestions of all people affected, with special attention to the victim, the non-offending spouse, and the families of each. It proposes an Action Plan based on the Healing Contract. The team requests that any Probation Order require his/her full cooperation with their healing efforts. If jail is imposed, they try to arrange regular work with the offender while in custody and prepare everyone for the day of release.

At all times team members work with, protect, support, teach and encourage a wide range of people. It is their view that since many people are affected by each disclosure, all deserve assistance and all must be involved in any process aimed at creating healthy dynamics and breaking the intergenerational chain of abuse. I watched them plan for a possible confrontation with a suspected victimizer, and the detailed dispersal of team members throughout the community to support those whom disclosure would touch reminded me of a military operation in its logistical complexity.

Virtually all community team members are themselves victims of long-standing sexual abuse, primarily at the hands of family members. Their perspectives on the dynamics of sexual abuse prevail. Even former victimizers who have been honoured for completing their healing process are asked to join the team. The personal experience of team members in the emotional, mental, physical and spiritual complexities of sexual abuse permits them an extraordinary rapport with victims and victimizers alike. In circles they share their own histories to coax others out of the anger, denial, guilt, fear, self-loathing and hurt that must be dealt with. Their personal experience permits them the patience necessary to embark on very long processes, and to see signs of progress which might escape the notice of others. It gives them the insight to recognize who is manipulating or hiding in denial, and the toughness to keep them there. This healing process is painful; it involves stripping away all the excuses, justifications, angers and other defences of each abuser until finally, confronted with a victim who has been made strong enough to expose his or her pain in their presence, that abuser actually feels the pain they created. Only then can re-building begin for both the abuser and the abused. The word "healing" seems such a soft word, but the process of healing within the Hollow Water program is anything but.

When the accused finally goes to court for sentencing, the Team is brutally honest about the sincerity of his/her efforts and about how much work still has to be done. That does not mean the accused who is still resisting the Team's efforts is abandoned to jail. Far from it. While western justice systems seem to have forged an unbreakable link between "holding someone responsible for their crime" and sending them to jail, Hollow Water fiercely denies the wisdom of that connection. I will let their 1993 position paper on the issue of jail speak for itself:

> CHCH's position on the use of incarceration, and its relationship to an individual's healing process, has changed over time. In our initial efforts to break the vicious cycle of abuse that was occurring in our community, we took the position that we needed to promote the use of incarceration in cases which were defined as "too serious." After some time, however, we came to the conclusion that this position was adding significantly to the difficulty of what was already complex casework.
>
> As we worked through the casework difficulties that arose out of this position, we came to realize two things:

(1) that as we both shared our own stories of victimization and learned from our experiences in assisting others in dealing with the pain of their victimization, it became very difficult to define "too serious." The quantity or quality of pain felt by the victim, the family/ies, and the community did not seem to be directly connected to any specific acts of victimization. Attempts, for example, by the courts—and to a certain degree by ourselves—to define a particular victimization as "too serious" and another as "not too serious" (e.g., "only" fondling vs. actual intercourse; victim is daughter vs. victim is nephew; 1 victim vs. 4 victims) were gross over-simplifications, and certainly not valid from an experiential point of view; and

(2) that promoting incarceration was based in, and motivated by, a mixture of feelings of anger, revenge, guilt and shame on our part, and around our personal victimization issues, rather than in the healthy resolution of the victimization we were trying to address.

Thus, our position on the use of incarceration has shifted. At the same time, we understand how the legal system continues to use and view incarceration—as punishment and deterrence for the victimizers (offenders) and protection and safety for the victim(s) and community. What the legal system seems to not understand is the complexity of the issues involved in breaking the cycle of abuse that exists in our community.

The use of judgement and punishment actually works against the healing process. An already unbalanced person is moved further out of balance.

What the threat of incarceration does do is keep people from coming forward and taking responsibility for the hurt they are causing. It reinforces the silence, and therefore promotes, rather than breaks, the cycle of violence that exists. In reality, rather than making the community a safer place, the threat of jail places the community more at risk.

In order to break the cycle, we believe that victimizer accountability must be to, and support must come from, those most affected by the victimization—the victim, the family/ies, and the community. Removal of the victimizer from those who must, and are best able to, hold him/her accountable, and to offer him/her support, adds complexity to already existing dynamics of denial, guilt and shame. The healing process of all parties is therefore at best delayed, and most often actually deterred.

The legal system, based on principles of punishment and deterrence, as we see it, simply is not working. We cannot understand how the legal system doesn't see this.

Their Position Paper speaks of the need to break free of the adversarial nature of court proceedings, the impediment to healing which arises when defence counsel recommend both complete silence and pleas of "Not Guilty," and the second "victimization," which occurs as victims are cross-examined on the witness stand. In their view, "[t]he courtroom and process simply is not a safe place for the victim to address the victimization—nor is it a safe place for the victimizer to come forward and take responsibility for what has happened."

Towards the conclusion of the Position Paper, the following passages appear:

We do not see our present position on incarceration as either "an easy way out" for the victimizer, or as the victimizer "getting away." We see it rather as establishing a very clear line of accountability between the victimizer and his or her community. What follows from that line is a process that we believe is not only much more difficult for the victimizer, but also much more likely to heal the victimization, than doing time in jail could ever be. Our children and the community can no longer afford the price the legal system is extracting in its attempts to provide justice in our community.

To this point, most of Hollow Water's work takes place away from the courtroom. The team works with affected people wherever and whenever they can. Virtually all their work takes place in a circle format, opened and closed by prayers, and respecting the "non-blaming" imperative the circle demands and fosters. Only their Assessments, Pre-Sentence Reports and Action Plans have been part of court proceedings thus far. In the fall of 1993, however, they will take their circle into the courtroom so the judge can hear directly from the people, the family/ies, and the community.

Glossary

Aboriginal peoples' rights
rights of Canada's Aboriginal peoples to preserve their culture, identity, customs, traditions, and languages, and any special rights that they have currently or may acquire in the future

acculturation
process of change in the cultural patterns of an ethnic group as a result of contact with other ethnic groups

anti-racism
an action-oriented, educational, and political strategy for institutional and systemic change that addresses issues of racism and the interlocking systems of social oppression

assimilation
to absorb groups of different cultures into the main culture

assimilation ideology
ideology that expects people of diversity to relinquish their culture and linguistic identity and adopt the culture of the host state

assimilationist
intolerant of immigrants' heritage culture, demanding that they relinquish the culture and adopt the host culture

authoritarianism
conduct that demands obedience to authority

bipolar disorder
mood disorder that involves emotional swings between depression and mania; formerly called manic depression

British North America Act
statute enacted on March 29, 1867 by the British Parliament providing for the confederation of Canada

Canadian Charter of Rights and Freedoms
part of the Canadian constitution that establishes the protection of basic rights and freedoms deemed essential to the maintenance of a free and democratic society and a united country

Canadian Human Rights Act
prohibits discrimination based on race, national or ethnic origin, colour, age, sex, marital status, disability, sexual orientation, or conviction for an offence for which a pardon has been granted

Canadian Human Rights Commission
federal body responsible for investigating and adjudicating complaints of violations of the *Canadian Human Rights Act*

child abuse
physical and psychological maltreatment of children by adults

child sexual abuse
sexual exploitation and maltreatment of dependent and developmentally immature children and adolescents

civic ideology
ideology that subscribes to multiculturalism ideology principles but does not support state funding to maintain and promote ethnocultural diversity

claims arising from Aboriginal title
claims based on the allegation that lands traditionally used and occupied by Aboriginal people were never surrendered to the Crown by Aboriginal people

claims arising from the surrender for sale of reserve land
claims occurring when First Nations seek compensation for, or the return of, land that had been surrendered to the Crown for sale for the benefit of the band

claims relating to the fulfillment of terms of treaties
claims that are usually a result of disagreement between the Crown and First Nations about the size and location of reserves set aside by treaties

code of silence
core value of withholding information from anyone who is not a member of the police culture

community policing principles
principles associated with the police services approach that provide for identifying and solving problems, resolving the underlying causes of disputes, preventing future recurrences, and eliminating the need for arrests and convictions except when necessary

comprehensive land claims
claims to territory that are not covered by treaty or land cessation agreements

constitution
the core system of rules and principles by which a nation or group is governed

constructive discrimination
discrimination that results from some criterion that seems reasonable but effectively excludes, restricts, or favours some people contrary to human rights laws

core values
values of self-control, cynicism, respect for authority, hypervigilance, and code of silence associated with the collectivist police culture

covenant chain
first agreement entered into between the five nations of the Iroquois and the British; a clear recognition by both sides that their political systems would remain separate even as their system of trade and alliance linked them together

cross-cultural communication
understanding the verbal and non-verbal communicative patterns of people from diverse cultures for the purpose of effective intercultural interchange

cross-cultural training
training in how to deal with other cultures, whether in another country or within one's own country

cultural awareness training
training in how to deal more effectively with cultural issues, either in general or in terms of a particular culture

cultural genocide
the deliberate and systematic destruction of the culture, tradition, language, and ways of being of a specific cultural group

culture
pattern of behaviour and results of behaviour that are shared and transmitted among members of a particular society

cynicism
belief that the primary motivation behind human behaviour is selfishness

delusions
ideas that are real only to the mentally ill person

democratic rights
rights to vote or run in an election and the assurance that no government has the right to continue to hold power indefinitely without seeking a new mandate from the electorate

depression
mood disorder characterized by feelings of despair and hopelessness

devolution
the return of control of programs and services to Native peoples

discrimination
process by which a person is deprived of equal access to privileges and opportunities available to others

diversity
the variety of human qualities among different people and groups

diversity awareness training
training in how to deal more effectively with diversity issues in all their forms

diversity equity
equity based on a belief that there are no superior or inferior cultural groups

diversity policing framework
affirms and values people of diversity; assumes a police–community climate that validates diversity; empowers voices of diversity within and outside the police force in goal setting, problem solving, and decision making; and promotes a police–community culture that is respectful of the rights of people of diversity, police safety, and the person

ego forcing
use of unnecessary force to boost macho self-image

elder abuse
physical, sexual, emotional, or psychological abuse or neglect, or financial exploitation, of an older person by caregiver

employment equity
strategy designed to make workplaces reflect society's diversity by encouraging the full participation of people of all diversities

equality rights
rights of all Canadians, regardless of race, national or ethnic origin, colour, sex, age, or mental or physical disability, to be equal before the law and to enjoy equal protection and benefit of the law

ethnic group
group of individuals with a shared sense of peoplehood based on presumed shared socio-cultural experiences and/or similar characteristics

ethnicity
individual or group identification with a culture of origin; may involve distinct elements that are shared, such as language, religion, and customs

ethnist ideology
ideology that expects people of diversity to assimilate, but the state defines which groups should assimilate and thus which ones are not rightful members of the state

exclusionary
intolerant of immigrants' heritage culture and of immigration in general

family violence
caregiver abuse of children or abuse of caregiver by children

fiduciary responsibility
the responsibility to hold something in trust for another

formication
hallucination that involves feeling that insects or snakes are crawling over or under one's skin

freedom from discrimination
part I of the Ontario *Human Rights Code*, which grants freedom from discrimination with respect to services, goods, facilities, accommodation, contracts, employment, and occupational associations, and freedom from sexual solicitation in the workplace and by those in a position of power

GLOSSARY

fundamental freedoms
freedom of conscience and religion; freedom of thought, belief, opinion, and expression, including freedom of the press and other media of communication; freedom of peaceful assembly; and freedom of association

gendered apartheid
viewpoint that considers women unequal to men and treats women as a subordinate class

hallucinations
sensory illusions that are disturbed or disturbing and are real only to the mentally ill person

harassment
comments or conduct toward another person that is unwelcome

homelessness
having no fixed, regular, and adequate address

host community
comprises groups of people who have the power and influence to shape attitudes toward the remaining groups in society

hypervigilance
belief that survival of police and of others depends on police ability to view everything in the environment as potentially life-threatening and dangerous

Indian Act
created in 1876 to consolidate all policies aimed at the administration of Indian populations in Canada

Indian agent
federal employee of Indian Affairs in charge of administration on reserves

indigenization
the incorporation of indigenous people into the justice system

integration
embrace of the host culture of settlement and continued maintenance of culture of origin

integrationist
supportive of immigrants' adopting features of the host culture while maintaining aspects of their heritage culture

interdependence
the state of being influenced by or dependent on one another

kinesics
physical communication, including look and appearance, eye contact, facial expressions, posture, body movements, and touching

legal rights
basic legal protections to safeguard Canadian citizens in their dealings with the state and its machinery of justice

mandatory arrest policy
arrest must take place

mania
mood disorder characterized by feelings of emotional high, agitation, and impulsivity

marginalization
simultaneous rejection of the culture of origin and the host culture

mediative policy
a non-arrest approach to family violence calls

mental illness
group of disabilities marked by disturbances in thinking, feeling, and relating

mental retardation
significant subaverage intelligence, significant limitation in adaptive functioning, and onset before the age of 18 years

misattribution
misinterpreting a message or behaviour

mobility rights
freedom to enter, remain in, or leave the country, and to live and seek employment anywhere in Canada

mood disorders
mental disorders that affect a person's mood, including depression and bipolar disorder

multicultural heritage
the unique and constitutionally enshrined character of Canadian society

multiculturalism
a policy relating to or designed for a combination of several distinct cultures

multiculturalism ideology
ideology that recognizes and supports people of diversity in maintaining or promoting their diversity, providing that their practices do not clash with the laws of the nation

official languages
English and French, as confirmed by the Charter, which guarantees that the federal government can serve members of the public in the official language of their choice

Ontario *Human Rights Code*
Ontario statute that protects the dignity and worth of every person and provides for equal rights and opportunities without discrimination that is contrary to law

Ontario Human Rights Commission
provincial body responsible for investigating and adjudicating complaints of violations of the Ontario *Human Rights Code*

Ontario *Police Services Act*
stipulates that police services shall be provided throughout Ontario in accordance with the safeguards that guarantee the fundamental rights enshrined in the *Canadian Charter of Rights and Freedoms* and the Ontario *Human Rights Code*

paralanguage
features of speech, such as tone, loudness, speed, and use of silence

paternalism
a system under which an authority undertakes to supply the needs and regulate the conduct of those under its control

persuasive disclosure
approaches people use to persuade others

pluralism
state of having many cultural groups in one country

police–community interface
represented by the motto "To serve and protect," the principle that police functions are presumed to be afforded to all community residents regardless of their culture, race, ethnic origin, religion, sex, age, sexual orientation, or physical or mental ability

police culture
attitudes, values, and beliefs in police organizations that influence police reactions and behaviours within the police services and on the street

police force approach
emphasizes a reactive, crime control mandate that measures police effectiveness by such indicators as number of random patrols to deter criminal activity, response rate to police calls, number of arrests and convictions, and citizen satisfaction surveys

police services approach
emphasizes problem solving, crime prevention, and partnerships between police and communities

prejudice
an adverse judgment or opinion formed beforehand or without knowledge or examination of the facts

pro-arrest policy
encourages arrest in family violence cases but leaves the discretion to the officers

proxemics
use of space, in terms of physical distance between people, as a form of non-verbal communication

psychosis
form of serious mental disorder in which an actual break with reality occurs

race
classification based on biological or cultural traits

race paternalism
a system under which the dominant group take authority to supply needs and regulate conduct of a minority group

race relations training
training in how to deal more effectively with race-related issues, from the perspective that racism is a social disease that can be eliminated with education

refugee policy
humanitarian policy, based on the United Nations definition of a refugee, that assesses eligibility for entry to a country based on refugee status

religion
a spiritual belief system

religious beliefs
tenets of particular faiths

religious practices
concrete expressions of religious beliefs

residential schools
church-run, government-funded residential schools for Native children designed to prepare them for life in white society

respect for authority
core value stemming from the prevailing paramilitary organizational structure of police services, which provides simplicity, clarity, and comfort for police in fulfilling their role and executing their duties

Royal Commission on Aboriginal Peoples (RCAP)
commission established in 1991 to investigate the issues facing Aboriginal people in Canada

Royal Proclamation of 1763
the cornerstone of Native land claims today; has been called the "Magna Carta of Indian Rights" and has been deemed by the courts to have the force of a statute which has never been repealed

schizophrenia
mental illness described as cancer of the mind that causes psychotic mental disturbances

scrip
a one-time payment to discharge treaty rights

segregationist
opposed to immigrants and other cultures, preferring that immigrants return to their countries of origin

seigniorial farms
a system in which a man, usually a soldier, was granted land in the name of France

self-control
suppression of verbal and non-verbal expressions of emotion

separation
individual rejection of the host culture and maintenance of the culture of origin

settlement patterns
the variety of ways people physically establish themselves in a country, whether born there or as immigrants

Sixties Scoop
the practice of removing Native children from Native communities and placing them in foster care or for adoption in non-Native homes

specific land claims
claims that relate to specific misdealings of the Crown with relation to land or resources

GLOSSARY

spousal abuse
behaviour that causes one partner in a relationship to be afraid of and controlled by the other

stereotype
conventional, formulaic, and usually oversimplified conception, opinion, or belief about a person, group, event, or issue considered to typify or conform to an unvarying pattern or manner

substance-related disorders
mental disorders caused by substance dependence and abuse, and by substance withdrawal

suicide
symptom of mood disorder that takes the form of ideation, threat, attempt, gesture, and completed suicide

systemic discrimination
the enforcement of laws and the enforcement of policies that are inherently prejudicial to a group or culture

thought disorder
mental symptom characterized by ideas and speech that are coherent only to the mentally ill person

treaty
an agreement between two states that has been formally concluded and ratified

values
standards or principles; ideas about the worth or importance of certain qualities, especially those accepted by a particular group

visible minority
individuals, other than Aboriginal people, who are non-Caucasian in race or non-white in colour

white machismo culture
culture in which whiteness, masculinity, and hierarchy are emphasized and diversity, women, gays and lesbians, and horizontality are devalued

Index

Aboriginal peoples
    criminal justice system, and
        alcohol, effect of, 289–92
        culture conflict, and, 294–95
        overrepresentation, 187–89
        proposed solutions, 295–301
        systemic problems, 292–93
    cultural beliefs, 72–75
    demographics
        birth rate, 231
        elementary and secondary education, 234–36
        life expectancy, 231–32
        median age, 232
        migration to cities, 233–34
        population growth rates, 230–31
        postsecondary education, 236
        provincial distribution, 233
        senior population, 233
    first contact, 171–80
    forced assimilation, 203–20
    health services, administration of, 245
    land claims issues
        background, 262
        case law, 262–65
        case study, 271–73
        Constitution Act, 1982, 265–68
        land claim categories, 274–76
        mutual recognition, achievement, 273–74
        Ontario, 274–77
        title, establishment of, 268–71
    living arrangements, 244
    living conditions, 243–44
    mental health
        alcoholism, 241–42
        substance abuse, 242–43
        suicides, 240
    off-reserve populations, 251–52
    physical health
        adult mortality, 238–39
        common problems, 239–40
        infant mortality, 237–38
    pre-contact, 147–70
    services and programs, delivery of, 250–51
    socio-economic issues, 225–54
    socio-economic status
        employment, 246–47
        income, 248–49
        social assistance, 250
Aboriginal peoples' rights, 12, 54
Aboriginal spirituality, 100–2
acculturation, 8
alcohol, Aboriginal people, and, 79–80, 241–42, 289–92
anti-racism, 114
assimilation, 9, 203–20
assimilation ideology, 4
assimilationist host, 8
authoritarianism, 109

Bahá'í, 90
bipolar disorder, 133
blacks in Canada, 81–82
Brian's Law, 132
British North America Act, 192, 262
Buddhism, 91

Canadian Bill of Rights, 9
Canadian Charter of Rights and Freedoms, 6, 10, 12, 47, 73
Canadian Human Rights Act, 10, 47
Canadian Human Rights Commission, 47
Canadian identity, development of, 22
Canadian Multiculturalism Act, 6, 10
Canadian society, 6
child abuse, 124
child sexual abuse, 125
Christian Science, 92
Christianity, 93
civic ideology, 4
claims arising from Aboriginal title, 277
claims arising from the surrender for sale of reserve land, 277
claims relating to the fulfillment of terms of treaties, 276
code of silence, 36

community policing principles, 39–40
comprehensive land claims, 274
Constitution Act, 1982, 265–68
constructive discrimination, 59
core values, 35
Corrections and Conditional Release Act, 300
covenant chain, 175
creation stories
    community organization, and, 156
    Cree, 169–70
    international organization, 157
    land and spirituality, concepts of, 155
    Mohawk, 164–68
    Ojibwe, 161–64
Criminal Code, 33, 296, 298
cross-cultural communication, 116
cross-cultural training, 113
cultural awareness training, 112, 298
cultural genocide, 219
culture, 70
cynicism, 35

delusions, 136
democratic rights, 48
depression, 133
devolution, 250
discrimination, 7
diversity
    awareness training, 41, 115
    cultural, 69–84
    defined, 3, 27
    family violence, and, 125–27
    initiatives, 110
    history of, Canada, 9
    human rights, and, 45–66
    police, and, 27–42, 107–19
    religious, 87–105
diversity awareness training, 41
diversity equity, 83
diversity policing framework, 41

ego forcing, 34
elder abuse, 125
employment equity, 112
Employment Equity Act, 10
equality rights, 49, 51
ethnic group, 22
ethnicity, 3, 71
ethnist ideology, 4
exclusionary host, 8

Family Law Act, 59
family violence
    adult abuse, 124
    barriers to leaving abusive relationship, 128
    child abuse, 124
    defined, 123
    diversity, and, 125–27
    explanations for, 127
    law, and, 124
    mental health issues, 130
    older adult abuse, 125
    police responses to, 129–30
    social responses to, 128–29
fiduciary responsibility, 199
First Nations, *see* Aboriginal peoples
formication, 131
freedom from discrimination, 56–58
fundamental freedoms, 47, 49
fur trade, 177

gendered apartheid, 127
Grassy Narrows, 225–30

hallucinations, 136
harassment, 59
Hinduism, 93–94
homelessness, 130
host community, 7
human rights
    Canada
        Canadian Charter of Rights and Freedoms, 47–56
        Canadian Human Rights Act, 47
        Ontario *Human Rights Code*, 56–62
    international, 45–46
    law enforcement, and, 62–63, 64–65
    post-9/11, 64
hypervigilance, 35

Immigration Act, 9, 11
Immigration and Refugee Protection Act, 11
immigration trends
    ethnic origins, 13–17
    implications for diversity, 20
    visible minorities, 17–18
Indian Act
    amendments to, 195–99
    gender discrimination, 194
    imposed system of government, 193–94
    passage of, 192–93
    tax exemption, 195

Indian agent, 195
indigenization, 296
integration, 9
integrationist, 8
interdependence, 101
International Covenant on Economic, Social and Cultural Rights, 10
Islam, 94–95

Jehovah's Witnesses, 96
Judaism, 96–98

kinesics, 117

land claims issues
	background, 262
	case law, 262–65
	case study, 271–73
	Constitution Act, 1982, 265–68
	land claim categories, 274–76
	mutual recognition, achievement, 273–74
	Ontario, 274–77
	title, establishment of, 268–71
legal rights, 48, 50

Magna Carta, 45
mandatory arrest policy, 129
mania, 133
marginalization, 8
mediative policy, 129
Mental Health Act, 131
mental illness
	defined, 130
	homelessness, and, 130–31
	police response to, 132–40
mental retardation, 137
minority, 71
minority language rights, 53, 54
misattribution, 117
mobility rights, 48
mood disorders, 133
multicultural heritage, 55
multiculturalism
	Canada, and, 5
	defined, 3
multiculturalism ideology, 4

non-verbal communication, 117

official languages, 51
Official Languages Act, 9, 51–53

Ontario *Human Rights Code*, 56–62
Ontario Human Rights Commission, 56
Ontario *Police Services Act*, 62

paralanguage, 117
paternalism, 302
persuasive disclosure, 118
pluralism, 27
police–community interface
	Aboriginal peoples, 296–97
	community perception, 108–10
	defined, 37
	police self-perception, 108
	race relations training, 111–19
police culture, 30
police force approach, 37
police profile demographics
	diverse communities, and, 32
	gender imbalance, 30
	knowledge of cultural groups, 31
police services approach, 38
policing, core values, 35–36
prejudice, 79
pro-arrest policy, 129
proxemics, 117
psychosis, 132

race, 71
race paternalism, 289
race relations training, 112
refugee policy, 11
religion, 88
religious beliefs, 88
religious practices, 88
residential schools
	abuse within, 209–13
	aftermath, 213–14
	assimilation policy, and, 204–5
	defined, 203
	health conditions, 208–9
	problems within, 205–8
	resolution, attempts at, 214–16
	wrong, recognition of, 216–17
respect for authority, 35
Royal Commission on Aboriginal Peoples (RCAP), 204
Royal Proclamation of 1763, 176–77, 183, 264

schizophrenia, 136
scrip, 195
segregationist host, 8

seigniorial farms, 178
self-control, 35
sentencing reform, 298–300
separation, 9
settlement patterns, 7
Shintoism, 98
Sikhism, 99
Sixties Scoop, 217–19
South Asians, 82–83
specific land claims, 274
spousal abuse, 124
state, concept of, 7
stereotype, 79
substance-related disorders, 132
suicide, 134–36, 240
systemic discrimination, 293

Taoism, 100
thought disorder, 136
treaty
	background, 183–85
	defined, 183
	numbered treaties, 185–87

Universal Declaration of Human Rights, 10, 46

values, 4
verbal communication, 117
visible minority, 17, 72, 76–78

white machismo culture, 30
women in workplace, 80–81
world view
	land ownership, theories of, 151–52
	migration theories, 149–51
	religious creation story, 148
	scientific creation story, 149

Acknowledgments

Statistics Canada information is used with the permission of Statistics Canada. Users are forbidden to copy this material and/or redisseminate the data, in an original or modified form, for commercial purposes, without the expressed permission of Statistics Canada. Information on the availability of the wide range of data from Statistics Canada can be obtained from Statistics Canada's Regional Offices, its World Wide Web site at http://www.statcan.ca, and its toll-free access number 1-800-263-1136.

Table 1.1: Population by selected ethnic origins, by province and territory (2001 Census) (Canada) 2005-01-25 from Statistics Canada website http://www40.statcan.ca/l01/cst01/demo26a.htm.

Table 1.2: Place of birth by period of immigration, Canada, 2001 from Statistics Canada publication *Analysis Series, 2001 Census*, Catalogue 96F0030XIE2001008; also available from Statistics Canada website http://www12.statcan.ca/english/census01/products/analytic/companion/etoimm/tables/canada/period.cfm.

Table 1.3: Top Countries of Birth, Canada, 2001 from Statistics Canada publication *Analysis Series, 2001 Census*, Catalogue 96F0030XIE2001008; also available from Statistics Canada website http://www12.statcan.ca/english/census01/products/analytic/companion/etoimm/tables/canada/pobtop.cfm.

Table 1.4: 1990s Immigrants by source country and proportion speaking a non-official language, Canada, 2001 from Statistics Canada publication *Analysis Series, 2001 Census*, Catalogue 96F0030XIE2001008; also available from Statistics Canada website http://www12.statcan.ca/english/census01/products/analytic/companion/etoimm/tables/canada/offlang.cfm.

Table 1.5: Distribution of 1990s immigrants compared with distribution of total population, Canada, provinces, and territories, 2001 from Statistics Canada publication *Analysis Series, 2001 Census*, Catalogue 96F0030XIE2001008; also available from Statistics Canada website http://www12.statcan.ca/english/census01/products/analytic/companion/etoimm/tables/canada/immsh.cfm.

Figure 2.2: Crime rate for Canada from Statistics Canada publication *Canada at a glance, 2005*, Catalogue 12-581-XPE, release date: November 10, 2004, page 7.

Table 2.2: Selected Criminal Code offences from Statistics Canada publication *Canada at a glance, 2005*, Catalogue 12-581-XPE. Release date: November 10, 2004, page 7.

Table 4.1: Top 10 ethnic groups in Canada, 2001 from Statistics Canada publication *Analysis Series, 2001 Census*, Catalogue 96F0030XIE2001008; also available from Statistics Canada website http://www12.statcan.ca/english/census01/products/analytic/companion/etoimm/canada.cfm#threefold_increaes.

Table 4.3: Native Ethics of Behaviour from Brant, C.C. Native Ethics and Rules of Behaviour. *Can J Psychiatry*. 1990. 35(6): 534-39. Reprinted with permission.

Table 6.1: Community Satisfaction with Police Services. Wortley (1994). Perceptions of bias and racism within the Ontario Criminal justice system: Results from a public opinion survey. Toronto: Commission on Systemic Racism in the Ontario Criminal Justice System. Reprinted with permission of Scot Wortley.

Table 7.2: Primary Needs of Abused Immigrant and Refugee Women. MacLeod and Shin (1990). *Isolated, afraid, and forgotten: The service delivery needs and realities of immigrant and refugee women who are battered*. Ottawa: Health and Welfare Canada. *National Clearinghouse on Family Violence*, Public Health Agency of Canada (1990) 8. Reproduced with the permission of the Minister of Public Works and Government Services Canada, 2007.

Figure 8.4: Trade Patterns Prior to European Contact. Adapted from R.C. Harris, ed., *Historical Atlas of Canada: Vol. 1—From the Beginning to 1800* (Toronto: Univeristy of Toronto Press, 1987), plate 14.

Appendix 11.2: Rita Joe, "I Lost My Talk" from *The Song of Eskasoni: More Poems of Rita Joe* (Toronto: Canadian Scholars' Press Inc./Women's Press, 1988) © Women's Press.

Figure 12.1: Incidence of Violent Death at Grassy Narrows, 1959-78; Table 11.1: School Dropout Rate at Grassy Narrows, 1977-78; and DIAND Expenditures at Grassy Narrows, 1969-77 from Shkilnyk, A. (1985). *A poison stronger than love: The destruction of an Ojibwa community*. New Haven, CT: Yale University Press. © 1985 Yale University Press.

Table 12.3: Size and Growth of the population Reporting Aboriginal Ancestry and Aboriginal Identity, Canada, 1996-2001 and Table 11.4, Population Reporting Aboriginal Identity in Selected Census Metropolitan Areas (CMA) and Census Agglomerations (CA) with an Aboriginal Population of 5,000 or More, 1996 and 2001 based on Statistics Canada. (2003, January 31). *Aboriginal peoples of Canada: A demographic profile, 2001 census (analysis series, 2001 census)*. p. 20. Catalogue no. 96F0030. Ottawa: Supply and Services Canada.

Figure 12.2: Life Expectancy at Birth, First Nations and Canada. Basic Departmental Data 2000. Ottawa: Indian and Northern Affairs Canada, 2001. http://www.ainc-inac.gc.ca/pr/sts/bdd00/bdd00_e.pdf. Reproduced with the permission of the Minister of Public Works and Government Services Canada, 2007.

Table 12.5: DIAND's Expenditures on First Nation Communitites, 1997-98. Indian and Northern Affairs Canada and Canadian Polar Commission Performance Report for the period ending March 31, 1998. Ottawa: Public Works and Government Services Canada, 1998. http://www.ainc-inac.gc.ca/pr/est/perrep.pdf. Reproduced with the permission of the Minister of Public Works and Government Services Canada, 2007.

Figure 12.3: Educational Attainment in First Nations and Canada, 1996. Hull, Jeremy, Aboriginal post-secondary education and labour market outcomes Canada, 1996. Ottawa: Indian and Northern Affairs Canada, 2000. Reproduced with the permission of the Minister of Public Works and Government Services Canada, 2007.

Figure 14.1: Victims of Crime, 1999; Figure 14.2, Aboriginal Adults in Custody, 1999; and Figure 14.3, Aboriginal Youth in Custody, 1999 adapted from Statistics Canada publication *Aboriginal Peoples in Canada— Profile Series*, Catalogue 85F0033MIE2001001. Released date: June 14, 2001.

Appendix 14.1: CBC.ca. Racist e-mail spurs probes among RCMP, police. November 22, 2005, http://www.cbc.ca/canada/story/2005/11/22/native-song-051122.html. © Canadian Broadcasting Corporation.

Appendix 14.3: Robert Ross, "Duelling Paradigms? Western Criminal Justice versus Aboriginal Community Healing" from *Justice as Healing: A Newsletter on Aboriginal Concepts of Justice* (Native Law Centre, Spring 1995), http://www.usask.ca/nativelaw/publications/jah/ross.html. Reprinted by permission.